MW01131105

Praise for

Billy Graham:
The Man I Knew

"Among the many things that stand out about my dad—the preacher—is that he had a desire to invest in younger preachers. His heart connected with those who had a passion for preaching God's truth to future generations. My longtime friend Greg Laurie is one of these guys. I've often said that the public Billy Graham seen on Crusade platforms and television was the same private Billy Graham at home. This certainly is revealed in *Billy Graham: The Man I Knew*, which is based on Greg's personal thoughts on the special times spent with my father and how his ministry impacted Greg's own life and evangelistic ministry. I am grateful for Greg's friendship, for his love for my father, and for his proclamation of the Gospel of the Lord Jesus Christ."

  —**FRANKLIN GRAHAM,** president and CEO of the Billy Graham
    Evangelistic Association and Samaritan's Purse

"In this page-turner of a book I learned things about my father that I never knew! Greg Laurie has done a masterly job of setting my father's life in historical and cultural context. I pray that *Billy Graham: The Man I Knew* will draw readers to the Gospel, where they will find the love of God that he preached so fervently and faithfully."

  —**ANNE GRAHAM LOTZ,** bestselling author of *Jesus in Me*

"God delights in using ordinary people to do extraordinary things. That a kid who grew up on a dairy farm in North Carolina would grow up to be the greatest evangelist the world has ever known is just the sort of thing that must make God smile. In *Billy Graham: The Man I Knew*, Greg Laurie will pull Dr. Graham out of the stained glass you might be tempted to put him in and inspire you to believe God wants to use you too!"

  —**LEVI LUSKO,** lead pastor of Fresh Life Church and bestselling
    author

"In our world of chaos and negativity, it is so refreshing to read in depth about the life of Billy Graham. His unwavering commitment to the Lord and to sharing the Gospel is unparalleled. He was never corrupted by fame or the magnitude of his platform. He was genuine, humble, and loved Jesus until his last breath.

"Greg Laurie has done a phenomenal job of capturing the heart and life of the legendary Billy. This is completely inspiring and well worth the read!"

—**JEREMY CAMP**, Grammy Award–nominated singer, songwriter, and storyteller

"Much has been said about 'the next Billy Graham.' It's not only a title that is passed around today, but Leonard Ravenhill wrote in a personal letter to a friend using that phrase as far back as the 1960s. People have been measuring against Billy Graham's impact for a half-century. He won't like me saying this, but I have shared multiple times publicly that Greg Laurie is the 'Billy Graham of Now' because of the unusual level of anointing I see on his ministry for salvations.

"So it is fitting that my hero Greg Laurie is writing about his personal friendship with Billy and the great impact Billy had on our world. I've ready many books on Billy Graham, but this one should be at the top of your list. Your faith will be edified by Billy Graham's pure heart for God and the Gospel."

—**MATT BROWN**, evangelist, author of *Truth Plus Love*, and founder of Think Eternity

"Billy Graham preached to more people than anyone in history, and his massive influence continues to this day as he is beloved by millions. But what was the man really like? Greg Laurie gives us an up-close look at the great evangelist and offers a new generation the story of one of the greatest Christians who has ever lived. Greg has done us all a great service in providing this fresh and inspiring biography of a spiritual hero."

—**DR. JACK GRAHAM**, pastor of Prestonwood Baptist Church in Plano, Texas, and host of *PowerPoint with Jack Graham*, which airs weekly on TBN

"This book introduces Billy Graham to a whole new generation. And the perfect person to write this is Greg Laurie. For years I have thought of Billy's anointing falling on Greg like Elijah's mantle fluttering down from heaven onto Elisha. This dynamic makes *Billy Graham: The Man I Knew* a most interesting read.

"I must confess I thought I knew all about Billy Graham's biography after studying him for half my life. Boy was I wrong! Pastor Greg revealed so many unheard stories and insights into Graham's life that the world has never heard. Reading every word of this book, from cover to cover, had me mesmerized.

"Let me tell you this is a book every Millennial has to read. The world has received a gift in Greg Laurie's friendship with Billy Graham documented in this compelling narrative."

—**BEN COURSON**, bestselling author, a TV and radio personality, an international speaker, founder of Hope Generation, and the senior pastor at Applegate Christian Fellowship in Oregon

"Billy Graham has always been a part of my life whether I was aware of it, agreed with him, cared about his message, or openly resisted his message. I do know that I was deeply moved by his words over the years, and like so many others, his message became a part of my life.

"I opened *Billy Graham: The Man I Knew*, and after a few chapters I was mesmerized. The combination of deep truths and vibrant moments kept me glued to teachings that my soul remembers crying out for so many troubled years ago. Traveling with him in these stories brought everything about eternal destiny into clear focus.

"As I read on, I got the sense that when Billy Graham entered a room you could almost hear two sets of footsteps. His walk was so in step with Jesus that God's presence could fill a room, an auditorium, or the hurting heart of a lonely person. He stood tall before multitudes, speaking hope and living truth into their lives while possessing that unique gift of simple humility that made it feel like it was just you and Billy in the room. The message was all that mattered, and people trusted him. A person could feel those blue eyes piercing their soul the length of a football field away.

"From the very beginning Billy listened to God, and because of that he always knew his purpose in life. There were pitfalls and spiritual pratfalls but never a falling away from the mission planted in his heart the day he accepted God's Lordship in his life.

"The authors in dealing with a story of such depth and magnitude have delicately melded the passion, detail, and absolute wonder of a life that bordered on down-home simplicity and ethereal wonder. In these pages Billy Graham's life unfolds, patiently and with quiet determination. It is then carefully folded back together into a Gospel tapestry as it beautifully progresses to the final chapters of an incredible life and ministry. Fresh beginnings and dramatic endings prevail throughout. It wasn't always easy, so as the old song goes, there were times that he traveled a road where even 'angels feared to tread.'

"He was common, he was consistent, and he was centered. Like King David he was a man after God's own heart, but upon reading *Billy Graham: The Man I Knew*, I realized that even more than that he was a man after my heart and yours.

"Billy Graham the man was summarized perfectly in one of the early chapters: '*In ordinary conversations and in the pulpit, he was able to take the complex and make it simple enough for a regular person to understand…a rare combination of a Statesman-Everyman—the farmer who was sought out by presidents, the country preacher who touched the world.*'

"And if you are looking for romance…herein lies the love story of the ages."

—**KEN MANSFIELD**, former U.S. Manager of Apple Records and author of *The Roof: The Beatles' Final Concert* and *The Beatles, the Bible, and Bodega Bay*

Billy Graham

BILLY
GRAHAM
THE MAN I KNEW

GREG LAURIE
WITH MARSHALL TERRILL

SALEM
BOOKS

an imprint of Regnery Publishing
Washington, D.C.

Scriptures marked AKJV are taken from the AMERICAN KING JAMES VERSION, public domain.

Scriptures marked ESV are taken from THE HOLY BIBLE, ENGLISH STANDARD VERSION®. Copyright © 2001 by Crossway, a publishing ministry of Good News Publishers. Used by permission.

Scriptures marked KJV are taken from the KING JAMES VERSION, public domain.

Scriptures marked MSG are taken from THE MESSAGE: THE BIBLE IN CONTEMPORARY ENGLISH. Copyright © 1993, 1994, 1995, 1996, 2000, 2001, 2002. Used by permission of NavPress Publishing Group.

Scriptures marked NASB are taken from the NEW AMERICAN STANDARD BIBLE®. Copyright © 1960, 1962, 1963, 1968, 1971, 1972, 1973, 1975, 1977, 1995 by the Lockman Foundation. Used by permission.

Scriptures marked NIV are taken from THE HOLY BIBLE, NEW INTERNATIONAL VERSION®. Copyright © 1973, 1978, 1984, 2011 by Biblica, Inc.™ Used by permission of Zondervan.

Scriptures marked NKJV are taken from the NEW KING JAMES VERSION®. Copyright © 1982 by Thomas Nelson, Inc. Used by permission. All rights reserved.

Scriptures marked NLT are taken from the HOLY BIBLE, NEW LIVING TRANSLATION. Copyright © 1996, 2004, 2007 by Tyndale House Foundation. Used by permission of Tyndale House Publishers, Inc., Carol Stream, Illinois, 60188. All rights reserved.

Scriptures marked WEB are taken from THE WORLD ENGLISH BIBLE, public domain.

Salem Books™ is a trademark of Salem Communications Holding Corporation
Regnery® is a registered trademark of Salem Communications Holding Corporation

ISBN: 978-1-68451-059-7
eISBN: 978-1-62157-999-1

Library of Congress Control Number: 2020945144

Published in the United States by
Salem Books
An Imprint of Regnery Publishing
A Division of Salem Media Group
Washington, D.C.
www.SalemBooks.com

Manufactured in the United States of America

10 9 8 7 6 5 4 3 2 1

Books are available in quantity for promotional or premium use. For information on discounts and terms, please visit our website: www.SalemBooks.com.

To Leo M. Terrill,
who shot this photo
shortly after dedicating his life to Christ
at a Billy Graham Crusade in Seoul, South Korea, in 1956

Contents

Introduction

" **J**ust call me Billy."

Just call me awestruck. This was, after all, The Man himself, a literal living legend and larger-than-life American icon. He had been on the "World's Most Admired Persons" list sixty-one times, more than any other person who has ever lived.

And there I was sitting across a table from him...at a Red Lobster, of all places.

He wore a baseball cap over that luxurious mane of wavy hair, but even with the bill pulled down over his face there was no mistaking those distinctive features.

A friend of mine once said he had the visage of a biblical prophet. If a Hollywood filmmaker wanted to cast someone in that role, they couldn't do better than Billy Graham.

But he never acted like a star. In fact, when you were with Billy, *you* got the star treatment from *him*. He always turned the conversation to you and genuinely listened to what you said. Why in the world would he care about me? But he did. He wanted to know about me.

I was in my late thirties and, after pastoring a church for nineteen years, had just begun my evangelistic ministry. At that point, Billy had been preaching for almost half a century.

There were many far more successful men who would have given anything to sit across from the man widely regarded as "the face of the evangelical world." Much worthier ones, too.

"Dr. Graham—" (I couldn't bring myself then to use his first name). "I came from a broken home," I began. "My mother was married and divorced seven times, and she was a raging alcoholic."

His blue eyes narrowed in sympathy and concern.

"So I lived with my grandparents for a time, and we would watch your Crusades on our black-and-white television."

How many times over the years must he have heard people tell him something like that? But there was nothing practiced or self-satisfied about the smile that lit up his face.

Just then our meals arrived, and I noticed that more than one person seated in our vicinity had recognized the famed evangelist. Some seemed shocked to see him in the flesh. He did not have a security detail and was dressed very casually.

As it happened, the town we were in was hosting not only a Billy Graham Crusade that week, but also—I kid you not—a convention of atheists. But if there were any card-carrying atheists at the Red Lobster that day, they were as dazzled and starstruck as the rest of us, and it wasn't long before other customers began filing over to say hello and shake his hand. He greeted each one with a smile and some kind words.

Just another day in the life of William Franklin Graham.

As I'd started to tell him, like millions of Americans who were born and raised in the second half of the twentieth century, I grew up with Billy Graham. When I lived with my grandparents, Charles and Stella McDaniel, we watched the Billy Graham Crusades on our TV.

We also watched *Bonanza*, *Wanted: Dead or Alive*, and *Gunsmoke*. My grandfather liked Westerns.

James Arness, who played Marshal Matt Dillon in *Gunsmoke*, reminded me of Billy, both physically and as a stalwart, upright role model who always did what was right and never drew his gun unless forced to. Marshal Dillon was the law in Dodge City.

Gunsmoke was shot on a soundstage in Los Angeles, and Billy Graham got his big start there, though not on the backlot of a movie studio. It took place in a large tent pitched at the corner of Washington and Hill streets, where he conducted the very first of the hundreds of Crusades that would change the world.

I'm not sure why, but early on I felt that God had also called me to be an evangelist—the kind that stands in front of crowds, large and small, and proclaims the Gospel. I wasn't sure I was up to that. Back before church-planting was as popular as it is today, I took over a study group for young people in Riverside, California, and it grew into a full-blown church; but evangelizing like Billy Graham did is different. Prior to becoming a Christian, I was more of a back-of-the-room kind of guy. My greatest aspiration was to become a professional cartoonist.

There was nothing I liked more than to retreat into the private universe of cartoon characters I had developed more or less as a survival skill. Long before iPads and smartphones came along, my diversion was a piece of white paper and a black felt-tipped pen. (What else was I supposed to do in a bar while watching my mom drink and get hit on by men?) My backup plan was to open a pet shop. I loved animals.

Standing in front of a crowd and preaching? Not for me.

Once during high school, my teacher assigned everyone a different famous quote from American history, and we were expected to stand up and give an extemporaneous speech based on it.

My quote was, "Do not fire until you see the whites of their eyes!"—the famous order of Colonel William Prescott at the Battle of Bunker Hill during the Revolutionary War, given so his men would make every shot count.

When it was my turn, I stepped in front of the class, cleared my throat, and recited my line. Then my mind went totally blank. After half a minute of embarrassing silence, I slunk back to my seat. Clearly, a life of public speaking was not in the cards for me.

But that was before I had something to say.

In 1976, our young church was exploding in growth. A newspaper article had been written about us. I made a copy of it and put it in an envelope along with a personal letter I'd written to the most famous evangelist in the world. I desperately wanted to meet Billy Graham and ask him some questions, and I figured the best way to pull this off was to deliver my letter to him personally at his Crusade in San Diego. Up until then, my only exposure to him was through TV and listening to him on the new cutting-edge technology called cassette tapes. Where I got that kind of confidence, God only knows.

I drove my trusty Corvair ninety miles south and sputtered into the parking lot of the stadium. It was overflowing with people of all ages. The atmosphere was electric, and the weather balmy. Billy was at his best that evening, and when he gave the altar call for people to come down to receive Christ, I went forward myself to get a closer look. It was as I stood on the field and looked at him that it dawned on me: *this is what I want to do when I grow up!*

The choir sang "Just as I Am," the very song that was sung when Billy had given his life to Christ decades before. After Billy led everyone in a final prayer, he began his descent from the stage.

This was my chance!

Members of Billy's entourage surrounded him, and as they passed by, I thrust out the manila envelope containing my letter and the newspaper clipping and beseeched, "Please give this to Reverend Graham!"

As an aide reached for it, I noticed what I had absentmindedly scrawled on the front, and my heart and high hopes crashed.

"To Billy *Gram*," it read.

Never mind!

I finally met Billy for real in 1985 and have been honored to serve on the Billy Graham Evangelistic Association's (BGEA) board of directors for more than twenty-five years now. I have had the privilege of meeting many well-known preachers and celebrities. I have shaken hands with four U.S. presidents and have stood in the Oval Office itself. But I have never met nor been in the presence of any other man like Billy Graham.

In the pages that follow, I want to relate all I know about this great man of God and his extraordinary life—how he grew up, his desires as a young man, his transformation into an obedient and humble shepherd of the Lord, his vision for humanity, and how he achieved so much in his ninety-nine years on this earth.

I also want to show you what I know of the unique challenges he faced. He had plenty of them, just like you and me.

A mystery dogged Billy Graham his whole life. The mystery was central to his very being, to the man he was and to the kind of life he led. But the solution to this particular mystery would not be revealed in his lifetime.

British journalist and talk-show host David Frost, whose father was a Methodist minister, enjoyed a long and lasting friendship with Billy. During one of their many interviews, the mystery came out when Frost asked him, "When you eventually meet God face to face, is there a question you'll want to ask Him?"

Without hesitation, Billy said, "Yes, I think so. I'm going to ask, 'Lord, why did you choose me to do this particular work?'"

Whoa! I sure didn't see that coming. I was expecting something like, "What is the meaning of life?" or something as generic. But his answer was typically Billy—totally honest, humble, open, and touchingly plaintive.

"I want to ask Him why, when there are so many wonderful people in this world that are His servants, He chose me."

Good question. Why did God select a dairyman's son whose dream was to play Major League Baseball to become history's best-known evangelist and the most powerful religious figure of his time? He was a preacher who counseled presidents, popes, queens, the world-famous, and the common man alike; a modern-day prophet who helped to heal our nation in the most trying of times—desegregation, Watergate, Hurricane Katrina, the Oklahoma City bombing, and the 9/11 terrorist attacks; a man of God who reached billions through several kinds of media. In fact, Billy Graham left such an impression on our country that in 2020, North Carolina had his statue installed on Capitol Hill—an honor afforded to only two residents of each state.

For all that, he deserved the title by which he was often called: "America's Preacher."

But Billy Graham wasn't just an American phenomenon. He was as well-known in Europe as he was in the United States, and in his six-plus decades of ministry, he preached in more than 185 countries and territories.

No matter where he appeared, Billy's message was simple and direct: "God loves you."

His ability to bring people to Christ and gather believers together was astounding; his love and thirst for Jesus were undeniable; his message of hope was forceful and inspiring.

For Billy, the mystery was at last revealed upon his entrance to glory. The rest of us can only sift through the events and signposts of his extraordinary life for clues, as well as for our own guidance and salvation. My greatest hope is that when you reach the end of this book you will ask yourself: *Why not me too?*

Billy had a sort of sainthood conferred on him over the years, especially since his death in February 2018. Far be it from me to say he didn't earn it, though Billy himself would probably be the first to deflect that kind of accolade.

In his youth, Billy was no stranger to mischief or sin. He had his share of scrapes and fistfights, had a tendency to show off to his buddies, and readily admitted his attraction to the opposite sex.

Billy was as good a man as any I've ever known—but he was a man, carrying the same baggage issued to you and me along with our birth certificates.

At first, this was going to be the third book in the *American Icon* series. The previous two I wrote were about Steve McQueen and Johnny Cash. I admired their careers from a distance and spent a great deal of time exploring their sometimes-private spiritual lives.

That's hardly necessary in a book about Billy Graham. He put it all out there for the world to see. The McQueen and Cash books were about their long and winding searches for spiritual fulfillment and peace. Billy exuded both and showed the world the way to find them.

The fact is, Billy Graham is the glue between my two previous *American Icon* books. At the end of McQueen's life, when he was going to Mexico for his final surgery because cancer had spread through his body, one of his final requests was to meet Billy Graham. Billy made it a point to see McQueen, despite his insanely busy schedule, and spent several hours at his bedside to discuss serious matters, including death and the eternity awaiting him. Billy went so far as to rendezvous with McQueen in his private plane on the tarmac and pray with him.

Billy impacted McQueen's life, but he was even more influential in the life of Johnny Cash. They prayed together, went fishing together, vacationed together, and Cash sang at many of Billy's Crusades. And just as with McQueen, Billy comforted Cash in his final days.

My goal with this book is to take Billy Graham's story in a whole new direction. I never knew Steve McQueen or Johnny Cash personally, but I got to know Billy Graham very well. I was blessed to know him, and my life was enriched by his friendship, counsel, and encouragement.

Because of this (and unlike other books about his life), I believe I can bring something unique and exciting to his story for you. Unlike the McQueen and Cash books, this isn't part of the *American Icon* series. As my friend Franklin Graham so rightly pointed out, "Daddy would have been embarrassed to be identified as any kind of icon. He was way too humble for that."

Instead, this is an intimate portrait of his father written by someone who knew him well, and the title should reflect that. Thus, *Billy Graham: The Man I Knew.*

This book isn't meant to be a definitive historical biography of Billy. It's meant to introduce you to him if you aren't familiar with him or all he accomplished. It's written through the eyes of a friend—a highlight reel. The book is a biopic of his shaping experiences and the people who impacted him. It tells how—in spite of a short season of doubt—he stayed true to his calling and his message through the tumultuous twentieth century and beyond. It's a story of an ordinary man who, through his love for God and his passion that the world should know Him, had a profound impact on his times.

He was a renaissance man who literally changed the world by bringing the Word of God to more people than any other living person. And if you couldn't see Billy with your own eyes, he still managed to reach you. His radio program *The Hour of Decision* (a name suggested by Ruth Graham) ran for sixty-six years on seven hundred stations around the globe. He also had hundreds of thousands of subscribers to his magazines (*Christianity Today* and *Decision*) and reached an additional five million people through his newspaper column, "My Answer." Then, of course, there were his thirty-three books, which sold in the millions during his lifetime (his 1953 book *Peace with God* sold two million copies alone).

His Crusades took him around the world—to Communist countries, to places where the government scoffed at God's existence and discouraged religion, and to not-so-exotic locales where people were hungry for the Gospel message.

At the height of his popularity, he received more than eight thousand requests a year to give sermons—and at times, an astounding ten thousand letters a day, according to the *Los Angeles Times*.

Billy Graham's impact was undeniable, but what's truly remarkable is that he accomplished these herculean feats during an era of travel that was not easy or comfortable. The interstate highway system wasn't completed until the 1970s. Before then, a cross-country trip could take as long as two weeks, versus the average five days it takes now. President Dwight D. Eisenhower (a personal friend of Billy's) was inspired to create the system when he joined a military convoy as a brevet lieutenant colonel in 1919. At the time, it took fifty-six days to travel from Washington, D.C., to San Francisco. There were no paved roads between Illinois and Nevada.

Flying in the 1950s and early 1960s wasn't much of an improvement. It was expensive. The average person could expect to spend 5 percent of his annual salary to fly from Chicago to Phoenix. It was also dangerous. Your chances of being killed were five times greater than they are today.

Crashes from fog were common. Engines fell off planes so often that the incidents weren't even recorded as accidents if the remaining engines landed the plane safely. Turbulence could snap your neck because plane interiors weren't designed for safety.

That was the world in which Billy Graham began his travels.

He also navigated a changing media landscape before the Digital Age. It would be interesting to see how Billy Graham would traverse the world of Snapchat, Twitter, Facebook, Instagram, TikTok, and YouTube today. His following was not built on posts, tweets, and memes, but on many hours of prayer, planning, sweat, and the devotion of an evangelistic team—that's what he called them, "the team"—that backed him time and again as he marched into spiritual battle.

Billy was as famous as the dozen presidents to whom he gave spiritual counsel, perhaps even more so because he was a light and inspiration to everyone. His words were powerful, but his simple outlook was filled with faith, and he offered hope in the worst of times.

Yet for all of his accomplishments and accolades, there are millions of Americans now who draw a blank when they hear the name "Billy Graham."

"There's a whole new generation who do not know who my father is," his son Franklin Graham recently confided to me.

As sad as that is, it's not surprising. Everyone fades from public consciousness over time, no matter how much they've accomplished. The only person I can think of who hasn't is Jesus Christ, but even that is being put to the test these days.

According to a 2018 Pew Research Center study, Christianity is in steady decline in the United States. When asked for personal information about religion on forms or applications, now more than 56 percent write "none." These religious "Nones" are people who aren't necessarily atheists, but they don't practice or ascribe to a particular faith. Six out of ten Millennials do not identify with any branch of Christianity at all. The faith that was once the backbone and bedrock of this country has been reduced to the fringes.

Nones are now the fastest-growing faith in America.

Generation Z, the demographic group following Millennials, is described as the "Hopeless Generation." We have gone from what is known as the Greatest Generation, who came of age during World War II, to the Hopeless Generation in the span of seven decades.

With the explosion of cutting-edge technology and comforts that make our lives so much easier, it seems as though we'd be happy, hopeful people. But the age of innocence seems long gone. Someone once said that man can live forty days without food, three days without water, but not even minutes without hope. We all need hope, and lots of it.

And that's the real reason I wanted to write this book: to introduce Billy Graham to a younger group of Americans who need real-life heroes and the truth of the Gospel. Look, it's a tough world out there, and it's changed dramatically. Studies show that Generation Z experiences higher levels of stress and serious symptoms of depression, anxiety, and pressure than previous generations, including Millennials. They are faced with situations that other generations simply did not have to deal with: online bullying, substance abuse, school violence, mass shootings, continual comparisons on social media to people whose lives look so much better than theirs, pressure to get into the right college, and societal judgment that they are entitled, overly sheltered, and brittle.

While it may be true that some young Americans are rejecting religion and patriotism, there is plenty of evidence to suggest the contrary. In August 2019, approximately one hundred thousand people filled Angel Stadium in Anaheim, California, for the weekend-long crusade our Harvest team has put on there for thirty years in a row. Among those in attendance, 63 percent were under thirty years old. I find that extremely promising.

As Billy Graham often did at his Crusades, I extended an opportunity for people to begin a relationship with God through Jesus Christ. More than eight thousand people responded, and 65 percent of them were either Millennials or from Generation Z. Some would describe that as "thousands of young people becoming more religious!"

The truth is that every generation has to come of age, but Millennials and Gen Z kids are apparently more interested in issues of faith and have more love for our country than is being recognized or generally reported.

Young people today, especially those who have never been introduced to the Bible or its characters, need modern-day examples of faith. The life of Billy Graham is a superb one. In this book, I've often described him as a modern-day Moses. Profiling this American legend and understanding his life, triumphs, and defeats offers a way for people to relate to the Bible.

Here's a glimpse into a remarkable person who was called to be a spokesman for God. What else is there to say about someone whose company, magnetism, and unstinting humanity could make a simple meal with him at Red Lobster an occasion more wonderful than a state dinner at the White House?

As always, thank you for accompanying me on this very personal and important journey.

Greg Laurie
July 2020

CHAPTER ONE

The Dairyman's Son

Billy Graham was a modern prophet of God. One of the most recognized and trusted faces of the twentieth and twenty-first centuries; a confidante and spiritual advisor to presidents, diplomats, and royalty; a civil-rights champion; a president and CEO of a major company; an inventive entrepreneur; and a pioneer of Christian cinema. He broke ground in radio and an emerging technology called television.

Think of Steve Jobs, who wanted to make his "dent in the universe," and in some ways did so with the creation of the smartphone. Think of Jeff Bezos, who created Amazon, the world's most successful business, and then took it in directions no one else could have foreseen. Think of Walt Disney, who imagined things no one had ever dreamed of, and you get a glimpse of the man who, in his own way, eclipsed them all.

William Franklin Graham was born in a much kinder, gentler time in America. Think William Faulkner and Mark Twain, but further east of the Mississippi. He was born on his family's three-hundred-acre dairy farm on the outskirts of Charlotte, North Carolina, on November 7, 1918 (four days before the World War I armistice) to parents William Franklin Sr. and Morrow Coffey Graham. Morrow, it was said, was made of pioneer stock, for she had been picking butterbeans in the field earlier in the day before Billy arrived.

From what I've discerned, they were hardworking and God-fearing people (they were devout Presbyterians) who ably provided for Billy and his three younger siblings: Catherine, Melvin, and Jean, who was fourteen years younger than Billy. They were initially raised in a white-framed farmhouse on a choppy dirt road. The land's soil was rich, and the farm was surrounded by woods, streams, and foliage such as oaks and cedars. The home was filled with lots of love, ample food, and plenty of laughter. A few years later, when Billy was around ten, they moved to a two-story colonial red brick house with a pillared porch and paved paths, about 150 yards north of the old property. The new home was an instant upgrade, with one of man's greatest inventions: indoor plumbing. (The luxury of walking down the hall in the dead of winter instead of outside to a freezing privy is not to be underestimated.) And it was a luxury—only 10 percent of American homes at the time had indoor plumbing and just 7 percent had electricity. These two innovations probably made the Grahams the envy of Mecklenburg County. (The house was later purchased by the Billy Graham Evangelistic Association, moved, and fully restored in 2007. It is now part of the Billy Graham Library complex in Charlotte, only a few miles from its original site.)

It was not the first structure on the property. Billy's grandfather, William Crook Graham, a former Confederate soldier with a patriarchal beard, built an unusually tall log cabin from American chestnut trees culled from the grounds around 1870, not long after the Civil War. The cabin stood strong for nearly 150 years and has been preserved on the Anne Springs Close Greenway a few miles south of Charlotte.

Billy, who never met William Crook, certainly heard about him. Many in the area knew of William's drinking exploits and sometimes outrageous behavior. "He'd get drunk and he'd stay drunk pretty much over Sunday," William's son-in-law once told Graham biographer John Pollock. He also mentioned the former soldier had accumulated lots of debt and made no attempt to pay it off.

Billy described his crusty and colorful grandfather in his autobiography, *Just as I Am*, as "a hard-drinking, hard-cursing veteran whose service with the Sixth South Carolina Volunteers left him with a Yankee bullet in his leg for the rest of his life." (Billy's maternal grandfather, Ben Coffey, also fought in the Civil War for the Confederates in the Eleventh North Carolina Regiment, Pettigrew's Brigade. He was wounded at Gettysburg in Pickett's Charge in July 1863 and is immortalized in the North Carolina monument at the famous battleground site.)

Graham's regiment also saw plenty of action, fighting in eleven engagements over four years. About half the unit was killed at the Battle of Seven Pines in Henrico County, Virginia. They took heavy casualties in most of their fights. Many of the men who weren't killed lost their minds. But Graham survived. Wounded at the Battle of the Wilderness and present at the surrender in Appomattox, he ended up walking back home after the war to Fort Mill, South Carolina, a distance of 230 miles—a mighty long way to walk even without a bullet in your body. He later acquired a farm in Sharon Township near Charlotte, North Carolina, for about one dollar per acre.

The land eventually became a dairy farm, but after surviving what Graham did, it's hard to go back to farm life. After living in the shadow of death for four years, he probably couldn't have cared less what anyone thought of him. Today he likely would have been diagnosed with post-traumatic stress disorder. It was not unknown back then, but people referred to it as "soldier's heart."

William Crook Graham was no saint, but he was a stubborn survivor. He fought, survived injury, and managed to get himself home alive through sheer strength of will. A Minié ball in his leg and a 230-mile walk ahead? A piece of cake after battles like Spotsylvania and Cold Harbor.

He also wasn't keen on religion (no surprise there), though he was mentioned in a 1914 *Charlotte Observer* article as a member of the Sharon Presbyterian Church. It was his Scottish wife, Maggie McCall—also a member and buried in the church's cemetery—who toiled and tended the spiritual needs of the Graham flock. She instilled solid Christian values in their eleven-member family, teaching them the Scriptures and ensuring they applied it to their lives. They weren't going to end up like Pap if she had anything to do with it. Every one of them was church-going, and several of their grandchildren and offspring—Billy being the first—became preachers.

William Crook Graham passed away on November 14, 1914, at the age of seventy-three. He didn't leave much to his children except unpleasant memories of binge drinking, boorish behavior, and a mountain of debt. The farm was in arrears; it was his sons William "Frank" (Billy's father) and Clyde who ultimately picked up the tab in order to keep the place, later known as the Graham Brothers Dairy Farm. Fortunately, they had more horse sense than their father and were harder workers. (The third brother, Billy's Uncle Tom, moved to Oklahoma and found success in the cotton-gin business.)

Frank, who only had three years of formal schooling, ran the day-to-day business affairs of the dairy farm while Clyde tended to the cows and milk-processing house. Frank's wife, Morrow, crunched the numbers and ran the Graham empire from their kitchen table.

It wasn't much of an empire in the beginning, but they were diligent, and it became one of the largest dairy farms in the area, boasting seventy-five cows and approximately four hundred customers. It was enough for Frank and Morrow to provide a nice roof over their heads and an automobile to shuttle them around (a '31 black Chevrolet with red wheels!). Being farmers, food was guaranteed to be on the table. The Grahams grew tomatoes, lettuce, eggplants, okra, and squash.

It seems a dairy farm was also a good place to work off nervous energy, which Billy had in abundance. Billy's father found myriad ways to harness his son's seemingly endless vigor, starting with sending him out to feed and milk the family cows at 2:30 a.m. The first time he slept in past 3:00 a.m., he got a rude awakening, courtesy of Frank.

"I used to have to get up by at least three o'clock," Billy told English broadcaster Guy Lawrence. "I remember one morning my father took a bucket of cold water and threw it in my face...I got up quickly that morning."

It was hard, dirty work, with stale and pungent farm smells lifting from the hay, dust, and cow dung. Milking cows is not for sissies. If you're not careful, you can get your teeth kicked in. You can also get knocked off your milking stool if you're competing with a calf for her mother's milk. You freeze in the winter and sweat in the summer. Billy was not fond of the daily chores, according to his brother, especially when he got hit in the eye by the swish of a cow tail. "Billy never liked (milking cows)," recalled Melvin Graham in a 1996 interview. "He only did it because Daddy made him...and he had to do it because he was still at home. I always did accuse him of leaving home when he was seventeen to get off the farm, get away from that farm work." He milked twenty cows by hand in the morning and another twenty after he returned home from school. That's a long day in itself, but after the milking, the shed had to be cleaned.

Billy was also enlisted to deliver milk, and that wasn't much safer. He recalled to British journalist David Frost a customer delivery that almost turned deadly.

"About three o'clock in the morning, I was delivering milk. The snow had fallen and the dog had gotten after me in this particular house, and I ran in a direction that I had never taken before to get back to the milk truck," Billy said. "A clothes wire had been strung and it caught me right in the neck. I did a double twist and almost severed my head from my body. Then the dog came and attacked me while I was down. I'll never forget that."

The farm instilled in the young boy a strong work ethic that would serve him well in later years. Another benefit of being a farmer was that during times of economic turmoil, they could live off the land and eat while others had to scramble for food and the other necessities of life.

Even still, the Grahams didn't go unscathed. No one did. Frank lost his entire life savings of four thousand dollars in the 1929 stock market crash. Sadly, he never recouped his money. Frank was forced to wipe the slate clean.

Financially, things only got worse as the Great Depression lurched forward. The Graham Brothers Dairy Farm managed to scrape by through wit and grit, working from sunup to sundown. When milk dropped to five cents a quart, Frank went into survival—but never panic—mode. Billy recalled how his father's keen sense of humor and ability to tell funny jokes never waned or showed the slightest sign of worry. My best guess is that Frank placed his trust firmly in God to pull his family through.

Billy would face many challenges as he grew older. I believe he learned how to be steady in a storm from his father. Farm people are notoriously tough. They are highly dependent on God's grace in times of plenty and in times of drought. A wise man must save when times are good so that he has some left over in times of drought. These are pieces of wisdom that are sprinkled throughout the Psalms.

While Frank and Morrow faced those crushing times head on, Billy was still young enough to escape such harsh realities. He grew to love baseball and dreamed that one day he would become a professional athlete. He had visions of grandeur: playing in Wrigley Field in Chicago and Yankee Stadium in New York—a place that he would fill to capacity years later, and not because crowds wanted to see him hit home runs. Billy devoured the sports pages each morning and memorized the box scores of his favorite teams. Billy batted lefty and had a fair throwing arm and a decent glove, but he showed no signs of superstar potential.

Later, when Billy entered his first year of high school, the famed Babe Ruth came to Charlotte to play in an exhibition game. Billy and his companions on the baseball team were in the front row to cheer on the greatest batter who ever lived, whooping it up at top volume for their hero. Frank had even made arrangements for Billy to shake the Babe's hand. It was a thrilling moment for the teenager. It should have been. Ruth remains one of America's greatest sports heroes.

Billy's other loves at that time were reading and tending to his animals; the family had a collie, cats (at one time up to twenty), and several goats. He recalled locking up the dog and a cat in the doghouse and leaving them together for the rest of the night. Billy said they were inseparable by morning. The pairing of the two animals left an indelible impression on him. "Maybe that is where the seeds of some of my ecumenical convictions got planted, wanting to help people at odds with each other find ways to get along," he recollected in his 1997 autobiography.

Billy also got an early upper hand on racial relations in the Deep South. His family employed an African-American housekeeper named Susie Nickolson for nearly twenty years, and she became an aunt/motherly figure to the Graham children. Nickolson pitched in with the cooking and cleaning (though Morrow chopped wood for the stove), and occasionally stepped in when a family fight was about to erupt.

"I remember one night Mother and Daddy had to go to a meeting and I had a friend over visiting, and Mother left, I think, two cans of pork and beans," recalled Catherine Graham in 1996. "Well, Billy Frank loved pork and beans...and we started fighting over those pork and beans with my friend there, and we were just in our early teens, and Susie stood over us wringing her hands, saying, 'Please, Mr. Billy, please Mr. Melvin, please Miss Catherine, please don't kill each other.' And so, that's the kind of family we were."

Billy grew especially close to Reese Brown, the farm's African-American foreman and blacksmith. Brown held the distinction of being the highest-paid farmhand in Mecklenburg County, but he earned every penny. Brown's paycheck, and the fact that he was personal friends with Frank Graham, drew critical whispers from other farmers in the area because of Brown's race.

But Brown was worth his weight in gold. Not only was he physically strong (he could hold down a bull when it had to be dehorned), but he was an unrelenting workhorse and set the tone with all of the other dairy employees. They could not slack around him. Brown was smart, loyal, dependable, and trustworthy.

He helped Billy in his cow-milking technique and later coached him as he learned to drive. In between, Billy received plenty of free life lessons. Brown, a U.S. Army sergeant during World War I, instructed Billy how to respect his elders and did not mind disciplining the lad if he stepped out of line. Billy, who fondly thought of Brown as an uncle, also played with his two children and gobbled down his wife's tasty buttermilk biscuits when offered. It might have been a working farm, but it was also a family farm.

While Brown helped shape his character, it was Morrow who helped shape her son's mind, introducing Billy to literature and nudging him to develop his mind as part of a daily habit. He read for pleasure on a daily basis. Because his mother taught him to read books, he basked in the superheroes of his day: Robin Hood, Tom Swift, the Rover Boys, and especially the adventures of the jungle lord Tarzan, locked in hand-to-hand combat with gorillas, tigers, and lions. He developed an effective Tarzan-style yell when hanging from a backyard tree, often scaring the horses and drivers who scuttled by on Park Road. Even that act didn't go to waste, his father later said.

"I think all that yelling helped develop his voice," Frank Graham later told a biographer.

Morrow also developed Billy's biblical knowledge, starting at age four. She constantly rehearsed her children on Bible-verse memorization and the Westminster Shorter Catechism, which teaches all humans "to glorify God and enjoy him forever." Billy recalled, "Every day was a different Scripture that she would read to us at the breakfast table. Then we would have a prayer. Either my father led the prayer, or usually in the early days, it was my mother."

In the evening, Morrow prayed for each of her children to serve the Lord in some capacity. She could not have anticipated the special plans God had in store for her rambunctious and gangly oldest son.

Some of the first few verses Billy memorized were John 3:16, Psalm 90:7, Proverbs 3:5–6, and John 14:6. The last one states: "Jesus said, 'I am the way, the truth and the life. No man comes to the Father but by me.'"

I find this interesting, because that verse would be emblazoned on massive banners on the various stages around the world where Billy stood to preach the Gospel.

John 3:16 was another verse he would quote thousands of times to millions of people. That verse, along with John 14:6, would be paramount to his preaching.

In the summer of 1932, Morrow wanted to deepen her understanding of her faith, so she joined a Bible class with the prompting of her sister, Lil Barker. She came to the belief "that the Lord has come in and lives in our hearts. I had never known that truth before."

She came to know another kind of truth: God hears prayers. A few weeks after Morrow joined the Bible study, Frank was nearly killed when Reese Brown was using a mechanical saw to cut wood for the boiler room. When Frank approached Reese to ask him a question, the foreman turned his head to listen because of the near-deafening noise of the saw. In an instant, the saw caught a piece of wood and hurled it with great force into Frank's face. He bled profusely and was whisked to the hospital. Doctors initially didn't give him very good odds to live, but Frank was a strong and willful man.

His condition was grave and remained so for several days. The surgeons had to skillfully rebuild Frank's face, and they said his chances for survival were grim. Morrow called family and friends to pray for Frank while she got down on her knees in her bedroom and, as she recalls, "just laid hold of the Lord. I got up with the assurance that God heard my prayer." And He did.

From this and other early life-shaping events, Billy learned that God both hears and answers our prayers.

It is in our youth that many foundational truths are learned.

Billy was living in a perfect environment with a stable and loving family that he would draw on for the rest of his life. Though it might appear idealistic, and to some even "Pollyannaish," Billy was being prepared by God for a life that would be equaled by few, if any.

Frank eventually recovered, but his appearance was slightly altered after the accident. Billy ascribed his father's full recovery to God's special intervention. He also observed that Frank became more introspective and got serious about his spiritual life. That harrowing incident was perhaps directly responsible for an episode in May 1934, which many people in Charlotte still talk about more than eighty-five years later.

Approximately thirty local businessmen wanted to devote a day to fasting and prayer because the Depression had cast a pall of antipathy in the region. They had met a few times before. On this occasion, they gathered under a grove of shade trees at the edge of a pasture on the Graham Brothers Dairy Farm.

Frank later told Billy that Vernon Patterson, a local paper salesman, offered up a daring and powerful prayer that day: that God would raise someone from Charlotte who would take the Gospel not just to the good people of North Carolina, but to a global audience. Billy was not an obvious choice to anyone, including himself.

The world's future leading Christian evangelist was in the barn that day pitching hay to the mules, along with one of the hired farmhands. The two heard the men singing from afar, and Billy's cohort wondered aloud what all the fuss was.

"I guess they're some fanatics that have talked Daddy into using the place," Billy said blithely.

Everything changed just six months later. A traveling evangelist and messenger of God with the Old Testament name of Mordecai Ham caught the gangly, blue-eyed teenager's attention.

Like the desert prophets of old, Ham would irrevocably change the boy from inside out.

It would be a few more years before Billy would leave the farm, which gave him time to mull over the theology of creation and death; God and the devil; good versus evil; the path of righteousness and free will.

Billy, like the farm, was fertile ground for growth.

CHAPTER TWO

No Angel

B y the time I started to develop a relationship with Billy Graham in the mid-1980s, I already knew a great deal about him. I had read almost every book and magazine article I could find about Billy because he was a remarkable person. He was the one man everyone in ministry wanted to emulate. He was my personal hero.

I was genuinely interested in Billy's life. It was also important for me to be up to speed with his story and not waste his time when I was with him by asking questions I could answer on my own. I was looking for insight into Billy for several reasons. I wanted to understand his personal walk with the Lord: What made him so mindful of God's presence in his life, what gave him the desire to be radically obedient, and what drove him to continue to do ministry when he was older—even though he was at times so weary and spent?

I devoured all this information. I was especially delighted to know that Billy was a typical all-American boy who wasn't born walking on water. He was obsessed with baseball, teased his siblings, didn't have blinders on when it came to pretty girls, and got into several scrapes with his schoolmates. He also wasn't crazy about sitting in the church pew on

Sunday mornings. Billy didn't find it that entertaining—so he made it entertaining, said his brother, Melvin Graham.

I got to know Melvin, who was every ounce the consummate gentleman, very well. He had more classic one-liners and amazing stories than you can imagine.

Melvin would often say, "When I was a boy, I had a drug problem." He would then pause for dramatic effect as the audience would try to process such a revelation coming from the brother of Billy Graham. He continued, "They *drug* me to church; they *drug* me to Sunday School." It was a line that played well over and over.

Another Billy story Melvin loved to tell is how he liked to throw paper wads in church. He said, "During the service, he'd sit kind of in the back, and he'd take a strong rubber band and he'd take a piece of chewing gum paper or something and wad it up tight, and...he'd shoot and hit [the women's] hats."

One of Billy's school bus drivers recalled to biographer John Pollock that the future evangelist had a fondness for pranks, and he was often the target. He said that when Billy got off the bus, he would stealthily reach underneath and flip the shutoff valve to the gas tank. The bus would roll on for about another hundred yards before the engine would conk out.

"I'd get out and shake my fist at him, but he'd only give me a laugh," the driver said. "It made him a hero to the other kids."

Part of the reason for Billy's sometimes unruly behavior was his fidgety nature and the fact that he didn't perceive any personal relevance in the Gospel message he often heard at that time. That message was usually delivered by Dr. W. B. Lindsay, the minister who presided over the Associate Reformed Presbyterian Church. Lindsay, a kind man, reminded Billy of a mortician; he found his sermons humorless, uninspired, and lethargic. He also discovered he wasn't the only one who thought so. Billy later recalled that Lindsay's wife dutifully sat in the front pew every week, fervently pointing at her watch when it was time for her husband to wrap things up.

Billy was blessed when it came to how and where he was raised. He was a child of the Roaring Twenties who came of age during the Depression that followed. Rural life shielded him from the bountiful sin the world had to offer. Barely.

The 1920s truly did roar. It was inescapable, even on a dairy farm in North Carolina. Only four hundred miles away in Montgomery, Alabama—a place similar to where the Grahams lived, steeped in Southern devotion and tradition—lived Zelda Fitzgerald and Tallulah Bankhead. Best friends in high school, (to no one's surprise) Fitzgerald became the "first American flapper," an outrageous socialite, a party girl, and the wife of F. Scott Fitzgerald, who dubbed the decade the "Jazz Age." Bankhead became a leading Hollywood star, famous for being sultry and having a husky voice prone to saying things like, "I'm pure as the driven slush." Her nickname was the "Alabama Tornado." Zelda often took off all her clothes at parties; Bankhead was even wilder. And these were Southern girls from good homes, not sharp-eyed princesses from Chicago or New York.

The point is, while Billy may have been down on the farm, the farm was not far from The Scene. Bountiful sin surrounded them. Prohibition was in full swing. Many people wished it would be repealed so they would drink *less*. While big cities had places like the Stork Club, every other town had house parties. People toted suitcases full of booze to each other's houses. Bootleggers likely drove down the road past the Graham farm late at night. The following words and phrases were all coined between 1918 and 1923: "junkie," "hitch-hike," "sexiness," "Hollywood," "comfort zone," "party crashing," "slinky," "cold turkey," and "brand name." Even in Charlotte—often considered the most church-going city in the United States—girls cut their hair short, wore scandalous dresses, used slang, drank, and smoked cigarettes. Even if you weren't in Charlotte around short-skirted girls chugging gin, the popular culture followed you home via the radio.

Being a typical eldest child, Billy was expected to set the example for his younger siblings. And if he didn't, his backside got graced by both of his parents. Frank used a belt; Morrow was partial to switches.

"My father and mother were both disciplinarians, and they didn't mind using the rod," Billy once told a reporter. "Maybe because I was the oldest child. I always felt I got much more of it than anybody else."

Perhaps he got "much more of it" because Billy was a hyperactive and mischievous kid prone to yanking girls' pigtails, tricking his siblings into trouble, or bringing a farm animal to school and setting it quietly on his lap while the teacher was none the wiser. As my friend David Aikman noted in his 2007 biography, *Billy Graham: His Life and Influence*, "(Graham) was a gangly knot of undirected energy running hither and yon through the family home, overturning egg baskets, knocking plates off the kitchen table, and even on one occasion, tipping a bureau chest down the stairs." Billy's parents were so concerned about his hyperkinetic ways that they took him to a local physician for examination. After a casual observation and an unusual line of questioning ("Did the boy eat a lot of sweets?" "Was he doing his chores?" "Was his father giving him enough busy work?"), the doctor assured them their child was simply built differently. Today, I have no doubt Billy would be heavily dosed with Ritalin or some other medication to slow him down. Thankfully, that wasn't common in his day. This was a blessing in disguise because that energy would be needed during his Crusades when he would spend weeks, sometimes months, praying and preaching.

Even in his older years, Billy had this energy, which I would describe as a supernatural power that God worked through him. I recall times when I was with him and helped with illustrations and current events to include in his Crusade message that coming evening at his request. He would call me up to his room, and I would rehearse what I wrote, almost "preaching" it to him as he might deliver it. He would lay out his long legs on his hotel bed with his thick glasses on, patiently listening. If he liked a point, he would slowly grab the hotel phone, dial the number of his secretary, Stephanie Wills, and tell her to include it in his message for that evening. Sometimes I wondered if he would have the strength to get out of that bed, much less mount the Crusade stage and preach. But he made it every time.

And though he needed assistance in his later years to get on the stage, once there, he owned it. That old spark of the younger Billy would come out as he began to speak, and people would hang on his every word— including me.

Billy Graham has often been described as a saint. But that word conjures up figures in robes, illuminated in stained glass, inaccessibly distant and impossibly perfect. It's tough to write a compelling book about someone who is widely perceived as such and keep it believable. But I am not merely writing what I have read. I am writing what I saw with my own eyes and heard with my own ears. While saints are to be emulated and admired, I've discovered they sure aren't a whole lot of fun to read about. I've never seen a smile on the faces of anyone in those glass windows. As Billy Joel famously sang in "Only the Good Die Young," he'd rather laugh with the sinners than cry with the saints. That sentiment seems to resonate with a lot of people, mainly because it's true. And who wants to read about someone who isn't real and relatable?

People will be surprised to discover that Billy Graham was not without sin or flaws, and his wife Ruth often reminded him of it. He had his moments of doubt, and he was so dedicated to his work that he spent days, even months, away from his family. Billy once said in an interview, "I do feel that I could have done so much more had I studied more or gone further in school, probably spent more time with my family. I have spent so little time with my family. And, thank God they're all wonderful children and wonderful grandchildren."

He also regretted not spending more time in prayer and Bible study— not just for his messages, but for his own spiritual growth.

Billy was, however, a model of integrity in his witness for Christ—an ordinary man who rose to an extraordinary challenge by his Creator. He made mistakes, yet he was obedient and consistent in his walk with the Lord, faithfully and humbly serving, and he never stopped listening to God's voice because that is where he found clear direction and guidance. No matter how ridiculous or outrageous a scenario, Billy always saw the task to the end, and he counted on the Holy Spirit to take care of the rest. He was called by God for a very good reason: he never questioned His word or authority. Billy's faith was bedrock, almost childlike. He didn't always understand what he was asked to do, but he knew he must trust and obey because the Bible requires a servant to be faithful.

Over time, I have found myself far more impressed with character than charisma, with persistence over power, and with faithfulness over fame. Billy Graham definitely had his priorities in order.

Though his past is well-documented, Billy rarely spoke to me about his upbringing, typically only doing so if I asked him about it. Like many successful people, he didn't live in the past. He was a forward-looking man. He knew you couldn't look back and continue to serve the Lord. Most of his time was spent studying the Word (six hours a day, according to Billy) so he could improve in sharing the message of the Gospel. He certainly never looked to prop up his legend, though he was truly a legendary man. Billy was very much interested in what was happening currently, which is why I think he allowed me to hang around him. He knew I was a younger evangelist, perhaps somewhat more in tune with the culture than he was. I suppose he also sensed my sincere desire to serve the Lord and knew I was looking for him to share his wisdom and guidance with me. Besides, it felt so good being in Billy's presence.

Almost like having a little bit of Heaven on Earth.

CHAPTER THREE

A Bespectacled Messenger

Any parent will tell you there is no such thing as the perfect teen. As the father of two sons, I speak from experience.

One of them was a handful right out of the womb, constantly pushing the envelope, while the other was shy, somewhat sheltered, and uncomfortable in his own skin. Both took years to find themselves and did so at their own pace.

A teen's years are often some of the most difficult challenges for families to face, ripe for producing conflict. It's a period of intense growth, not only physically but emotionally, intellectually, and spiritually. Hormonal changes come with puberty, which means teens have to deal with issues of identity, dating and sexuality, drinking, drugs, and social status among their peers.

Teens are often a combustible mix of boundless enthusiasm and total ignorance. "Feel like jumping off a thirty-foot cliff into a river bottom?" "Sure, go for it. What could possibly go wrong?" "Mom's station wagon can get airborne—let's go!" Or maybe this scenario: "Let's mix everything in the medicine cabinet and see what happens!"

I guess you could say that Billy Graham's behavior in his teenage years was tame by today's standards, but he had a few episodes that would curl any parent's hair—like the time he drove his dad's car into a muddy sinkhole. By then Graham was a freshman in high school, and like many young men that age, he was speeding and showing off for his buddies. Obviously distracted, Billy drove the family car right into the mud. Tucking his tail between his legs, he knocked on a neighbor's door, went inside, and called his dad, asking him to bring a team of mules to pull out the car (the 1930s version of a tow truck!). Frank Graham was usually a very quiet man, but he made it clear to his eldest son upon arrival that he was not pleased.

When Billy commenced his secondary education, "country kids" like him were required to transfer to Sharon High School at the edge of town. Billy recalled in his autobiography a scene that very well could have been in Francis Ford Coppola's *The Outsiders*: "We newcomers glared at the students who were already there, and they glared back. It took at least six months for us to get used to each other. That first year at Sharon, I got into more fistfights and wrestling matches than in all the rest of my schooldays put together. And a couple of times, I got beaten."

He was also beaten by alcohol, though that was by design. When Prohibition was repealed in December 1933, his father brought home two bottles of beer, placed one in front of Billy and the other in front of his sister, Catherine, then directed them to drink up. They did so and found the bitterness displeasing to their taste buds.

This approach worked like a charm because Billy and his sister never developed a taste for beer or any other alcoholic beverage, allowing them to abstain throughout their adult years. Billy said as an adult he also abstained for another reason.

"The Bible says if I do anything to make my brother stumble or fall, then I'm not to do it," Billy said. "If people saw me sitting at a table drinking, in America at least, then they might say, 'Well, Billy does it; it's alright for me' and they may become alcoholics as a result of it. So I have to be careful of my witness."

Billy's two vices as he entered high school were oddly matched: the opposite sex and chewing tobacco. The latter fell by the wayside quickly. The former was a little harder to shake.

The tallish, high-spirited teen became a heartthrob to young ladies at Sharon High School. With his height, stylish threads, wavy blond hair, and fierce blue eyes, Billy cut a striking figure. He could be seen holding hands and kissing girls in the hallways. Billy was a serial dater, often seeing two girls successively the same night. He seemed to have a different girlfriend every day, his sister Catherine noted. That doesn't surprise me. Teenage Billy sounded like a fun and charismatic guy to be around.

Case in point: Billy sometimes borrowed a yellow convertible from a relative so a young woman he frequently dated could stand up and vigorously clang a cowbell as he hurtled along at breakneck speed down one of Charlotte's country lanes. This tells me that people were going to notice Billy Graham, whether they wanted to or not.

While Billy had dated and kissed several girls, he showed uncommon restraint by not taking things further. Sure, he was tempted in the same way his male peers were, but he said the Lord had used his parents' love, teachings, and discipline to keep him on the straight and narrow. In the back of Billy's mind, the only person he was going to have sex with was the woman he was going to marry. But even that got put to the test.

During his senior year, while participating in a school play, Billy was wheedled one night into a dark classroom by a female cast member with a heavy-duty reputation for taking things too far. Before Billy knew what hit him, she was begging him to make love to her. Billy recalled in his autobiography, "My hormones were as active as any other healthy young male's, and I had fantasized often enough about such a moment. But when it came, I silently cried to God for strength and darted from that classroom the way Joseph fled the bedroom of Potiphar's philandering wife in ancient Egypt."

Billy certainly was not naïve to the ways of the world. Sex was a topic he and his teenage buddies often discussed when they got together. And he got advanced tutoring from a ranch hand named Pedro Evans, whom

Billy recalled as a rough-around-the-edges but fairly good-natured character. Pedro often confided in him about his sexual exploits with women, but Billy later suspected they were "probably embellished for my wide-eyed benefit."

Pedro also tried to mentor Billy on the fine art of chewing tobacco. The highly addictive habit was introduced to a lot of teens, particularly in the South, through professional baseball players. That included Billy's hero, Babe Ruth, who not only indulged in, but also endorsed chewing tobacco and smoking cigarettes.

The habit didn't take hold for Billy because when Frank caught him with a chaw in his mouth, Pedro was fired. Billy also did not escape his father's wrath and said he received a "thrashing to remember."

Clearly, by age fifteen, Billy had seen and experienced sin firsthand, although immorality was not part of his makeup. Still, Billy had no desire to live his life for Christ. Perhaps he figured that would happen when he matured. Church was all well and good, and Billy would continue to attend and not complain to his parents, for he knew that "they would have whaled the tar out of me."

The problem, as I see it, was that Billy Graham simply wasn't ready for the Lord. Committing one's life to Christ is a decision that we each must personally make. God was preparing Billy for the moment he would really hear the Gospel, as He does every person. But what we do with that moment is entirely up to us.

In late summer 1934, Charlotte's Christian Men's Club invited Dr. Mordecai Fowler Ham, a man *Time* magazine labeled a "fiery-eyed, long-fingered Kentucky revivalist" to Charlotte to blaze away in a sprawling "tent tabernacle," which lasted twelve weeks between August 30 and November 25, 1934. Actually, it wasn't a tent, but a twenty-thousand-square-foot cheap pine board building that Ham had to get a special variance to build because it wasn't fireproof.

But blaze he did. Modern dance was only one of his targets. In Ham's estimation, dances, whether held in a private home or a public dance hall, were one of the devil's greatest agencies. Four out of five girls who went astray in big cities did so because they started dancing. "Sin," "Hell," the "inevitable decline of Western civilization," cigarette smoking, night riding, and petting were other subjects he opined on for hours.

Ham vowed to stay until he drove the devil and his angels out of Charlotte. "Ham compared Charlotte to Sodom, which he said was little better than the Charlotte people who oppose his campaign in trying to save men's souls," wrote the *Elizabeth City Independent* on October 12 that year.

Ham, a tallish, balding, white-mustached man who wore "granny glasses" and impeccable clothing, developed a reputation for seeking out the worst sinners at the worst of times. He was a man with intense convictions who harangued revelers during New Orleans' Mardi Gras; confronted a four-time murderer at a revival, then led him to Christ; and got a Chattanooga mob boss and bootleg czar with a first-degree murder rap to give up his life of crime and turn to Jesus.

Ham routinely got legislators to shut down saloons, gambling halls, and brothels, but not without blowback or some form of retribution. He often used his Bible to deflect blows from angry atheists, infidels, and moonshiners. Guns were routinely shoved in his face, and knives were pulled. Armed escorts, including U.S. Marshals, were common on many stops.

The evangelist's bravado caught up with him when he was mowed down by an automobile and dragged for half a block. No one thought it was by accident. Ham required a team of fourteen doctors over a period of six weeks to bring him back from the brink of death. Upon discharge, he immediately picked up where he left off, and the threats continued, which included kidnapping his little daughter.

Ham was tougher than a two-dollar steak. And his unbridled passion for winning souls led to approximately three hundred thousand decisions for Christ in his evangelistic career.

In addition to unsaved souls, Ham was also known for going after clergy when he felt they were getting too complacent. He had a term for these folks: he called them "halfway fellows."

Ham once told a reporter:

> There are a lot of Christians who are halfway fellows. They
> stand in the door, holding on to the church with one hand
> while they play with the toys of the world with the other. They
> are in the doorway and we cannot bring sinners in. And, until
> we get some of God's people right, we cannot hope to get
> sinners regenerated. Now they always accuse me of carrying
> around a sledgehammer with which to pound church mem-
> bers. Yes sir, I do pound them, every time I come down, I
> knock one of the halfway fellows out of the doorway, and
> every time I knock one out, I get a sinner in.

Frank and Morrow Graham initially put off attending Ham's revival
based on the tacit disapproval of their minister at the Associate Reformed
Presbyterian Church, who thought Ham was a rabble-rousing trouble-
maker. They skipped the first week or so of his revival, which started in
late August. But finally, a neighbor couple escorted them to one of Ham's
sermons. The Grahams were instantly hooked on the old-fashioned
revival, which was drawing two to three thousand people a night. They
began attending almost nightly.

Billy, on the other hand, was openly leery of Ham and refused to go.
Surprisingly, he held a very cynical view of evangelists. Like many in his
day, he thought they were crooked quick-buck artists who preyed on
peoples' emotions. Billy was a smart kid, if you ask me!

In actuality, Ham may not have been crooked, but this reputation
certainly preceded him. When he arrived in a new town, his MO was to
search out the biggest and most vile sinner and take them to task. When
he rolled into Charlotte, considered one of the most churchgoing cities
in the country, and sniffed around, he soon discovered the "Queen City"
had an underbelly. He was informed by local preachers that sexual
immorality was rampant, especially among young people. Ham claimed
that students from Charlotte's Central High School had been visiting a

nearby house of prostitution during lunch hour, and he had the affidavits to prove it, which he gladly turned over to the city council.

The story broke in both the *Charlotte News* and *Charlotte Observer.* The crusade became the talk of the town. Locals felt the honor of Charlotte's youth had been besmirched. Students were upset and angry, as were a few of Charlotte's most high-powered lawyers, who leaned heavily on Ham through newspaper op-eds to end the crusade. (After police raided the brothel and the owners were convicted, the threats against Ham suddenly disappeared.)

Central High School students were especially infuriated at the evangelist and demanded a public apology. And if they didn't get one, they were going to march on the tabernacle and physically evict him from the platform. Suddenly, Billy was intrigued, though still not ready to commit.

But who could get him to go?

The answer came in the form of twenty-four-year-old Albert McMakin, a recently married man who worked several years on the Graham farm. McMakin had given his life to Christ a year before and was on fire for the Lord. He had been attending Ham's services regularly, and one October night, he was planning on loading his old vegetable truck with as many people as he could fit to hear another nightly sermon. When he came across Billy that day, he extended the invitation.

"Why don't you come out and hear our fighting preacher?" McMakin suggested.

"Is he a fighter?" Billy asked. The notion of Ham as a scrappy street-fighter willing to take on all comers captivated him. "I like a fighter."

McMakin threw in the extra incentive of letting Billy drive his truck into town, even suggesting that he could perhaps pick up Pauline Presson (a girl Billy was sweet on) and take her to the service. Billy, a few weeks shy of his sixteenth birthday, took the bait.

"I figured he was the same way that I had been, a moral boy with a head knowledge taught by his own people, but not having come face-to-face with the Lord Jesus Christ," McMakin said of Billy.

When they arrived that night at the corner of Central and Pecan Avenues (today it's the parking lot of a French bistro in the Central Square Shopping Center) in downtown Charlotte, the tent tabernacle was nearly filled to capacity. Billy and the rest of the folks crammed into the truck that night and traipsed through a parking lot filled with cars and people, feeling the same kind of electricity that would later infuse rock concerts in the 1960s and '70s. Once they entered the tent, it was like a whole new world: wood shavings and sawdust on the floor, light-bulbs strung along the overhead rafters, the angelic choir all dressed in white backed by the rollicking playing of pianist Rawley Treadway, and the empty podium awaiting Ham, whose sonorous voice would deliver a thundering Gospel sermon. The group sat in the rear of the auditorium. It was one of the largest crowds Billy had seen up to that point in his life (though later, when he was at his peak, he would routinely speak to audiences ten to fifty times this size).

The large crowd, the singing, and the excitement served as a great buildup for Ham, who started each sermon by opening his Bible and wasted no time launching into his message. He spoke loudly and with clear diction—so loudly, in fact, that everyone in the tent could hear him without the assistance of a PA system. Decades later, Billy remembered that special moment in his 1997 autobiography.

"I have no recollection of what he preached about, but I was spell-bound," Graham wrote. "In some indefinable way, he was getting through to me. I was hearing another voice, as was often said of Dwight L. Moody when he preached: the voice of the Holy Spirit."

As an evangelist, this is what I hope and pray for: that non-believers hear the voice of God when I preach. To be effective, my message is intentionally streamlined. In the minds of some, it might seem simplistic. I would use a slightly different word: simple.

The evangelist effectively preaches to solicit a decision from the moment his message begins. And the crowning moment is the invitation, or the altar call. This is when the non-believer is invited to commit his life to Christ.

Billy understood this well and, in my opinion, was the greatest evangelist who ever lived (excluding the apostles, of course). In fact, Billy Graham would become the gold standard for all evangelists. And it would all begin when the young Billy Frank heard the bespectacled messenger, Mordecai Ham.

Billy didn't give his heart to the Lord that night, but something rattled him. Driving back home in the truck, he was deep in thought. His friend Albert McMakin took notice of his spiritual struggle.

"He didn't know really what was wrong with him. He moved around from one place to another," McMakin recalled. "I could tell he was under conviction, but I kept my mouth shut because I felt God was handling this affair, and I could very well cause him not to go with me if I said much."

As it turned out, McMakin didn't need to worry. Graham was hooked. Ham's crusade was the best draw in town, and Billy began attending his sermons on a nightly basis over the next several weeks. It wasn't just the spectacle; he grew to enjoy Ham's choice of lively topics, which included a potpourri of mankind's worldly sins.

Ham's sermon on Hell most piqued Billy's curiosity because as a young man, he had never heard his preacher even broach the subject. Today Ham might be called a hellfire-and-brimstone preacher. Many people might complain there are too many people cut from that cloth, but quite frankly, I don't believe there are enough of them. I see preachers on TV, but I can't remember the last time I heard a message on God's judgment and the inevitable hellfire awaiting them.

That's not all preachers should discuss, of course, but when they leave it out completely, they are not delivering an authentic Gospel message. The fact is, Jesus Christ Himself spoke more on the topic of Hell than all the other preachers of the Bible put together.

The more Billy listened to these sermons, the more he became convicted. Naturally, this led to confusion. He had been baptized, practically memorized the entire Shorter Catechism, and had been confirmed in the Associate Reformed Presbyterian Church. He was kind to everyone (except maybe his school bus driver and the little old ladies in church wearing those frilly hats), respectful to his parents, and truly didn't have a mean bone in his body. Lying, cheating, and stealing were foreign concepts to Billy.

Good boy, most certainly. But was he actually saved? Not yet. But that would happen very soon, and the world would be a much different place because of it.

CHAPTER FOUR

The Old Has Gone, the New Has Come

B illy Graham was under conviction. I can tell you from personal experience that it's very unsettling.

It's not easy to run from the Holy Spirit once He convicts you. When it's happening to you, it's undeniable. And it's constantly on your mind.

Historically, the Bible points to many examples of this. John the Baptist confronted Herod Antipas because of his illicit marriage to Herodias, his brother's wife, and he fell under the conviction of the Holy Spirit. Unfortunately, he did not respond to the Gospel, despite hearing the truth from John, one of the greatest prophets. And then there was Paul, the biggest sinner of them all, who persecuted Christians and even had them killed. He was convicted by Jesus on the road to Damascus when Jesus said to him, "Saul, Saul, why are you persecuting me? It is useless for you to fight against my will" (Acts 26:14 NLT).

Everyone contemplating a life with Christ will come under conviction. Billy Graham was no exception. Neither was I. We were just about the same age when God began speaking to our hearts. In my search, I was living an empty and meaningless life, partying heavily with drugs and drinking. At the age of seventeen, I felt like I was seventy. Then, after seeing a group of Christians who were not ashamed of their faith but were simply living as followers of Jesus, I ended up at one of their Bible studies. It took place on the front lawn of my high school. I sat closely enough to eavesdrop on what they were saying, but not so close that people would think I was actually listening—or worse, joining them.

A young evangelist from Calvary Chapel of Costa Mesa in California spoke that day. His name was Lonnie Frisbee. As I listened, I came under the conviction of the Holy Spirit; it suddenly dawned on me that Jesus was the One I was searching for all this time. When Lonnie gave the invitation that day for people to come to Christ, I responded.

Billy's inward struggle also dogged him as the Holy Spirit spoke to him about certain sins in his life. And it made him feel terribly guilty.

He certainly was not anywhere near the worst of sinners, but God does not grade on the curve. Billy still carried a great burden because he was separated from God. He realized that his efforts at self-improvement were futile, and he had led a purposeless life.

But what he feared most was that powerful finger Ham seemed to be pointing in his direction when he attended the evangelist's fiery sermons. One night, Billy was so sure that Ham had pointed him out that he ducked behind the wide-brimmed hat of the lady sitting in front of him.

Billy's brother, Melvin, said Ham's line, "Get your heart right with the Lord or you'll wind up in Hell," resonated the most.

"He made it very vivid," Melvin recalled. "And he scared my brother, too.... And it had an effect on me, but it had more or less a delayed effect on me, I would say. You know the Gospel message affects different people different ways. Some people can turn a deaf ear time after time and just dismiss it. Others get convicted, and I've seen people cry. I've seen people weep deep sobs of conviction. I've seen people laugh and enjoy themselves."

I'm also positive Billy was shaken to his core. And yet, he couldn't stay away. He realized that he did not have a personal relationship with Jesus Christ.

"In a word, I was spiritually dead," Billy later said.

One could argue that Billy was also ripe for conversion. He was ready to fall from the tree, be picked up by Jesus, and become whatever the Lord wanted him to be.

On the night of November 1, 1934, the Holy Spirit set the path for Billy Graham to make a decision that would irrevocably change his life and literally impact billions of people all over the world.

While attending the meetings, Billy developed lasting friendships with Grady and Thomas Walter (T.W.) Wilson, brothers who attended Central High School, the institution under Ham's assault. Grady considered himself a Christian but, like Billy, was questioning the depth of his commitment to Christ. The Wilsons were the sons of a local plumber who was friendly with Billy's father through the Christian Men's Club. Their father, Thomas Walter Sr., had been present at the prayer meeting on the Graham Brothers Dairy Farm, beseeching God for revival and to bring a messenger of God to the world.

The two brothers were polar opposites: Grady was short and stocky, but a happy-go-lucky lad—a natural comedian whose sense of humor kept everyone grounded when things got too tense. T.W., on the other hand, was tall and bulky and not someone to be trifled with.

I never had the pleasure of meeting Grady because he passed away in 1987, about a year or so after my association and friendship with Billy began to deepen. I do know from Billy's own words that he and Grady were especially tight.

Billy once said, "Grady Wilson was one of my closest friends and associates for over fifty years. No one outside of my family has ever been any closer than Grady.

"He was a unique servant of God. I doubt if there will ever be another one like him."

I did, however, get to know T.W. as a friend. He, too, was a real comrade to Billy and did whatever was needed to make his life a bit more comfortable—including keeping threats at bay and even washing Billy's socks in the hotel-room sink when the need arose.

T.W. was a capable and gifted preacher and could have been a successful pastor had he chosen that route. But he felt he had a higher calling to come alongside Billy and be as Barnabas was to Paul or Joshua was to Moses. T.W. may have showed a gruff exterior to some, but he was a very tender-hearted man who simply loved Billy and felt called to protect and serve in that capacity.

Billy knew he was safe when T.W. and Grady were around. They kept him grounded and "knew him way back when" as boyhood friends. Billy could count on them for their loyalty, counsel, friendship, and a good laugh when needed. They had his back.

We often celebrate the well-known people God uses like Billy, but we sometimes forget to laud those who work behind the scenes, as many did for Graham with an undying devotion, respect, and affection. Billy built an amazing collective—known worldwide as the "Graham Team"—that stayed with him to the end. He thought he would precede them all to Heaven, but he outlived every one of them—including his beloved wife, Ruth.

Though familiar with the Wilson brothers, who attended Caldwell Memorial Presbyterian Church, Billy never had an opportunity to spend time with them until the Mordecai Ham revival. Their friendship deepened after those shared late summer/early fall nights and continued for the rest of their natural lives. The Wilsons became a part of Billy's evangelistic band of brothers who protected him, helped him think strategically, and did a lot of heavy lifting so Billy could stay focused on public ministry and outreach.

One of Billy and Grady's early strategies to thwart Mordecai Ham's ire from the pulpit was to join the choir, which sat on the platform risers behind the preacher's podium. Neither could sing a lick, but they could silently pantomime and use the hymn books to cloak their faces.

They discovered they were not entirely alone. Billy's first cousin Crook Stafford also sang in the choir. Slightly older than Billy and an accountant by trade, he was a kindly figure growing up, Billy recollected. He also bucked Billy up in his spiritual walk, often shuttling him to and from the evening services. Crook was there for all the right reasons; Billy was still on the fence.

But Billy's ploy to hide within the sanctuary of the choir instantly crumbled with Ham's first words on November 1, 1934:

"There's a great sinner in this place tonight!"

The words seared his heart, and Billy was wracked with instant guilt. His armor had been penetrated, and he was deeply convicted, which was God's intention.

Ham gave another earth-scorching sermon, asking congregants to surrender their lives to Christ before it was too late. At the end, Ham offered the invitation to anyone who felt the desire to accept Christ. His long-time musical director (and business partner), William J. Ramsay, led everyone in the hymn "Just as I Am."

Just as I am, without one plea,
But that Thy blood was shed for me,
And that Thou bid'st me come to Thee,
O Lamb of God, I come, I come!

This was a well-known hymn in the South and was later popularized by Billy in his Crusades, sung as hundreds of thousands of people streamed forward to make their public professions of faith to follow Jesus Christ.

"Just as I Am" also brings back a very personal memory.

My mother, Charlene, called me one night when she had been drinking. She was the classic prodigal daughter; she ran away from home and eloped while still a young girl. Her parents, Charles and Stella, were rigid Southern Baptists and strict disciplinarians.

In between her seven husbands, Charlene had a fling with a sailor from Long Beach, during which I was conceived. She had no interest in being a mother, and I was sent to live with her parents. Over the years, our relationship was strained even though I loved her dearly.

At the time of my mother's phone call, I was a young pastor, and I prayed constantly for her to come to Christ. Slurring her words from a night of boozing, she asked if I would sing "Just as I Am" if she went forward to commit her life to Christ at one of my services. I would have sung anything if she had taken that bold step. When I brought it up to her the next day, when she was sober, she had no recollection of our conversation and wouldn't talk about it.

Her salvation would come at a later date, but Billy's was like a burning fuse: it couldn't wait.

Ramsey followed "Just as I Am" with another classic hymn, "Almost Persuaded, Now to Believe," written by Philip Paul Bliss, an American composer, conductor, and writer of hymns. Bliss was a rare artist and entrepreneur who found success in publishing, conducting, and teaching as a concert pianist. But he gave it all up when he met the evangelist Dwight L. Moody and became a full-time missionary singer.

Billy knew none of this, of course, but the song moved him in such a way that by the time they reached the last verse, he walked down to the front of the aisle and stepped onto the platform to make a declaration for Christ. (Grady Wilson made his decision for Christ on another night that same week, as did Billy's cousin Crook Graham.)

The lyrics of that sweet hymn beckoned Billy to come forward:

> *Almost persuaded, harvest is past!*
> *Almost persuaded, doom comes at last!*
> *Almost cannot avail;*
> *Almost is but to fail!*
> *Sad, sad, that bitter wail—*
> *Almost, but lost!*

Billy recalled in his autobiography that the walk to the platform was painful, almost like it was done in slow motion. Once he reached his destination, hundreds of people were making professions of faith. Many of them were crying, including a lady next to Billy who had the full waterworks going. Billy was surprised; he was so devoid of any emotion that he second-guessed himself. Was this the right move?

A very similar thing happened when I walked forward to give my life to Jesus. A few others walked up with me. A woman on my left was filled with happiness while the person on my right was weeping over his sin. I, like Billy, strangely felt nothing.

I thought, *It figures. God rejected me!*

But nothing could be further from the truth. That is the day I mark as the day of my conversion.

The lack of emotion made Billy wonder, and he even contemplated retreating to his spot in the choir. That's when I believe God sent another messenger to him.

J.D. Prevatt was a Charlotte tailor, a Graham family friend, and a strong Christian who loved people and wanted to be used by God. Prevatt was a short man with dark eyes and jet-black hair who spoke with a thick European accent and ushered at Ham's services. He quietly appeared by Billy's side on the platform, sliding his arm around his shoulder in a show of support. He gently explained God's plan for Billy's salvation in a way the teen could comprehend.

"My tailor friend helped me to understand what I had to do to become a genuine Christian. The key word was *do*," Billy wrote in his autobiography. "Those of us standing up front had to decide to *do* something about what we knew before it could take effect."

Prevatt prayed for Billy, then suggested that Billy follow his lead and pray too. Billy then repented of his sins and invited Christ into his heart. But there was the last hurdle, which is the same for all who are seeking the Christian walk: Was Billy truly ready to make a change?

Billy actually answered that question when he checked the "recommitment" box on the decision card he filled out that night in cursive. That card, which has been preserved by the Billy Graham Evangelistic Association for more than eight decades, gives me a personal thrill every time I see it.

Wrapped in a green cover called *The Pocket Treasury*, this simple card is a historic document today. When you look at it, it's shocking to think about the way the entire world was impacted by the prayer of that young farm boy from Charlotte—a boy who would soon become a man, and a man who would change the world.

In fact, Billy's impact on the world made his hometown famous. No wonder he's called "Charlotte's favorite son."

That night, Billy felt a sense of serenity. And so did his father, Frank, who hugged him on the platform and told him how proud he was. Later that evening back home, when Billy walked into the kitchen, his mother lovingly embraced her newly minted son.

"I'm a changed boy," Billy proudly told a pleased Morrow.

He eventually headed upstairs to his room and tried to make sense of what had transpired a few hours before. Billy then went to his knees to pray. He closed his eyes and thanked God for his salvation.

Before Billy drowsed off, he contemplated what his life would be like now as a committed Christian. He drifted off to sleep with a degree of uncertainty, wondering if this new feeling of spiritual bliss would last.

It would, in ways that a sixteen-year-old farm boy could never begin to imagine.

CHAPTER FIVE

Rose-Colored Glasses

The next morning, after wiping the sleep from his eyes, Billy Graham realized he was indeed a new creature because he had been born again. He saw and experienced the world in a whole new light.

That morning and in the days that followed, it seemed that the birds sang louder and more sweetly. The sun shone brighter. The sky was bluer, and the clouds were whiter. Over time, his love for the Lord, his family, and his friends grew deeper. He experienced greater compassion for people and saw them in a new light. He recognized more than ever his own and humanity's great need for Jesus Christ.

Billy said that before his conversion, he claimed he was alternately oversensitive, envious, and irritable. After his life-changing experience, he was deliberately courteous and kind to everybody around him. (I can't imagine Billy Graham being anything other than kind and courteous in his lifetime.)

Beyond that, Billy now looked forward to the church activities he'd once dreaded. Bible verses he had memorized suddenly had new meaning. Dr. Lindsay's once-boring sermons suddenly became so interesting that Billy took notes. He became more studious at school. He happily sang hymns while he milked cows. The Lord was definitely changing him from the inside out.

Yes, there is a period in which new believers see everything through rose-colored glasses; but when hardship or difficulties hit, that's when they grow in their faith. Being a Christian doesn't exempt you from the trials and tribulations of life. In fact, new believers will go through a phase when their faith will be tried and tested. But if it is genuine, it will not be weakened by those trials; it will be strengthened.

This could be compared to physically working out. You effectively break down muscle to build it back up again. Trials are like God's gym, where the Lord strengthens us spiritually for what lies ahead. The Bible reminds us, "Consider it a sheer gift, friends, when tests and challenges come at you from all sides. You know that under pressure, your faith-life is forced into the open and shows its true colors. So, don't try to get out of anything prematurely. Let it do its work so you become mature and well-developed, not deficient in any way" (James 1:2–4 MSG).

Billy Graham was no exception.

In the days following his conversion, he was ridiculed at school by a few friends while some of his closest buddies passed on attending Ham's revival with him. Billy was also embarrassed by a teacher in front of his classmates. Billy later confessed to feeling some resentment toward this teacher.

The Bible is filled with promises that Christians love to claim, but one Scripture that is rarely quoted is: "Everyone who wants to live a godly life in Christ Jesus will suffer persecution" (1 Timothy 3:12 NLT).

No one wants to be ridiculed or made fun of, but it often goes with the territory of being a true Christ-follower.

Billy had no one to consult during this transitional period. He quickly learned there was a great need for mentorship and accountability with other believers.

He also learned how imperative it is to read the Scriptures daily early in your walk with the Lord, allowing God to speak to you directly. Reading and listening are essential for growing that personal relationship with

Christ. New Christians are like newborn babies: they need to learn to take nourishment from the Scriptures and walk in the light of the Lord. Billy was bold when he took his stand for Christ, but he wasn't growing in the knowledge of God's Word and the wisdom he needed as quickly as he wanted. That would come later, in college, but high school still presented opportunities to hinder him.

As a new Christian, he was walking in as much light and truth as he knew, but he had not yet experienced the fullness of Christ because he lacked fellowship with other young believers. The Bible speaks of this in Proverbs 27:17 (NIV): "As iron sharpens iron, so one person sharpens another."

However, Billy began to experience a spiritual and moral resolve to do what was right. He began by severing his relationship with Pauline Presson, the beautiful and charismatic young woman whom he had been dating for some time. Pauline had attended one of Ham's revivals, but it didn't take hold of her like it did with Billy.

"Billy realized that he had to break up with her if he were to remain a committed Christian," said friend Grady Wilson. "He certainly hated to part ways with that girl, but I have to hand it to him. He did it!"

Billy refused to do anything that would dishonor the Lord, and he was quick to take up for Christ if he felt others dishonored Him. Once while waiting in a Charlotte garage with Grady Wilson to get a tire patched, a mechanic who banged his thumb let out a mighty grumble.

"Christ!" he screamed.

Billy's hackles instantly went up.

"Sir, don't do that," he said. "Don't ever do that again!"

The mechanic, who didn't appreciate being taken to task by a teen, narrowed his eyes and replied that it was a free country and he could do whatever he pleased.

Billy retorted no—not around him.

The mechanic slowly pulled out a tire iron and stepped toward him. Billy's quick mind shut him down. He told the man that his father was Frank Graham and that he took all his Deere trucks there for mechanical work—and that mechanic could expect a precipitous drop in business if he did not lower the weapon. The man obviously weighed Billy's words, then went back to his workstation in silence.

Billy was displaying the typical zeal of a new convert, albeit without much grace. This would be tempered in time with winsomeness and a genuine love for people who held beliefs different from his.

Many years later, when he was receiving invitations to meet everyone from popular TV talk show hosts to presidents, Billy had a very different sort of encounter with a non-Christian that he handled with charm and wit while never compromising his strongly held convictions. This is, in my opinion, a quality other Christians would do well to emulate.

In 1969, Billy was interviewed by the atheistic Jewish comedian, writer, and director Woody Allen. They debated on television not only the Ten Commandments, but the very existence of God. At one point, Allen offered to bridge the gap between them.

"If you come to one of my movies sometime, I'll go to one of your revival meetings," he told Graham.

"Now that is a deal!" Graham replied.

Allen subtly joked that Graham might even be able to win him over.

"You could probably convert me because I'm a pushover—I have no convictions in any direction," Allen said. "If you make it appealing enough and you promise me some sort of wonderful afterlife with a white robe and wings, I might go for it."

"Well, I don't promise you a white robe and wings, but I can promise you a very interesting, thrilling life," Graham replied.

"One wing?" Allen quipped.

It was a wonderful exchange, especially in light of today's current political climate where opposite sides refuse to communicate and it's not unheard for someone to tear off their mike and storm off the set.

Both men enjoyed swatting around ideas, smiling all the while and laughing at each other's jokes. Woody cracked that his worst sin had been impure thoughts about Art Linkletter, a famous TV personality at the time. He asked Billy what the worst sin was. Billy was light on his rhetorical feet; he didn't so much parry and riposte as he warmly and winningly laid out his beliefs.

"Every sin is the worst sin in God's eyes," he answered. But, he added, "in God's sight you are beautiful."

Allen, the short and rumpled mensch who sported Einstein hair and thick glasses, shrugged and smiled, playing up Billy's last statement for the camera. Both had a great time and enjoyed each other's company.

Billy adopted a similar stance with his friends at school, showing concern for those who drank, gambled, or danced a little too closely. He drifted from old friends and started hanging out with a group dubbed the "Preacher Boys," which included the Wilson brothers and a few others who clung tightly to their newfound faith.

He formed a Bible club, stopped going to the movies, and spent his time trying to please the Lord. Billy's grades improved, and he became nicer. However, some old habits were hard to break: he still dated and raced his father's Plymouth a little too fast.

It's safe to say that Billy was following Grady Wilson's lead in those days. Grady had become president of a Christian club on the high school campus, the Christian Life Services Band. Through that, he fielded invitations to speak at small local Baptist churches. According to Wilson, Billy was raw and untutored but had no shortage of zeal. He started off preaching in jails and on street corners before finally graduating to revivals. His first was at the Eighteenth Street Mission in Charlotte. Billy and Grady's girlfriends at the time were sitting in the front row. Grady kept time with Billy's pocket watch and preached on "God's Four Questions," a sermon he had borrowed from an unknown preacher.

During the sermon, Wilson kept winding the watch until he eventually broke the stem. At that point, he went way off track. After ninety minutes, Wilson announced, "Now we come to God's second question." Wilson wryly recalled how Graham's eyes bulged and how he nearly leapt out of the pew. But Billy also marveled at his friend's gift of gab, his memorization of the Scriptures, and his ability to stand in front of a group of people and preach the Gospel.

Billy wanted to be as good as Grady, so he preached on Charlotte's sidewalks and in front of a busy department store. They were painfully embarrassing episodes, and Wilson didn't give him very high marks at the time. He noticed that his friend was scattered in thought and took up time, mostly rattling on in order to avoid uncomfortable silences.

Everybody has to start somewhere.

I remember the first time I sought to speak publicly. It was as though time stood still and my mind went blank. And during my first attempts to share my faith with a friend, I was interrupted by a curious man who barraged me with a series of what I thought at the time were unanswerable questions. I was both dumbfounded and embarrassed. I learned from that experience and began to study my Bible a lot more closely.

Billy became Grady Wilson's de facto chauffer, accompanying him around Mecklenburg County to jails, missions, and a home for unwed mothers. They also rode shotgun with Jimmie Johnson, a twenty-five-year-old evangelist from Alabama whom the Graham family befriended. Johnson invited Billy and Grady to hear him preach at a jail in Monroe, North Carolina, about forty-five minutes from Charlotte. When Johnson finished, he asked Billy to testify for the Lord. The petrified teen did as he was asked and promptly put his foot in his mouth.

"I'm glad to see so many of you *out* this afternoon," Graham said.

An audible groan came from Wilson and about a dozen of the inmates, whose only other option for the day was going back to their cells, a place they spent enough time as it was. Wilson said the speech that followed wasn't much better. Billy was so nervous while speaking that he twisted the hem of his coat until it looked like a rope.

False starts like Billy's often dissuade people from becoming preachers, but he possessed the internal fortitude to become better. And he did. (I remember an occasion when I was a young preacher. At the end of my message, at a key moment, I referred to Jesus calling Simon "Peter." I got tongue-tied and called him "Peepers." It was an awkward moment which produced a few guffaws, but everyone in the ministry has them.)

Another time, Billy accompanied Grady on a trip to a home for wayward girls, and his testimony was so compelling that many young ladies made a profession of faith. One of them Billy recognized—she had previously lived with a tenant family on the Graham Brothers Farm. She vowed to him that she'd get on the straight and narrow and follow Christ. Billy fished out a five-dollar bill he had in his pocket, handed it over, and wished her the best. Hints of what was to come were beginning to show.

When traveling preachers came through town, Billy paid rapt attention not only to their sermons, but to their preaching styles, making mental notes of what worked and what didn't. He often practiced in front of a mirror, vowing to get better, until he developed a style that felt comfortable to him. While his future as a preacher was uncertain, one thing he did know for sure was that he no longer wanted to farm.

No one could blame Billy for that. With his spiritual growth came a new outlook and aspirations. Many of the evangelists who stayed with the Grahams were graduates of Bob Jones College in Cleveland, Tennessee, like Jimmie Johnson. They encouraged Billy to consider higher education in spite of his not-so-stellar grades. When Dr. Bob Jones himself spoke at Sharon High School, Billy's parents were in the audience and became sold on that option. T.W. Wilson was already studying there, and his brother Grady was about to enroll. Billy wouldn't be entirely alone if he attended.

Grades really weren't the issue, though; money was. To rectify that, Billy took a job with the Fuller Brush Company after his high school graduation in May 1936. Once again, he followed in the footsteps of Albert McMakin, who had first taken him to hear Mordecai Ham. McMakin had landed a job as a regional manager with the company after leaving the Graham Brothers Dairy. He asked Billy if he'd be willing to join him in selling high-end brushes door-to-door through the summer to potentially earn some quick cash for college tuition. They roomed in boardinghouses throughout the Carolinas, where they could usually get a night's lodging and a meal for a dollar a day. They often dined with hard-bitten salesmen and endured pesky insects during the day and the occasional bedbug at night. The summer humidity was sweltering; the food could be unsavory—and sometimes unsafe.

Billy recalled one place where the biscuits were so dense that he almost lost a tooth. Harking back to the days he wanted to play pro ball, he angrily tossed a biscuit at the cook through the kitchen door so fast his idol Babe Ruth would have whiffed at it.

Albert and Billy's territory was South Carolina, and they'd usually stay in a town or city a few days at most. After the first week, Billy got homesick. So he asked Grady and T.W. Wilson, also eager to earn money for college, if they would join him. He didn't have to ask twice. The Wilson brothers jumped at the opportunity.

The Connecticut-based Fuller Brush Company was started in 1906 by entrepreneur Alfred C. Fuller, who initially worked out of his sister's basement with a $375 investment. Fuller's founding credo was, "Make it work, make it last, and guarantee it no matter what."

By the time Billy Graham started knocking on doors, Fuller had turned the company into a multi-million-dollar enterprise with a force of more than a thousand people. In 1922, the term "Fuller Brush Man" was coined. Every salesman announced, "I'm your Fuller Brush Man!" when the front door opened. It became an American institution. A Fuller Brush Man appeared in cartoons with Mickey Mouse and Donald Duck. Comedy-mystery movies featuring Red Skelton and Lucille Ball (*The Fuller Brush Man* and *The Fuller Brush Girl*) were huge hits. Alfred Fuller knew his salespeople were the key to his success, and his management team focused on them. Every American was familiar with Fuller Brush Men. In the age of Amazon and e-commerce, the company still operates today.

The job ended up changing Billy and the Wilson brothers in many ways. It helped them overcome their bashfulness, it developed their stamina, they had to think and learn on their feet, and they had to produce. The men received no base salary, walked about six miles a day, and only averaged a sale in one of every five homes. The job was not for everyone—seven out of ten Fuller recruits failed in the first three months.

The sales strategy was simple enough: sweet talk your way enough to get your actual foot in the door. Then hold it there so the customer couldn't close it and invited you in. Billy and the others found out in short order that intrusion didn't always work. Customers had no problem slamming the door on their feet.

Another sales strategy was giving away an item, typically a ten-cent bottle or utility brush. The items were offered as a choice and the costs were always deducted out of the salesperson's paycheck. It was just the cost of doing business.

Billy developed a clever and simple greeting.

"My technique was to offer the lady a free brush and, of course, in those days that appealed," Billy recalled. "I would have to empty my whole case of brushes to get to the bottom and the woman's curiosity was aroused by looking at the brushes and she would say, 'By the way, what's this? How much is that?' Well, I knew I had a fish on the string."

But that approach wasn't foolproof. Some of the more cunning women who answered the door quickly snatched the brush and *then* slammed the door shut, leaving the salesman both ego sore and a dime poorer.

The four men, however, were successful. Mostly because they found a novel way to gain entry into homes.

"We combined our selling with our witnessing for Christ," Grady said. "We would gain entry into a home, sell our brushes, and give away our faith."

But not everyone wanted to hear what they had to say. Billy recalled a time when he rang a doorbell and the lady of the house did not open. Instead, she went to the window upstairs, looked out, and then doused Billy with an entire pail of water.

Other times it got much more dangerous. One night in Lancaster, South Carolina—a textile town with several mills and plenty of rough customers—Billy and Grady encountered a group of roughnecks on a downtown street. The boys had developed a radar for men who were looking for trouble. But Billy, who was no stranger to fighting, grew bolder with each step.

"Grady, did you bring your gun along?" he asked loudly.

"Buddy, we're okay," Grady said, picking up his cue. "Go ahead."

The men quickly backed off and ran.

I love this story because it shows both the spiritual and practical side of Billy—his combination of deep spirituality and basic street smarts. I observed this personally. Billy was that rare combination of a man of great faith and also a man who intuitively understood people and how they operated.

The group ended up having a lot of fun that summer. To keep things loose, they pulled pranks on each other and other people in the boardinghouses. They short-sheeted the others' beds and put shaving cream in each other's shoes. Or they might quickly yank a guy's chair out from under him as he was sitting down to eat and delight in the embarrassed victim ending up on his fanny.

Despite their shenanigans, they grew in their spiritual walks on this journey. The men routinely held prayer meetings wherever they stayed, read the Bible together, and held each other accountable, which helped them resist the temptations that traveling salesmen often faced on the road.

Billy ended up becoming the best salesman of the four. That was partially due to the fact that Grady and T.W. Wilson took off on many afternoons to fish or swim. They'd rendezvous in the evenings to discuss their sales strategy or find out which local girls were available for dates. But Billy was never tempted to play hooky and had the constitution of an iron horse, knocking on doors from sunrise to sunset.

He said that summer's experience selling brushes bolstered his self-confidence, helped him gain financial independence, and was crucial for his personal and professional development in the years to come.

"I was naturally sort of a shy fellow and I didn't particularly like to meet people," Billy recalled. "That got me over that. It allowed me to talk with people and to sell people."

Billy was pulling in fifty to seventy-five dollars a week in the aftermath of the Depression. In days when a dollar got you a room and a meal, that was a sizeable bounty for anyone, let alone a teenager. He began to question whether he should go to college and become a preacher or continue raking in the dough as a salesman. He certainly knew which was easier, the odd pail of cold water notwithstanding.

CHAPTER SIX

God's Not Deaf

Young Billy Graham was serious about his faith.

He sensed a calling on his life and wanted to do everything he could to prepare himself for it. But how could he have anticipated that he would have a global impact that would last decades and impact billions of people?

In his heart, he was a faithful person who simply wanted to honor God. When people would heap praise on Billy, he would sometimes respond, "I'm just a country preacher!"

That was not false humility, but a statement of fact. The reality was that God was going to take this simple dairyman's son and mold him into one of the most powerful communicators of the Gospel in all of human history.

What young Billy would experience at Bob Jones College was not the kind of preparation he was hoping for, but it would, in fact, be an education for him. Unfortunately, much of what he learned was what *not* to do in his ministry.

Billy first heard about Bob Jones College at a school assembly during his senior year. He had originally considered the University of North

Carolina, but his parents, who wanted him to attend a Christian school, practically thrust him in the direction of Bob Jones. It was a small fundamentalist school in Cleveland, Tennessee, with a reputation for its commitment to the Scriptures and strict moral standards.

Today the term "fundamentalist" is largely negative, ranging from the term "fundamentalist Christian" to even "Islamic fundamentalism"—but the origin of the term is worth noting. In the late nineteenth and early twentieth centuries, theological liberalism was encroaching on the Protestant Church. A multivolume group of essays called *The Fundamentals*, edited by R.A. Torrey, was published in 1910. Torrey was an associate of the great evangelist D.L. Moody and is still highly respected in evangelical circles today, especially for his books. The people who agreed with these basics of the Christian life were called *fundamentalists*. In time, this became a pejorative term used to describe someone as very narrow-minded and overly rigid. The term "evangelical" was later adopted to describe someone who is theologically conservative but not a fundamentalist per se. (Although with "evangelical" losing much of its meaning in modern culture, perhaps it's time for a new word.)

This early fundamentalism was part of the culture of Bob Jones College when Billy applied during his senior year of high school. He was quickly accepted, and in September 1936, he made the three-hundred-mile journey with his father and the Wilson brothers to the tiny, isolated campus in the eastern Tennessee hills. Shortly after Billy arrived, he learned the school was not accredited and did not compete with other colleges in athletics.

"I didn't have the slightest idea what kind of school it was," Billy confessed decades later. "All I knew was that it was Christian."

The college opened in Florida in 1927 with eighty-eight students. Jones refused a salary and supported the school with his own income, savings, and evangelistic campaigns. It was immediately beset by problems: a real estate bust had hit Florida two years before, followed by a hurricane and the Great Depression. In 1933, the college was forced to move the campus to Tennessee, where Billy attended.

Jones was a preaching prodigy from an early age. He became a Sunday school superintendent at age twelve, holding evangelistic meetings and seeing about sixty people make a profession of faith each week. Interestingly enough, like me and Billy, Jones had horrible stage fright when he began preaching. Just about no one starts out perfectly spreading the Word.

When Jones became a college president, he wasn't perfect either. He pounded his students with his own special brand of legalism. He created an environment with so many rules and regulations that it resembled a strict military academy. The place was absolutely stifling to a young man like Billy Graham. When Billy decided to leave the college after one semester, Bob Jones Sr. declared him an abject failure and told him so to his face.

To make matters worse, his son, Bob Jones Jr., later said when Billy was a famed evangelist that he was "doing more harm to the cause of Jesus Christ than any living man."

These criticisms were due to the fact that Billy not only worked with theologically conservative churches, but also those that may have skewed more to the liberal side. Billy also wanted meetings that were open to all races, which went against the grain of the segregationist policies Bob Jones College had at that time. Both Bob Jones Sr. and Jr. were on the wrong side of history.

At the time Billy was drawing their criticism, he had developed a friendship with famed Civil Rights icon Martin Luther King Jr., asking him to lead his Crusade at Madison Square Garden in July 1957 in prayer. This was a controversial decision, but Billy always wanted to build bridges between cultures and beliefs. He would later have clergy of all stripes on his platform, including Catholic priests. The thing many missed, however, was that Billy Graham never watered down his preaching—and, in fact, had the opportunity to lead some mainline church leaders to Christ.

Jones wasn't very open-minded and didn't seem to like the free exchange of ideas. He blatantly told his students what to think, what to do, and how to act. He didn't take kindly to dissent or questions, and he operated his school like a boot camp.

In the end, Billy acknowledged a debt to Bob Jones Sr., who influenced his own passionate sermons and oratorical gestures, according to many of Graham's biographers. But knowing Billy as I did, he would never be one to criticize someone else in public regardless of how he felt about them privately.

It should come as no surprise that academics were hardline and doctrinaire, and student life was draconian at Bob Jones College. Men wore ties and women sported skirts. Physical contact with the opposite sex—even holding hands—was verboten, as was sitting on the same piece of furniture. Dating was limited to fifteen minutes of chaperoned conversation once a week. During that painful visit, students were "watched like a hawk," Billy recalled. Participation in most secular forms of entertainment, such as movies or dancing, was prohibited. Chapel attendance was mandatory on Sundays. And mail was monitored by staff for anything spiritually or physically untoward.

A sign on the wall of both the men's and women's dormitories—brick barracks, actually—welcomed new students to Bob Jones College with this message: "GRIPING NOT TOLERATED!" Billy may have had second thoughts about how bad the milking shed actually was, wondering if he should go back home.

Very few students questioned Jones's dictatorial control to his face—and if they did, he had no problem showing them the door. When they did speak about Jones with each other, it was always in hushed tones and with fear in their voices.

While it is true that young people need standards, rules, and absolutes to live by, it seems that Bob Jones College did not foster the passion and heart one should have first in their relationship with God that motivates them to reach out to others. It seemed more about rules than relationship.

I can't say I blame Billy for eventually leaving such a place. I don't know that I would have even made it for a semester, as he did.

As far as academics went, Billy earned fair marks and hoped that he'd get better as he went along. However, he never properly learned to study in high school and had to retake an exam in summer school to graduate, so things did not improve in that area. He discovered in short order that the blistering pace of college academics took it up another notch and then some. In high school, students read only single book chapters on a weekly basis. He discovered that college students read entire books in one week—plus wrote papers, took exams, and debated in class.

Illness also prevented Billy from excelling. He suffered from colds and recurring cases of the flu because of the damp, dismal autumn weather. He also contended with allergies and bronchitis throughout the first semester, though some friends claimed it was not illness at all. Add to this fact that Billy was also depressed and homesick.

He did try his best, studying almost every waking hour. He also liked hearing "Dr. Bob" preach at chapel and enjoyed his homespun philosophies ("If a hound dog barks for Jesus, then I'm for the hound dog!"), but it wasn't enough to get him over the hurdle of life at Bob Jones College. T.W. Wilson said at that point, Billy was lost and confused.

"He didn't have any purpose or goal in life," Wilson said. "He felt that he ought to preach. And yet he didn't know how to go about it."

Perhaps even more troubling was that even though Billy knew he was a real follower of Jesus now, he was being tested. He lost his feeling for Christ; he wasn't getting anywhere in his prayers. His struggle continued for weeks.

We need to remember that everything we go through in life is preparation for something else. We certainly have precedent for this in Scripture. Moses was schooled in the desert before his confrontation with Pharaoh. The same was true of Elijah, who was called to a brook that eventually dried up. This was a dry but preparatory time for the man who would shake the world.

According to Grady Wilson, Billy thought some humor might improve his grim circumstances at Bob Jones College.

"Although converted, Billy and I hadn't lost our identity and we still loved to cut up. No one could accuse us of long-faced Christianity," Grady said. "Billy and I started at Bob Jones with a bang. The rules were restrictive and tight, and we really didn't fit in." But they gave it the old college try.

The freshmen resorted to sophomoric pranks and shenanigans to lift their spirits. They hit each other with pies or snuck black pepper out of the kitchen and rubbed it under unsuspecting noses. During Bible conference time, many of the male students slept in the gym to make room for visitors. That's when they'd gently place a toad on a visitor's foot or inside their shoe.

As much as Billy was dishing it out to others, he was getting battered in the classroom. He was having an especially rough go with mathematics and failed to grasp the differences between calculus and analytical geometry. At one point, Billy rose out of his chair and asked his professor if it was possible to drop the class. The answer was yes, but Billy would have to accept an F.

He said he'd gladly take it. With that, he rose from his desk and walked out of the classroom.

Billy also received poor grades where it concerned his health. He suffered from flu and bronchitis that first semester and had a hard time concentrating on his studies because he wasn't feeling well. Grady noted that loud, emotional prayer particularly bothered Billy, especially when he was studying. He grew annoyed when a group of fellow students in a nearby room were praying a little too loudly for his tastes. He banged on the wall and yelled, "Hey, God's not deaf!"

And neither was Bob Jones Sr., who kept an ear to the ground for disgruntled students displaying any hint of disloyalty to him or the school. He once told a high-spirited student that he was possessed of demons. To be fair, the man saw demons in Mickey Mouse. Demons were not in short supply to Bob Jones.

In the early months of school, Billy had befriended a fellow student named Wendell Phillips. The two young men were rambunctious, mischievous, and had a healthy disdain for the school's strict rules and its uptight leader. The college expelled students after 150 demerits, which were easy to rack up, considering punctuality, cleanliness, and loitering in the halls were infractions. Phillips told Graham biographer William Martin, "We both had about 149," and the two were skating on thin ice.

Jones frequently called students to his office for "come to Jesus" meetings, where he either set them straight or sent them packing. He had sensed the two men's growing discontent over the semester and had heard they'd inquired about another Bible college. That was treasonous to Jones, who sent for them. Once there, Phillips was "biting his nails and hanging his head sheepishly as Dr. Bob began censuring him for his wavering and fickle attitude toward school, particularly his school," according to Billy.

As for Billy, Jones told him point-blank, "If you leave and throw your life away at a little country Bible school, the chances are you'll never be heard of. At best all you could amount to would be a poor country Baptist preacher somewhere out in the sticks." This was a standard speech given to academic underachievers and those who didn't follow Jones's rigid authority.

It was the last straw for Phillips, who made the first move and quit before the semester was over. He drove to Tampa, Florida, after reading about the Florida Bible Institute, and fell in love with the campus. Afterward, Phillips penned an enthusiastic letter to Billy about the beaches, the sunsets, the palm trees, the orange groves, and the encouraging teaching staff and administrators. Overall, it was a much more pleasant setting than Bob Jones College, and he urged Billy through many follow-up letters to join him.

But Billy wasn't as hasty as Phillips. He used the Christmas break to reflect, decompress, and regenerate his health. A Charlotte doctor suggested a warmer climate would be better for Billy's respiratory issues. By chance, a Plymouth Brethren Bible teacher visiting the Grahams suggested Billy consider transferring to Florida Bible Institute—the very same place Wendell Phillips had been touting. Morrow had talked Frank into taking the family to Florida to visit her sister and husband for Christmas. They had just bought a large boarding house with their cousin Mildred in Orlando, and the holidays were the perfect excuse for a trip. Still reeling from the flu, Billy joined his parents and siblings on their outing. It was just ninety minutes from Tampa—but, for some inexplicable reason, they did not make the trek to the campus. However, Billy didn't need to see it. Once he stepped foot on Floridian soil, he was sold on the Sunshine State. (Billy continued to have a soft spot for it throughout his life. When I joined his board of directors in 1994, we had many of our BGEA board meetings at Marriott hotels there, and Billy enjoyed soaking up the sun between meetings.)

Billy applied to Florida Bible Institute and prayed for a good outcome. Those prayers were answered when he received an acceptance letter in January.

Billy could now put his disastrous first semester at Bob Jones College behind him. Or so he thought. It wasn't the last time he would hear stinging criticism from its rigid patriarch. The two men and the university would go on to have what has been described as a "mixed history" for many decades to come.

Jones would be proven wrong over time, and Billy was being groomed by the Lord for much greater things. However, more preparation was needed.

CHAPTER SEVEN

New Horizons

The Scriptures are filled with God's promises, and throughout his life, Billy Graham would learn to rely on them.

His short tenure at Bob Jones College left him less than content. Many others in his situation might have abandoned their dream of serving the Lord or left college altogether. Billy had the personality to be a great salesperson, and the Fuller Brush Company opportunity was still wide open to him. Had he chosen to follow the money trail, he certainly would have been a tremendous success in the business world. Later in life, when he became a household name through a combination of his preaching in tandem with leading-man good looks, Hollywood came knocking, even offering him a million-dollar movie contract. But Billy was not interested. He also was asked by many to run for political office. Had he chosen to, I have no doubt Billy could have run for the presidency at the height of his popularity and won. But he always responded with the words, "I have a higher calling."

And he did. It just wasn't obvious to him yet.

Even though he was disillusioned after a terrible first semester, Billy still had not lost the compelling desire to continue studying

God's word. All he needed was a positive influence showcasing the joy of Christ's teachings.

Billy had high hopes for the Florida Bible Institute. His parents encouraged him not to give up on college, nursed him along physically and spiritually, and helped him get back on the right track. He was excited about the opportunity to learn at a new school and longed for a deeper relationship with God and a better understanding of the Scriptures.

Because God intervened, the world was given the greatest evangelist of the twentieth century and a true American icon. At Florida Bible Institute, Billy Graham not only received a fresh start, but also finally found his calling.

Less than a month after their first visit, the Grahams once again made the trek from Charlotte to Florida. They arrived in Temple Terrace, fifteen miles east of Tampa, in mid-January 1937. It was a charming village that had been incorporated only a dozen years prior. Named after coal, lumber, and citrus baron William Chase Temple, the city was planned and developed in the 1920s as a Mediterranean Revival golf course community.

With its rolling landscapes, orange groves, and shady oak trees, Temple Terrace was part of an exclusive residential subdivision on the banks of the Hillsborough River. This distinct place drew some of the wealthiest patrons around the country to stay at the luxury Spanish-style hotel and play tennis or golf. In no time, it became a winter retreat for wealthy Northerners, but then the bottom fell out with the Wall Street Crash of 1929, and that was that. Temple Terrace was now practically a ghost town with unfinished roads, unpaved sidewalks, and many luxury homes abandoned by fleeing occupants.

The institute's founder and president, Dr. William Thomas Watson, had taken over the bankrupt property for back taxes. The school opened in 1932 and produced its first graduating class two years later.

Watson transformed the place into a nondenominational institute, conference center, and Christian resort hotel with its seventy students (forty women and thirty men) putting in sweat equity to help defray the costs of their tuition, room, and board, which amounted to about a dollar a day. Frank Graham covered the room and board by sending Billy six dollars a week, but he expected Billy to get a job to pay for his other living expenses.

Students were still on holiday break when the Grahams arrived. This gave Billy time to take in the splendor of the beautiful campus and ease into the place.

Reverend John Minder, a tall ginger-haired man who was Watson's friend and classmate from New York's Nyack Bible College in the twenties, was the first to spot the Graham family as they pulled up.

"I had just stepped outside the back door when a Chevrolet drove up and stopped; a young man got out and stretched," said Minder, who was the dean of men and later Billy's special advisor and counselor. "The father got out, came over to where I was and said, 'Hi, I'm Frank Graham. I came down to enter my son, Billy, in school.'"

Frank and Morrow helped Billy unload his luggage and stayed for lunch before heading back to Charlotte. Billy was in good hands when they left. He had immediately taken up with former roommate Wendell Phillips, and later that night, he renewed his friendship with another schoolmate, Roy Gustafson, a senior in the music department. In time, Gustafson became a trusted friend and longtime evangelist with the Billy Graham Evangelistic Association, as well as a mentor to Billy's son Franklin when he rededicated his life to the Lord in the 1970s. (In fact, Franklin named one of his sons after him.) Gustafson recalled Billy holding a large Boy Scout knife and acting like an overgrown schoolboy upon their first meeting. He said Billy was "like an animal that had been in captivity and had finally got its freedom. He and Wendell ran all over the golf course!"

I got to know Roy very well, and he was a no-nonsense, very practical, yet very spiritual man. He spoke at our church quite a few times, and I traveled with him to Ethiopia for a pastor's conference as well. Roy was also very witty, usually ready with a clever quip in any conversation.

Billy felt as if he had inherited a new family with his new classmates. He was especially taken in by a young woman in the class above his. The vivacious and intelligent Emily Cavanaugh, with her dark hair, sparkling eyes, and natural athleticism, made his knees buckle. They were tennis partners and table-tennis rivals, and they joined the Tampa Gospel Tabernacle youth to spend more time together. Emily also accompanied Billy on his preaching assignments later in the semester.

Billy said he fell in love with Emily the moment he saw her, and he spent every free moment he could with her. He moved quickly and proposed to her that summer. And Billy expected an answer when they returned for the next semester.

With the relaxed feel of the grounds, the *esprit de corps* among the students, the Florida sunshine, a sense of purpose, and now with the charming Miss Cavanaugh on his arm, Billy was loving life.

It all came together for him at Temple Terrace—the biblically based curriculum, the friendly faculty, the free debate of ideas, the low teacher-to-student ratio, the personal mentoring, and affordable tuition. He also embraced the visiting lecturers who ventured to the campus, many of whom were charismatic, world-renowned evangelists—all confirming for Billy that he was exactly where he should be.

I can totally relate to what Billy was feeling at the time. The Bible was a mysterious book to me when I first began to read it. But suddenly, the words on its pages came alive, and I not only began to understand what it was saying, but I also found the moral grid that I'd never had growing up.

Billy developed a love for Scripture in Florida that he carried with him to his final breath. He loved to hear sermons from the Word of God as well. I remember when his health was in decline and I went to visit him at his home in Montreat, North Carolina. I was in town speaking at the conference center that he and his wife, Ruth, established. It was named the Billy Graham Training Center at the Cove. I had conducted a series on the topic of Heaven at that particular time, and Billy asked me to share what I had taught that week. As I did, I could see his eyes light up.

He just loved God's Word. And at Florida Bible Institute, he could revel in it without fear.

Billy's studies got underway in late January 1937, and he and the student body got a scare early in the semester. Dr. Watson called an emergency meeting to apprise them of the school's financial situation: they were floundering in red ink. He implored them to spend the rest of the day in prayer and meditation. They complied, and a few hours later, Dr. Watson had good news. He had just received a telegram from a man named Kellogg (quite possibly American industrialist W.K. Kellogg of the cereal empire), who told Watson an inner voice guided him to send a ten-thousand-dollar check to the school. Billy, who would experience several miracles like this throughout his career, said this particular episode regarding prayer made a big impression on him.

Everyone at Florida Bible Institute prayed, studied, and worked together. In fact, the students were the school's workforce and ran the entire operation. They waited tables, prepared food, washed dishes, performed housekeeping duties, and even took care of the grounds. Billy started out washing dishes. One classmate said Billy actually liked the chore because "the fellows would wash the dishes and all the girls would dry." Billy jokingly referred to himself as the school's first "automatic dishwasher" because he outpaced the women drying the dishes. He later graduated to server and then found work on the golf course.

Billy actually preferred outdoor work and enjoyed mowing lawns, raking leaves, and trimming hedges. He eventually eased his way to the links as a caddy, which gave him access to some of the era's most renowned Christian scholars, administrators, preachers, and evangelists. Billy soaked up every ounce of wisdom they offered. Such was the case with William Evans, former director of the Bible department at Moody Bible Institute. Billy once carried his clubs around for a day and received a one-dollar tip for his services. But even more valuable was the verbal tip Evans dispensed at the end of the day: if Billy applied himself to his studies, one day he would be in the fortunate position to offer someone else a tip too.

Florida Bible Institute also kickstarted Billy's love of golf, which he later utilized for developing friendships with future allies: presidents, diplomats, captains of industry, entertainers, and others who proved useful in spreading the Gospel.

Billy once told me to use golf to establish relationships in the same way. Although, for all of its virtues, the golf course lacked one thing: Billy admitted to me, "The only time my prayers are never answered is on the golf course." Given what can be heard on golf courses when someone is having a bad day, perhaps God decided long ago to close His ears to imprecations issued from links, though I'm sure Billy's were not among them.

Billy mulled over Evans's words because after a year at the institute, he realized he was selling himself short in the area of academics.

"I had no purpose. I was interested in the Bible, I had been converted," Billy said. "But I was still carefree, happy-go-lucky."

That would change shortly.

In addition to their classroom work, the students were called upon to do "practical work," which meant getting embedded in the community. They frequently spoke to and counseled prisoners in jail, senior citizens in trailer parks, vagrants, and the occasional passersby on street corners. They also assisted in church services, missions, and teaching Sunday school in local houses of worship. Eighteen-year-old Billy also spoke regularly at various trailer parks, an infamous Tampa jail called "The Stockade," and was put in charge of a children's Bible class, overseeing the spiritual lives of a half-dozen kids.

This is the testing ground where most people in the ministry get started: doing simple things and being faithful in doing them. Jesus said, "If you are faithful in little things, you will be faithful in large ones. But if you are dishonest in little things, you won't be honest with greater responsibilities" (Luke 16:10 NLT).

I literally had a broom handed to me when I volunteered to help serve in ministry at the church. I went to visit Pastor Chuck Smith at Calvary Chapel of Costa Mesa at the age of eighteen. I had only been a believer for a year or so, and I told him that I would like to serve the Lord.

He basically put me to work as a janitor. I was not discouraged by that though, and I just felt I ought to do the best job possible. One day I was asked to replace a doorknob for the front office of Chuck's church, and I felt like I was on a special mission for God. I was, however, over- whelmed by the myriad choices at the hardware store and even prayed for guidance. I returned with a doorknob that was the wrong size! The point is, I was learning the importance of doing what needed to be done, no matter how large or small it was. I taught the same lesson to my son Jonathan when he started in ministry. Now he is a pastor at our Orange County campus.

It's like the famous poem about a battle being lost all because of a missing horseshoe nail. The devil is not in the details. God is.

After hearing Billy speak at a dog track in nearby Sulphur Springs in early 1937, John Minder invited him to accompany him on a three- hour jaunt north to Lake Swan, a sprawling 150-acre property near Melrose, Florida. Minder's family opened the Christian complex, situ- ated close to the lake shore, in 1927. It boasted recreational facilities, lodging, meeting rooms, and a large hall that could be used for services, conferences, and other community events.

The two men had grown close in a short amount of time. The nurtur- ing Minder took a vested interest in Billy's future. Minder had already been personally responsible for an uptick in his academics and saw great potential in Billy. In return, Billy soaked in all he could from Minder, tak- ing his courses in pastoral theology and hermeneutics. He responded well to Minder's much gentler approach than that of his predecessor, Bob Jones.

Billy recalled in his autobiography taking a drive with Minder to see his friend, Cecil Underwood, a part-time Baptist preacher and interior decorator. Underwood was in charge of the Peniel Baptist Church, five miles west of Lake Swan. When they arrived, Underwood was setting up the pulpit for the next night's sermon. Shortly after they exchanged greetings, Underwood asked Minder to speak that evening at Bostwick Baptist Church in Palatka, a nearby church for which Underwood had taken responsibility.

"No," Minder replied. He had a much better idea: "Billy's going to preach."

I would love to have seen Billy's reaction when Minder offered him up to preach right then and there. This is one of those moments a preacher both dreams about and dreads.

When God has gifted you and you have something to say, you want to take that opportunity when it presents itself. At the same time, you find yourself not feeling up to the task. Add to that the weighty responsibility of knowing you are, in fact, speaking for God Himself (no pressure there!).

Billy's theological repository was extremely limited at the time. It consisted of four borrowed sermons. When Billy stammered that he had never delivered a sermon in front of live bodies before, he didn't get much sympathy from Minder and Underwood. They actually laughed in unison before saying they'd pray for him.

There wasn't much Billy could do other than grin and bear it. He wanted to preach, and here was his moment.

Billy's nerves ensured no rest for him the night before. He spent the evening studying, praying, and rehearsing aloud. When it came time to speak, Billy was confident one of his sermons might last twenty to thirty minutes.

The white clapboard church built in 1909 was populated with characters out of central casting. They were a humble congregation of thirty to forty people—cowboys and ranchers in denim overalls and staunch women in cotton dresses. For whatever reasons, they even brought their hounds with them for the evening service.

The meeting room where Billy was to deliver his first sermon was, shall we say, modestly sized. A pot-bellied iron stove was strategically placed near the front door to keep the cold weather at bay. The song leader was a non-career type. That means he held a variety of odd jobs, from collecting junk to fishing. He led the congregation in hymns, pausing occasionally to spit tobacco juice out the front door. I'm surprised there wasn't a spittoon in the place.

Billy found none of this humorous because he was a bundle of nerves. Underwood gave him a proper introduction as the skinny, tall teen took his place behind the small wooden pulpit. Neither his message nor the delivery took the world by storm, but hey—it was a start.

Billy zipped through all four of his sermons in eight minutes, falling way short of the goal he had set for himself. He then quietly sat down, feeling totally deflated. He questioned in his heart if he truly was meant to preach the Gospel. But Billy wasn't as bad as he imagined, according to Underwood.

"He had a bit of difficulty, but he got through all right," Underwood said to Graham biographer John Pollock. "He ran out of words. He ran out of thoughts. His delivery was impressive, even that first sermon, because of his sincerity."

Florrie Wilkinson Hoeltzel was just nine at the time and recalled in a 2011 interview with the *Florida Baptist Witness* that Billy's appearance was "big doings in those days" because having a visitor at a country church was not an everyday occurrence. "I never thought at that time, regardless of what age I would have been, would I have ever thought that I heard the first sermon that a worldwide evangelist preached…just the memories of seeing him and now knowing what he became in God's Kingdom and God's work—I've prayed for him all these years."

Today a historical marker sits in front of Bostwick Baptist Church to commemorate what took place on March 28, 1937, on Easter Sunday night in that tiny church—all eight minutes of it.

Steven Spielberg was rejected by the University of Southern California School of Cinematic Arts multiple times. Oprah Winfrey was publicly fired from her television job as an anchor in Baltimore for getting "too emotionally invested" in her stories. Walt Disney was canned by the *Kansas City Star* because his editor felt he "lacked imagination and had no good ideas." Colonel Harland David Sanders was fired from dozens of jobs before putting a chicken in every frying pan.

Billy had a long way to go. And no signs pointed the way. But big doors swing on small hinges, as he would soon discover.

CHAPTER EIGHT

God Speaks,
on the Eighteenth Hole

Billy Graham worried he had bombed in his first sermon, but this wasn't the most pressing matter at hand. Getting him back into the pulpit before he had time to stew about his mistakes was essential. Nobody knew this better than John Minder, who gave Billy his next assignment the following weekend.

As I read about this incident in John Pollock's excellent 1966 biography on Billy, I became convinced that Minder, as an academic dean, instructor, and mentor, knew exactly what was best for Billy's personal development and growth. I was at the very same place in my life after I accepted Christ and decided I wanted to become a preacher.

In Malcom Gladwell's 2008 bestseller, *Outliers: The Story of Success*, he strongly suggests that 10,000 hours of appropriately guided practice is the "magic number of greatness" despite one's aptitude. Greatness requires repetition and endless practice for almost everyone. Very few people in all of human history have ever done anything perfectly right out of the gate. Of the 500 pieces of classical music considered masterworks—composed by 76 people—all but three were written after the tenth year of the composer's career. Golfer Tiger Woods trained for

13 hours a day when he was young. He did a morning workout, worked on his swing, played 18 holes, worked on his game some more, then did a second workout in the evening. The Beatles played on stage in Hamburg, Germany, 270 times in a year and a half. By the time they had their first big hit in 1964, they had played live 1,200 times. As a teenager, basketball legend "Pistol" Pete Maravich practiced up to 8 hours a day, then went on to become college basketball's all-time leading scorer with a phenomenal 3,667 points for Louisiana State University. For 10 years he thrilled NBA crowds with his shooting expertise, bombarding the nets with more than 15,000 points. "If I play ten hours a day for ten years, and you play one hour a day for ten years and we meet on the basketball court, you're dead," Maravich said. Greatness requires repetition and endless practice for almost everyone.

The difference between preaching and other disciplines is that there is a God-given anointing that overrides human ability. Yes, the more you preach, the better you become. However, if one's heart is not right with God, you may grow in your "craft" but lack effectiveness. And Billy was a long way off from ten hours in a pulpit, let alone ten thousand.

When they returned to Temple Terrace, Minder asked Billy to preach to the young members the next evening at the Tampa Gospel Tabernacle, where he was the pastor. Once again, Billy panicked. He enlisted his roommate Woodrow Flynn to help. Flynn preached his outlines to Billy in their small room, then Billy spent the rest of the evening studying and praying. In the morning, he paddled a canoe across the Hillsborough River to a desolate island where Billy rehearsed his sermon to a coterie of animals: birds, squirrels, rabbits, water moccasins, and alligators roaming the place. The private retreat later became his favorite spot to practice.

The Bible does say, "preach the Gospel to every creature," so it seems like it was a good place for young Billy to get comfortable speaking out loud. Public speaking is uniquely challenging. For many, it is the most terrifying thing they can imagine doing—even more than dying.

Billy's Sunday sermon once again left him deflated and questioning himself, but his audience didn't seem to agree with his assessment. They loved his sincerity and authenticity. Minder gave him another vote of confidence when he asked Billy before the 1937 summer semester was over to take charge of the Tabernacle's youth program. It was a confirmation that the Lord was indeed with and using him.

When Billy returned to Florida after summer vacation, he endured a pair of emotionally stinging blows that shook him to his core and put his faith to the ultimate test.

The first was the discovery that two Christians on campus that he had greatly admired were accused of serious "moral defections." It was a major scandal at the small school. Billy and a group of students tried an intervention with the couple by following them to a private residence for a confrontation, but they were rebuffed.

The incident was emotionally traumatic for Billy, who learned first-hand how a person can publicly advocate for Christ while privately acting the opposite way. Billy vowed that he would never allow his words or deeds to besmirch Christ's name, nor commit any act that could be construed as hypocrisy. Deep down, Billy knew he had to guard his heart or he could fall into the same trap and out of favor with God. It's like Oscar Wilde once wrote: "I can resist anything but temptation." Billy said this incident "caused me to look to God rather than to men. I realized that any man could have feet of clay. Paul said, 'Put no confidence in the flesh.' This was an early lesson that helped me tremendously through the years."

The next lesson was something Billy could not prepare for.

His relationship with Emily Cavanaugh gave him immense joy, and they saw each other almost daily. They played sports together, went on romantic canoe trips and preaching excursions, and met each other in the student lounge for dinners on most nights. And Billy snuck in kisses here and there.

They worked together, played together, worshipped together, and sang in the choir together. God was truly at the center of their lives. Shortly after she paid a visit to Charlotte and met his parents, Billy wrote Emily a letter asking for her hand in marriage. And while Emily didn't give an immediate answer, she hinted at the possibility. One evening, after they attended a local black church service and stopped off at an ice cream parlor for a late dessert, she said something that tickled his ears.

"I have something to tell you," Emily said. "I want to say 'yes' to your letter last summer."

Billy was overjoyed, and from that moment on, considered them engaged despite the fact that he could not afford to buy her a ring. It was just as well.

Soon after Emily said yes, her behavior suggested otherwise. Billy noticed that she seemed to be emotionally pulling back at the turn of the year, and her reticence persisted through the spring. It finally manifested itself at an annual end-of-the-semester social event in May 1938 called Class Night.

Earlier that day, John Minder escorted Billy and several classmates to a local florist shop to buy corsages for the ladies. As college students on limited budgets, the florist presented them with an affordable option: twenty-five cents for the flowers. But Billy was in love and money was no object that night. He spent double that amount for Emily's corsage. And when she didn't wear it to the event that evening, Billy was hurt.

During a lull in the night's activities, they strolled down to their favorite spot on the river and settled into a hanging swing. It didn't take long for it to all spill out: Emily explained that she was in love with someone else and would not be marrying Billy. He was being dumped. To add insult to injury, her new beau was a fellow Florida Bible Institute student. This had happened right under Billy's nose.

Mr. Dreamboat was Charles Massey. Billy knew him (it's usually that way). He recalled Massey as one of the most gifted student preachers he'd ever heard. Whenever he had free time, Billy would spend it watching and learning from Massey. He and Emily also played doubles with Massey in tennis whenever his Michigan girlfriend came to town. Quietly and surreptitiously, Emily and Massey had become more than just an item: they were going to tie the knot.

"She wanted to marry a man who was going to amount to something," Graham's brother Melvin later said. For her, Billy was not that man. And he certainly wasn't a Harvard man, which is where Massey was headed once he graduated from Florida Bible Institute.

After the tears subsided, Billy plumbed the depths of his soul and began to look more inwardly. For the next few weeks, Billy worked off his inner aching with nightly walks, winding through Temple Terrace's empty streets and circling back through the institute's golf course.

Despite the fact that he was a Christian enrolled in a Bible college, the idea of dedicating his life to the ministry frayed his nerves. He had seriously contemplated whether or not he should be preaching for a living.

After another late-night stroll, Billy ended up on the east end of the eighteenth hole of the Temple Terrace golf course. He stopped, got down on his knees on the wet grass, and humbly prayed.

I've seen Billy pray many times, and I can tell you he was always humble about it. And when Billy got down on his knees that night, he meant business.

"Oh God," he cried, "if You want me to serve You, I will."

Billy listened for God's voice and, although he didn't hear anything audibly, he received his answer. Lightning didn't rend boulders asunder. No bush burned. There were no columns of smoke or fire. It wasn't loud, and the eighteenth hole of the Temple Terrace golf course certainly wasn't where he might have expected such an encounter, but the message was clear: he was being enlisted by God to preach.

"One of two things can happen in a time like that," Billy said in reflection. "You can resist and then become bitter, or you can let God break you. And I determined to let God have His way."

After that epiphany, Billy no longer questioned who he was, what he should be doing, or if he had made the wrong vocational choice. He had finally found his calling, and the rest of his life would be dedicated to Christ.

From then on, despite the fits, starts, and stumbles, and continuing throughout the years of mega-Crusades and meetings with the powerful, famous, and heads of state all over the world, he never looked back or questioned the journey he agreed to take.

CHAPTER NINE

Ready to Roar

There's an internal metamorphosis that takes place when a Christian makes that conscious leap of faith and decides to place everything in God's hands. It's called surrendering. Sadly, many believers don't ever make it this far.

The reasons are plentiful. Surrender is hard because it is the opposite of what our stubborn, wayward hearts are inclined to do. By nature, we are sinful, manipulative, and controlling. That can change if we consciously turn our lives over to Christ for Him to do with as He wills.

In Matthew 16:24–25, Jesus tells us to surrender to His loving authority. He told His disciples, "If anyone would come after me, let him deny himself and take up his cross and follow me. For whoever would save his life will lose it, but whoever loses his life for my sake will find it" (AKJV).

And that's what happened to Billy.

After surrendering, he experienced a newfound love and peace he'd never known before. A burden had been lifted, and it gave him greater joy to serve. He saw in himself a new desire to witness and share Christ, a new song in his heart, and an unspeakable joy.

Billy had to die to self to live for Christ. He surrendered his life, his will, his privacy—and later, time with his wife and children—in order to further the Gospel. Every preacher, pastor, and minister must relinquish a great deal of themselves, often at the expense of their own families.

Billy wasn't there yet because he didn't know what God had in mind for him. But turning over his life and his will to Christ would take him to unfathomable heights.

In the days that followed, Billy continued to walk the empty streets of Temple Terrace and pray—sometimes for three to four hours at a stretch. In rare moments, the Lord gave him a glimpse into the future: in brief flashes he saw a stadium-sized crowd gathered to hear the Gospel. At the time, Billy was still too humble to think that the crowds were there for him.

The Bible certainly has its fair share of stories about individuals who experienced prophetic dreams or visions, most notably Daniel, Paul, Isaiah, and Ezekiel. I had similar impressions about my future.

Attending a Billy Graham Crusade at the age of twenty rocked my world. Not because I came to Christ there, but because I realized that type of ministry was what I wanted to do when I grew up. But even then, I never dreamed I would end up speaking in stadiums like my hero, Billy Graham.

Young Billy also had a long journey to reach his destination, but he sensed something big was about to happen. His son Franklin later described his father as a "turtle on a fencepost." The essence of this Southern colloquialism is that a turtle would not get to such a place on his own. Billy was put there by the hand of God.

By that point, everybody had noticed the dramatic change in Billy. He was serving with greater confidence and an intense desire to make an impact. He was preaching, volunteering, searching the Scriptures, and studying the Bible for clarity and understanding. Once in this mindset, Billy had no time to fret over girls. His greatest relationship now was with his Lord and Savior—a relationship that began to bear fruit almost immediately.

When the school year was over, almost all of the students left for the summer. Billy made a conscious decision to stay behind in Temple Terrace and help Dr. Minder with whatever needed to be done—conferences at Lake Swan, delivering sermons, attending engagements, or performing odd jobs around the campus. He also applied to churches to be their minister, but experienced one rejection after another. No one wanted someone who was green in the pulpit. The fact is, Billy could not have made a wiser choice to prepare for service. There is no better place to learn about ministry than in ministry—getting in the trenches and doing what needs to be done to help people come to faith and grow spiritually.

When God shuts a door, sometimes He opens a window. In this case, God provided an opportunity for Billy to prove himself when he spotted a man he knew as "Mr. Corwin" walking the campus grounds. Corwin ran the Hispanic ministry of the West Tampa Gospel Mission and often called on the institute to lend a helping hand. For whatever reasons, Billy felt invisible around Corwin, who never requested him.

Billy fell to his knees behind a bush and prayed hard that Corwin would ask him to preach at the mission the following day. When Billy rose and dusted himself off, Corwin approached him. He told Billy someone had canceled on him, and he needed help at the mission the next day. Was Billy available?

Prayer answered. Immediately!

The Bible says, "You have not, because you ask not." But prayer is not about getting God to do what we want Him to do. It's not getting our will in Heaven, but rather God's will on Earth. The Lord prompted Billy to ask for what the Lord actually wanted Him to do. Billy could have refused to pray (and many do), but he would have missed a tremendous open door. The Lord does not usually give us a full roadmap in life. Rather, He usually leads us one step at a time.

The following day, Billy showed up to speak to a large group of Hispanic teens at the mission. Corwin must have been impressed because he asked Billy to come back several times. Billy's confidence soared, and he took it upon himself to start preaching on the street, and sometimes in front of seedy bars and rowdy saloons.

When a preacher is willing to put himself in situations like that, it prepares him for what is ahead. One cannot control the reactions of random people on the street. They may applaud you, but they more than likely will ignore you, and sometimes turn on you. How you react to all of that helps you as a communicator to get into "fighting shape" for greater battles.

Slowly but surely, word got out about Billy's work. Invitations came trickling in. One was from a Baptist church in Venice, a small community of about five hundred people on Florida's Gulf Coast. This particular invitation sounded a little more unconventional than most: the congregation held its services in a converted meat market. Jesus had no problem preaching in an open field and feeding thousands with a few loaves of bread and a handful of fish, and Billy didn't see a problem preaching here either.

This service was "meaty" however you sliced it. Of the approximately eighty-five people in the congregation, almost a third responded to Billy's invitation to "commit their lives to Christ." If an evangelist has a 10 percent response to his preaching, that is considered a great success. But to have a third of an audience respond? That is "revival-like"!

Billy was awestruck. Humbly, he did not believe it was his sermon or the invitation that got so many to come forward; he credited the powerful prayer preceding the afternoon service that set it all in motion.

Billy told me once that he felt he had a gifting from God to give the invitation. He did not regard himself as a great preacher, though I strongly disagreed with him on that point. Having said that, he did have a supernatural ability, or what the Bible calls "an anointing," to call people to Christ. You can't learn that in a classroom or from a book. It is a gift from Heaven, and Billy already had it as a young man. Though every Christian is called to share their faith, not every believer has the "gift" of the office of the evangelist. There is only one person in the Bible who is uniquely identified that way. His name was Philip. He started out literally waiting tables (Acts 6:5) and ended up being called by the Lord to bring others to Christ. He is best known for his conversation with the visiting dignitary from Ethiopia who went to Jerusalem searching for God. Philip led him to Christ on a desert road (Acts 8).

Speaking of preordained, a second invitation came that summer from Dr. Minder's friend Cecil Underwood. He made arrangements for Billy to preach at a week-long engagement at East Palatka Baptist Church, a few miles from his debut effort at Bostwick Baptist Church. Even though Billy didn't shine his first time in the pulpit, Underwood connected with him again when he spent a couple of summer months working with children at the Lake Swan Conference Center. He must have sensed Billy's growth from the year before and specifically asked for him.

This trip was pivotal in many ways: it gave Billy the opportunity not only to preach, but to lead a week-long series of evening meetings. Second, Underwood made arrangements for Billy to preach live every morning on WFOY radio in St. Augustine, a half-hour drive from the church. This was especially crucial for him. Those first stints in a broadcasting booth afforded Billy vital experience and familiarity with the medium, which he would later use to his advantage.

Billy prepared fifteen full sermons and memorized each one cold. Unlike the previous year, he didn't lose any sleep when it came to preparation, and he was brimming with confidence. This was an entirely new Billy, and he was loaded for bear.

Palatka must have been hungry for the Word because the locals showed up in droves for Billy's services, bolstered by his appearances on WFOY. Every night approximately 150 people came to hear him preach. Taking a cue from Mordecai Ham, Billy was fired up, feisty, and ready to save souls. He was also ready to rumble.

Early into the week, Billy quickly became annoyed with a group of young people who took their seats in the back pews. They were a disrespectful bunch, talking loudly and joking around while Billy preached. One young boy's blatant disrespect drew Billy's ire. He barked at the lad from the pulpit, even threatening to march to the back of the room, seize him by his neck, and bum-rush him out of the building. Patience is not infinite for anyone. (Ask Jesus how He felt about moneylending inside the temple.)

Over the years, Billy's response to instigators mellowed. I remember one time when he was preaching in London and a few protesters showed up and disrupted the meeting, with thousands in attendance. They unfurled a huge protest banner with not-so-kind words and dropped it down in full sight of the audience. I was on the other side of the arena, and I was so angry that I wanted to run over and take care of them myself! The ushers slowly approached them and finally escorted them out of the building. Billy kept right on preaching and never missed a note. I can tell you from experience, there are few things that bother a preacher more than someone causing a distraction. I suppose the only thing that would be worse is a completely indifferent audience.

One of Billy's early services at the church drew the attention of a local reporter who wrote: "Old timers say that last night's meeting in East Palatka was the greatest meeting of the history of the church…Billy Graham, the young nineteen-year-old student of the Florida Bible Institute, is causing quite a sensation."

That sensation manifested itself in bountiful decisions for Christ. Approximately eighty people asked for salvation during that week, many of them later joining and supporting the church. This is important because many will walk forward in an invitation, but not as many will go forward spiritually. "The Great Commission" as given by Jesus is not just to preach the Gospel. Jesus said, "Go and make disciples of all nations, baptizing them in the name of the Father and of the Son and of the Holy Spirit, and teaching them to obey everything I have commanded you. And surely I am with you always, to the very end of the age" (Matthew 28:19–20 WEB).

There really is no better place for spiritual growth and discipleship to take place than in the church.

Preachers can get discouraged—or encouraged—just like anyone else. For a businessman, a sale, a closed deal, and financial profit are yardsticks of success. For an evangelist, success is when people come to the Lord. Our "profit margin" is much different. In my opinion, this was a milestone event for Billy. This experience and others to follow would throw some fuel on the flame of Billy Graham.

His confidence soon grew to fearlessness. He was now a crusader, a warrior for the Lord, a Joshua who would wade into any fight or any dark alley. Sundays were now reserved for Tampa's worst: he held more than a half-dozen services that day, preaching to the down and out, the indigent and poor, and those crippled by addictions. He went back to preaching to people in prisons, trailer parks, and anywhere else there was a need with renewed vigor. He once recalled preaching in front of a saloon on Tampa's rowdy Franklin Street. During the day it was an entertainment and shopping district, and at night it was filled with drunks, prostitutes, and other sinners in need of the Good News.

"I stood right in the door, preaching to people sitting at the bar. The barkeeper came out and ordered me away, and I wouldn't go," Billy later said. "He just shoved me down, and I half fell and half tripped into the wet street. I got my clothes messed up. I remembered the words of Jesus, and felt that I was suffering for Christ's sake. It was quite tactless the way I went about it, zeal and no knowledge; but those were experiences that helped develop."

Criminals, addicts, street people, and night hawks. These weren't housewives with buckets of water. Billy had entered a new world, far from children and summer Bible camps, and he reveled in it. He was Joshua reborn, a lion of God who didn't blink or hesitate.

And he was ready to roar.

CHAPTER TEN

Knees Down! Chin Up!

Billy Graham was beginning to experience a new Holy Spirit power in his life and in his ministry. He was growing by leaps and bounds. It was most apparent in the pulpit when he was delivering a sermon and during his prayer times. He had encountered every milestone that a preacher must reach in order to get to the next step, and he met every challenge with great enthusiasm and humility.

He studied God's Word. He preached the Gospel in churches and on street corners. He made home and hospital visits to people who were sick, and he held hands with the dying. He got down on his knees at his lowest moment and surrendered his total will to his Savior. When he failed in the pulpit, he got right back in the saddle and tried harder. And finally, he led a successful week-long revival. While at Florida Bible Institute, he paid his dues and then some.

What I love most about Billy's character was his spiritual intensity. He practiced so hard during the day that by the time he entered the pulpit, he was pretty much spent. He stayed at college during the summer to assist his mentor and soak in whatever he could to learn more. His mind never relented, to the point where he became a light sleeper. He bought a car in college that he could not afford because he needed transportation so he could preach the Gospel in rural areas. He was his own worst critic when it came to his sermons. He was never satisfied with his messages or delivery. He would not give a sermon until he had practiced it many times. His dedication and hunger for more were nearly unquenchable.

I have mentored many young preachers and pastors since I entered ministry in the 1970s. Some excellent talent has passed through the doors of my church. However, I have yet to see anyone match Billy's hunger and determination. That's something that can't be taught. Billy was very open to instruction throughout his entire life, which seems to be a rare quality, especially among men as accomplished as he was.

I would describe him as selfless. His first instinct was to put others first, and you can't fake that. Billy was genuinely interested in others and always felt he could learn from them. He was a lifelong pupil, always asking questions. He would often begin a conversation with the words "Tell me about yourself!" And he meant it.

He would listen intently. If he repeated your story to someone else, he would have it down, note for note. When he was with theologians and academics, he would pepper them with questions and absorb the information. When he was with senators, congressmen, governors, and even presidents, he would learn about geopolitics. When he was with common folk, he listened just as intently.

But when Billy spoke, it was never in a braggadocious manner. It was very down-to-earth.

In ordinary conversations and in the pulpit, he was able to take the complex and make it simple enough for a regular person to understand. There was always a rare combination in Billy of a Statesman-Everyman— the farmer who was sought out by presidents, the country preacher who touched the world. I think his ability to listen and learn was his most valuable quality. When we became friends, he would ask for my opinions on different topics, and in time he asked me to assist with his sermon preparation. I honestly was amazed that he would care what I thought, but that is a tribute to him. I was in my late thirties at the time, and I worked to freshen up his cultural illustrations at his request. But with the actual content and delivery, Billy Graham did not need anyone's help...except the Lord's.

Billy knew deep down he still had deficiencies, and that is why, over and over, he had to turn to God for help. He recalled in the book of Exodus when God called Moses by way of a burning bush. Even though Moses was full of inadequacies, God used him mightily.

Billy quickly learned his job was to pray, study hard, practice, practice, practice, and trust God with the outcome. It was God's job to fill in the gaps and make sure Billy's preaching of His Word accomplished what He wanted.

After the triumph of his first revival meeting, Billy sought God even more. He strongly felt the need to be baptized by immersion and made arrangements with Dr. Minder to get it done. This was important to Billy because he felt the act "signified my dying to sin and rising again to a new life in Christ." Different denominations baptize differently—some with splashes of water on the head, some by full immersion in an ocean, river, stream, in a baptismal, or even a swimming pool. Early Christian baptism was by total immersion, which was the practice of the New Testament church.

Cecil Underwood agreed to perform the baptism and suggested to Billy that he consider changing his religious affiliation to Southern Baptist—the largest Protestant denomination in the United States.

After much contemplation (and with his parents' approval), Billy decided to take the plunge on December 4, 1938. Underwood immersed him in Palatka's Silver Lake with people from his church witnessing the act. Shortly after that came ordination into the Baptist Association in February 1939.

Being ordained gave Billy authority to perform and officiate over several functions such as weddings, funerals, baptisms, and other church activities. This opened up many avenues to him, including the offer to preach a two-week evangelistic service at Welaka Baptist Church. It presented a challenge to Billy in that it was not only the longest revival thus far, but also because Welaka was a blue-collar fishing village with plenty of tough customers.

Welaka reminds me of a few places where I have spoken over the years. One time I was invited to speak to thousands of people in Ohio at what was described to me as a "Woodstock-like" Christian gathering at a local farm. I was just getting started in ministry and jumped at the chance. I was picked up at the airport and rode to the location in the bed of a pickup truck with a bunch of other folks. That's not even legal in California!

It was incredibly hot and humid, and I cooled down by taking a plunge in the river. The meeting was underwhelming, to say the least. Instead of thousands, around thirty people showed up, most of them in rocking chairs they brought with them. Some cooled themselves with funeral fans. It was a humbling reminder to me that I was "not all that and a bag of chips." Despite the small crowd, quite a few of them came forward at my invitation to receive Christ into their lives, so I was thankful for that.

Billy would have more than a few of those experiences as a young preacher.

His development as a leader and preacher was also bolstered when John Minder asked him to be his summer replacement at the Tampa Gospel Tabernacle. For six weeks, Billy ran the place, which must have given him a real sense of what it was like to be a full-time pastor. He took advantage of the empty sanctuary to practice his sermons. Sometimes it was an audience of one—the janitor—and Billy even sought feedback from him. The man pushing the mop had plenty of feedback to offer him, which he tactfully accepted. Billy was wise to accept counsel from others and did so throughout his life.

Billy's ordination brought good tidings, including a spot as vice president of the young people's ministry for the Christian and Missionary Alliance (CMA) churches in Florida. As a result, almost all the CMA churches invited him to speak to their youth in the summer months, establishing crucial connections for him in Florida and Georgia. Some people just have a knack for networking, and Billy had it in spades.

When young men come to me and tell me they feel a call to preach, I have them start with Sunday School. Youth have short attention spans. If you can hold their attention, you indeed have a gift from God. Anyone can be boring, but only a few seem to be able to get and hold the attention of an audience. Some of the best preachers I know today started out as youth pastors.

The ordination benefitted him professionally and financially, in some cases—enough to buy him a used car and put some spending money in his pocket. But he knew deep down it still wasn't enough. He wanted to do more for Christ.

After Billy's decision to turn his life over to the Lord years before, his thirst for knowledge increased. He read the newspapers on a daily basis, stayed up on current affairs, devoured history books, and was consciously curious about everyday life beyond the confines of the institute. He didn't want to be the kind of Christian who lived in a bubble. He even purchased a set of used encyclopedias and developed a habit of reading them to round out his worldly education. Often, he referenced them if he didn't know the answer to something. But he turned to God when the realization hit him that he needed more education than he was receiving at Florida Bible Institute.

God provided the answer when a group of winter visitors descended on Temple Terrace during Billy's senior year of college. Billy befriended Chicago attorney Paul Fisher, who frequented the institute's hotel. In early 1940, he visited the campus along with Elner Edman, a business associate, and Edman's mother. Fisher's brother Herman was chairman of the board at Wheaton College near Chicago, Illinois, and Edman's brother Raymond was a history professor and interim president at the school. After the Edmans sat spellbound hearing Billy preach, they encouraged him to further his education. Naturally, they suggested Wheaton, a top-tier Christian liberal arts college and graduate school held in high esteem. (V. Raymond Edman eventually became one of Billy's great mentors, often praying with him when they visited. He wrote Billy many encouraging letters, which often carried the refrain "Knees down! Chin up!")

Billy's parents also knew of Wheaton's stellar reputation. However, family finances made that prospect a pipe dream. But as evangelist Billy Sunday once said, "There is more power in a mother's hand than in a king's scepter." When Morrow got on her knees to pray for Billy, it seemed as though God immediately went to work.

The men asked Billy to caddy for them during a round of golf. The conversation eased its way to Billy. They had seen him preach and were impressed. Out of Billy's earshot, they said they thought he was the most talented preacher at Florida Bible Institute. However, Fisher said he needed more education. Billy knew that as well, nodding his head in acknowledgment. But what Fisher said next was something Billy could not anticipate—he offered to pay his room and board at Wheaton for a year. Elner Edman matched Fisher's largesse, stating he'd pay for a year's tuition. Billy was floored by their generosity, and his mind immediately went into pros-and-cons mode. *Would the college even admit him or transfer credits from Florida Bible Institute? What would his high school transcript reveal? Could he survive a Windy City winter after living in sunny Florida?*

He took the decision to God and ultimately came to the following conclusion: "The more I prayed, the more I was certain God was leading, and that I must further my education at all costs."

Billy applied for admission and was accepted into Wheaton, thanks to his new and influential friends. But the decision didn't come without a degree of pain and humiliation. Many of his Florida Bible Institute credits would not carry over. After Wheaton calculated what it could accept, they gave Billy the rank of a second-semester freshman. To be sure, it was a setback, and Billy was disappointed. Yet something kept tugging at him to leave the comfortable trappings of Florida and head north on a new journey.

Billy's Florida sojourn ended in May 1940. America was on the cusp of its greatest crucible. Adolf Hitler's armies *blitzkrieged* across Europe in the blink of an eye, conquering Poland, Belgium, France, Holland, and Scandinavia with ease. A year later Japan would follow, engulfing colonies and countries across Asia and bringing war to the gates of India, the jewel of the British Empire. London was bombed, and daily air battles raged over England that summer and fall. Nazi armies looked across the English Channel, certain in the knowledge their armor would soon be clanking across English fields. President Franklin D. Roosevelt resisted becoming involved, even though German submarines were sinking merchant ships all over the Atlantic Ocean. Phone calls for relief from Winston Churchill, Britain's new prime minister, became more and more desperate. However, within a year, the U.S. could no longer avoid the conflict—and the "Greatest Generation" would need great moral leaders to see them through it.

An eerily prophetic address was delivered at Billy's Class Night, just before spring commencement. Obviously distressed by the tensions abroad and their transformative impact on the world, valedictorian Vera Resue called for a spiritual and moral leader to emerge and lead the country through its darkest hour: "God has chosen a human instrument to shine forth His light in the darkness. Men like Luther, John and Charles Wesley, D.L. Moody, and others who were ordinary men, but men who heard the voice of God.... It has been said that Luther revolutionized the world. It was not he but Christ working through him. The time is ripe for another Luther, Wesley, Moody. There is room for another man on this list."

No one in the room knew, even the young man who sat listening a few yards away from Resue, that the new Moses God was calling was among them.

CHAPTER ELEVEN

The Twenty-One-Year-Old Freshman

I get the idea that Billy Graham's idea of paradise wasn't Wheaton College. He probably wasn't looking forward to cold winters in Illinois or studying at a new place where he knew virtually no one. He was leaving an area where he was most comfortable—the weather was ideal, his living accommodations were to his liking, the food was plentiful, and he had grown very close to his classmates. Also, he was being mentored by knowledgeable and caring instructors, and this alone enabled him to grow personally and spiritually in a rapid manner. He was beginning to come into his own in Florida when he had to leave.

Billy loved the sun. It was not uncommon to see his bronzed face behind the pulpit. That was a genuine tan from being outdoors, where he jogged and hiked to stay in shape. I spent many hours with Billy in the Florida sun where we often held our Billy Graham Evangelistic Association board meetings.

Billy was wrestling with the idea of leaving a place so well suited for him, but he knew God was calling him to something bigger—and his way lay through Wheaton College. While he wasn't enthralled with the idea of starting over again, he experienced a great inner peace because he knew this was where God wanted him. And there was no place that Billy Graham would rather be than at the center of God's will for his life.

Unbeknownst to Billy, there was a pretty young woman in Wheaton who was praying for a special man to come into her life, but it would have to be someone who loved the Lord as much as she did. God, in his own time, was bringing together two people whose ministry would have a huge impact on the world.

In September 1940, Billy made the long trek to Wheaton College, where he majored in anthropology. Wheaton was at the time a quaint suburban city located twenty-five miles west of Chicago. It was a beautiful campus surrounded by lots of elm and maple trees—eighty acres in all—filled with eighteenth-century limestone and red brick buildings. Considered the Harvard of evangelicals, the private institution was built in 1860 by abolitionists and was a stop on the Underground Railroad. By the time Billy arrived, the college was mostly attended by the children of the country's wealthiest and most prominent Christian families and a smattering of foreign students.

For the first six weeks, Billy felt sure he'd gotten off at the wrong stop. He wrote to a former mentor that Illinois was an adjustment, and he found Wheaton "a new and strange place."

Translation: Billy was miserable.

Billy admitted that his Southern roots made him feel inferior to these sophisticated Northerners, whose dialect he found hard to understand and vice versa. He also missed his friends in Florida and his preaching rounds. For many days he questioned whether or not he had made the right choice, wondering if it had been a big mistake.

Billy knew only one other student at Wheaton: Howard Van Buren, a slightly older high school buddy from Charlotte. They were even saved at the same Mordecai Ham revival. Van Buren was an outstanding student who later became a heart surgeon. Billy served as a groomsman at his wedding, most likely because he played a crucial role in Billy's working up the nerve to ask his future bride out on a date.

Also eroding Billy's self-confidence was his age. He was almost twenty-one—a few years older than the majority of his freshmen classmates. Even though Billy considered himself a natty dresser, he had to turn it up a notch at Wheaton. He wrote in his autobiography that when he first arrived, he felt like cartoon hillbilly "Li'l Abner" with his lanky frame, loud attire, and scuffed brogan shoes. So one of the first things he did was buy a five-dollar turquoise tweed suit at a local Chicago-area flea market. But five-dollar suits perform about as well as five-hundred-dollar cars. Billy's literally shrank on his body when he proudly wore it to a football game a month into the semester. It rained that night, and the pant legs crept up to his ankles and the seat of his pants grew so tight that he burst the seams. He walked home puckered, but with purpose.

Thinking that joining a sports team might help give him some social currency and build friendships, Billy tried out for wrestling. David Dresser was a senior at a nearby high school and routinely worked out at the Wheaton gym (he later attended the college). Dresser was asked to wrestle with Billy, which didn't go well.

"He was so much taller than I. We started out in the referee's position and I was on top," Dresser recalled in a 2010 interview. "I remember I could barely get my arm over his back. And so I grabbed his left arm, rammed my head in his armpit and flattened him out. I can't remember much beyond that. I don't think we wrestled very long because it was obvious I wasn't going to give him much of a workout."

Billy eventually found a spot on the roster. But at six foot two and 160 pounds, he was awkward, and his inexperience showed. He lost his first two matches, then called it quits. Nothing seemed to be working for Billy at Wheaton.

Whatever inadequacies Billy saw in himself were not apparent to others—especially a striking, brown-haired, hazel-eyed young woman named Ruth Bell. The twenty-year-old beauty was a second-year student at Wheaton and first took notice of Billy at the entrance of East Blanchard Hall in the early fall of 1940. He was hard to miss—a handsome beanstalk with wavy blonde hair and piercing blue eyes, gliding down the steps with those long, slender legs. He made a definite impression.

"He was tall and lanky and just dashed past," Ruth remembered.

For whatever reason, Billy's eyes did not lock onto Ruth's. He was headed somewhere, seemingly in a hurry.

There's a young man who knows where he's going, Ruth thought.

A few days later, Ruth met with a group of students for prayer in Williston Hall before heading out to teach a Sunday School class at a remote church. What struck her most that day was a prayer that took place in another room.

"We would take turns praying, and all of a sudden I heard a voice from the next room," Ruth recalled. "I had never heard anyone pray like it before. I knew that someone was talking to God. I sensed that here was a man that knew God in a very unusual way."

Ruth would soon get to know that mysterious, commanding voice on the other side of the wall.

Billy didn't remain an outsider at Wheaton for too long. His outsized personality, friendly nature, and the fact that he owned his own car saw to that. He was wisely recruited by the school's Student Christian Council for field work. The council dispatched ministerial squads to churches and missions on weekends. Billy tagged along and waited patiently to deliver his first sermon. He got that opportunity at a church in Terre Haute, Indiana, about a three-hour drive from the campus. Billy impressed everyone and word about his talent soon got around.

Requests for his speaking services poured in. Despite his hunger to preach, Billy declined most of them and instead chose to focus on his academics. This move paid great dividends as his B+ grade average finally showed that he could handle the academic rigor of a top-tier college.

One of the few invitations Billy did accept was a Sunday service at the Masonic Lodge in downtown Wheaton. Dr. Edman had preached there when he was teaching history at the college. However, when he was named its president a few months before Billy arrived, he vacated his ministry with the United Gospel Tabernacle (known to locals simply as

"The Tabernacle"). After Edman's departure, the church supplemented services with student preachers. Billy's first sermon there went over so well that he was given a fifteen-dollar honorarium, followed by repeat invitations to speak.

In no time, Billy's services drew capacity crowds numbering in the hundreds. His attendees were a mix of college students, school staff, working professionals, executives, and high-profile academics from Wheaton.

W. Glyn Evans attended Wheaton from 1941 to 1945 and heard Billy preach at the Tabernacle. Like most others on campus, he was impressed.

"Other fellow students there were talking about this Billy Graham. How great a preacher he was, how wonderful he was. So I was anxious, of course, to hear him," Evans recalled in 2010.

Evans said he took along a housemate who had not professed Christ yet as Savior, but who was willing to go one Sunday evening. He recalled Billy being stick thin, but with a thick Southern accent and a booming voice that didn't need the aid of a PA system.

"(Billy) was not a person to entertain. He didn't use many jokes in his sermons and he wasn't there to be buddy-buddy," Evans recalled. "He was there, it struck me as being, as a messenger of God with one goal in mind. Very sincere, very commanding, very dedicated…just a straightforward, simple presentation of the Gospel. But it was very effective."

Evans said Billy preached about the forgiveness of sins (John 1:7) and that his housemate went forward that night with tears rolling down his cheeks.

"This student who went forth was standing right next to me to sing the final hymn (and) said he was going forward," Evans recalled. "And I was shocked because we had tried to witness to him before and (he) had not moved an inch. But that sermon by Billy just touched his heart."

Evans's association with Billy didn't end there. The two ended up in the same geology class and ended up talking about other matters.

"We weren't too interested in geology, but we were awfully, greatly interested in theology," said Evans, who pastored at a nearby church part-time while attending Wheaton. He really got to know Billy during a two-hour drive to the Wisconsin Dells, where he and a couple of classmates took a field trip to deliver a lecture on the famous rock formations.

"He not only did the driving, but also the speaking. And all the way up there we got wonderful interpretations of various parts of Scripture," Evans said. "And I said to myself as I was listening to Billy talk, *This man is a born preacher!*"

It's important to remember that Billy was not naturally drawn to preaching at all, starting with his resistance to hear Mordecai Ham. Even after his conversion, evangelism was not something he immediately liked. Had he followed his own trajectory, he might have been a dairy farmer, like his father and brother Melvin, or a successful salesman with the Fuller Brush Company. God chose Billy to do His work. Billy did not choose it for himself.

The Tabernacle recruited Billy to become its resident pastor in the fall of 1941. Dr. Edman suggested serious contemplation before Billy gave an answer. The responsibility was heavy duty, preaching two Sunday services and conducting a Wednesday night prayer service. It was quite an obligation for a young man attending college. Billy eventually accepted the position, a decision that turned out to be a mixed blessing.

The time in the pulpit kept Billy from getting rusty and exposed him to all the right people, but it came at the expense of his grades. The equation was simple: the more time he spent at the Tabernacle, the less time he spent on his studies. The eighty-seven-point grade-point average he was so proud of that first semester precipitously dropped. But a few months later, that became almost inconsequential.

On Sunday evening, December 7, 1941, after Billy preached another sermon at the Tabernacle, he, like millions of other Americans, learned that Pearl Harbor, a U.S. Naval base in Hawaii, had been attacked by Japanese forces. Billy didn't have much context about the attack, but the seriousness of the situation soon sank in.

Americans thought about the war in Europe, but not about becoming involved in it. War in the Pacific certainly wasn't on anyone's mind.

But within hours of the attack on Pearl Harbor, the country went into a full-on war posture that is unimaginable today. The Office of Production Management said to the Big Three automakers, "You now build airplanes." Using auto parts, they began manufacturing aircraft in less than a month. Our modern equivalent would be when some of our automobile companies went from making cars to ventilators because of the coronavirus pandemic.

The war was not part of the culture; the war *was* the culture. Everything was now viewed through the prism of the war effort. Only two or three days after the attack, thousands of men rushed to enlist in the U.S. Armed Forces. So did women, who found employment serving as nurses, driving trucks, repairing airplanes, and performing clerical work. Some were even killed in combat or captured as prisoners of war.

Many of the movies of that time had war themes. Women went to work in factories. Children participated in scrap drives—paper drives, metal drives, rubber drives, and grease drives. Everybody in this country found a way to chip in.

On December 8, Dr. Edman assembled the entire student body for an impromptu service at the school chapel. Edman had enlisted in the U.S. Army to serve his country in World War I just a month after he converted to Christianity at age eighteen. He intimately knew the horrors of conflict and that many of the young men in front of him would be recruited or would voluntarily enlist to fight the Axis powers of Nazi Germany, the Kingdom of Italy, and the Empire of Japan.

Billy, like millions of other young men of that era, felt the need to do something. Anything. His initial reaction was to drop out of Wheaton and sign up for the war effort. He wrote the War Department about becoming a U.S. Army chaplain, but was informed he needed to finish college first, and then he would have to take a seminary course. For the next three semesters, everything Billy did was with much greater purpose.

"Life and death were not abstractions to us anymore, and the Wheaton township of seven thousand residents shared with the rest of the nation the anxiety and grief of war," Billy wrote in his autobiography.

It was a turning point for him, the nation, and the world. Whatever plans anyone on the planet had for the future were now on hold indefinitely.

CHAPTER TWELVE

Saved by a Bell

Shortly after Billy Graham surrendered his will to Christ on the eighteenth hole of the Temple Terrace golf course, he vowed that the next woman he kissed would be his wife. As hard as it was for a man in his prime, Billy put off his feelings for women so he could focus his energies solely on his studies and preaching. But his resolve practically crumbled when his friend Johnny Streater told him about an eye-catching, spiritual woman he knew by the name of Ruth Bell.

Billy had met Streater, a fellow student who ran a college moving service using his personal pickup truck, during his first semester at Wheaton. He extended Billy a job offer and a whopping fifty cents an hour to help him haul furniture and household items for those on a budget.

Billy's wardrobe also looked like he was on a budget, said Jane Levring, who attended Wheaton in the 1940s. She recalled when Streater and Billy moved her into North Hall.

"I noticed what they were wearing and this guy, that I found out later was Billy, had on these old country shoes," Levring recalled in 2010. "You know, they were high-topped leather. They're just right in fashion now with what the fellows are wearing but back in those days, most of the boys wore saddle outs with something like that. And I looked at his shoes and I thought, 'My goodness, he must be from the farm.' And sure enough, he was!"

Streater was more sophisticated than Billy. He was a U.S. Navy veteran, and after graduation, he intended to become a missionary to China along with his fiancée, Carol Lane. One day while driving around Wheaton, he and Billy got on the subject of women. Almost by default, Streater mentioned that the nicest girl on campus was (of course) his fiancée. But then he went on to espouse the qualities of a young Christian woman named Ruth Bell, a junior.

"She's so spiritual that she gets up at four o'clock each morning to read her Bible and pray," he said. "I want you to meet her...she's the girl for you!"

Billy was intrigued. About a month later, he had the opportunity to make her acquaintance.

That's when he and Streater were in front of Williston Hall, the women's dorm, preparing to move some furniture for a client in a nearby suburb. Ruth was in the hallway, talking to a group of her friends.

The two men certainly didn't look their finest—sopping wet in their sweaty work clothes, and probably smelling as bad as they looked. Perhaps that's why Billy lacked confidence when Streater introduced him to Ruth. That didn't seem to matter much to her; she smiled as she gazed into those intense blue eyes. In that moment, Billy felt totally out of his league, recalling that Ruth resembled to him a "slender, hazel-eyed movie starlet."

Billy, who never lacked for confidence when it came to the opposite sex, couldn't work up the nerve to ask Ruth out on a date. It would take another month for him to do that. He later admitted, "At that moment I was in love. Not only in love but something told me inside that 'she'll be your wife.'"

And he was in love for a good reason: Ruth McCue Bell was a very special girl.

Born on June 10, 1920, to medical missionaries Dr. L. Nelson and Virginia Bell, Ruth spent the first seventeen years of her life in war-torn

China. Nelson was a surgical chief and administrative superintendent of a three-hundred-and-eighty-bed Presbyterian hospital in the eastern Chinese province of Kiangsu, about three hundred miles north of Shanghai. Her mother was a nurse.

Ruth's parents not only shared the Gospel, but lived it, and young Ruth had a heart for the Lord from a very early age. Ruth recalled seeing her father read the Bible and kneeling in prayer when she awoke each morning.

"(My parents) ran a tight ship but a loving home," Ruth said. "I had the privilege of being brought up by happy Christians, and that makes a tremendous difference."

Any doubt about the difference missionaries made in the lives of the locals was dispelled by the story of Ruth's Chinese nurse, Wang Nai Nai. Known as *amah* (grandmother) to Ruth and her three siblings, she was a beloved figure.

"We children were not the only ones who loved her. Everyone did. And with good reason: she loved everyone," Ruth recalled.

Wang Nai Nai's past was proof of the Bells' Christian love and understanding. For years, she and her husband had located, kidnapped, and sold young girls to houses of prostitution in Shanghai. But then she had a conversion experience, and her life radically changed. She experienced the peace that surpasses all understanding, and Ruth often recalled Wang Nai Nai sitting on a low stool, singing from a paper-bound Chinese hymnal.

"And to my innocent child's mind, she was the picture of a saintly old soul at worship," Ruth said in her later years.

That peaceful recollection contrasted with their immediate surroundings. Ruth remembered being enveloped by disease, despair, and the ravages of civil war. She grew up with air raids, explosions, and seeing mutilated bodies in the streets. In fact, she couldn't recall a night when she didn't hear gunshots or explosions in the distance as she went to bed.

It was a turbulent time in China's history. The country was filled with warlords, bandits, the Japanese, the Communists, and the Nationalists all fighting each other. Often these conflicts spilled over to foreigners, and missionaries were not exempt from the violence. The country had a population of about four hundred million. Men still wore long pigtails called *queues*, which in the Imperial era signified their allegiance to the ruling dynasty. Wealthy women had their feet bound so they were as small as possible, a sign of beauty and prosperity. Only about 30 percent of the population could read or write. Outside of cities like Shanghai, there was no electricity, running water, or sanitation. Almost all work, including large-scale construction, was done entirely by human muscle. Notorious criminals were placed in cages to die in public as a message. With nooses around their necks, their toes barely reached the bottom of the cage. They could stand in agony or be slowly strangled.

The ruling Manchu dynasty had been overthrown by a warlord and an intellectual shortly before the Bells arrived. Chinese feudal society simply was not modernizing quickly enough, leading to a defeat by the Japanese twenty-one years before the Bells arrived. The Imperial armies fought with crossbows, halberds, and spears. When it rained during battles, they put up huge gray umbrellas and simply waited for the weather to clear up. After the 1911 revolution, the country was in chaos, with order reigning only in European enclaves like Shanghai and Japanese-controlled Manchuria in the north. River piracy, for instance, was a serious problem until World War II. While the Bells were there, Roy Chapman Andrews—the inspiration for Indiana Jones—was running around the Western deserts, searching for dinosaur bones and swapping shots with bandits on horseback.

Ruth undoubtedly saw shocking things, which would have been impossible to avoid. But having been born there, she would have been inured to much of the daily and commonplace cruelties she saw, like farm kids learning the facts of life at very young ages. When she accompanied her *amah* to the market, it would have been completely different than the same experience in Iowa. Pangolin, turtles, crabs, and strange fish in tubs; bats and blood spurting from the necks of chickens and snakes; the cry and babble of thousands of voices selling and cajoling; smells and smoke and frying oil and the jostle of crowds—this was Ruth Bell's "normal." It's known as the "wet market" and still exists in some provinces of China today.

But to her, it was simply home.

From those firsthand experiences, Ruth grew up quickly. She wrote beautiful poetry that was wise beyond her years. She was also extremely well-read; Billy often referred to her as the real theologian of the family who could dig into Greek texts and interpret the most difficult Scripture for him.

When the mission's compound could no longer further Ruth's education at thirteen, she was sent to a boarding school in Pyongyang, which is today the capital of North Korea and run with an iron fist by dictator Kim Jong-un.

The night before Ruth left Shanghai for Pyongyang with a handful of other teens from the compound, she was desperately unhappy. She cried herself to sleep, praying that somehow she wouldn't have to go, even wishing that she would die before morning light. But God didn't answer that prayer, and for good reason. Her voyage to Pyongyang the next day would bear fruit in the decades to come.

Almost sixty years later, in April 1992, Billy Graham was invited to Pyongyang as an honored guest of North Korea's late president, Kim Il-sung. It was a curious time for North Korea with the collapse of the Soviet Union, the failure of its economy, and famine on the horizon. Kim was looking to improve ties with the United States, and Billy saw an opportunity to build a bridge by bringing the Gospel to the atheist country.

Before World War II, Pyongyang was filled with churches and missionaries and was called "the Jerusalem of the East." But then it became Communist, and anyone preaching anything other than collectivism was persecuted. Merely possessing a Bible could lead to criminal charges.

None of that mattered to Billy. He felt the embers of faith were still there in North Korea and wanted an opportunity to preach the Gospel. When he arrived, he gave the North Korean dictator a Bible. Kim in turn asked Billy to go fishing with him.

But the roots of this historic trip started with Ruth. When Kim Il-sung heard of her ties to North Korea, he was intrigued.

"That was one of the reasons that we could get in and talk to the leaders that made it possible for us to go," Billy later said at a press conference. "And we had a wonderful reception."

It's amazing the things God allows in our present in order to bear fruit in the future.

That 1992 trip to North Korea led to a return in 1997. Ruth called it one of the highlights of her life.

"Almost nothing remains from my school days here during the 1930s," she told her hosts. "But two things have not changed: the beauty of the two rivers that flow through the city of Pyongyang and the warmth and hospitality of the people."

As a teenager, Ruth found peace a few weeks after arriving in Pyongyang when her homesickness turned into illness. While in the infirmary, she carefully read all 150 psalms, and suddenly her faith became very real to her. This episode commenced her spiritual "boot camp," and it taught her to find solace in God's presence while separated from her loved ones.

Ruth never lost that spiritual spark, and, in fact, it grew to a great fire in her heart. She loved to study the Bible. In her little study, the Bible was always there, along with many other commentaries open next to it. When I would visit the Grahams' home years later, I noticed two signs she had that showed both her servant's heart and her humor. Over the sink was a sign that said, "Divine service will be conducted here…daily." At the front door was a foot mat that read, "Not you again!"

I had many occasions to speak at the Billy Graham Training Center at the Cove, which was not far from Billy and Ruth's house in Montreat, North Carolina. Billy was often out of town on one of his Crusades, but Ruth was a real homebody and would swing by and attend a service. I have to say, speaking in front of her was intimidating, to say the least. She wrote my wife, Cathe, beautiful letters in left-slanting writing. I remember one she wrote in October 1989 after hearing me speak at the Cove. It read, "When you look over a flock of sheep, just remember that the old ewes are just as hungry as the lambs. This one is no exception. And boy did I get fed!"

Ruth studied in Korea for three years and viewed that time as a special training period.

"During those months of separation from my family, I learned things that only God could teach me," she said. "Little knowing that He was about to prepare me for a lifetime of goodbyes."

Ruth completed her high school education in Montreat while her parents were on furlough in 1935 and 1936. She returned to China the summer after her high school graduation and wanted to stay with her parents rather than further her education. She felt college was simply going to be a waste of time, as her future was already mapped out in her mind. She had no intention of marrying, and her adventurous life as a missionary in Tibet would fulfill all of her needs.

But on August 13, 1937—the day Ruth was to leave for Wheaton College—the Chinese capital, Shanghai, fell to the Japanese. The troops of the Rising Sun rampaged across China, slaughtering millions. The infamous Rape of Nanjing happened that year. To this day, historical movies portraying Japanese villains are popular in China. As a result of these actions, Ruth's trip was delayed when the Japanese mined the Yangtze River and obliterated the Nanking-Shanghai railway system, essentially choking off all the major modes of transportation.

General Chiang Kai-shek, leader of China's national government, fought the Japanese for eight years. Japan couldn't control the immense Chinese countryside, and guerillas fought the Empire in rural provinces. The people suffered under both armies. Tens of thousands of Chinese died after Chiang pulled back into the hinterlands and used scorched-earth tactics like blowing up dams and torching entire cities. As occupiers, the Japanese were as brutal as the Nazis, mass-murdering civilians in reprisals. Essentially, the conflict remained at a stalemate until Japan surrendered after World War II and Chairman Mao Tse-tung's Communists defeated the national forces.

On September 1, the American ambassador recommended that all missionaries promptly evacuate to the United States, but the Bells waited a few weeks before fleeing through a maze of trains, rivers, canals, and secret waterways. They encountered air raids, bombings, and other potentially deadly attacks, hunching in dugouts, train stations, and other forms of shelter. A tugboat took them to a United States troopship that dumped them off in Quindago. The missionaries' story portrayed in the 1966 film *The Sand Pebbles,* starring Steve McQueen and Candice Bergen, closely mirrors this adventure. It could easily have been a page or two ripped from the Bells' life.

Ruth arrived safely at Wheaton College in the fall of 1937, two months after the semester started. She studied the Bible and art in preparation for being a missionary in Tibet. She also had many male admirers.

Her housemother, Julia Scott, wrote of her at the time: "Very attractive, beautiful to look at and excellent taste in dress. The most beautiful Christian character of any young person I have ever known. And she has the intellectual qualities to make a success in any work she would choose to undertake. She ranks very high in the qualities of poise, forcefulness, and courtesy."

I couldn't have said it better myself.

Had Ruth chosen to, she could have had a very successful international speaking ministry. But after falling in love, she believed her primary calling was to be a wife to Billy and the mother of their children. She was clearly his equal, and he deeply valued her counsel and companionship.

Billy and Ruth were literally meant for each other. Theirs was truly a love story for the ages. Even in their later years, you could see their deep affection for and dependence on each other.

The two of them did not walk on air—but they had amazing chemistry, and Ruth could bring Billy back to earth with very practical and sound advice. Wisely, he listened.

It's no wonder that Ruth was especially popular with students on campus and had no shortage of men asking her for dates, said Jeanne Smith Burton, who was Ruth's roommate at Wheaton when she first arrived.

"She was very outgoing in her relationships with people...very vivacious, you know, not pulled back at all," Burton said. "She was so popular and guys were always wanting to date her. She probably spent more time going on dates than the rest of us." (Her sister Rosa kept count on a piece of paper: Ruth dated fifty-two men at Wheaton before she met Billy; he, in turn, dated only two women while in college.)

Billy waited a few weeks to ask Ruth out. The Christmas holidays beckoned, and a presentation of Handel's *Messiah* at the Pierce Chapel offered an ideal first date. Billy was hanging out with buddies Johnny Streater and Howard Van Buren at the campus library inside Blanchard Hall when they spotted Ruth studying for one of her finals. Billy was suddenly gripped with fear.

The three men whispered and strategized (incurring a few harsh looks from the school librarian) how Billy, who was uncharacteristically low on courage and self-confidence that day, should ask her out. They decided the best course of action was for him to compose and deliver a note. Putting his best foot forward, he marched across the room and placed the note in Ruth's hand while he waited for a response. She looked up and nodded her head affirmatively, agreeing to go.

Their date was on a Sunday afternoon, and it was a typical wintery Chicago day: cold and snowy. The music inside Pierce Chapel was beautiful and enchanting. The glee clubs, which put on the presentation, sang their collective hearts out, but Billy barely heard a word. With Ruth Bell sitting next to him, his nervous system was out of whack and his mind raced.

I knew the couple in their later years, and Billy would talk about his latest aches and pains if you asked him how he was feeling. Ruth, even if she was not feeling well, would never discuss her ailments.

Yet as grandparents, Ruth was the one who fell ill. I went to visit her and Billy with my friend Dennis Agajanian, who performed on many of their Crusades. Billy asked Dennis to play them a song; he broke into an instrumental version of "The Hallelujah Chorus."

I drank the moment in as Ruth seemed to be positively glowing despite her frail condition. Billy lovingly looked at her and said, "That's the song they played on our first date!"

Their first date could have easily ended when the performance was over, but they went for a cup of tea on campus and engaged in their first real conversation. Billy could not get over how beautiful and spiritual Ruth Bell was. In that conversation, the rumor Billy had first heard from Johnny Streater about Ruth's getting up at the crack of dawn to go over her morning devotional was confirmed. Many years later, her Wheaton roommate Bessie Lea Eichorn would tell a reporter, "Finances were tight for all of us and particularly for Ruth as a 'missionary kid,' so she worked in Lower Dining Hall. She had to be there very early (each) morning to prepare breakfast, but she always had her hour of daily devotions before she left. Sometimes, when I was up early, I would see the light under her door at four a.m."

Ruth was equally impressed with Billy on that first date.

"There was a seriousness about him; there was a depth," Ruth said. "He was much older in every way than the other students on campus, not just in age. He was a mature man; he was a man who knew God; he was a man who had a purpose, a dedication in life; he knew where he was going. He wanted to please God more than any other man I'd ever met."

But Billy was a man, and he was made of flesh and bone...and plenty of tenderness. When they finished drinking their tea, Billy escorted Ruth to her doorstep at Williston Hall. In the hushed quiet of the snow, he reached for her hand, his heart beating so hard he was sure she could hear it. This was a bold move in the 1940s. His breath hung in his throat, waiting to feel her fingertips brush against his.

Billy recalled: "I tried to hold her hand, and she pulled it away. And I'll never forget that and how rejected I felt. I said, 'Well, I've failed with this one, anyway.'"

He was crushed.

Unbeknownst to Billy, he hadn't failed completely. Privately, Ruth was impressed with him, and was more interested than she let on—something her former roommate Jeanne Smith Burton attested to.

"(Ruth) had her eyes on him more than he had his eyes on her," Burton recalled decades later. "She decided that he was the one she really wanted to date."

On the way back to his dorm after their date, Billy was disheartened. But when Ruth got to her dorm room, she fell to her knees and prayed to God: "If You let me serve You with that man, I'd consider it the greatest privilege in my life."

In August 1943, her wish would come true above and beyond anything she could dream. With their hands at last entwined forever, they would embark on a life neither could imagine at the time. Together they would raise a family, experience adventures across the globe, minister to others, and befriend the world's most powerful and influential people in every field. Their marriage would last until Ruth's death in 2007.

CHAPTER THIRTEEN

A Marriage Made in Heaven

It's no accident that Billy Graham and Ruth Bell got together at Wheaton College. It was all part of God's grand plan from the time those two were in their mothers' wombs. He would use their formative years to grow their faith and trust in Him and let them know they had to choose wisely when it came to picking a mate. God has a plan for us before we have a plan for ourselves.

The two most important moments in a person's life are when they are born and when they realize what they were born for. When Jeremiah was but a boy, God declared to him,

> "I knew you before I formed you in your mother's womb. Before you were born I set you apart and appointed you as my prophet to the nations."
>
> "O Sovereign Lord," I said, "I can't speak for you! I'm too young!"
>
> The Lord replied, "Don't say, 'I'm too young,' for you must go wherever I send you and say whatever I tell you. And

don't be afraid of the people, for I will be with you and will protect you." (Jeremiah 1:5–7 NLT)

Billy was called to be an evangelist to the world, and like Jeremiah, to even have a "prophet-like" calling.

Ruth Bell Graham was called to be his wife and the mother of their children. But even more, she was called to be the love of his life, his strongest supporter, and his most-trusted counselor.

Anyone who spent time with Billy and his team soon discovered that he was deeply loved by many. They all looked forward to the moment when he would call them or ask their advice.

One time I was at a Billy Graham Evangelistic Association board meeting with a Crusade approaching (they were always looming large). I said to him at the end, "Billy, if you need me to do any research or help you with your message, just let me know."

That sounds presumptuous, I know, but I had been actively assisting him by that point. I went back to my hotel room and was getting ready for bed when the phone rang. This was not surprising, as Dennis Agajanian often called me after a BGEA board meeting to ask me how it went.

Dennis liked to pretend to be Billy when he called, and on this occasion (in a pretty spot-on imitation) he said, "Greg, I've been thinking about what you said, and I would like some help with my messages." I was channel surfing and not really paying attention, and I said, "Uh-huh…Whatever…" as I waited for Dennis to identify himself.

Suddenly, it dawned on me that I was not speaking with Dennis because he had no way of knowing I had offered to assist Billy with his messages. I was blowing off Billy Graham himself!

I quickly snapped to attention. "Yes, Billy, whatever I can do!" Thankfully, I had many opportunities to serve him in this capacity.

But the one person whose opinion carried the greatest weight was always Ruth.

In no time, Billy fell head over heels for her. His friend Johnny Streater, the man who introduced them, was alarmed at how hard and fast this occurred. He advised him to dial it down a notch or two.

Ruth was so beautiful and refined that Billy was afraid someone else would snatch her up. But Streater and others cautioned that his zealousness would surely put her off. After Billy caught his breath and came back down to Planet Earth, the two began courting the old-fashioned way. He took her on picnics, strolls around the campus, canoe trips on the Fox River in nearby St. Charles, and even to a graveyard to read headstones—though some might find the latter not so romantic. Ruth sensed in him a passion for preaching the Gospel so intense that he found it hard to take the time to stop and smell the roses.

"He was so very serious about life in general," she said. "He didn't have enough time to go to ball games. Every date we had was to a preaching service of some kind. Yet for all his terrific dedication and drive there was a winsomeness about him, and a consideration for other people, which I found endearing."

Like all young couples in love, this was their "honeymoon phase" where everything they said and did was adorable. Mistakes were overlooked, annoying quirks ignored, and glaring personality flaws were seen as something that could be overcome with the right training. However, one nagging issue kept coming up—not arguments, but lengthy discussions in which they didn't exactly see eye-to-eye. Ruth wanted Billy to go with her as a missionary in Tibet. Billy's major in anthropology signaled to Ruth that he might consider that. But the brochure was much better than the vacation.

In the recesses of his heart, Billy knew he was called to preach the Gospel. Yes, he had designs on foreign missions at the global level and was ready to serve overseas, but there was no indication that God had called him to be a missionary per se. Like many men of his era, he had an old-fashioned view of marriage: the wife would benefit more from being in the home, looking after the family, and raising their children.

Even though they were tiptoeing around the idea of engagement, they tabled the issue of mission work for the time being. However, it didn't go away or sit well with Ruth. She was reared in the missionary life, and rather than reject her parents' vocation, Ruth embraced it, nurtured it, and dreamed about it. Even her heroes were missionaries.

Ruth was particularly intrigued by the lives of Amy Carmichael and Mildred Cable, extraordinary women who devoted their lives to their work in foreign countries. Both were from the United Kingdom, both came from wealthy families, and both were unbelievably tough.

Unsurprisingly, given her background, Ruth was fascinated by them. She envisioned an exotic life like theirs, seeing the world and spreading the Word. She had her heart set on this dream, but Billy's dream for his life seemed to conflict with it. Interestingly enough, Mildred Cable's most famous quote was this: "God provides the men and women needed for each generation." Perhaps God's need for experienced camel riders was waning, and His desire for people who could master all modern media was waxing.

That fall, Ruth returned to Wheaton with a new resolve to go to the mission field after graduation, still wanting Billy to accompany her. He gave her the courtesy of committing to pray about the issue, but he came back more sure than ever regarding his call to preach.

They were two strong individuals at an impasse.

"We've both got such strong wills, I almost despaired at ever having things so peacefully wrong," Ruth wrote in a letter to her parents at the time. "But I couldn't want him any other way and I can't be any other way."

They were just like me and my wife.

When Cathe and I first started dating, we had constant conflict. It was her very sense of who she was and what she thought that drew me to her (not to mention her beauty).

She was very organized, and, thanks to her upbringing by well-to-do parents and being raised overseas like Ruth, she was also very well-mannered.

I was the opposite. I was raised by wolves. (Well, not exactly, but you get the idea.) My unruly mother traversed the country marrying, divorcing, and marrying again, and I was dragged along for the ride. The result was that I had to grow up quickly and fend for myself. After I came to Christ, I wanted to live a life that mattered, and like Billy, I felt called to preach the Gospel.

Cathe and I broke up three times. But we always came back together. We have been married for forty-six years as of this writing and are still going strong!

Ruth Graham once said, "A good marriage is made up of two good forgivers." And she was right.

After getting to know Ruth, I have to say, in her own unique way she was just as impressive and remarkable as Billy. Cathe and I just loved spending time with her and listening to her childhood stories. She was such a down-to-earth, yet deeply spiritual woman. And she had a wild sense of humor.

Once when she was driving her car in North Carolina, she hit the accelerator instead of the brake, sending her car crashing through a fence. No one was injured, but in a heated telephone conversation from California, Billy angrily demanded she surrender her driver's license. She argued with him, stating it wasn't that big of a deal. After taking a moment to pause, Billy tried a different approach.

"I don't recall reading in Scripture that Sarah ever talked to Abraham like this," he said.

Ruth zinged him back: "Well, I don't recall reading in Scripture that Abraham ever tried to take Sarah's camel away from her."

However, prior to these years of wedded adventure, the stress of their dating situation was starting to get to Billy. He crumbled into a chair after a Sunday evening service and bemoaned to one of his professors that Ruth was so out of his league in terms of looks, brains, poise, and any other category he cared to imagine. He felt totally out of his depth.

Even though Ruth was still struggling with her decision, she started coming around to the idea that the Lord had not called Billy to be a missionary.

One day he finally asked her point-blank: Did she think that God had brought them together?

Ruth paused, giving his question much consideration. She loved Billy and didn't want to lose him. Ruth allowed God to speak to her heart and redirect her thoughts and desires, which would allow the two of them to become one. She finally admitted that yes, God had indeed brought them together.

Billy reasoned with her that the Bible points out that the husband is responsible to God and is the head of the wife. She nodded.

"The Lord leads me and you follow."

Ruth agreed with that statement in faith. However, what Billy would come to know after their marriage was that while Ruth allowed him to be the head of the home, some might say she was the neck that turned the head and the heart that melted him.

(She wrote in her 1982 memoir, *It's My Turn*: "A Christian wife's responsibility balances delicately between knowing when to submit and when to outwit. Adapting to our husbands never implied the annihilation of our creativity, rather the blossoming of it.")

Their relationship was interrupted by an extended absence when Ruth's older sister Rosa was diagnosed with tuberculosis and forced to drop out of college. She was admitted to a TB hospital in New Mexico. Ruth cared for Rosa for several months until her parents came back from China on furlough in the summer of 1941 and took over. Ruth then headed to Montreat, North Carolina, where she stayed with close family friends.

That summer, Billy continued to preach and was usually on the road. While in John Minder's church in Florida, he received a letter from Ruth with the news he was hoping for.

He pored over the letter, but the three words that caught his attention were these: "I'll marry you." With that, Billy let out a mighty holler.

When he settled down, he read the letter repeatedly. Ruth explained how God had given her a clear message: they were meant to be man and wife.

Billy's abundant happiness did not translate into a strong sermon that night. He was on Cloud Nine and didn't seem to care. However, he redeemed himself when he finished a week-long preaching series at a Charlotte church. The congregation gifted him a sum of $165. Billy wrote in his autobiography that he "raced right out and spent almost all of it on an engagement ring with a diamond so big you could almost see it with a magnifying glass!"

Billy's next move was to beat a hasty retreat to Montreat in his Plymouth. When he got there, he drove off the main road toward the house. Then he spotted a strange woman off in the distance walking down the road—perhaps a genuine mountain woman taking in some fresh air.

"She had long, straight hair sticking out all over, an awful-looking faded dress, bare feet, and what looked to be very few teeth," Billy said. "I passed by her, but when I suddenly realized it was Ruth playing a trick on me—her teeth blacked out so that she looked toothless—I slammed on the brakes. She got in and we went on to the Currie house deep in the woods."

As the sun slowly faded and the moon was rising on the opposite side, Billy kissed Ruth on the lips for the first time.

Billy then pulled out the ring, and Ruth accepted his proposal. They were officially engaged.

Billy visited her that summer at the Bells' home in Waynesboro, Virginia, a Shenandoah Valley community near many Civil War battle sites. The town was named after Revolutionary War general "Mad" Anthony Wayne and was where the Bells initially settled after leaving China for good.

A few miles outside of Waynesboro, Billy briefly stopped to slip into a suit and tie, hoping to make a good impression on his future bride's parents. He looked sharp, but he was visibly stunned when Ruth came out to greet him with a hug and kiss. He was extremely nervous to meet her parents and stiffened up when they made their approach. Billy loosened up enough at dinner; afterward, he was deposited on the doorstep of a hotel in town. Billy was relieved that Dr. Bell was thoughtful enough to pay the tab in advance of his departure the next morning. They made a great first impression, and over time, the Bells became the in-laws from Heaven. (Billy often referred to his father-in-law as one of his greatest mentors and advocates.)

But Billy and Ruth suffered a minor setback when they returned to Wheaton that fall. For whatever reasons, doubt crept back into Ruth's mind about being called into the mission field. Those dreams died hard for her, and no doubt this angered her. All her life, that was the only future she had envisioned. Suddenly, all of that was gone—perhaps too suddenly. The ground beneath her feet was shaken. Now she expressed doubts she and Billy should even be dating, suggesting they call it quits.

Upon hearing that declaration, Billy kindly asked for the ring back. His strong, unemotional request threw her for a loop; she was not ready to relinquish her beloved ring. Ruth would just not give it back. In a way, that was good because Billy felt that put an end to all doubt.

Though officially engaged now, the two were wise and did not rush into marriage. They waited it out a year until graduation. They roomed with others at private homes near campus. Billy was reunited again with Jimmie Johnson and Grady Wilson, who had both parted ways with Bob Jones College and continued their studies at Wheaton. Billy maintained his fervent pace by incorporating studies, services at the Tabernacle, preaching at churches as far as Flint, Michigan, networking with professors and prayer groups, and moving furniture with Johnny Streater. Sometimes his exhaustion spilled over into the classroom on Monday mornings. He frequently dozed off in front of his anthropology teacher, Dr. Alexander Grigiola, a balding but charismatic Russian immigrant who held two doctorates and a medical degree and was fluent in several languages.

"Do not disturb our dear Billy," he'd say in his thick Russian accent when Billy was catching some Zs. "He's tired in God's service!"

Relief came in the form of a future job offer. While Billy was lecturing at Wheaton in early 1943, he noticed a dark-haired man in his thirties, nattily dressed in a suit and large Li'l Abner shoes.

He was hard to miss because he was so out of place and was sitting there right in the front row. He later showed up on Billy's doorstep, pulling up in a sleek and cavernous Lincoln Continental. He introduced himself as Robert Van Kampen, president of the Chicago-based Hitchcock Publishing Company and treasurer of the National Gideon Association.

Van Kampen was there to offer an opportunity to the young man: taking over as pastor of the Western Springs Baptist Church where he served as a deacon. The church was located in an upscale middle-class suburb twenty miles southwest of Wheaton. His offer was forty dollars a week (much better than Billy's Tabernacle gig, which paid nothing). Van Kampen's timing was impeccable because Billy was going to need an income once he graduated and married Ruth.

The other advantage was that Billy was familiar with the church. He had preached there as a student, and Western Springs wanted him to begin that summer. He also was told he could have time off to travel to evangelistic conferences—music to his ears!

This offer provided an avenue for Billy to pursue post-graduate work at Chicago University as well as the year's pastorate the Army required for a chaplain position (he had still not given up his dream to serve his country). In Billy's haste, he forgot to tell Ruth and accepted the job offer on the spot. Naturally, he received an earful from his future wife when he told her about Van Kampen's visit. She reminded him that it would be good practice from that day forward for them to discuss and pray together over any major decision affecting their lives. While he had his heart in the right place about being a good provider, the other half of being a good, communicating husband had escaped him.

Once they got down to the business of the offer, Billy and Ruth viewed it as temporary, a stepping stone in their lives. The real milestones had yet to occur.

In June 1943, Billy and Ruth graduated from Wheaton College as a couple. They were ready for their next adventure.

Two months later, on August 13, 1943, they were married near Ruth's parents' new home in Montreat, North Carolina, twenty miles east of Asheville. They exchanged nuptials in the Gaither Chapel at 8:30 p.m. amid family, friends, candles, and aromatic clematis. Dr. Minder presided over the wedding. Billy wrote this beautiful and loving letter to Ruth on that momentous day:

> *To love thee, to cherish thee to protect thee so long as we both shall live. To be tender, kind, and patient and true is the deepest desire of my heart tonight.*
> *My Darling, I love you with a love that knows no bounds and together under the leadership of the Holy Spirit we shall walk life's road together.*
> *May we be calm in His presence.*
> *May we rest our souls in Him.*
> *May we feed on the fullness of His Word.*
> *May we die to all things of time.*
> *Bill*

After a brief honeymoon in the Blue Ridge Mountains, the newlyweds drove back to the Chicago area and finally arrived at their new digs in Hinsdale, Illinois, an apartment selected and furnished by the church.

They discovered they were situated one block from the main line of the Burlington Railroad. The first week they lived there every train sounded as if it was barreling through their living room. They learned to pause conversations when the rumbling began and finish when the train had passed by.

It was a good metaphor for their lives together. Whatever came barreling down the track, disrupting their plans and interrupting them, they could survive it. They were the man and woman God had indeed provided for a new generation.

CHAPTER FOURTEEN

It Takes a Village

With a college degree in hand and his bride on his arm, Billy Graham was ready to take on the world.

By the summer of 1943, the couple had a functional car, a furnished apartment, and a full set of china, crystal, and silver. They both had college degrees. And now Billy was fulfilling his destiny by preaching the Gospel.

He had gotten a late start in life and made some turns off the beaten path. It took him seven years to finish college. While selling Fuller brushes was not his divine vocation, he had made a success of it and learned valuable lessons which served him the rest of his life. Had he been satisfied with his time in Florida, he might have become another Mordecai Ham, or just another country preacher holding revivals in small churches. But God was grooming Billy for an international reach that would touch both the common folk and the elite, and the future was as shiny as their wedding silver.

At twenty-four, Billy was full of robust health and possessed a positively optimistic outlook. He'd need to cling to those traits after he saw the state of the Western Springs Baptist Church. Membership numbered around fifty people, and the church had only raised enough money to construct what essentially amounted to a basement sanctuary.

"The building had a low ceiling...it was a small neighborhood church," remembered Grosvenor S. Rust, who attended Wheaton College with Billy. "It was a very unassuming place. It wasn't an outstanding building at all."

Rust was being generous. Ruth told her husband it looked like an air raid shelter.

The congregation, though, was wonderful to the Grahams upon their arrival in July 1943. The young couple sat through several heartfelt speeches welcoming them to their new church. They took up an offering and presented to the Grahams an envelope containing forty-eight dollars. Wedding cake was also served. It was here that Billy, for the only time in his decades-long career, would have the experience of a full-time pastorate.

When Billy was home, the newlyweds took hikes, strolled through the nearby arboretum, played golf, watched movies, and occasionally splurged for dinner at a restaurant—a rare treat on a pastor's budget.

Ah, I remember those days well. When Cathe and I started what was to be Harvest Church, we lived at poverty wage. We were so young that when Cathe moved into our first rented home, she was shocked to learn that you actually had to pay for water! (She had lived a relatively sheltered and pampered life with her parents up to that point.)

Our furniture, courtesy of the Salvation Army, was threadbare, and we could barely afford to put food on the table. Despite our lack of funds, we look back on those days with great fondness.

The windows of the old home we rented were all painted shut. One day we were doing some work on it to make it somewhat livable, and a window framed in wood was not completely closed, so I figured I would remedy the situation with a hammer. After a couple of hard bangs, one of the panes of glass in the top of the window dislodged, landed smack on my nose, and split it open to the cartilage. Cathe found me with my hands over my face, blood spurting from between my fingers. It was a clean break, and the doctor placed stitches on the front of my nose. I did not have time to go back to have them removed, so Pastor Chuck Smith removed them in his office on our wedding day. Forty-six years later, Cathe still never lets me go anywhere with a hammer in my hand.

The early stages of marriage can also underscore a spouse's deficiencies. Billy had a few habits that got under Ruth's skin: he kept a messy desk and hung wet towels on the bathroom doorknob. In turn, Ruth was no gourmet chef—pickled peach Jell-O was just one of the many failed dishes she served him. They also possessed opposite temperaments (she was easygoing and optimistic; he was highly disciplined and drove himself unmercifully), had different tastes in many things, and didn't always hold the same viewpoints. She was raised to speak her mind, whereas Billy's bloodline wasn't used to dealing with strong, outspoken women. They definitely had their differences of opinion and had to learn to sort them out.

"I think it is very important for young couples to disagree, but to learn to disagree pleasantly and to respect one another's opinions," Ruth said. "If you agree on everything, there's not going to be much room for growth…I don't think happy marriages are ever accidental. They are the result of good, hard work."

Ruth also had this helpful piece of advice for women in her later years: "It is not wise to disagree with a man when he is tired, hungry, worried, preoccupied or pressured…. Nor does it pay to argue with your husband unless you are looking your very best. The woman who argues with her hair in rollers has ten strikes against her to begin with." I'm telling you, Ruth was a hoot!

In addition to keeping a tidy household, Ruth especially proved her worth as she spent considerable time combing through material in search of ideas for Billy's sermons. It was something she enjoyed and something he deeply appreciated. She could also be his harshest critic, but that often worked in his favor. Such was the case when Billy penned an op-ed for *Ladies' Home Journal* on the Women's Liberation Movement in the early 1970s.

"After I wrote the article, I submitted it to my wife, because she's a marvelous critic," he said. "She handed it back to me all blue-penciled and said, 'I don't agree with most of this.' So I re-wrote it."

Billy was quick to let everyone know that his wife was the real secret weapon in his ministry.

This is an area where I could really relate to Billy. My wife, Cathe, has a deep love for Scripture and is constantly giving me sermon ideas or pointing out things she thinks I should say when I preach. At times I am resistant because I may have a message pretty much finished. But I'm happy to admit that her ideas and insights are always significant, and I love how they connect with people when I share them.

Despite their teamwork, there was friction in the early months of their marriage when Ruth refused to switch denominations. She was Presbyterian at birth, and her family was deeply steeped in that denomination. Her father ranked highly in the church and founded the *Southern Presbyterian Journal*, a publication that championed conservative Presbyterian views. There was also great pressure from the congregation for her to be rebaptized by immersion. Ruth studied the Scriptures and politely dismissed the idea. Her feeling was the focus should be on worshipping Jesus, not what people labeled themselves. More than a few of the church elders gave Billy grief, calling Ruth a "disobedient wife." To Billy's credit, he didn't stew or allow her decision to impact their marriage. In time this turned out to be a blessing because it improved Billy's ability to work with men and women of various denominations, which he did throughout his Crusades.

Attendance at the church grew steadily, in spite of the fact that there were very few Baptists in the area and many men were off fighting in the war. The growth was not accidental. Billy pounded the pavement in a vigorous campaign to build up its numbers. When he wasn't preaching or organizing house-to-house visits to those deemed uncommitted, he got to know local shopkeepers and launched the Western Suburban Professional Men's Club. The club held monthly dinners ($1.90 per ticket) in the winter months at a restaurant called the Old Spinning Wheel in Hinsdale.

Billy invited high-ranking businessmen as well as national and regional figures to these affairs. They included Walter Maier of *The*

Lutheran Hour radio program, Wheaton College president Elner Edman, New York City attorney James E. Bennet, and Pulitzer Prize–winning cartoonist Vaughn Shoemaker of the *Chicago Daily News*. Often more than three hundred men showed up for fellowship, singing, and to hear a prominent Christian give his testimony.

Billy amazed his congregants with his ingenuity and energy. In addition to preaching twice on Sundays, he attended youth meetings and started a church newsletter. He also held a mid-week prayer meeting, and he and Ruth taught Child Evangelism classes on Wednesday afternoons in the winter, spring, and fall months. They were said to be the largest of their kind in the Chicago area. A Boys' Brigade was also created, and some forty boys met every week for games, military drills, talks, crafts, and many other activities. Plans were in the offing for a bookstore that would sell Christian literature, books, stationery, and gifts. All that in addition to pastoral calls whenever the need arose. Ministry is never dull or slow.

Billy's efforts were appreciated, but congregants especially got a kick out of his thick Southern accent, loud ties and socks, and colorful sermons. And they admired Ruth for her poise and intellect. The Grahams were a good team. Their youthful energy and exuberance were exactly the boost the church needed.

Shortly after Billy took over the pulpit, another unexpected opportunity presented itself in October 1943. Torrey Johnson, a radio broadcaster and the dynamic pastor of Chicago's burgeoning Midwest Bible Church, invited Billy to take over one of his Christian radio programs, *Songs in the Night*, which aired Sunday nights on WCFL. It was a powerful 50,000-watt station in the Windy City that serviced the Midwest and even got picked up in a few Southern and Eastern states.

The forty-five-minute live broadcast was an immediate hit, but Johnson found the program too demanding at the close of his Sunday service. Like many other preachers, Johnson had a full plate. He juggled teaching a Sunday School class, appearing on a church-sponsored program called *The Chapel Hour*, and conducting the evening service. He was also the backbone of the fledgling youth movement that would soon be known as Youth for Christ and fielded speaking engagements around the country. Johnson said he had prayed about his situation, and Billy Graham's name kept coming to the fore.

His offer came with a stipulation—the church would pay Johnson $150 a week to sponsor the show, with an initial contract of thirteen weeks. That was definitely going to be a challenge because the church was already maxed out with Billy's weekly salary. But Billy rightfully envisioned what the show could do for the church and assured his deacons the money would be well spent. Some weren't so sure and initially vetoed the idea. After some back and forth, Bob Van Kampen provided seed money that would cover the first five shows. The quartet from the Wheaton College women's glee club (later called the Village Carollers) also stepped up and agreed to sing for free on Sunday nights.

What Billy was really hoping for was to attach a big-ticket name to the show—someone who could draw instant attention. The only name that fit that bill for him was George Beverly Shea, a well-known gospel singer in the Chicago area. Little did either man know they would minister together for the next sixty years.

At the time, Shea was a famous Christian soloist and broadcaster who appeared on *Club Time*, the second-oldest hymn program on commercial radio. Additionally, he had a string of Gospel hits, including "I'd Rather Have Jesus," and was a Decca Records artist—a major record label at the time.

Billy approached Shea at WMBI, a Moody Bible Institute radio station in downtown Chicago where he worked as program manager. Once there, Billy encountered an overly vigilant receptionist who tried to block him from meeting Shea. After all, he couldn't just walk in off the street to see her boss without an appointment! Billy felt otherwise. He wasn't going to go away without talking to the man, whom he could see sitting in his office.

No, I've come to see him, Billy thought. *I'm going to see him!*

Billy sat in the reception area and waited until the time was right. When he saw Shea's door crack open for a split second, he darted in, sneaking quickly by the secretary. Compared to skeptical housewives who already owned a brush, thank you very much, this was child's play to Billy.

He apologized to Shea for imposing, but he had something important to say.

Shea held his hand up to the secretary, who had tried to intervene, and gave Billy his time. He had heard of the young preacher. Billy took a moment to explain that Torrey Johnson had offered him his Sunday night radio show. He added that he needed Shea's star power to make it a success.

Shea didn't know what to think, but Billy didn't give him much time to digest the information. Billy ran down the show for him and where his spot would be. When Billy finished his spiel, he got his commitment from Shea. However, Billy was convinced it was only because Shea felt he would never leave the office without a "yes." And he was probably right. Billy was a hard man to say no to. After all, he was your Fuller Brush Man.

With Shea on board, everybody went to work. Ruth pitched in and helped Billy write the scripts, which consisted of a brief meditation about a current news event or something topical, followed by a Bible message to demonstrate how the Scriptures are relevant to everyday problems. The program was also supported by choir music and a featured spot for Shea, the star soloist.

The inaugural show aired on January 2, 1944. The first two programs were broadcast out of Chicago, but on January 16, *Songs in the Night* was heard for the first time from "the Village Church," the new name for Western Springs. Billy suggested to the elders they make the name change in a bid to draw more people living in the surrounding area. The elders agreed—albeit reluctantly—but saw their membership numbers continue to swell.

It took some tweaking and the burning of much midnight oil, but soon they had the show down to a science, and it started to take off.

People began filling up the 125-seat sanctuary, and they received many letters from people all over the Midwest explaining how the show touched them. The *Chicago Tribune* even wrote a piece, giving the broadcast some cachet and casting Billy as a local celebrity. Generous donations kept the show in the black and running.

The show's popularity led to more speaking engagements for Billy, mostly in cities in the upper Midwest. Despite initially being told by the deacons that he was free to travel, this clearly wasn't the case. Billy got upset when someone remarked that the church would have to cut his pay if this continued. He was not pleased with the elders' going back on their word and told them they could start looking for his replacement if his paycheck was reduced.

Still, the offers came pouring in, including another call from Torrey Johnson in the spring of 1944. He was now heading a new committee originally called Chicago Youth for Christ to reach the servicemen and young people who congregated at Michigan Avenue in downtown Chicago on Saturday nights. The first meeting was held on May 27—ten days before D-Day. It took place in Chicago's Orchestra Hall, which seated close to three thousand people.

Many committee members weren't sold on Billy. They had their pick of more seasoned and better-known speakers, but Johnson insisted Billy was their man; he could be counted on to preach an authentic Gospel message. Billy was so overwhelmed by the gesture that it translated to a rare case of nerves once he peeked through the backstage curtains and saw the sea of faces. He later described it as "the worst fit of stage fright in my life." Billy had never spoken to an audience that size before. But once he stepped up to the podium, he killed it. He mesmerized the crowd, and when he gave the invitation to accept Christ, many responded. More importantly, it opened a picture window into a future that showed Billy all sorts of possibilities.

Billy had finally found that space God was calling him into. All through his ministry, he preached with such power, ease, and confidence in what he was saying. I think Billy Graham was the greatest preacher in contemporary history and certainly the most effective evangelist of all time. He was born for it, and God had it all planned from the beginning.

Those Orchestra Hall rallies blazed through the summer, continuing to draw large and enthusiastic crowds, mostly G.I.s and teens looking for an excuse to venture into the city and blow off some steam. Based on its success, Johnson began organizing Youth for Christ rallies in other cities like Indianapolis, Philadelphia, and Detroit. He invited Billy to speak at those as well. Billy was happy to oblige, enjoying the travel and speaking to large crowds.

Despite the Village Church's newfound success and popularity, Billy's frequent travels began to irritate his congregants, who wanted him at their beck and call. They grumbled that he was putting his career in front of the well-being of his own flock. In the beginning, no one said a word because Billy's efforts were growing the church and giving it national name recognition. Tithing had increased to the point where church leaders had paid off the mortgage on their basement sanctuary, and Billy burned the contract in a pie pan during a special ceremony. They also were able to modernize the church auditorium, install a pipe organ, and launch a program to help support several missionaries.

Despite the church's big strides, the sniping began to wear Billy down. From time to time, he let the deacons know he was in great demand. In fact, he had received numerous job offers from churches, radio stations, and colleges. They included a larger church in Fort Wayne, Indiana, and another in Chicago with an office, staff, and music. And it came with a *much* more generous salary. There was even a nice home for the pastor, which came gratis. Also tendered was a proposition from Wheaton College, Billy's alma mater, to become a field representative. Every offer was substantially better than his current situation and would certainly be considered a step up.

Finally, things reached a boiling point, and Billy addressed the underlying hostility in one of his Sunday sermons. He told the congregation they needed to check themselves.

"Some of you need to confess to the sin of troublemaking," he said. "A person tries to build a testimony for God and all you do is tear it down. You had better confess before God has to remove some people. As for me, I'm here to do this job for God and with His help, I'll get it done."

A hush fell over the congregation. Billy rightly spoke his piece.

Maybe it was apparent to some of them that Billy was bound for bigger and better things than their small church. Despite other weighty job offers, Billy still very much wanted to join the war effort. He had twice applied for an army chaplaincy and was refused on the grounds that he did not meet their weight requirement—he was three pounds under. Finally, in August 1944, he was accepted by the War Department and ordered to report to Harvard Divinity School in Cambridge, Massachusetts.

At that point, America was well into fighting its way inch by bloody inch up the Pacific Islands toward Japan. Billy joined the army two months after D-Day. The Germans were not leaving without a fight. A month after Billy was accepted, the Americans and British made the largest parachute drop in history at Arnhem, Holland, in a bid to hasten the end of the war. It was the Allies' worst defeat and one of the Reich's greatest victories. Pastors jumped at Arnhem and were literally in the worst of the fighting with SS bullets flying past them as they ministered to the wounded and dying. General Dwight D. Eisenhower knew the war in Europe was not going to be over by Christmas—or for a long time afterward.

Billy was not ready for the army. Despite his best intentions, it was simply not meant to be. He began experiencing stress-related paralysis of the throat in September, and a month later came the official diagnosis: Billy had contracted the mumps. Later it morphed into orchitis, which often accompanies the mumps. The illness laid him up for six weeks. At one point, Billy was delirious with fever, his temperature soaring as high as 105 degrees. He could only keep down liquids and strained baby foods, and he lost a lot of weight. He dipped to a dangerously low 130 pounds. Doctors who made daily visits didn't think he'd survive. When the crisis eventually passed, Billy was told he and Ruth might not be able to conceive children. That was proven wrong almost immediately.

The Grahams headed to Florida for a few days of relaxation, thanks to a generous female radio listener. She had heard about Billy's illness and sent the Grahams a one-hundred-dollar check. They used the money to take a much-needed vacation in December 1944. They drove to Miami and stayed at a budget motel near the beach.

While there, Billy discovered that Torrey Johnson and his family were also staying in town about three blocks away. Billy sought him out and thanked him for his past support. Johnson then invited Billy to go fishing.

Unbeknownst to Billy, God was putting a unit of like-minded men together—an evangelistic team that was unlike anything seen before or since. With George Beverly Shea as his soloist and Torrey Johnson at his side with his Youth for Christ connections, Billy was getting ready to be launched like a rocket.

Once they got settled in the boat, Johnson pitched to Billy an aspirational plan to ratchet up the Youth for Christ ministry beyond the U.S. borders. Johnson would head the new Youth for Christ International that would bring revival to young people around the globe while Billy would serve as its national organizer and one of its lead preachers. Best of all, it came with a nice bump in pay—almost twice his current salary.

It was not only a great opportunity but also a lifeline that Billy needed during a time of great stress. Billy accepted the offer after consulting with Ruth. However, he had one condition for Johnson: "Not one bit of paperwork." They shook hands on it. Billy then resigned from the Village Church after twenty-one months and got a release from the army to be discharged from his chaplaincy assignment.

In mastering radio, preaching to increasingly larger crowds, and becoming a minor celebrity in the Midwest, Billy Graham had taken the first steps toward widening his message and his audience.

Unbeknownst to Billy or anyone else, he had started the gradual climb toward wearing the mantle of "America's Preacher."

CHAPTER FIFTEEN

London Fog

With his first and only pastorate behind him, Billy Graham was literally off and running with Youth for Christ. He was developing an unflagging fondness for evangelism, raucous audiences, and a chance to see the world.

He traveled more than 135,000 miles, visiting nearly every state in the union and all of the Canadian provinces in his first year with the organization. (United Airlines designated him its top civilian passenger.) He was traipsing the globe and establishing a frantic travel schedule that he would maintain for the rest of his life. Not many people are suited for this type of life, but Billy most certainly was. He possessed strength, stamina, and the curiosity to see the world, meet people who were searching for meaning and purpose, and preach the Gospel of Jesus Christ. Billy was exactly where he was supposed to be.

When we are in the beginning and even the middle of life, it's hard at times to make sense of why the Lord opens some doors and closes others. But when we are older, we can often look back, begin to connect the dots, and realize our lives were not a series of accidents, but rather providence.

Billy was standing on the shoulders of other renowned evangelists like Billy Sunday, Dwight L. Moody, and Charles Finney, a key figure in the Great Awakening—the religious revival that swept the nation in the early nineteenth century. They, in turn, had built upon the itinerant preaching tradition of the eighteenth-century revivalists of the First Great Awakening, which included the likes of Northampton Anglican minister Jonathan Edwards, Methodism founder John Wesley, and British minister and evangelist extraordinaire George Whitefield.

And you can trace their roots back to the apostles Peter and Paul.

It's what I call "Proclamation Evangelism," and frankly, it has fallen out of favor in recent days. It's rare to hear someone give an overt evangelistic message complete with an invitation for the hearer to make a decision for or against Jesus Christ.

Though every Christian is called to evangelize, there is a specific gift of evangelism—and Billy had that in spades. He never really was cut out to be a pastor, as wonderful as that calling is. Plain and simple, Billy was called to reach people with the Gospel.

Youth for Christ International preachers had a much narrower focus than their evangelist predecessors and set their sights on a specifically targeted audience. A new era was dawning, as World War II had created an entirely new culture in America.

The American economy roared after the war like never before. A shoe salesman could earn enough to afford a three-bedroom house, car, and a spouse who didn't work. If factory workers couldn't afford a second home, a cottage by the shore was well within reach. Developers built homes specifically priced for returning soldiers. The G.I. Bill meant millions of ex-servicemen went to college for free, increasing their earning power even more.

Widespread affluence and education were only two parts of the three-legged postwar stool. The third was children. Men returned from Europe and the Pacific and started families, leading to the biggest population explosion in American history: the Baby Boom.

The word "teenager" was created in the 1940s by advertising executives. As breadwinners earned more, their teenaged children earned their own money and spent it on clothing, cars, and music. Rock and roll erupted with its themes of rebellion and young love. Artists like Little Richard, Fats Domino, Jerry Lee Lewis—and, of course, Elvis Presley—created the soundtrack of a generation.

Movies and television amplified a revolution against traditional middle-class values. In the 1953 movie *The Wild One* starring Marlon Brando, an adult asks the young biker, "What are you rebelling against?" "What've you got?" Brando replies. Having been raised without the hardships of the Great Depression or the horrors of World War II, young people in the 1950s questioned everything. That included religion.

The world was rapidly changing, and Billy could sense this. And that is why Youth for Christ tried to demonstrate in its campaigns that Christianity was exciting and didn't have to be dull or boring. It cleverly presented "Old-Fashioned Truth for Up-to-Date Youth" in messages "Geared to the Times, Anchored to the Rock." To show that its speakers were relevant and not out of touch, the Saturday night rallies were bright and raucous, the complete opposite of Sunday morning services. They featured fast-paced entertainment from magicians, ventriloquists, and a horse named MacArthur, who would "kneel at the cross" and tap his foot twelve times when asked the number of Christ's apostles and three times when asked how many Persons constituted the Trinity. One can be critical and say this was all rather gimmicky, but rapidly changing worlds call for rapid changes. Sometimes that falls on counting horses.

Spiritual entertainment came in the form of testimonies from athletes, military heroes, business and civic leaders, and celebrities. The rallies also included youth choirs, quartets, trios, and soloists, depending on the city. The preachers also got in on the act by sporting bright suits and sports coats, hand-painted ties, argyle socks, and shiny shoes.

"We used every modern means to catch the attention of the unconverted—and then we punched them between the eyes with the Gospel," Billy quipped.

The strategy was hugely successful, and the results were gratifying: thousands of youth flocked to the rallies, sometimes packing theaters, arenas, or stadiums, including seventy thousand at Chicago's Soldier Field on Memorial Day in 1945. Many made decisions to repent of their sins and follow Christ. The rallies proved so popular that Billy and his ministry colleagues kept adding dates and bookings.

Billy loved the travel, but it soon began putting a strain on his fledgling marriage. He confessed it caused him much heartache; saying goodbye to Ruth in the driveway before each departure got harder each time, but he grew more in love with her by the day. During this period, when boarding a train, he was handed a telegram from Chicago. He placed the paper in his pocket to read later when he got settled. As the train neared Indianapolis, he remembered the telegram, pulled it out, and was stunned: Ruth was expecting. So much for the doctors' proclamations he'd never sire children—he and Ruth eventually had five kids.

To deal with the long periods of separation from Billy and to receive a helping hand, Ruth moved back in with her parents in North Carolina. It was a temporary, albeit happy arrangement. It also proved to be a blessing because on September 21, 1945, while Billy was at a rally in Mobile, Alabama, she gave birth to their first daughter, Virginia, also known as "Gigi." Ruth developed coping mechanisms to deal with Billy's extended absences, but it didn't get any easier over time. She remained an ardent supporter of his work, even if it meant raising their children virtually alone. Ruth reasoned, "I'd rather have a little of Bill than a lot of any other man."

That was also the year another member of the legendary team that would last for decades entered the picture. Cliff Barrows and his new bride, Billie, attended a youth night at a Ben Lippen Bible Conference in Asheville, North Carolina, that summer to hear Billy speak. The song leader who'd been scheduled was unable to attend, so Billy asked Barrows, who was on his honeymoon, to take his place. Barrows was reluctant, but Billy was persuasive.

"When we met, Billy looked at me with a smile," Barrows recalled. "He grabbed both of my hands and said, 'No time to be choosy!'" He also sweet-talked Barrows's wife, Billie, into playing the piano.

It was the start of a beautiful friendship and a rich, lifelong ministry together.

The following year was even more demanding as Youth for Christ International made its first concerted effort to expand overseas. Teams were sent to Japan, Korea, Africa, and Australia in the spring of 1946. Graham and a cohort of others—including gospel singer J. Stratton Shufelt, Canadian Youth for Christ evangelist Charles "Chuck" Templeton, and Hearst newspaper reporter Wesley Hartzell—set off on a forty-six-day tour of Europe and Great Britain, where they sponsored rallies and met with church leaders in hopes of establishing new chapters. Hartzell's presence was a real boost as his stories underscored Billy's patriotism and high moral standards as a model for youth. After the Soldier Field rally, all twenty-two Hearst papers carried a full-page story Hartzell wrote. More coverage followed, including a *Time* magazine article quoting President Harry Truman saying, "This is what I hoped would happen in America" after he saw a rally in Olympia, Washington. Publishing magnate William Randolph Hearst didn't need a stethoscope to read the American public's pulse. The wily old tycoon picked up on the fact that this young preacher had a way about him, and he filed that away for future use.

The voyage abroad got off to a shaky start when a scheduled stop in Gander, Newfoundland, was thwarted by a furious snowstorm, forcing the team to land at a nearby U.S. airfield. Mistakenly believing that Billy's bunch was an entertainment troupe or a USO knock-off, the social director at the small military base thought they were manna from Heaven. He penciled them in for a late-night performance. Not wanting to disappoint the man and his personnel, Torrey Johnson didn't have the heart—or the guts—to tell him they were a Gospel team. But if it was entertainment they wanted, entertainment they would get!

The culturally starved audience, which included the base commander, packed the Quonset-hut auditorium and whistled and cheered loudly as Templeton served as master of ceremonies. Gander, on the edge of the desolate Labrador Sea, was home to a base that served as a stepping stone for planes flying to Europe during the war. Las Vegas or Nashville it was not. Entertainment revolved around fishing, drinking, and staying warm.

Templeton started off with a few jokes and colorful anecdotes about his past, and then introduced the other acts. The audience politely laughed. They also cheered at Shufelt's version of "Shortnin' Bread," but things quickly soured. At the sight of Torrey Johnson, they began demanding something else.

They wanted to see legs.

They did not mean Johnson's or Shufelt's legs. Specifically, they wanted to see women's legs. When Shufelt took the microphone and began to sing again, he was soundly howled off the stage. The time for pleasantries were over.

Backstage, the men gathered in prayer, and at one point, Johnson wanted the team to cut bait and exit stage left. They ultimately decided that Billy would deliver the bad news as opposed to the Good News and apologize for not being the entertainment they had expected. He then offered up his testimony, and like Strat, the boo-birds voiced their displeasure. Wrong time, wrong place.

The base commander no longer wanted legs, but heads. He was raging and read Johnson the riot act. He threatened to toss them all in their jail, but the men did some fast talking—and praying—and were able to get back on their way and leave hundreds of bored G.I.s to fish and watch the snow fall.

On this trip, Billy befriended and roomed with Canadian Charles Templeton, whom he helped to recruit to Youth for Christ. The child of a single mother, and with only a ninth-grade education, Templeton was hired by the *Toronto Globe* as a sports cartoonist—and, I might add, was a very good one as well. He had a deft eye, attention to detail, and realism in his art. Different newspaper jobs attract different personalities. Political and crime reporters tend to be hard chargers. Cartooning pulls in eccentrics and oddballs. (I suppose I must include myself among them, as I, too, was once a cartoonist.)

A cartoonist is often a satirist, which means you try to find humor in hard and dark times. Templeton no doubt developed this skill as a reaction to his upbringing. It was a way to cope with and process what was happening around him. I, too, was the son of a single mother and spent a lot of time sketching out my craft on plain white paper in smoky bars.

Templeton's life as a sports cartoonist mainly consisted of long hours, bars, alcohol, loose women, and parties. One night, he arrived home at three in the morning after a social mixer featuring a stripper. He reeked of cigarettes, booze, and BO, not unlike many other weeknights. As he was heading to his bedroom, Templeton briefly caught his reflection in the mirror. He froze for a few seconds, which made him take stock of his life. His mother then awoke, and they had a brief conversation about where his life was headed. As she spoke, he was taking moral inventory. He went to bed that night totally depressed, but then he got on his knees and prayed.

"Lord, come down," he cried. "Come down. Come down…"

That was almost a decade before Youth for Christ.

Almost immediately, Templeton resigned from the newspaper, purchased an old car, and started preaching wherever he could. His popularity grew swiftly. Shortly after he married his soloist, they rented an abandoned church in Toronto for one hundred dollars a month, establishing the Avenue Road Church of the Nazarene without a congregation. The church consisted of mainly family and friends in the beginning. In a matter of months, it was filled to capacity.

Templeton also took to the road, barnstorming the U.S. and Canada, regularly filling large halls and indoor arenas. He began winning souls at an astounding rate. One newspaper account said Templeton led 150 people to Christ a night at his evangelistic peak.

Templeton was smart, witty, and a lot of fun, according to Billy. Templeton's knowledge of the history and culture of the places they would visit in Europe impressed Billy all the more.

In the years to come they would travel the world together, filling football stadiums and even arranging the first racially integrated public meeting south of the Mason-Dixon line. Many thought that Templeton—not Billy—was the one who was going to overturn the world with the Gospel.

The trip that began in Newfoundland was Graham's first abroad and took place about six months after World War II concluded. He also sensed the Communist threat posed by the Soviet Union, which filtered into his messages when he got back to the States.

The evangelistic team arrived in London on March 19, 1946, where they encountered shortages, blackouts, and rationing of food, gas, and other essentials. Even something as simple as eggs was considered a luxury during this period—and Billy ate a lot of tasteless powdered eggs to prove it. London was blackened, bombed out, and in ruins. People went hungry and did without, much as they had during the war. For most of the 1950s, they drove 1930s cars. Reconstruction, in some cases, wasn't finished until the late 1970s. The East End had been heavily bombed. Shells of buildings remained there twenty years later. This was the case for most of Europe. Unexploded ordnance is still found to this day.

Despite the utter devastation from the Nazis, Billy found the people delightful and happy. They were ecstatic that the war was over. No more air raid sirens sent them scurrying into the underground or shelters, no more buzz bombs or doodlebugs, no more destruction. Mainly, there was no more death coming without warning.

British businessman turned evangelist Eric Hutchings remembered the arrival of the team in London and was shocked they weren't dressed in their usual Youth for Christ attire.

"When they came off the train they were all dressed in black because a well-wisher in America told them if they were to go over big in England they must dress like morticians: black hats, black Hamburgs, black ties, and black suits," Hutchings said. "I recall saying to them, 'Do you dress like this in America?' And they said, 'No.' So I got them a hotel room before the reception in Manchester, and they changed. And when they came down, in the words of Winston Churchill, 'Never in all the history of human apparel had so much color been aggregated on so few.'"

This was a no-frills tour, and the Youth for Christ team mostly stayed on couches or guest rooms in the homes of their sponsors, dumpy hotels, or anywhere they could plop their hats. They remained busy, holding three to four meetings a day, every venue packed and filled to capacity. Billy sensed these people were still emotionally wounded from the war and were "starved for hope and hungry for God."

Hutchings said the response to the two rallies in Manchester was so overwhelming that people could not fit in the venues.

"Billy was amazed at the numbers that were turned away. We could see the earnestness in his soul, his directness in his speech, his candor, his honesty, his compassion. Billy had a great future should the Lord tarry," Hutchings said.

Naturally, there were some bumps along the way. The Americans left a mixed impression on some of their more reserved European counterparts. Billy's Southern accent and rapid-fire delivery also caused a few wrinkles, said Canon Thomas Livermore, the British minister who actually invited the Youth for Christ team to England and became the head of the British branch of the organization.

"Billy Graham at that time was preaching at a tremendous pace…this we found rather difficult," Livermore said. "I heard English people say at the time he seemed so breathless that they wanted to take breaths for him! And in my congregation, I had expert shorthand writers, stenographers who tried to get down his sermons, but they estimated he was speaking at about 240 words a minute. And their shorthand wouldn't measure up to that."

It's no wonder. Billy was influenced by radio commentator Walter Winchell, whose machine-gun style held people spellbound during World War II. Billy would find his own voice and cadence in time.

Livermore said that despite Billy's delivery, people from all walks of life—dock workers, teachers, college students, clergy, and intellectuals—thoroughly enjoyed his sermons.

"They enjoyed the way he said things. They laughed at the right moments, and they were serious when the messages called for that," Livermore said. "He somehow understood how to talk to our people."

The Youth for Christ team held 101 meetings in 46 days and traveled approximately 20,000 miles, speaking to almost 100,000 people. They led some 1,500 people to Christ.

Billy felt called by God to return to England after the tour ended. So did several ministers who had heard him speak, and they invited him back. Torrey Johnson was all for it and saw the need, but he told Billy he'd have to raise the funds himself.

Over the course of a few months, Billy had raised enough money for a team to spend six months abroad. He originally asked Stratton Shufelt and his wife to join him as the song leaders. But a few weeks before their departure, they said they couldn't leave their two little girls. So Billy turned to Cliff Barrows and his wife, Billie, who agreed.

Cliff led the singing, Billie played piano, and Billy preached. He also assumed the role of a leader behind the scenes. George Wilson came along to manage their finances. Ruth also went on the trip, later joining the team in early December; her role was to pray and keep her husband in line. That was the easy part. Leaving their one-year-old daughter with her parents and extended family in Montreat for several months was not so easy.

Upon their arrival by ship in October 1946, the group conducted rallies in England and Wales. Shortly into the trip, many cost-cutting measures were employed. They shared rooms, slept on floors, and often bunked at places with no heat. In Wales they stayed in the home of a couple who served them a modest breakfast consisting of a hot tomato and coffee. Lunch wasn't much more tasty: watery chicken soup with bread. The group came to understand and appreciate what their hosts had endured on a daily basis during the war.

When Ruth finally arrived in London, she had her first taste of powdered eggs and breaded sausage—and almost gagged. She also got a taste of some London fog at one of their first services. The city's signature miasma—the result of bad weather, industrial pollution, and the overabundance of coal fireplaces—was trapped by the windless, wintry air, and seeped its way inside the church. It was so thick you could cut the air with a knife, like a pool hall or poker room. Billy could barely see the back of the sanctuary from the church platform. The list of road bumps Billy encountered while preaching grew longer.

Whatever hardships the Youth for Christ team endured, they found inspiration wherever they went. They witnessed the personal sacrifices of their host families and forged lifelong friendships. As a result, they saw churches filled that normally drew only ten to twenty people and observed normally reserved people enthusiastically coming to Christ—including Eric Hutchings, a successful businessman at the time.

Hutchings had organized a meeting in G. Campbell Morgan's chapel in London, and he said Billy had a special word for him and other Christians on this particular tour.

"He challenged those who were ready to give themselves to the Lord full-time, anywhere, to come forward. I must confess, I was very annoyed. I saw my wife go forward," Hutchings said. "I was very satisfied with Manchester and all our big rallies and yet Billy had been used to challenge her to give herself completely. And I could feel the hand of God was closing in on me, because previously in a hotel in Birmingham, Billy had pointed his finger at me and said, 'One day, God will dig you out of your security and home, and everything, and fling you around the world as an evangelist.' And I said, 'Billy, you're crazy!' And I clearly recall his words now, 'I may be crazy, but sometimes I'm right.' However, by '48, Billy's prophecies had come true."

Billy was also under conviction. He met with several British evangelists and students of evangelism history such as J. Edwin Orr and Stephen F. Olford, whom Billy once praised as the one person who most influenced his ministry.

Zambian-born Olford was the son of Plymouth Brethren missionaries; his near-fatal motorcycle accident led to his dramatic call into the ministry. He met Billy in Cardiff, Wales, and explained how he had come to a deeper spiritual commitment.

"I gave him my testimony of how God completely turned my life inside out—an experience of the Holy Spirit in His fullness and anointing,"

Olford told Graham biographer William Martin. Olford said Billy's eyes grew big and moist as he said, "Stephen, I see it. That's what I want. That's what I need in my life."

The two men knelt and prayed for total dedication of the heart; Billy was empowered in a new way by the Holy Spirit. To Olford and others on the trip, Billy's preaching grew more dynamic and compelling, and audiences responded in kind.

After two months away from Gigi, Ruth was ready to go home. Billy still had two months of meetings, so Ruth flew home alone in February 1947.

Billy faced a hardship of another kind when she left: dwindling finances. To his horror, he discovered from George Wilson they were near broke. In desperation, he wrote to R.G. LeTourneau, who was the only wealthy American he knew. Billy explained his predicament to the industrialist, who made his fortune on earth-moving equipment and engineering vehicles, asking for seven thousand dollars. Two weeks later the much-needed cashier's check arrived and saw them through to the end of the trip.

Tired but satisfied with the work he accomplished in Great Britain, Billy returned home more invigorated and inspired. He came back from the trip with a deeper hunger for Bible study.

Billy also felt emotional stirrings to expand his preaching beyond youth rallies. Although he would remain on the Youth for Christ payroll, he envisioned broader audiences beyond teen campaigns. He assembled what would become his A-list ministry team: Cliff Barrows (emcee and song leader), George Beverly Shea (soloist), and Grady Wilson (associate evangelist). A few years later he would add T.W. Wilson as a second associate evangelist to the roster. Billy was poised to lead this Crusade team into history.

But then Billy's life and ministry took a strange detour when a Baptist preacher on his deathbed asked him for a big favor.

CHAPTER SIXTEEN

Evangelism Races, Education Plods

Ruth Bell Graham once proclaimed that only twice did her husband's long and esteemed career go off track. The first was when he became pastor of Western Springs Church. The second was when he took a position as the president of Northwestern Schools in Minnesota. The common denominator in both instances was that Billy did not consult with her on the decision. The latter occurred at the tail end of his tenure with Youth for Christ and actually short-circuited his stay with the ministry.

Billy had been invited to speak at a conference in Medicine Lake, not far from Minneapolis. The conference was sponsored by Dr. William Bell Riley, a Baptist preacher of great renown. After a harrowing flight to get to Minnesota, he probably wished that invitation never came.

The way Billy later told it in his autobiography, the flight took place in the summer of 1946, originating in Seattle. He then switched planes in Vancouver, Canada, boarding a Lockheed Model 18 Lodestar, a World War II–era passenger plane first pressed into service a few years earlier. Billy was one of about a dozen passengers on the flight, which was mostly smooth—until somewhere over Alberta, when a flight attendant informed him that they needed to refuel and all the airports within range were shuttered because snow had blanketed the region. Billy grew increasingly alarmed when she told him the pilot had no plan but was in the process of figuring one out. Finally, the pilot came over the intercom and told everyone he was going to put the plane down as soon as possible.

All the passengers were warned things were "going to get bumpy." They were told to lean forward, bury their heads between their knees, and hope for the best as the pilot frantically looked for a spot to land the plane. He assessed that because the plane was so low on fuel, most likely there would be no fire. If they crashed, at least they wouldn't burn to death. The passengers probably didn't receive this news the way the pilot hoped.

As predicted, the plane landed hard. The panic-stricken passengers shrieked in horror as the plane bumped up and down in a plowed snowfield, then finally came to a stop. Everyone checked themselves and the people around them, and save for a few bruises, no one was seriously injured. The pilot's radio was still functioning, and he was in communication with authorities in a nearby town. They were, however, told to sit tight. They spent the rest of the evening in the plane until help arrived at first light.

It came in the form of a wagon with a team of horses, which took them to an awaiting bus and into town. The airline comped the passengers' overnight accommodations and put them up in a local boardinghouse. Billy was so exhausted from the harrowing experience that he collapsed into bed and instantly fell into a slumber. About an hour later, he received a rude awakening from a Canadian Mountie pounding on his door.

Billy was informed that a bank robber had been registered to his room, and he needed to go with the lawman until the mess was cleared up. Luckily for him, the flight attendant and the pilot vouched for him. He was free again, albeit growing less enchanted with Canadian authorities every minute.

After the plane crash, the night spent in frigid wreckage, and the false arrest, Billy finally got to Minnesota, where he had to muster the gusto to deliver the keynote speech at W.B. Riley's conference the next day! There may be no rest for the wicked, as the Bible says, but often there's no rest for the righteous either.

In 1902, Riley founded the Northwestern Bible and Missionary Training School, a Christian educational complex that by the 1940s included a Bible school, a seminary, and a liberal arts college in Minneapolis. Northwestern Schools trained ministers, evangelists, teachers, missionaries, and Christian laypeople from around the world.

Known as the "Grand Old Man of Fundamentalism," Riley was one of the most diligent evangelists of his day, a gifted orator, and an early pioneer of the Vacation Bible School movement. He also authored more than sixty books and countless articles. In the 1920s, Riley was quite the evangelist himself. Thousands would show up to hear this tall and commanding man with a resonant voice preach the Gospel.

Riley retired from his pastoral duties in 1941 to devote himself full-time to Northwestern Schools, which counted more than seven hundred students.

The elderly Riley was also a big booster of Youth for Christ and saw Billy as a rising star in the field. The eighty-six-year-old's health was failing him, and he was desperately in search of someone to carry on his life's work and continue to lurch his college forward.

He first met Billy years before at Temple Terrace. Riley heard him preach there and said to an administrator, "that young man rarely misses the mark." He saw Billy again at a Youth for Christ rally in February 1945. Riley sat on the dais of the old Minneapolis Auditorium to watch Billy up close. The aging warrior was impressed with what he witnessed that evening: this young evangelist helped lead dozens of people to Christ. He deemed Billy "a comer" and pursued him to take his mantle.

Riley was convinced Billy had the right stuff: he was someone who could bolster student recruitment, find prayer support, and was charismatic and energetic enough to raise funds for the college.

When Riley initially approached him to fill his shoes, Billy suggested Torrey Johnson, then the president of Youth for Christ, for the role and offered to serve underneath him. But Johnson declined. After that, Riley gave Billy the full-court press. And each time Billy politely refused, stating it was a job he neither felt comfortable with nor called to do.

Sometimes the way we discover God's will for our lives is by first figuring out what we are *not* called to do—the process of elimination.

For two and a half years, Riley, a stubborn and very persuasive man, pursued Billy through an intense letter-writing and telegram campaign. Riley hoped to raise one million dollars for a set of new buildings to move and expand his campus and saw Billy as the only person with the fire and energy to do so. He also hoped Billy's influence would help get his schools accredited. But his correspondence only served to make Billy more incensed as he felt compelled to reply each time. In the process, his patience was wearing thin.

"I sent him a letter from Winona Lake (Indiana)," Billy recalled. "And I said, 'Dr. Riley, I would appreciate it if you would not write me anymore. Or disturb my heart or conscience anymore.' I said, 'Please let's cease negotiations.'"

But Billy did take a meeting with Riley at his Golden Valley home in August 1947. Since Riley asked him to speak at the Minneapolis conference, how could Billy possibly say no, especially to a man of God who was ailing and near death?

The stately Riley, who was lying on the living room couch when Billy entered his home, reminded him of an Old Testament prophet with his leonine mane of white hair, hawkish nose, and piercing eyes. It was thundering outside when Riley, pointing his bony finger at Billy with great certainty, proclaimed him his successor.

"He looked at me with fire in his eyes that day. He said, 'As David was appointed King of Israel, before David realized he was to be the king, I now appoint you,'" Billy recalled Riley saying.

Billy said even though Riley's words felt like a "patriarchal blessing," God had not shown him the way on this huge life decision. Shouldering the burden of another man's vision was a responsibility he did not want but didn't outright refuse, either.

Certainly, the idea was appealing—take an educational institution in a different direction from the competition and send young people on fire for Christ to the ends of the earth to introduce the lost to the Lord. From young minds come fresh ideas, often causing huge paradigm shifts. No doubt that intrigued Billy just a little.

But the request came at an odd time in Billy's life. Ruth was pregnant again with a second child (Anne Morrow Graham), and they had just borrowed $4,500 from a local bank to purchase a two-story home. It sat across the street from the Bells' abode in Montreat, North Carolina. Ruth and her mother had a wonderful time decorating it, scouring mountain junk shops and antique stores in the area. She was beginning to feel comfortable with the idea of domesticity, raising their children while her husband trotted the globe, after surrendering her dreams of becoming a missionary.

The idea of running an academic institution also caused Billy anxiety. He knew that evangelism took priority, and although a college president might travel widely to promote his campus, conflicts were bound to erupt. Not just his own, but with others. He would not only have to lead a faculty and staff and get them to back his vision (if he even had one at that point), but there would be a board of directors he'd have to answer to—never a fun prospect for anyone. He was also expected to raise $250,000 to complete and oversee construction of the main building on campus, which he had no idea how to do. Then there would be the day-to-day management of an academic institution—something he also had no idea how to execute.

Not to mention the personnel issues or personality conflicts that were sure to come!

Billy clearly respected Riley and did not want to disappoint him. Yet at the same time, he knew what the Lord had called him to do, and that was to preach the Gospel, not push papers, negotiate with a board of directors, or build up a student body.

In a way, Riley had one part right—Billy was like a young David before he became king. David showed up at the front lines of the war between the Israelites and the Philistines. There was a nine-foot, six-inch beast of a man bellowing from the Valley of Elah named Goliath. The giant man's challenge was for Israel to send one of its best to face him on behalf of both armies.

King Saul, the logical choice to take on Goliath, was not taking the bait. Nor were any of his other warriors. Enter David.

He could not imagine such a challenge going unanswered, so he volunteered to face Goliath. After all, as a shepherd, he had plenty of experience protecting his sheep from all manner of wild beasts, plus he had become quite adept with his sling and a well-chosen stone.

So King Saul offered his armor, which David tried on—much to the entertainment of the others watching. David realized he could not fight the battle wearing armor designed for another. He had his own weapons and skills to use. Best of all, he had big faith and a big God. The shepherd boy became the stuff of legends that day as he felled that giant with one stone, shot like a missile into the forehead of Goliath.

Dr. Riley was like Saul trying to get Billy to wear his armor. But God had other plans.

Predictably, Ruth was less than thrilled with the whole idea. She knew Billy was not a professional scholar, and sluggish academia was not suited to his temperament. Billy was used to moving quickly and getting instant results. No university works like that. He would soon come to discover what a faculty member advised him early in his tenure: "evangelism races, education plods."

Billy told Riley that he'd accept the job on an interim basis until the board found a permanent president. That seemed to satisfy Riley for the time being, but Billy left the house in the pouring rain and a state of anxiety.

After a few weeks of serious contemplation, Billy decided that if Riley should die within the next ten months, he would accept the position and stay until a new candidate could be selected. It was a generous time-frame given Riley's ailing condition. He died four months later on December 5, 1947.

The news came to Billy through his friend George Wilson. The midnight call interrupted his visit with Stephen Olford, his influential British friend. They were in Hattiesburg, Mississippi, at the time for a Youth for Christ rally. Billy kindly asked Olford to take over his speaking schedule while he flew to Minnesota to deliver Riley's eulogy. Olford readily agreed.

After the service, Richard V. Clearwaters, a prominent local pastor who led the opening prayer, angrily approached Billy in an aggressive manner. Clearwaters, a professor and board member at Northwestern Schools, fumed to the young man that *he* should have preached at the funeral—and he also should have been named Riley's successor at Northwestern.

But Riley knew that Clearwaters was a separatist, and Billy was a unifier. Clearwaters was instrumental in the Conservative Baptist movement and would go on to found the Central Baptist Seminary and Pillsbury Bible College in 1956, both of which were separatist and fundamentalist.

Billy eventually discovered there were many individuals and various factions jockeying for Riley's hallowed mantle.

Even though Clearwaters was hostile toward him, Billy found it hard to disagree with his logic. He had only graduated from Wheaton College four years before with a bachelor's degree in anthropology, while the position usually required a doctorate. Others, like the board of directors—fifty in all—and the school's faculty might have felt the same way: Who in the world was this young outsider? They'd know soon enough.

On December 17, 1947, Northwestern held its next board meeting. The directors followed the founder's mandate and named twenty-nine-year-old Billy Graham as its next leader. He was believed to be the youngest college president in U.S. history.

It was a decision Billy soon came to regret and one that Ruth found hard to support. Early in Billy's tenure, a Northwestern administrator called Ruth, thinking it would be wise to make nice with his boss' wife. He politely asked when she would be moving to Minneapolis. Ruth had no intention of uprooting her or her two children's lives in their new Montreat home to be by her husband's side. And she made that very clear.

"Never," came the reply.

CHAPTER SEVENTEEN

Inexperienced, but Enthusiastic

Have you ever seen the movie *The Candidate,* starring Robert Redford and Peter Boyle? It was made in 1972, but it still resonates today.

Here's the premise: Redford plays Bill McKay, a reluctant candidate from California running for the U.S. Senate. He has no chance against his opponent, a smooth-talking incumbent, Crocker Jarmon (brilliantly portrayed by character actor Don Porter), who thinks he has the race in the bag. It galls the opposing party to allow Jarmon to go unchallenged, so McKay agrees to throw his hat into the ring. He knows he's going to lose, but this allows him the freedom to say whatever he wants to voters. Because of his straight talk, his grassroots candidacy catches fire and much to his surprise, McKay wins the election. But he's like the dog that chased a car and caught it. He has no idea what to do with it.

At the end of the film, McKay, bone-tired from his months of campaign stumping, is surrounded by his team of volunteers and admirers, who are ready to celebrate. However, McKay is in no mood for revelry and pulls his campaign manager aside. He is clearly flustered, and one question weighs heavily on his mind.

"What do we do now?"

I get the feeling that's the headspace Billy Graham was in when the realization hit him that he was now a college president. So he did what many wise people do in that type of desperate situation: call someone smarter than yourself and hire them. That's why the first phone call he made the day after Riley's death was to his old friend T.W. Wilson. He had him installed as the school's vice president and chief administrator.

Wilson was living comfortably with his wife, Mary Helen, in Alabama at the time. He must not have given Billy the answer he wanted because he called T.W. ten nights in a row until he acquiesced. T.W. was a gifted evangelist in his own right and felt he was no more qualified to run a college than Billy. Plus, moving to a place like Minnesota with its harsh winters didn't sound appealing. Billy never drew his salary as president of Northwestern because he was still on the Youth for Christ payroll, and it's my best guess this likely went to pay for Wilson's position. He also stayed in an old hotel or boardinghouse whenever he was in Minneapolis for business. I'm astonished by the sacrifices Billy made, but not by his selflessness.

One of Billy's first few days on the job underscored his lack of administrative experience. That's when the school librarian, Dorothea Williams, told Billy she could no longer stay at her current position given her meager salary. Upon hearing what Williams made, Billy readily agreed she should make more and authorized an immediate increase. Billy's largesse spread quickly among the faculty and staff, who often took on second jobs to make ends meet. Pretty soon, everyone had their hands out.

"I didn't know that would grow like ten pins through the rest of the faculty and staff, and everybody had to have a raise," Billy recalled at Northwestern's seventy-fifth anniversary in 1977. "And we didn't have the money."

In addition to the pay-raise fiasco, Billy made a few other gaffes. In his first letter to faculty, he addressed these academic types in his own folksy way: "Dear Gang." He also hired an English professor to teach math simply because he liked the man. The students quickly discovered their knowledge easily surpassed the professor's, and some hasty arrangements had to be made to cover Billy's faux pas. Others also complained that Billy showed up at board meetings fully expecting on-the-spot decisions for agenda items that required months of exhaustive research. Often his fallback position was to look at his watch, then instruct T.W. Wilson, his dependable second-in-command, "T, you better do the rest. Goodbye."

What Billy couldn't avoid or shrug off was the school's severe lack of funds. W.B. Riley had tried in vain to build an administrative and academic headquarters after running it out of the First Baptist Church building, which was several blocks away. A majority of the funds he raised for the building went into the excavation and foundation pilings. When Riley passed, there was no money to complete the project. It fell to Billy as president to raise the necessary $250,000 to finish the structure, later known as Memorial Hall.

The only thing Billy inherited at Northwestern of any value was a team that helped him meet his lofty goals and objectives. This included Riley's longtime secretary, Luverne Gustavson. She immediately proved to be indispensable, and Billy later hired her when he formed the Billy Graham Evangelistic Association, where she would stay during their most historic period, riding it out for almost fifteen years until taking another job in 1964.

"When she gave advice and counsel, we always listened because of her vast experience and ability," Grady Wilson said.

Gustavson was equally taken with her new boss. Nobody came into Billy's office without him praying for them before they left, she noted.

Billy also inherited George Wilson, a layman and the business manager at Northwestern as well as the owner of a downtown Christian bookstore. He had a ministry of his own and was the director of the Youth for Christ rallies in Minneapolis, where W.B. Riley was first introduced to Billy. He later proved to be vital in establishing a radio station at the school under Billy's watch. As a board member for the BGEA, I interacted with George on multiple occasions. He was a very serious man, but very dedicated to the task at hand.

Another crucial Northwestern employee was Jerry Beavan, who served as the school's registrar and taught at both the college and the seminary. Initially, Billy was unsure of his abilities, but Beavan's organizational skills were self-evident. Billy also took advantage of Beavan's journalism experience and had him write press releases for the early Crusades. In 1950, he was named Billy's executive secretary and then director of public relations—and ultimately, director of Crusade planning. Some believe it was his vision to expand Billy's itinerant evangelistic ministry in America into an international evangelistic outreach, and in 1952, he began work on the legendary London Crusade of 1954. Billy even referred to him as "the architect of world evangelism as we know it today." I was born in 1952. So when I was in diapers, Billy and his team were changing the world.

Billy could also count on the founder's widow, Marie Acomb Riley, who served as the dean of women, to keep an eye on Northwestern Schools while he was gone. In his 1997 autobiography, Billy credited her authority, managerial hand, talent, and total dedication to the campus for helping him run things smoothly. Billy referred to Mrs. Riley graciously, as he did everyone, but his relationship with her would become one of the major points of contention that led to his eventual departure from Northwestern in 1952. They did not always get along, but Billy would never publicly expose that tension.

However, nothing going on behind the scenes at Northwestern had any impact on the student body. All they noticed was their new president's magnetism, fervor for saving souls, and boundless energy and enthusiasm. And they loved him.

"I greatly admired Billy from his first introduction in Northwestern Chapel," said Allen Dale Golding, who was the senior class president for the Bible school in 1950. "He was an impressive presence, even before he was world famous."

Pauline Hutchens, class of 1951, recalled a time when she was sitting in the lobby of the chapel and Billy suddenly appeared. She remembered: "He came in through the door with his entourage (the executives). He had such a presence—he was tall, blonde, and handsome. He said hello. And I haven't forgotten it."

That rings very true for me. I remember as a younger man when I was at the National Religious Broadcasters conference before I had met Billy, and he walked through the room. He had his associates around him, and he really stood out. Of course, everyone knew who he was, especially the people at that convention. You could hear the whispers, "There's Billy Graham!"

Layton Brueske, also class of 1951, said even though Billy had a killer schedule that would wipe out most mortals, he never appeared frantic or in a hurry.

"He really threw himself into the social, spiritual, everyday contact with students to the best of his ability," Brueske said. "How he did it, I don't know. He was a busy man."

Billy wasn't like most people. To many it seemed as if he had an internal engine that not only powered him through life but couldn't switch itself off. Under his leadership and guidance, the school moved six blocks to a newly constructed site in Loring Park, which was dedicated in November 1948. The new campus included three dormitories and a Fine Arts building fashioned from early twentieth century homes and apartment buildings with the newly constructed Memorial Hall as the main academic building with classrooms, offices, and a chapel. A space for a future radio station was set aside.

Billy also assumed Riley's role as editor-in-chief of the *Northwestern Pilot* and contributed several articles to each issue. In one column alone, Billy quoted philosopher Arthur Schopenhauer, Abraham Lincoln, and a famous rear admiral. His writings boosted the subscription rate by one thousand. (Whether you live in the era of subscriptions or clicks, gaining one thousand new pairs of eyeballs is impressive.)

"He was handed an institution with three schools and told to run it," Beavan said. "It would be like if you were suddenly put in the pilot's seat of an airplane and told to fly it. And he'd had no training in that area at all. But he had some great vision."

That vision also included developing a new catchphrase to signal Northwestern's exciting mission.

The school's motto, "Blazing New Trails with the Old Faith," didn't resonate with Billy. While resting at his home in Montreat, Billy and Jerry Beavan collaborated on a new slogan: "Knowledge on Fire." To them, it conveyed that Northwestern would not only lead the way in training men and women for the evangelistic field, but would present to them a challenge and a goal. There was a lot of community buy-in, which brought a renewed sense of mission to the school.

That included trying to build a new drama program under the auspices of the speech department. Billy hired Mark W. Lee, whom he had known from his days at Wheaton, to get the program off the ground after a shaky start.

"(Billy) had invited me to the college to be on the faculty and he had decided that he would try to make Northwestern into another Wheaton. He had an admiration for Wheaton," Lee recalled in 2013. "I came up for an interview and was immediately approved. He wanted drama. And Wheaton had drama."

Billy got more drama than he wanted when Jerry Beavan told him in front of Lee that the school lacked the funds to build such a program.

For the rest of his life, Lee said this was the only time he ever saw Billy without a smile on his face. Here's how he remembered the conversation:

Billy said to Beavan, "We're going to have drama."

"But there's no budget for it," Beavan said.

"Well, we're working on that," Billy replied.

Firmly, with irritation rising in his voice, Beavan answered, "We can't have it."

"We will have it, and you will do it," Billy said.

Beavan relented. "All right."

Lee put on three full-scale costumed productions his first year at Northwestern—*Crown of Thorns*, *The Passing of the Third Floor Back*, and *Barter*—a trio of Christian-themed plays, and in a newly decorated auditorium, no less!

After that was settled, Billy realized another of Riley's big ambitions: to construct a Christian radio station and get it up and running. Riley's vision was in total alignment with Billy's, who saw radio as a medium to reach the masses.

Think about all the places you see TVs now: doctors' offices, airports, bars, almost every restaurant, and most offices. That is nothing compared to the reach of radio before TV. Everyone had a big radio in their living room, and people gathered around to listen to their favorite shows the way they do with television now. Radio was the king of all media.

Billy recognized the power of mass media, but in a way no other evangelist did. Just as there would be a drama program at Northwestern, the radio would win souls for Christ.

A novel approach to raising the funds for the enterprise took shape at a chapel service in early 1948. Billy challenged the student body to give a dollar a week to get the radio station off the ground. It was an odd request, given that throughout history students have been notoriously broke. The usual pattern is to find alumni with deep pockets and big egos, convince them only they can save the world, and then promise to splash their name on everything. But in this case...

"The challenge really worked, and the students gave over a thousand dollars a week," said Kyle Wilson, who graduated from Northwestern in 1951. "Students and staff put Northwestern on the air through that weekly offering."

In a year's time, the students raised forty-four thousand dollars—equivalent to more than three quarters of a million today. The station went on the air nearly a year later in February 1949 with an opening prayer by Billy and a tranquil rendition of the hymn "Blessed Quietness."

Billy was sure to repay the students in access to the studio. Not only were they active in the construction of the station, but they were involved in providing some of the on-air content. Some became on-air personalities while others worked in the engineering room. The school's quartet appeared twice a week on a radio program. It became a training ground in media for many students and a living laboratory like many of today's colleges. And its mission was always clear: lead people to the Lord and nurture them in their spiritual growth through Christ-centered media.

The feedback from Twin Cities residents was overwhelming, recalled Gustavson, who corresponded with many of the listeners.

"I could hardly keep up with the correspondence to answer people who were so thrilled to hear his voice on the radio," Gustavson said.

Much to the delight of his faculty and staff, Billy was able to give them a raise, and the school's finances were in good shape. This was achieved by raising tuition and the increase in enrollment, which included several international students. By the end of Billy's tenure at Northwestern, the student body had almost doubled from 700 to 1,300.

Mark W. Lee said the formula for his success was simple.

"Billy was able to put forth this image of energy and belief," Lee said. "You didn't believe that there was a one percent loss in his convictions. He had that feeling inside: 'Well, you're a professional and you ought to know what is needed to be done. Now let's get it done!' kind of thing."

Some historians have written that Billy's years at Northwestern were a bust. I don't agree. Billy moved mountains. He brought a very fresh perspective to academia, a staid field where things are expected to move along slowly. He made a paradigm shift at Northwestern. An entire campus moved. Buildings and dormitories rose. A two-wave radio station was constructed and opened. An entire drama program was created from scratch. Magazine subscriptions rocketed. The student body doubled. Donations poured in. Coffers filled. Accreditation seemed forthcoming. The spiritual needs of the community were met like never before. The Northwestern Kingdom truly was on fire for the Lord.

"When Billy Graham left Northwestern, he felt that he had fulfilled his obligation to W.B. Riley. But despite his successes, Graham never truly settled into the position as Riley had hoped he would," said Greg Rosauer, assistant professor and archivist at the University of Northwestern-St. Paul, as the school came to be called in 2013. "It was still clear to Graham that God meant for him to be an evangelist. In one sense, his time at Northwestern assured him of and enabled him to realize that calling."

The only person whose needs weren't being met, it seemed, were Billy's.

In a candid letter written in 1948 to secretary Luverne Gustavson, Billy revealed that his evangelistic travels with Youth for Christ combined with his Northwestern duties were physically draining him and sapping his soul.

"When I neglect my correspondence from time to time in these campaigns, it is because I am so busy, I hardly know what to do. I am speaking four or five times a day and trying to prepare all of these messages and keep my body fit and my soul prepared before the Lord, and it is awfully hard to get to the work, but I am trying to fill it between the cracks."

Indeed, the cracks were beginning to show in Billy's life. Later that year, it would lead to what no one who knew him would ever believe possible: a potential crisis of faith. And a time of deep soul-searching that almost took Billy Graham permanently out of evangelism.

CHAPTER EIGHTEEN

Two Evangelists, Two Crises of Faith

C hristians stumble while walking with the Lord. They just do. We're human, after all. The Bible is filled with examples of men who had a crisis of faith.

Moses said in Numbers 11:14–15 that the job God had given him was too much. He had a great sense of insecurity and failed to trust God for the moment, but God used him in spite of his weaknesses.

Elijah's crisis came in 1 Kings 19:3–4 because of his fear of Jezebel, queen of Israel. But in spite of this, he encouraged others to believe in the one true God.

Job's great crisis of faith can be found in Job 3:11 when he questioned God about why he was even born. Still, Job ended up saying, "Though God slay me, yet I will trust Him."

Jonah's crisis of faith came about because of his pride.

Yet these men persevered, and they continued to love God and ultimately chose to trust rather than turn their backs on Him.

In my lifetime, I have seen great men and women of God—faith leaders—who fell spiritually from grace. I have discovered that how we respond to the crisis is what determines our future maturity as a Christian.

It could be any number of things that cause a person to get off track: greed, substance abuse, an extramarital affair, an outsized ego, intellectual superiority, a crisis of faith, or an actual loss of faith. The key is to repent, turn from sin, and return to Christ having learned and grown in faith.

Sometimes pastors stay in the pulpit when they have lost their zeal for Christ. It's not unlike the builder whose own house lies in shambles. They forget that true ministry starts with a heart turned toward God. The service to the Lord is the overflow of that.

It can be surprisingly easy for a spiritual leader to go through the motions but lose the emotion. All perspiration, no inspiration. And one's calling can turn into a career. I have seen it. Sometimes these are the ones who find themselves "burning out." I find personally that when I walk closely with the Lord my service for Him comes rather easily, and I have been doing this now for over forty-five years. I have never grown tired of the Lord's work, but like anyone else, I can grow tired *in* it. One needs to learn to pace himself and take time to recharge both spiritually and physically.

Character is fundamental because our actions can easily drown out our words—and if we lack integrity, we have pretty much lost everything.

Awhile back I came across an interesting headline in *Forbes* magazine. It read, "Success will come and go, but integrity is forever." Billionaire Warren Buffett recently stated that when you're looking for someone to hire, you should look for three qualities: intelligence, initiative, and integrity. He added, "And if they don't have the latter, the first two will kill you, because if you're going to hire someone without integrity, you want them lazy and dumb."

Having spent time with Billy Graham up close, I can tell you without hesitation he was a man of tremendous integrity. But know this too—Christian leaders are constantly under attack. Nothing delights Satan more than taking down a Christian leader because he knows it will have a domino effect on the flock.

Though Billy never lost faith, there was a time in his life when he truly examined if what he'd believed his entire life was true. That came at the prompting of his friend and fellow Youth for Christ associate Charles Templeton.

Billy was still barnstorming the country for Youth for Christ and tending to his duties at Northwestern while Templeton, his one-time rival for the title of "world's most up-and-coming-evangelist," had just resigned from his job in Toronto in order to pursue an advanced degree at Princeton Theological Seminary.

Billy, too, had been contemplating taking a leave of absence from all his duties to get his Ph.D. He inquired with several universities, asking what would be required of him, but the courses and amount of time it would take him discouraged him.

Three weeks before the fall semester began, Templeton flew to North Carolina to speak at a summer conference in 1948. While there, Templeton spent a day with the Grahams. And the state Billy found him in was alarming.

From the moment Billy and Templeton met, they had been fast friends, though they couldn't have been more opposite: Billy was reared in the South by Christian parents with a firm belief in God and His Word. Templeton grew up in grinding poverty and was the child of a single mother. Billy was always a country preacher in his heart. Templeton was a street-smart Northerner who led a sinful life before his adult conversion. Billy was warm and ingratiating. Templeton was eloquent and cerebral. Billy preached with vigor and great conviction. Templeton effectively used his keen sense of observation and humor in his sermons. Billy never doubted the veracity of the Scriptures. Templeton was skeptical by nature and questioned everything. Billy had a warm smile. Templeton grinned like a wolf.

They were about as city-mouse-and-country-mouse as you could get. But I can see how that relationship easily caught fire. No one can understand a preacher like another preacher. It's one of the reasons I loved and admired Billy so much.

Double that when the other preacher is an evangelist. It's a unique calling, and to continue to do it with passion and effectiveness is no small feat. When someone rises to the top, as Billy did, and meets someone else who has weathered the many storms leaders face, there is a mutual and instant respect.

But in the months that followed their return from Europe in 1947, Templeton had been fighting a losing battle with his faith. He felt there was a shallowness to Youth for Christ's mission because everyone associated with the organization measured success by the amount of people they drew each night.

"There seemed to be little concern with what happened to the young sters who responded to our appeals," Templeton wrote in his 1983 book, *An Anecdotal Memoir*. "If the after service dragged on, we tended to get impatient, wanting to wrap things up and get back to the hotel or restaurant for our nightly steak and shop talk. Billy, too, was troubled by it, and we talked about it many times. It undoubtedly contributed to his move from Youth for Christ to conduct his own campaigns."

The tipping point for him was a *Life* magazine photo of a young black woman in North Africa. The region had experienced a terrible drought, and she was holding her dead baby in her arms, looking up at God for an explanation. Templeton studied the photo intensely and wondered how it was possible to believe in a caring Creator when all her child needed was something as simple as rain?

"How could a loving God *do this* to that woman?" Templeton demanded to know.

As a result, Templeton could no longer accept many of the basic teachings of the Christian faith despite his longing for a personal relationship with God. In the beginning of his walk, he accepted the beliefs of the people around him and the evangelical subculture. He also read everything he could get his hands on, especially delving into philosophical and theological works that included the likes of Thomas Paine, Voltaire, Bertrand Russell, Robert Ingersoll, David Hume, and Thomas Huxley.

Templeton later wrote that Christianity "is not a faith for the scholar or the contemplative." That is not true, of course, but it was in his mind.

While I am all for reading and educating yourself, even arming yourself against the enemy by what scholars have written, there is an inherent danger in being tempted to become intellectually superior rather than resting and relying on faith.

I suspect such was the case of comparing and contrasting the lives of Billy Graham and Charles Templeton. Billy searched and examined the Scriptures, and they rang true to his heart. The power of God's Holy Spirit in him bore witness to this. Templeton succumbed to the lure of intellectual superiority.

Having faith does not mean one checks their brains at the door. Some of the greatest minds of all time had a deep faith in God and belief in Scripture. The great British professor and author C.S. Lewis immediately comes to mind, among many others. But ultimately, you must accept an authority higher than your own.

And that ultimate authority is God Himself as He reveals Himself in His Word, the Bible. People have asked me, "What do you do when you come to a passage of Scripture you don't agree with?" My answer is simple. I respond, "You change your opinion because God's Word is true."

Slowly and against his will, Templeton said his mind began to challenge and rebut all of the things he once believed, including the Genesis account of creation, the virgin birth of Jesus, and the Holy Trinity. He realized that his faith was disintegrating. Then a pastor he knew threw him a life preserver by telling him that if he wanted to continue being useful in the ministry, he should quit preaching and return to school.

When Templeton arrived in North Carolina and met up with Billy again, he had a year of seminary under his belt. Templeton and Billy spoke at length about his departure from Youth for Christ. Billy was distressed for Templeton because he wasn't just leaving the organization; he was leaving his very faith behind.

Templeton said he could no longer believe the biblical account of creation and that he sided with the scientists: Earth had evolved over millions of years.

"It's not a matter of speculation, it's demonstratable fact," Templeton said. Billy refuted those words and said there were plenty of reputable scholars that backed him.

"Who are they?" Templeton asked. "Men in conservative colleges?"

"Most of them, yes. But that's not the point," Billy said. "I believe in the Genesis account of creation simply because it's in the Bible. I've discovered something in my ministry: when I take the Bible literally, when I proclaim it as God's Word, I have power." Billy added that he didn't have the time to examine all sides of each theological dispute and simply accepted the Bible as God's Word.

Templeton admonished Billy for committing "intellectual suicide" and coldly told him that his preaching, style, and jargon were "fifty years out of date." Billy's faith, Templeton said, was too simple.

He pushed for Billy to go to Princeton and study with him. Billy refused on the grounds that he couldn't attend a college in the States (because he was still a college president). However, if they got accepted to a university in another country, such as Oxford in England, Billy said he'd consider it. With that, Billy stuck out his hand to Templeton, ready to shake on a deal. Templeton refused to take it. It sure doesn't sound like their parting was sweet.

One thing was for sure: Templeton's departure left Billy stunned and shaken to his core. It also left him asking questions about his faith and reading habits. For the first time since his conversion, he was questioning the truth and dependability of the Scriptures.

Can the Bible be trusted completely? Billy secretly wondered.

Thus began an intensive study of the question, soaking in the writings of theologians and scholars on all sides of the issue as well as the Bible. Billy carried this emotional baggage with him for months. It came to a head at the College Briefing Conference at Forest Home, which was held from August 5 to September 5, 1949. He had agreed to speak there, but his spirits were in the doldrums, and Billy felt as if he didn't have much to say.

While at the retreat center, approximately eighty miles east of Los Angeles, he sought the wise counsel of Henrietta Mears. She was the director of religious education at First Presbyterian Church of Hollywood and one of the great Bible teachers of the twentieth century. A former high school chemistry teacher from Minneapolis, the bespectacled spinster-matriarch was given to big hats with pinwheels, brooches, and frilly dresses.

Mears had a profound impact on the ministries of Billy Graham, Bill Bright, Dawson Trotman, and Jim Rayburn. She also mentored and counseled an actor by the name of Ronald Reagan, who later became the fortieth president of the United States. Billy once said of Mears, "I doubt if any other woman, outside of my wife and mother, has had such a marked influence on me. She is certainly one of the greatest Christians I have ever known."

Billy prayed and consulted with Mears at Forest Home regarding his search for a deeper understanding of the Bible. He certainly went to the right person. Mears explained that the Bible is without fault or error and is infallible. It was indeed the Word of God.

Billy stated in his autobiography that after his consultation with her, he felt as though he had been "placed on a rack," with Templeton stretching him one way, Mears the other. While alone in his room, he pored over every verse of Scripture where Christ was quoted.

He also examined what Jesus specifically thought of the Scriptures. As far as Billy could tell, Jesus never doubted a word. In fact, Billy noted that Christ actually substantiated many colorful but oft-doubted stories told in the Old Testament, including those of Noah and Jonah. That was certainly encouraging.

Even with that knowledge, Billy was still uncertain. If he didn't have the answer soon, he knew he'd have to pack it in and leave the ministry. He reasoned that he could always go back to North Carolina and milk cows for a living. But after all he'd been through, was that truly God's destiny for him?

It was a true crisis of faith, and Billy was wracked with doubt.

"Lord, what shall I do?" he asked. "What shall be the direction of my life?"

One sleepless night he got up to take a walk in the woods and brought along a Bible. Billy's mind was swimming as he wandered into the rugged terrain. If he was at an emotional crossroads, this was the place to be.

Forest Home was a blessed place, to be sure, with a rich and moving history. In 1876, fourteen men from around the world knelt on one of its mountaintops to pray that somehow through the years to come, God would use the mountain and the valley below for His work. After the 1938 floods, Mears bought the resort for thirty thousand dollars—one-tenth of its asking price. She turned it into a place where people could get away and encounter Jesus. Billy was about to have such an experience.

Spotting a tree stump on his walk in the dark that night, Billy placed his Bible on the flat surface and dropped to his knees to pray.

In a life filled with prayer at every opportunity, from giving thanks in solitude to blessing visitors in his office to addressing God in the company of thousands, it was perhaps *the* greatest prayer of his entire life.

"Oh God, there are many things in this book I do not understand. There are many problems with it for which I have no solution. There are many seeming contradictions. There are some areas in it that do not seem to correlate with modern science. I can't answer some of the philosophical and psychological questions Chuck and others are raising.

"Father, I am going to accept this as Thy word—by faith! I'm going to allow faith to go beyond my intellectual questions and doubts, and I will believe this is to be Your inspired Word."

It was heartfelt, and surely a prayer that God heard and answered. This was to be a pivotal moment in Billy's life that he would never forget and would later recount many times. When he finally stood up, Billy no longer had any doubts. His mind was free and clear, and his mission to serve God to the best of his ability reset. He said years later regarding that moment, "That was the beginning of a whole new era in my ministry."

Weeks after that spiritual experience, Billy Graham traveled to Los Angeles to commence the campaign that would propel him to international prominence. Templeton thinks history would have taken a much different course had he not rejected Billy's invitation at Montreat.

"I have often pondered what might have happened if I had taken his hand that day and we had gone off to school together," Templeton wrote in his 1983 memoir. "I am certain of this: he would not be the Billy Graham he has become, and the history of mass evangelism would be different than it is."

That is probably true. And it's also true the world would be a much bleaker place, for Billy Graham was used by God to bring millions of people around the world hope, solace, faith, and most of all, Christ Himself.

Heaven is fuller today because of it, and Hell lost more than a few future residents.

As for Templeton—well, he also entered a new era: a decades-long sojourn in which he drifted away from God and into the wilderness.

He eventually left the ministry, got divorced, and watched his beloved mother slowly die of cancer—though he didn't dare tell her that he had turned his back on the Lord. He abandoned all the people he befriended during his nineteen years with the church, including the three dozen men and women who were in the ministry or mission fields because of him. He and Billy drifted apart, though they spoke on the phone every now and then.

Outwardly, the next few decades of Templeton's life looked successful. His career bounced between television, music, screenplays, politics, advertising, and journalism before he became a bestselling novelist in 1977. His first attempt, *The Kidnapping of the President*, was adapted into a 1980 feature film starring William Shatner, Hal Holbrook, Van Johnson, and Ava Gardner.

He continued writing books, hosting a radio show, and mainly stayed in the spotlight as Canada's most famous apostate. His last book,

1995's *Farewell to God*, was his parting shot at Christianity and listed the reasons he left the faith.

"I oppose the Christian Church because, for all the good it sometimes does, it presumes to speak in the name of God and to propound and advocate beliefs that are outdated, demonstrably untrue, and often, in their various manifestations, deleterious to individuals and society," Templeton said at the time.

Shortly before *Farewell to God* was published, Templeton was diagnosed with Alzheimer's. He was essentially given a death sentence and wondered how Alzheimer's could exist if God was loving. In what should have been a time to get reacquainted with his Maker, Templeton seemed to push Him away even more.

Farewell to God led to a poignant 1998 interview with my friend and author Lee Strobel as he was working on a book that also would become a bestseller: *The Case for Christ: A Journalist's Personal Investigation of the Evidence for Jesus.*

Strobel, a former atheist, was an award-winning legal editor of the *Chicago Tribune*. After a long struggle with his wife's conversion, he sought to disprove it, putting his legal mind to work. But in the end, Strobel himself came to put his faith in Christ and now is celebrated as one of evangelicalism's greatest apologists.

He tailed Templeton to a penthouse apartment in a modern high-rise building in Toronto. Then eighty-three with thinning gray hair, Templeton suffered through recurring bouts of depression. On the twenty-fifth floor, Templeton's third wife, Madeleine, ushered Strobel inside. He recalled in his book that Templeton had just emerged from a nap, his hair slightly disheveled, sporting brown pajamas, black slippers, and a light housecoat. He shook hands with Strobel in his bedroom and announced he was not feeling well. Then he corrected himself.

"Actually, I'm dying," Templeton said resolutely. He told Strobel his memory wasn't as sharp as it used to be and that it was only a matter of time before Alzheimer's claimed it completely.

A few minutes later, they settled in the living room and got down to the business at hand. How, Strobel wanted to know, did Templeton go from preaching the Gospel alongside Billy Graham to agnosticism?

Templeton spoke of the heartbreaking *Life* magazine photo of the African woman holding her dead baby, the concept of Heaven and Hell, atheism versus agnosticism, and the possibility that he could be wrong about God's existence.

"No," Templeton strongly declared. "*No.* There cannot be, in our world, a loving God."

What about Jesus? Did Templeton believe He actually existed?

"No question," Templeton replied without giving it much thought. Jesus was "the greatest human being that ever lived." Furthermore, Templeton called Him a moral genius, said His ethical sense was uncanny, and that He was intrinsically the wisest and greatest person he'd ever read about.

Strobel, taken aback, said, "You sound like you really care about Him."

What Templeton said next floored my friend.

"Well, yes, He's the most important thing in my life. I know it may sound strange, but I have to say...I *adore* Him!" Templeton added that everything decent or pure he ever knew, he learned from Jesus. He ruminated that He was not only kind, caring, and compassionate, but also tough when the occasion called for it.

"And if I may put it this way," Templeton said as his voice began to crack, "*I...miss...Him!*"

Of course he did.

Charles Templeton was not as much of an agnostic as he famously claimed; he was, in fact, a prodigal son. And like the story Jesus told, the prodigal missed his home.

Uncontrollable tears flowed down Templeton's face, Strobel recollected. He turned away and looked down as he quivered and wept for a few moments before collecting himself. Then the shield went back up.

"Enough of that," he said dismissively. He picked up his coffee, taking a sip, holding it tightly "as if drawing warmth from it," Strobel wrote in *The Case for Christ*. "It was obvious that he wanted to pretend this unvarnished look into his soul had never happened."

To Strobel, it was apparent that Templeton hungered for his faith again. Many scribes over the years wrote Templeton off as a cautionary tale—a God-haunted man who surrendered his spiritual life to intellectualism. That is partly true. But it's also quite possible that in his last days, Chuck Templeton had a change of heart or even possibly reversed his liberal theology. Something in me believes that Jesus did not abandon Charles Templeton and was there to receive him when he finally passed. How am I so sure? Read on…

Toronto Star columnist Tom Harper interviewed Madeleine Templeton about her husband's "transcendent deathbed encounter" in June 2001. Madeleine, who identified at the time as part deist and part agnostic, said Templeton was gazing upward from his deathbed when he saw angels.

"Look at them, look at them!" he cried out suddenly and excitedly. "They're so beautiful. They're waiting for me…I'm coming."

The next day—June 7, 2001—he was dead.

Madeleine told Harper what she witnessed was "such a tremendous comfort."

I have no doubt that when Billy died in 2018, his old and dear friend Charles Templeton was there sitting near the throne of God to welcome him to the Kingdom.

CHAPTER NINETEEN

Kissed by William Randolph Hearst

L os Angeles in the late 1940s was Southern California at its zenith. Thousands of World War II veterans moved there for the sun, the mass-produced housing financed by the G.I. Bill and the Federal Housing Administration, and the lucrative aerospace and defense jobs. The war may have been over, but the Cold War was not. The suburbs boomed.

Los Angeles has always been a city of extremes. At that time, the American dream was thriving. People had brand-new houses with lawns. Men wore fedoras and double-breasted suits. Ladies wore lipstick and hose. If there was a lawn mower in the garage, there was a refrigerator, washer, and dryer in the house.

And when people have all the necessities of life, they like to spend on luxuries. At one end of that scale were the new car hops—places like Bob's Big Boy—where you could pull in and have a burger brought to your car. I still remember Bob's Big Boy from my childhood; a giant statue of the character Bob held a giant burger aloft in front on everyone. Movies were huge too. The studio system was in full swing, cranking out glamour on the big screen and keeping star peccadillos out of the papers. Howard Hughes, the richest man in the world, was still handsome and sane and dating bevies of starlets, including Bette Davis, Ava Gardner, Olivia de Havilland, Katharine Hepburn, Hedy Lamarr, Ginger Rogers, Janet Leigh, Rita Hayworth, and many more.

At the other extreme, L.A.'s seedy underbelly was also on full display. Mobster Mickey Cohen, nicknamed the "King of Los Angeles," could be seen with top L.A. politicians as well as Frank Sinatra, Robert Mitchum, Dean Martin, Jerry Lewis, and Sammy Davis Jr. Meanwhile, one morning in 1947, a pretty twenty-two-year-old waitress and aspiring actress named Elizabeth Short was found slain: the killer had cut her in half and disfigured her body. The "Black Dahlia" murder remains one of the oldest unsolved cases in Los Angeles County and one of the most famous murders in American history as well.

Nationally, things were unsettling in a different way. On September 23, 1949, President Harry Truman announced that the Soviet Union had detonated an atomic bomb. The United States was no longer the sole possessor of nuclear weapons. That turn of events felt even more ominous because the Soviets had embraced the deadly, aggressive, atheistic ideology of Communism. The threat felt frightfully real, especially to Billy Graham. That fall, mainland China fell to Mao Tse-tung's Red Army. Communists possessed both the determination and the ability, in Billy's words, "to holster the whole world."

At home things looked just as grim: militarism, racism, materialism, and rampant sexual immorality spread tentacles through the American culture.

At the time, Billy still held his post at Northwestern and was ministering intermittently for Youth for Christ, as he would until 1952. But he was also beginning to launch his own solo ministry career—and Los Angeles would prove to be the city that made him a household name.

Like the rest of the country, Los Angeles seemed like it could use an inspired Gospel message. Was this city of angels, devils, gangsters, movie stars, starlets, sunshine, and palm trees ready for a spiritual awakening? Even if it was, did the people want to hear it from an unknown thirty-one-year-old Southerner with an accent who didn't know the first thing about hard living? Ex-G.I.s cutting their grass with a sweating beer waiting on the porch didn't need to hear about Hell from some farm boy from North Carolina. They'd already seen plenty of it—but that was about to change.

The watershed Los Angeles campaign that rocketed Billy Graham from an up-and-coming evangelist to an international media sensation was originally planned by its local organizing committee to be a down-home affair.

A group of local businessmen calling themselves "Christ for Greater Los Angeles" invited Billy to hold meetings in the fall of 1949. They represented a group of approximately two hundred churches in the city and had already sponsored several campaigns. While fairly successful, none of them grabbed many headlines or stirred the soul of the community.

Billy had met the committee before. They had held a joint rally with Youth for Christ at the Hollywood Bowl in June 1947. The event drew thousands of spirited teens, and Billy's preaching that night was inspired, recalled committee member Lawrence Young.

"There was one thing that impressed me particularly, and that was that even before the invitation to repent of sins and receive Jesus Christ as personal Savior was given, young people were trekking down and kneeling at the altar," said Young, who worked on the publicity team. "Billy was already having this kind of effect in his ministry…we had a great movement of the Spirit that night."

Invitations were also extended to Billy's associates, Cliff Barrows and George Beverly Shea. Billy didn't normally put conditions on his campaigns, but this was, after all, Los Angeles—a place where credibility meant more than in most cities. Billy knew this campaign had to be different if they were to make an impact. Their most recent affair—a ten-day campaign in June in the railroad city of Altoona, Pennsylvania—had been amateur hour at best. Local preparation was minimal and ministers bickered and refused to share the platform because of their doctrinal differences. Protesters, including a radio preacher, held up placards admonishing Billy for cooperating with other churches. While advertisers touted free parking and four thousand upholstered seats in the Jaffa Shrine, which was owned by local Shriners who rented the large auditorium out for special civic and religious events, they forgot to mention that the cavernous building lacked air conditioning, and the summer heat was stifling.

Clearly, the devil was in the details, and the spiritual attack was intense. Grady Wilson recalled Altoona as the greatest flop they ever experienced.

Billy was determined that things would be different from that day forward. He insisted on three things if he were to venture to the West Coast. The first was broadening local church support to include as many churches and denominations as possible.

I've been doing our own Harvest crusades for more than thirty years, and this is important because you can get so much more done when Christians lay aside their minor differences for what they hopefully have in common: a desire to preach the Gospel to their communities. Believe it or not, just getting pastors to talk to each other is challenging, let alone actually getting them to work together.

It's a bit like herding cats. But when it works, it's a beautiful thing.

The second condition was that the committee had to substantially raise its advertising and promotion budget. Eventually a budget of thirty thousand dollars was decided on, which showed great faith and generosity on the part of the committee. Billy had had good experiences with radio before. He knew he had to come in big. L.A. was the birthplace of massaging your message with the media.

Finally, the committee was to construct a much larger tent than originally intended. Billy's experience in citywide campaigns informed him and his team that the crowds grew bigger as the days ticked off.

The committee initially agreed to everything except raising the advertising and promotional budget. Even though these were money people, getting hardened Californians to part with their cash to put on an evangelistic event was as tough as convincing them to move to Cleveland.

Campaigns were temporary events, and most budgets required much more sweat than equity. Besides, even at the biggest meetings, getting more than fifty people to respond to the invitation at the end of each night was a huge deal. Getting more than two thousand people to come a night was an audacious stretch.

Initially for some of the older folks on the Christ for Greater Los Angeles Committee, Billy came off as brash. However, Billy had higher and bolder hopes for the Los Angeles campaign. He dreamed big and wanted them to take that leap of faith with him.

With all the terms finally agreed upon, Billy asked for one last thing: the committee had to put the public leadership and the platform duties of the campaign entirely in the hands of the local clergy. Billy's reasoning was that the committee represented too limited an evangelistic constituency to make a meaningful impact. This was a very significant and insightful thing for an evangelist like Billy to understand.

As a pastor, I know what it's like for people who are part of what we call "para-church" organizations to basically plan an event, come to your town, and then expect you to support it. It is valuable and important to seek the counsel of the local pastors who have labored in a community because they know things an outsider does not.

Billy always believed in the local church and supported it. He also had deep and abiding friendships with many pastors throughout his life—and he understood that if he could get the shepherds on board, their flocks would follow. He would ask different pastors to play a role in the evening, getting them personally invested.

That made all the difference and distinguished Billy from other traveling evangelists and revivalists of his day.

Billy trembled in fear at the idea of only a handful of churches being involved, resulting not only in low attendance, but in failing to follow up with new Christians after the Crusade. He was totally convinced that if revival broke out in Los Angeles, it would reverberate around the nation and the world. And he was right.

The committee finally agreed to all of Billy's terms. Once he was satisfied that they would live up to their obligations, a three-week campaign was set to begin on September 25 and run until October 16, 1949.

Shortly before it commenced, Henrietta Mears invited Billy to her Beverly Hills home to address the Hollywood Christian Group. It included prominent actors and actresses such as Jane Russell, Donald O'Connor, Colleen Townsend, Roy and Dale Rogers, Hugh O'Brian, and Stuart Hamblen, a rough-and-tumble Western star turned prominent radio personality. (Marilyn Monroe once attended a group meeting with co-star Jane Russell when filming *Gentlemen Prefer Blondes*, but she never returned.)

The forty-year-old Hamblen connected with the young evangelist at the meeting. Billy said he took an instant liking to the six-foot-two, 220-pound cowboy, who hosted a popular two-hour morning radio show. Hamblen, the top radio personality on the West Coast, said in a semi-serious tone that if he gave Billy his full blessing, he could fill the tent. He later had Billy on the show and then got pulled into the undertow of the campaign.

According to Lawrence Young, the committee was strategic in the tent's placement. At the corner of Washington and Hill streets sat an empty lot at the fringe of the Los Angeles business district. Preparations for a building on the lot were in motion, but Young said things miraculously worked to the committee's advantage.

"We were praying about it. It just looked as if there were no possibilities in getting that lot," Young said. "And then, things just began to fall into place and the lot was available. We got the biggest tent in the West and set it up."

The tent (later known as "the Canvas Cathedral") was so cavernous—with a capacity for six thousand—that it could have had a counter psychological effect had it not been for savvy committee members.

"We knew that we might have small crowds, at least to start with, so we put the chairs in, and spaced them as widely as we could," Young said. "We didn't deceive people, but we wanted to have the feel of a pretty good crowd."

Judging by the lack of publicity, crowds were going to be hard to come by. The campaign pointed in the direction of failure despite the fact that three hundred churches and approximately one thousand prayer groups had been formed in and around Los Angeles. The committee had hired Lloyd Doctor, the public relations director for the Salvation Army, who conducted a press conference just days before the start of the campaign. A handful of reporters showed up, and Billy engaged them, but nothing showed up in print. An old-fashioned tent revival in downtown Los Angeles simply didn't warrant coverage to these hardened scribes.

A few days later, Doctor arranged for a meeting with Los Angeles Mayor Fletcher Bowron, who made a brief statement supporting the "Crusade of 100,000" and posed for a photo with Billy. The *Los Angeles Times* carried a small back-page photo and story of that meeting. It carried the headline "Bowron Backs Young Evangelist's Revivals," but it didn't carry much weight. Save for the advertisements the committee ran in the church section of the paper, that was the only media attention the campaign received the first few weeks.

Stuart Hamblen came through with an invitation for Billy to appear on his show, though he was initially hesitant to accept. Hamblen's show was sponsored by a tobacco company, and Billy wondered if the committee might disapprove of—or frown upon—the idea. But the more he thought about it, Billy reflected on the fact that Jesus spent time with sinners, much to the dismay of the religious leaders of His day. And at the time, Hamblen was one of Hollywood's biggest sinners, which was saying something.

Hamblen's drinking and gambling (he owned horses and bet on them) short-circuited a once-bright movie career. The entertainer was one of the first singing cowboys to smoothly transition from radio into films. Hamblen co-starred with Gene Autry, Roy Rogers, and John Wayne while simultaneously becoming the first artist signed by the American subsidiary of Decca Records in 1934.

But Hamblen, who sought solace in the bottle and smoked like a chimney, did not wear fame well. His drinking escapades often landed him in jail for public brawling and other wild behavior, including shooting out streetlights. He didn't hit rock bottom for a while because his sponsors were able to bail him out, although his alcoholism increasingly hampered his concert performances. And truth be told, he was still struggling when he met Billy. However, Hamblen's loving wife, Suzy, a strong Christian woman who bore his children, continually prayed that he would find peace.

Billy and Hamblen had an easy rapport. At the end of the show, Hamblen encouraged his listeners to come and see Billy preach. He said he'd also be there front and center.

That was a pleasant surprise to Billy, and at 3:00 p.m. on Sunday, September 25, Hamblen and Suzy sat front row and center. Getting him there, however, was a different story. Earlier that afternoon, as the time was swiftly approaching and Hamblen was hemming and hawing, Suzy appeared, all ready to go out the door.

"You ready to go?" she asked. "You told everyone you were going to be there. You don't want to disappoint your fans."

So Hamblen showed up, and early in the service, Billy announced, "There is someone in this tent who is leading a double life." Hamblen felt the conviction of the Holy Spirit and was convinced that Billy was leveling the finger at him. You see, the cowboy star was the son of Dr. James Henry Hamblen, an itinerant Methodist circuit preacher and the founder of the Evangelical Methodist Church denomination. Hamblen angrily stalked out of that meeting, but came back a few nights later.

Each night he showed up, his rage would manifest. He once got so angry that he shook his fist at a bewildered Billy as he exited the tent. Hamblen's old self was putting up a mighty battle, but Billy's inspired words kept wearing him down. But the question of whether he would make a commitment lingered.

Getting others to show up was also a task because of the weather, said committee member Lawrence Young.

"It was very slow going, the weather was cold, you couldn't get people to come," Young said. "Well, not that many people came."

The campaign drew nightly crowds of three thousand to four thousand people—better than expected—but the tent was never full and certainly not packed to capacity. And Billy felt he was simply preaching to the choir.

It was like that night after night for three weeks, just plodding along.

The campaign was coming to a close on Sunday, October 16. Committee members were unsure whether it should be extended. The choir, counselors, and other workers were exhausted, and they risked not only burnout but a disappointing ending.

Sure, there were shouts of joy, decisions for Christ, and opportunities for people to renew their faith during those first three weeks. It was a good campaign, but it certainly wasn't over the top. Revival was not in the air—just the infamous L.A. smog.

All the commitments had been kept, as had the budget, and everyone was confident the tent would legitimately be filled the last night, giving Billy and crew a nice send-off. But the evangelistic team was unsure about whether to call it quits, so they prayed throughout the last week, asking God for a clear sign.

They certainly received one, but it was not exactly what they had expected.

After the last service, Stuart Hamblen called Billy's hotel room at 4:30 a.m. in tears, begging to see him immediately. Hamblen had been on an all-night bender, and when the alcohol finally wore off, he and Suzy were knocking on Billy's door. Billy asked Ruth to go to another room with Grady and Wilma Wilson to pray hard for Hamblen.

The rugged cowboy poured out his heart for thirty minutes while Billy patiently listened. After a brief discussion, they dropped to their knees to pray. Hamblen finally gave his life to the Lord, which Billy took as a sign that the campaign must continue.

The Church Federation of Los Angeles announced its support for the extended meetings, which gave it a big boost, as did Hamblen's public declaration of faith in the next service. Afterward, he called his minister father in West Texas to tell him of his decision. His father was so over-joyed that Billy could hear him whooping over the phone.

Hamblen also gave his testimony over his radio program, telling listeners how he accepted Christ and now felt a new sense of inner peace. Not long after his conversion, Hamblen put pen to paper and wrote "It Is No Secret (What God Can Do)," a gospel song inspired by a conversation he'd had with John Wayne at his home. Hamblen had told the movie star how his problems seemed to dissipate once he accepted Christ. Wayne was so taken with Hamblen's testimony that he said Hamblen should write a song about his experience. Hamblen got home around midnight and sat down at the organ. Two hours later the classic was finished. "It's No Secret" was not only a favorite at Billy Graham Crusades (sung beautifully by Bev Shea), but has been heard in churches across America and around the world and translated into more than fifty languages. Elvis Presley even recorded a version for 1957's *Elvis's Christmas Album.*

The West Coast rumbled, and people were buzzing with excitement after Hamblen's public profession of faith. The campaign was now a full-on happening. The Canvas Cathedral became L.A.'s new hot spot.

When Billy arrived at the tent for the next meeting, he was stunned by the scene: thousands of people had descended on the large tent. It was teeming with reporters and photographers with flashbulbs popping. Billy, not quite sure what to make of this, asked one of the reporters what was happening.

"You've been kissed by William Randolph Hearst," he was told.

CHAPTER TWENTY

Cowboys, Heroes, and Mobsters

The day after this pivotal night of the Crusade, Billy Graham was on the front page of all the Hearst newspapers, including the *Los Angeles Examiner* and the *Los Angeles Herald Express*. His life and ministry would never be the same.

Billy's star literally ascended overnight, and he was showered with media attention, drawing comparisons to the great evangelist Billy Sunday. His name and photo appeared in prestigious publications such as *Life*, *Time*, and *Newsweek* and in hundreds of metropolitan newspapers around the country because the Associated Press picked up the story as well. Some were calling it the greatest religious revival in the history of Southern California—which has seen quite a few.

Billy found himself an instant celebrity in a town that minted stars.

For decades, theories abounded as to why William Randolph Hearst, the founder of "yellow journalism," inexplicably lent a helping hand to Billy Graham by ordering his reporters through a telegram to "Puff Graham"—a journalistic signaling to write feel-good stories about the golden-haired evangelist. The two-word directive from Hearst launched an international ministry that has remained steady over the decades.

But why did the affluent entrepreneur do this? After all, he was no saint, and he did not appear to have any personal interest in Christianity.

In fact, Hearst curried favor with neither man nor God. He was absolutely ruthless. First, he battled Joseph Pulitzer in a war to own the most successful paper in New York. Hearst went low, running lurid headlines and stories about crime, corruption, sex, scandal, innuendo, and lots of cartoons and sports ("if it bleeds, it leads," he famously said). Eventually, he came to own thirty papers in major American cities. All the editorial views were his, and Heaven help you if he didn't like you or your ideas. He inflamed U.S. tensions with Spain over Cuba. He claimed to have started the Spanish-American War. Historians reject this for many reasons, but even if he didn't start the war, he tossed gasoline on the fire.

Even more puzzling was the fact that Hearst had never met Graham, but they came close. According to Charles Templeton, Hearst extended an invitation in 1947 to the Youth for Christ team to spend a weekend with him at his storied palace in San Simeon, California, better known today as the Hearst Castle.

The architectural masterpiece sprawls across the top of a hill overlooking the Pacific Ocean and has panoramic views of the mountains. It is filled with European antiques and rare artwork. Hearst used it as his primary residence for the latter part of his life, and in this setting he and his wife entertained guests and socialized with celebrities, movie stars, captains of industry, and his mistresses. My wife, Cathe, and I toured the place during our honeymoon. It is spectacular.

Hearst greatly respected Youth for Christ because the leaders were proudly American, staunchly conservative, and weren't shy in expressing anti-Communist sentiments. Even stranger, Hearst was seventy-nine at the time, in poor health, and had grown reclusive. The idea of spending a weekend in such extravagance was awfully tempting, but Youth for Christ backed off because they did not want to be seen as being in the aging mogul's back pocket.

So why would Hearst lift a finger to help Billy Graham? It certainly was a mystery, given that the two men never met, spoke by phone, or corresponded as long as they lived.

Some say Hearst did it because Graham held the same unflinching condemnation of Communism as the publishing magnate. Others believed Graham promoted a lifestyle that was good for all Americans. Some have stated a maid tipped off the mogul when he asked her what she was doing that evening. The more cynical ones held to the belief that Graham made for "good copy" and sold newspapers. (Years later a story circulated that Hearst's sons revealed that their father attended the tent revival in disguise in a wheelchair with his longtime mistress, silent film actress Marion Davies, in tow.)

I happen to think it's a much deeper reason: divine intervention. The Bible has demonstrated time and again the many examples of unlikely figures helping godly people.

King Artaxerxes supplied the resources for Nehemiah to rebuild the walls of Jerusalem.

King Cyrus led the Medo-Persian forces to overcome Babylon, and the Bible mentions him by name as "accomplishing what God pleased" (Isaiah 44:28 NIV).

The Bible also reminds us that "The king's heart is like a stream of water directed by the Lord; He guides it wherever He pleases" (Proverbs 21:1 NLT).

William Randolph Hearst was certainly a "king" in his day, and the Lord moved him to launch Billy Graham.

The additional attention showered by Hearst's journalistic henchmen pumped new life into the campaign, which was extended repeatedly. Suddenly, crowds were no longer a problem.

Night after night, the meetings continued to draw overflow crowds. The tent's capacity was expanded to more than nine thousand seats. No outside writer could quite explain what was happening inside the tent, but God was definitely present.

In late October 1949, one of Cynthia Zamperini's neighbors invited her to one of the meetings. The neighbor was concerned because Cynthia and her husband, Louis, were in the process of filing for divorce. Cynthia was at her wits' end. Louis was a former world-famous Olympic runner, World War II B-24 bombardier, and prisoner of war whose life was later brilliantly chronicled in Laura Hillenbrand's bestselling book *Unbroken*. He had suffered from alcoholism and depression—the result of PTSD due to two plane crashes, forty-seven days adrift in the ocean in a life raft, and a long stint in a Japanese POW camp.

Louis fervently prayed one day while clinging to that life raft. *God, if I survive this ordeal and get back to America alive, I'll seek You and serve You*, he promised. Suffice to say, God came through on His end, but Louis did not. And the guilt consumed him when he got back to the States.

I was blessed to befriend Louis toward the end of his life. I became aware of him when I read a newspaper story about his harrowing ordeal at sea and in the Japanese POW camp, capped off by how he came to Christ. The article was accompanied by a photo of him riding a skateboard. He was in his nineties!

I searched him on the Internet, found out he was alive, sought him out, and interviewed him on multiple occasions, including once at Angel Stadium in front of fifty thousand people.

Louis was the real deal, and he remembered his story in vivid detail, recounting it blow-by-blow with amazing recollection. He was one of the most colorful and amazing people I have ever met.

One of the things we enjoyed was eating at El Cholo, our favorite Mexican restaurant in Corona del Mar, California. Louis confided in me that one of the things that kept him going through the hell he endured was thinking about his favorite item on the El Cholo menu— the hallowed #1 plate, consisting of a rolled taco, cheese enchilada, and beans and rice.

Louis also told me about that deal he made with God and how he reneged on it. He promised the Lord that he would follow Him if he was delivered from that miserable life raft, bobbing around the ocean and encircled by sharks. The Lord answered his prayer, though not in the way Zamperini had hoped. He was picked up by a Japanese ship and taken to a POW camp, where he was singled out for torture because of his Olympic fame. But he did survive, and a deal is a deal.

Louis's wife, Cynthia, was absolutely God-sent. She and Louis met on a Florida beach in January 1946. They were engaged after two weeks and married after two months. But their whirlwind courtship quickly soured. It was apparent to Cynthia that her new husband had serious psychological scars. He was hounded by the demons of his past, suffering from flashbacks and nightmares. He turned to the bottle to ease his suffering, but it only made things worse. One night he dreamt he was strangling "The Bird," the sadistic Japanese commander who had tormented him in the POW camp, only to find when he woke up that he was strangling his now-pregnant wife. Cynthia begged him to seek professional help, but what he suffered from did not have a clinical diagnosis; the term PTSD didn't come into use until the 1970s when Vietnam-era soldiers started coming home. Louis went out drinking almost every night. His behavior was boorish and draining; Cynthia felt she had no alternative and filed for divorce.

Billy's Crusade was all the buzz in Los Angeles, and word eventually filtered down to Cynthia. She asked Louis to take her to hear Billy, but he wasn't having it. She went alone, and at the end of the service, she accepted the invitation to receive Christ. She had a palpable glow when she entered the house that night that even Louis could see. She sat him down, told him she'd had a spiritual awakening, and that she wasn't going to divorce him. He was happy she wasn't giving up on them, but he wanted no part of Christianity.

Cynthia convinced Louis the following night to attend the Crusade. And he went—reluctantly.

God's hand was on Billy in a special way that night, and when he finished preaching, Louis couldn't take it anymore.

"I got under conviction and was so mad because of the Scriptures he read," Louis said. "I grabbed my wife and said, 'Let's get out of here.

Don't ever bring me back to a place like this again.' But the next day she persuaded me in going back. I said, 'Okay, I'll go under one condition. When the fellow says, "Every head bowed and every eye closed," I'm getting out.' She said, 'Fine.'"

I suspect Cynthia did everything she could to get Louis back into that tent, knowing the Holy Spirit was working on him. That night, Billy preached from 1 John 5:11–12: "And this is the record, that is, the witness of God, eternal life and this life is in His Son. Now, he that has the Son has life; he that has not the Son has not life."

When Billy read those verses, they zapped Louis right in the heart.

"Of all my near-death experiences, my life never passed before my eyes," he said. "But when Billy Graham quoted Scripture, my life did pass before my eyes."

It wasn't pretty. He saw scenes from the POW camp, but equally as ugly was his life after he got home. And he didn't like what he saw: a sloppy drunk. There was never a shortage of alcohol for Louis because, when he showed up in a bar, everyone wanted to buy the war hero a drink. Whatever anger he held on to from the past, he finally let go. When he received Christ as his Lord and Savior, he instantly felt the love and peace of God. And he was finally delivered from all his demons.

"I knew I was through getting drunk," Louis said. "I knew I was through smoking, and I knew I'd forgiven all of my guards including The Bird. Never dawned on me again that I hated the guy. That was the first night in all those years I'd never had a nightmare, and I haven't had one since."

The change in Louis's life was so complete that he returned to Japan to share the Gospel with hundreds of the Japanese troops he'd once despised. This time, the tables were turned—they were the ones behind bars, having been prosecuted for war crimes. Louis ministered to them, seeing many of them come to Christ.

He traveled around the world, shared his faith, spoke at several Billy Graham Crusades, and forged a strong relationship with Billy that lasted until his own death at age ninety-seven on July 2, 2014. I can tell you this: Louis was a bold witness for Jesus to the very end.

He also remained very fit. Louis told me one of the secrets was never taking elevators; and when we had him speak at our church, he powered up the stairs like a teenager. Because he was a former Olympian, he would sometimes challenge passersby to a race. He would say, "Hey, want to race an Olympic athlete?" They took the bait, thinking they could easily beat an old man, but much to their shock, he would win...and then he would share the Gospel with them. That was Louis.

A week after the Zamperinis came to faith, another troubled couple made their way into the big tent to walk the sawdust trail. Jim and Alice Vaus compulsively decided to attend a Sunday service in early November 1949. They had heard of the meetings, and Jim, who knew Stuart Hamblen, had read about his born-again experience in the papers.

They drove past the tent slowly, taking it all in. It was hard to miss the sign above the tent: "Greater Los Angeles Revival—Billy Graham." Thousands of people were milling around. There was excitement in the air. The couple looked at each other for an answer.

"Well, honey, let's go," Jim suggested.

That was a surprising decision, given where Jim Vaus's life was at that time. He was a private detective and electronics surveillance expert who was doing contract work for the Los Angeles Police Department and the mafia. He surreptitiously wiretapped and collected evidence to convict a Hollywood madam, low-level criminals, and various mafiosos.

In time, he discovered there was more money working for mafiosos than collecting evidence against them. He ended up working for Ben "Bugsy" Siegel in Las Vegas, but after Siegel's 1947 murder for skimming money from the New York bosses, Vaus moved to Los Angeles. Later, he got involved with Mickey Cohen, who had Vaus spy on the cops—a precarious position, since Vaus was still working for the LAPD.

Vaus witnessed several people get killed through his nefarious activities with Cohen and skirted death a few times himself. A man in that business instinctively knows it's not long before his number eventually comes up; perhaps that's why Vaus thought going to Billy's service that night might not be a bad thing. Or it could have been the fact that, like Hamblen, Vaus was raised in the faith. His father, James Arthur Vaus, was a Baptist preacher, as well as a dean at the Bible Institute of Los Angeles. At one time, Vaus had seriously considered following in his footsteps. He even attended Wheaton College for a semester and got involved again in church life when he moved to Hollywood. He attended Hollywood Presbyterian Church, eventually led the men's singing, and even dated Henrietta Mears's niece for a time! God definitely moves in mysterious ways and strange circles—sometimes with characters out of a Dashiell Hammett detective novel.

When Pearl Harbor was attacked, Vaus was drafted. He served as a radar man but then was court-martialed for misappropriation of government property—he lent a slide projector to the church. He was sentenced to ten years at a military prison where he worked as an electrician and taught school mathematics and elementary radio. After the war ended, he received a pardon from President Harry Truman in December 1946. Upon his discharge, he started an electronics engineering business, and well, we know where he ended up from there. But where was he headed?

When the Vauses entered the tent, Jim quickly took notice of the standing-room-only crowd of 6,500 people. Alice was nine months pregnant and ready to give birth at any moment, which got them an instant escort to the front. A kindly couple gave up their seats so Alice could listen in comfort. Jim? Not so comfortable once he settled in. He decided he was going to remain emotionally detached and keep his mental distance. But that proved to be nearly impossible once Billy took the stage.

That night, Billy preached on the passage in the Gospel of Mark where Jesus queries: "For what shall it profit a man, if he shall gain the whole world, and lose his own soul?" (Mark 8:36 KJV).

When the invitation came, the six-foot-five, 250-pound Vaus put out the vibe that he was not to be approached by any of the counselors. One—Billy Schofield—didn't get the memo or didn't care. He tapped Vaus on the shoulder.

"Brother, are you saved?" Schofield asked. "Don't you want to go forward?"

Vaus remembers staring daggers at the man and contemplating violence.

"All I could think about was that if he says one more word, I had it figured out, the place where he was going down and the place where I was going out. And he didn't say anything else," Vaus said.

A moment of silence passed, then Billy stepped to the platform and spoke.

"There is a man in this audience tonight who has heard this message many times before, but he has never given his life to Christ, and this may be his last opportunity," Billy said softly. Vaus rightly sensed God was speaking directly to him.

"OK, I'll go," he said to Schofield, then invited Alice to join him. Billy saw the hard-to-miss Vaus and his wife making their way up to the front and bought them some time by asking Barrows to have the audience sing one more verse of the final song to give them time to reach the altar. Billy's perception of others and his discernment was uncanny; to me, this showed serious skill.

As Alice recommitted her life to Christ, Jim knelt down in the prayer tent and handed his over: "God, if You'll mean business with me, I'll mean business with You. If You can take the tangled mess of my life and straighten it out, all I have is Yours. I'll hold back nothing."

Vaus's conversion also made the November 8 headlines of the *Los Angeles Times*: "Wire-Tapping Vaus Hits Sawdust Trail." Three nights later, he stepped on the platform where Billy stood to make a public profession of faith.

A few days later, he paid Billy a visit and asked: Would he like to meet mobster Mickey Cohen?

A situation like this often presents ethical issues for laypeople. At this point, I must confess my fondness for films about organized crime. In fact, one the greatest guests I've ever interviewed at one of my crusades is former mafia boss Michael Franzese. He was the son of the notorious underboss of New York's most violent and feared Colombo crime family. At his most affluent, he generated an estimated five million to eight million dollars a week from legal and illegal businesses. It was a life filled with power, luxury, and deadly violence.

When I later got to know Michael, he told me he was put in solitary confinement (known as "the hole") in prison, and a guard gave him a Bible that he began to read. Sometime after Michael asked Christ into his life, he was given cassette tapes of my preaching, which he listened to continually. When Michael got out of prison, he mentioned this when giving his testimony. We finally met and became good friends.

Billy's take on wanting to meet Mickey Cohen was probably different from mine. He often said he'd go anywhere to talk to anyone about Christ.

Vaus, Billy, and Cliff Barrows quietly exited the tent one night after a meeting in order to dodge the press. They drove in Vaus's nondescript car to avoid being tailed, then headed to Cohen's home on Moreno Drive in Brentwood.

As they inched closer to the house, Billy spotted a car parked across the street with a suspicious man sitting inside. (Cohen was under surveillance and his wires were tapped by the LAPD; additionally, there was a contract out on Vaus's life.) When they stepped out of the vehicle, Cohen greeted them at the front door. He was surprisingly genial...and short. Billy instantly thought of Zacchaeus in the New Testament, the diminutive tax collector who scaled up a tree in order to get a better view of Jesus over the heads of others.

Billy was surprised that the underworld figure had a case of the nerves over meeting him.

"I don't think Cohen had ever met a clergyman. He was very nervous and he said, 'What do you want to drink?'" Billy remembered. "I said, 'Well, give me a Coca-Cola.' And so he brought me a Coca-Cola."

The hospitable but anxious mobster poured himself one as well. Vaus explained to Cohen the transformation he had undergone a few nights before, giving Billy an opening to talk about the Gospel and how Cohen could have salvation through Jesus Christ.

Cohen, who was Jewish, responded that he respected Billy and what he'd done for Vaus. Never mentioning his life of crime, Cohen said he wasn't a stranger to good works. He ticked off all the charitable organizations he had supported over the years, including the Zionist movement in Israel. He dug through several shelves and cabinets, finally fishing out a dust-covered Bible the Israeli government had given him for his financial gift of three hundred thousand dollars. It was important to Cohen for Billy to know he had a Bible.

Their meeting was interrupted by a phone call. It was an Associated Press reporter looking for verification on a story he was working on. He wanted to know if Cohen was having a private meeting with evangelist Billy Graham.

"No!" Cohen boomed. "And if that guy ever showed up around here, I wouldn't let him in, anyway." He hung up the phone and looked at his guest. "You understand, Billy?"

Billy did indeed. He was a quick study. But he was also a dutiful servant of God. He wasn't afraid to end the meeting with a simple request: that they pray.

Cohen did not end up becoming a Christian, but he and Billy parted on friendly terms. They would meet again in 1957 during Billy's famed New York City Crusade, and they also had a nice reunion with Jim Vaus, who remained an outspoken and committed Christian the rest of his life, dedicating his life to youth ministry. Billy would tell reporters that he constantly prayed for Cohen because he had the potential to become one of the greatest Gospel preachers of all time. Billy was the ultimate optimist, another endearing quality of his.

Despite Billy's promise not to say a word about their meeting, a newspaper had been tipped off. The headline read: "Wiretapper in Confession as Evangelist Tries to Save Cohen." Looking back, Billy thought the man inside the car across the street was a reporter. Regardless, he couldn't stay out of the headlines.

As the campaign was extended into its fifth week, the team rearranged the seats to accommodate three thousand additional people. Then they doubled the size of the tent, which ran almost five hundred feet long. On Billy's thirty-first birthday on November 7, approximately fifteen thousand people showed up—the campaign's largest crowd.

On November 20, the campaign finally ended after eight weeks. An estimated four hundred clergymen stood on the platform with Billy for the final service, facing a crowd of about eleven thousand. "The revival that started here won't end with the folding of this tent," Billy said in conclusion.

When Billy's train had arrived in Los Angeles in mid-September, he was brimming with enthusiasm. Heading home, he'd lost 20 pounds and suffered from exhaustion. And it was no wonder—he had preached 65 sermons to a total of 350,000 people, a quarter million more than the committee's original goal. Around 6,000 people either gave their lives to the Lord for the first time or made recommitments. In addition to his soul-stirring sermons, Billy spoke to countless civic, school, and business groups, registering three to four appearances a day. He gave countless interviews and sold thousands of Hearst's newspapers. Even celebrities wanted in on the action. He met with Spencer Tracy, Katharine Hepburn, Jimmy Stewart, and director Cecil B. DeMille, who offered him a screen test for his planned remake of *The Ten Commandments*.

Once Billy settled into his seat on the train, the other passengers treated him like a returning war hero. At every stop, reporters climbed aboard to request an interview. Whatever he said found its way into print; he had crossed over into another realm.

"Something was happening that all the media coverage in the world could not explain, and neither could I," Billy reflected of the Los Angeles campaign. "God may have used Mr. Hearst to promote the meetings…but the credit belonged solely to God. All I knew was that before it was over, we were on a journey from which there would be no looking back."

I have a personal family story that connects me to the tent as well: one of the counselors that night was none other than my Uncle Fred Jordan.

Uncle Fred went on to found the Fred Jordan Mission, which still reaches out to thousands of homeless and hurting people on L.A.'s Skid Row today. Billy's legacy from that Crusade not only lives on—it thrives.

CHAPTER TWENTY-ONE

King of All Media

For the generation that survived the Great Depression and the Second World War, the 1950s was their reward.

Average family income grew as much in the decade after the war as it had in the previous fifty years combined, almost tripling. The ability to improve one's quality of life came to be seen as a basic right. A man with one job could support a wife who didn't work, own a home and a car, raise a family, and go on vacations.

Ten percent of the population bought brand-new homes in the suburbs and shiny new cars. After production moratoriums on automobiles during the war, factories began churning out long, low, wide, flashy cars decked out with tail fins, chrome, and eye-popping paint jobs.

You gotta love those '50s cars! Especially the ones from 1955–1958. It truly was a golden era for automotive design. What could be more exaggerated than those fins jutting from the back of the Cadillac, which from tip to tail seemed to measure about thirty feet? These cars were not always practical, but they were cool.

Seventy-seven percent of homes featured a TV set—black and white at first, then color. They watched Westerns like *Gunsmoke, Bonanza*, and *The Cisco Kid*. They watched game shows like *The Price Is Right* and *Truth or Consequences*. Sitcoms like *I Love Lucy, Father Knows Best*, and *Leave It to Beaver* mirrored their lives and outlooks.

Despite TV, reading was still immensely popular among all classes. Writers like Ernest Hemingway, John Steinbeck, Ayn Rand, and Ray Bradbury were read by gas station attendants and the wealthy alike.

In 1955, Disneyland opened in Southern California, signaling a surge of optimism and investment in entertainment. It doesn't get any happier or more wholesome than Disneyland.

Smiling above it all was Second World War hero and retired U.S. Army General Dwight D. Eisenhower. "Ike" was president from 1953 to 1961 and was viewed by most as a paternal figure. Ike was a moderate conservative (except when he threatened to drop the bomb on the Chinese until they agreed to peace in the Korean War). He launched the idea of an interstate highway system, played golf, and kept life quiet. Ike was who everyone wanted and needed after the two previous and tumultuous decades.

Communism was on the minds of many. In February 1950, a U.S. senator from Wisconsin named Joseph McCarthy presented a list to the U.S. State Department of hundreds of people in government, entertainment, academia, and labor unions he alleged were members of the Communist Party, thus ruining their lives. When Russia launched its first satellite in 1957, Americans determined that the Soviets and Maoist China were a threat to their safety and way of life.

Hollywood played up that fear by releasing a raft of science fiction movies that either revolved around the bomb (think giant ants created by nuclear testing) or alien invasions (like *The Blob*). Outside of that genre, James Dean, Marlon Brando, and Marilyn Monroe were the era's biggest movie stars. All three embodied some form of defiance. Dean and Brando were rebels, and Monroe just oozed sex appeal without saying a word in a time when couples like Lucy and Ricky Ricardo pointedly slept in separate beds on TV.

In general, culture zigged against the mainstream. Elvis Presley shocked the nation by singing what had been considered black music and suggestively wagging his hips on TV. Jackson Pollock painted huge canvases with wild splashes of color, rejecting any kind of conventional representation. In literature, a group of writers and poets called the Beatniks turned against anything valued in American society, like religion, sobriety, materialism, and conformity. All of them set the stage for the wider rebellion of the 1960s.

Once Billy had spent a few weeks recovering from the Los Angeles campaign, he regained his strength and hit the ground running. He wasted no time in putting his newfound celebrity status to productive use. Within a year, his team had organized the Billy Graham Evangelistic Association, based in Minneapolis, to plan and finance his fledging ministry and its citywide campaigns, which were called "Crusades" from that point forward. Later, he would launch a popular weekly radio program called *The Hour of Decision* (which later became a weekly TV series) and a busy movie production company called World Wide Pictures. Books and a nationally syndicated newspaper column were also in the pipeline.

Billy quickly followed Los Angeles with a Crusade in Boston, drawing overflow crowds and extensive media coverage. Billy was intimidated by the area's reputation as the educational capital of the United States, home to the country's most elite colleges and universities. They included Harvard, Yale, Dartmouth, Brown, Tufts, and Amherst College. The clergy, academics, students, and laypeople in the region had a very liberal attitude, which didn't jibe with Billy's view of the Bible. Many saw Billy as a throwback, even stating he was setting religion back at least a century.

But he didn't need to worry. He was warmly received by the media, the Roman Catholic Church, and college students. The seventeen-day Crusade (doubling the original length) was an unqualified triumph.

Next was a Crusade in Columbia, South Carolina, a friendlier region to the evangelist's message. That three-week Crusade, which took place from February 19 to March 12 and drew an estimated 180,000 people of mixed races, marked the start of Billy's friendship with South Carolina governor Strom Thurmond. The 1948 presidential candidate promoted Billy's meetings in the area and urged him to stay in the cavernous governor's mansion.

That was fortuitous for Billy, because Thurmond's other houseguest was magazine magnate Henry R. Luce, publisher of *Time* and *Life*, both of which had already written about Graham and continued to do so for years. Luce was known as "the most influential private citizen in the America of his day," and he had a lot in common with the Grahams. Like Ruth, Luce's parents were missionaries, and he was a committed Christian. He hoped Billy's revival in Los Angeles would catch fire nationwide and planned to give him the needed ink if that occurred. The men spent several hours discussing spiritual awakening and the spread of Communism. An enduring friendship soon developed. A week later, *Time* ran a large spread on Graham, touting him as an emerging national figure worth listening to.

Billy used his influence to promote his messages. No target was bigger than the highest office in the land. He wrote to President Harry Truman—a Southern Baptist like himself—asking for a meeting, but was rebuffed. While in Boston in early 1950, he told a reporter he hoped to "get President Truman's ear for thirty minutes, to get a little help" in spreading the Gospel. He later sent a telegram urging the president to declare a National Day of Prayer and repentance as a step toward international peace. When Communist forces invaded North Korea a few weeks later, he sent another urgent telegram, stating that millions of Christians were praying for God to give Truman wisdom and urging him to force a "showdown with Communism now." They could not let down South Korea, which was home to more Christians per capita than any other nation in the world.

Shortly afterward, Democratic congressmen Joe Bryson of South Carolina, Herbert Bonner of North Carolina, and House Majority Leader John W. McCormack of Massachusetts arranged for Billy to finally meet President Truman in the Oval Office at noon on July 14, 1950.

Billy was thrilled, but he didn't go alone. He expanded his invitation to include his team members—Cliff Barrows, Grady Wilson, and Gerald Beavan, his new press secretary, whom he'd lured away from Northwestern Schools. The men came dressed to the nines in their most flamboyant attire: double-breasted pastel suits, wide hand-painted ties, and white buck shoes—a not-so-subtle fashion nod to Truman, who was a haberdasher before getting into politics. Looking back, Billy recognized they were probably a little over the top (a reporter described Billy's suit as "pistachio green"): they turned many a head as they walked down Pennsylvania Avenue toward the White House.

Once the men arrived, they were politely but firmly told by Truman's secretary they had twenty minutes with her boss. The insinuation was crystal clear: don't deviate or linger past the allotted time. Truman had a lot on his mind, given this was a month after the start of the Korean War. Meeting four evangelists dressed like a barbershop quartet was not his priority.

The president cordially greeted the men, but his face seemed to give him away. The flashy suits and buck shoes no doubt gave off the wrong impression to the commander in chief.

When he gathered his wits, Truman told the men he had heard about their great success, congratulated them, and the conversation from there unfolded quickly. Billy updated him about campaigns in Los Angeles, Boston, and South Carolina, reiterating that he had publicly called upon him to declare a National Day of Prayer. Truman nodded but didn't specifically acknowledge the request. Billy then switched gears, commending the president for his quick actions regarding Kim Il-sung's invasion of South Korea despite news reports that it was disastrous. The room grew a bit…warm.

Billy was eager to hear about Truman's religious background and prodded him about that. Truman replied that as a fellow Baptist he lived by the lessons of the Sermon on the Mount, in which Jesus declared that those who seek humility and hunger for righteousness shall be blessed.

In his zeal, Billy corrected the president. He told him in front of all of his men that it was faith in Christ and His death on the cross that Truman really needed.

Billy didn't realize he was doling out unsolicited advice to the world's most powerful man. He was thirty-one. Truman was sixty-six at the time.

When he took the oath of office the day after President Franklin Roosevelt died suddenly of a massive stroke—just eighty-two days into his new role as the nation's vice president—Truman had told reporters, "Boys, if you ever pray, pray for me now. I don't know if you fellas ever had a load of hay fall on you, but when they told me what happened yesterday, I felt like the moon, the stars, and all the planets had fallen on me."

After Roosevelt died, Truman consoled First Lady Eleanor Roosevelt, asking if there was anything he could do for her.

"Is there anything *we* can do for you?" she replied. "For you are the one in trouble now!"

Three months after he assumed the presidency, Truman met with Winston Churchill and Joseph Stalin—two of the most important men in the world—at Potsdam. He swam with sharks. A month after that, he ordered nuclear weapons dropped on Japan. It was the hardest decision he'd ever made in his life. Now, perhaps in his perception, there was a young stripling standing in his office wearing a pistachio-colored suit and buck shoes and telling him the way things were.

The famous Missourian stood up, a clear signal that their time was up. Billy and his men were, in effect, getting the presidential boot. But before that happened, Billy asked if they could pray before they left. He then put his arm around Truman, unknowingly breaking another rule of protocol. It was just Billy's way, but it sounds like Truman wasn't a touchy-feely kinda guy.

"And of course that was taking advantage of the president's gracious-ness in receiving us," Billy said years later.

Billy peeked at his wristwatch when he finished the prayer and was horrified. He went five minutes over the allotted time. And from a public-relations standpoint, things were about to get a whole lot worse.

An entire press corps pounced on Billy and his men when they stepped onto the White House grounds, wanting to know details about their meeting with Truman. Unschooled in presidential protocol, they happily recounted details and recreated for the press how they knelt in prayer for a picture that appeared in newspapers nationwide. It was a major faux pas on Billy's part; he was still as green as his pistachio-colored suit when dealing with the press.

It didn't take long for Truman's press secretary to leak to Drew Pearson, who had a nationally syndicated column called "Washington Merry-Go-Round," that Billy was "persona non grata" for breaching the details of the private conversation. Truman was offended that Billy "made a show of himself" and quoted him without authorization; he considered him a user. Billy could see his point of view and later admitted it was a terrible mistake on his part.

"I did not know that you didn't quote the president or anybody like that," Billy said. "And I learned a great lesson that has helped me through the years—not to quote famous people."

To add insult to injury, Billy's request for a signed photograph of Truman was never fulfilled, and the thirty-third president never invited him back to the White House. It was a hard lesson learned.

Billy learned to keep the confidence of some very well-known people, especially those in power. And he learned well.

When I first got to know Billy, I pumped him endlessly for details about people he had met who literally walked out of the pages of history. He was very tight-lipped about what the famous told him, which to me was a very impressive quality. And he wouldn't talk about those who weren't famous at all, except for one time: John F. Kennedy.

Years later in 1967, Billy met with Truman at his home in Independence, Missouri, and profusely apologized for his naiveté. He said Truman was quick to forgive the incident, realizing that the evangelist had not been briefed by his team about what to say after he left his office.

Billy vowed he'd never repeat the same mistake if given another opportunity by a person in power or influence—and he didn't. He gave spiritual counsel to subsequent presidents and was always sure to keep their confidence.

Billy's ministry surged at a Crusade in Portland, Oregon, in September 1950. That's when *The Hour of Decision* and Billy Graham Evangelistic Films were birthed.

More than five hundred thousand people attended the Portland Crusade, which lasted six weeks. There, Bob Pierce—an evangelical missionary, documentary filmmaker, and the founder of World Vision, whom Billy met through Youth for Christ—suggested to Billy that he produce films that would be evangelistic in nature. While studying at Wheaton College, Billy had seen a "Christian" film and thought it was seriously lacking in quality and content, unlikely to appeal to a secular audience. He felt there was a huge vacuum in this arena but never envisioned himself as a filmmaker. Sensing that something special was taking place with the Crusades, Pierce suggested to Billy that filmmaker Dick Ross should tag along. Ross, the owner of Great Commission Films, and a small crew shot a sixteen-millimeter color documentary called *The Portland Story* (later retitled *Mid-Century Crusade*). It was shown in churches throughout the Pacific Northwest and was well-received.

Based on that success, Billy made Ross the president of Billy Graham Films (which was officially changed to World Wide Pictures in 1980). The team also felt that more people might go see a fictional movie about a Crusade. The end result was *Mr. Texas*, the story of a rodeo rider who attends a Crusade in Fort Worth and ultimately receives Christ.

Billy wanted to make some noise by renting out the Hollywood Bowl in early October 1951 to screen *Mr. Texas*. It was a splashy affair, attended by top director Cecil B. DeMille, Paramount Studios executives

Y. Frank Freeman and Walter Wanger, and film stars Redd Harper and Cindy Walker.

For Billy to start a Christian film studio at this time was nothing short of revolutionary—a huge risk, and not without controversy. Today Christian films are a regular part of our culture, with some doing impressive numbers like the 2018 blockbuster *I Can Only Imagine*, which was directed by my friends Jon and Andy Erwin and made over eighty-five million dollars at the box office.

That all started with Billy.

Even though *Mr. Texas* was low-budget, the screening at the Hollywood Bowl rivaled any studio premiere: red carpet, velvet ropes, twenty-five searchlights crisscrossing the sky, and a mammoth forty-foot screen. More than thirty thousand people showed up, with five thousand of them sitting on the lawn after all the seats were filled.

The reviews by the mainstream media were terrible, but that didn't stop more than five hundred people from coming forward at Billy's invitation after the screening, much to his surprise. Nor did it stop World Wide Pictures from making more movies.

The company built its own sound stages and post-production facilities in Burbank, California, literally a block away from the Walt Disney Studio. In all, it produced more than two hundred dramatic and documentary films—including some classics like *The Restless Ones* (1965), *The Hiding Place* (1975), and *Joni* (1979).

The company knew it would never compete with the major studios, so it was forced to be clever in its distribution. Some of the films had limited theatrical releases, but most were shown on national television in time slots that normally went to Graham's Crusade broadcasts. In addition to presenting the Gospel in a new and creative way, these films led to countless decisions for Christ over several decades.

"I became a Christian at Lake Tahoe where *Mr. Texas* was shown in a small Presbyterian church," one viewer, Pat Whitehouse, recalled in 2014. He later joined the seminary and counseled at a Billy Graham Crusade in San Francisco. "I was running from God. In the film, Billy

Graham said, 'Has Christ become the master of your life?' I prayed to receive Christ."

As far as Billy was concerned, that was the best review the film could ever receive.

Another major win for Christ manifested at the Portland Crusade, but it started in Boston. That's when Billy heard about the passing of Dr. Walter A. Maier, a Lutheran theologian, university professor, and radio preacher from St. Louis. His show, *The Lutheran Hour*, ran from 1930 and ended with Maier's sudden death (a heart attack) on January 11, 1950, at age fifty-six. He was one of only two preachers on national radio at the time.

Billy had met him during his pastorate at the Village Church when Maier appeared as a guest speaker at his popular speaker dinners. Shaken by the news of Maier's death, Billy immediately dropped to his knees in prayer in his hotel room. He beseeched God to find someone equally as impactful to fill his shoes.

Billy didn't give it much thought again until later that summer. He and Cliff Barrows were eating lunch at a New Jersey diner when they were practically accosted by a burly man who grabbed Billy's hand and shouted, "Hallelujah! What an answer to prayer!" His name was Dr. Theodore Elsner.

Elsner, a Philadelphia preacher, said Maier's death placed a big burden on his heart, and after much prayer, he had concluded that Billy was his logical successor. Elsner urged Billy to contact his son-in-law, Fred Dienert, and Walter Bennett, Elsner's Christian radio agent. Billy gave a noncommittal response and went about his business. There was no time in his already insanely busy schedule for this sort of commitment. But a few weeks later, Dienert and Bennett showed up at a Michigan conference where Billy was speaking.

The two men introduced themselves. Billy immediately connected the dots after they relayed their intentions of having him fill Maier's shoes. He thanked them for the vote of confidence but politely waved them off, stating he was too busy. They left with their heads down, but they showed up again at Billy's Portland Crusade.

This time, they actually ambushed Billy, asking for a few minutes of his time. Billy wouldn't even acknowledge the two men and ignored them throughout the Crusade, taking extra effort to avoid them. They finally cornered him one night as he exited his hotel, wishing him well as they departed for Chicago.

Billy must have admired their spunk because he laid a near-impossible condition on the two men before they left: if they could raise twenty-five thousand dollars before midnight, he'd do the show.

As outlandish as it was, the promise was as good as gold to these men, who laughed with Billy as they departed for the airport. Billy even told that evening's audience of seventeen thousand people about the hallway encounter and the whammy he placed on the two men. Everyone had a good chuckle, but the joke turned out to be on Billy.

After the service, several friends and well-wishers stopped by Billy's green room. Almost every one of them said they had felt moved by the Spirit of God to get Billy on the air and left cash, checks, and pledges in a shoebox. The total was twenty-four thousand dollars—a grand short of Billy's goal.

Billy and the group felt it was tantamount to a crying shame, but said nothing as they took in a meal, as was their custom after the service. When they got back to the hotel at 11:30 p.m., the desk clerk informed Billy he had two letters for him. They were postmarked two days earlier and sent by a pair of businessmen he barely knew: Howard Butt (a Texas grocery chain heir) and Bill O. Mead (a baker turned international businessman). Each man's correspondence said they would like to hear Billy on the radio, and each individual enclosed a check of five hundred dollars.

That brought the night's tally to exactly twenty-five thousand dollars.

Billy was speechless—but it was impossible to deny that this was clearly a positive sign from God to do the show. He then bowed his head and said a silent prayer. It was one of the few times in Billy's life that he was overwhelmed with emotion. Even though he'd already seen a few miracles in his relatively short life, he hadn't expected this. Needing a breath of fresh air, Billy took the elevator down to the lobby. When the doors opened, there stood Dienert and Bennett. They said when they'd reached the airport, an inner voice told them to skip the flight and head back to the Crusade.

Billy smiled at his new partners and embraced them warmly. He then told them to sign him up for the first thirteen weeks, never knowing the show would last much longer.

In its first five weeks, *The Hour of Decision* earned the highest audience rating ever accorded a religious program. Within eighteen months, it was rated higher than most news commentators in daytime Sunday listening. It also became one of Christian radio's most beloved and longest-running programs of all time, and it eventually grew into one of the most widely distributed radio broadcasts in the world.

Billy effectively used it to help launch a five-week Atlanta Crusade in late 1950, held from October 29 to December 10 at the city's old Ponce de Leon Ballpark. The Crusade drew more than half a million people, and approximately eight thousand souls were won for Christ. It was considered the largest religious gathering in the history of the South up to that time.

The new thirty-minute radio show debuted on November 5, 1950, and featured music that was directed by Cliff Barrows and built around Billy's sermons. It aired on more than 850 radio stations across the country and in five different languages in fifty-five countries on six continents. It ran from 1950 to December 2016, ending with the death of Cliff Barrows, who took it over when Billy grew too infirm to continue. ABC-TV carried the program from 1951 to 1954, and the newspaper industry soon followed.

In 1952, Billy's column, "My Answer," which was distributed by Tribune Media Services, ran six days a week in newspapers across the United States. At its peak, it had a circulation of twenty million readers, and it was still running at the time of Billy's death.

In 1956, Billy, along with Carl F. H. Henry, launched *Christianity Today*. The monthly magazine gave balanced, accurate reporting and biblical commentary. It also brought context to the social culture and theological trends and issues facing Christians. Strategically, Billy wanted the publication to be based in Washington, D.C., to give it a measure of authority. At its peak, *CT* had 190,000 subscribers in seventy-five different countries. In 1960, Billy initiated another magazine called *Decision*, a monthly which provided hard-hitting stories from around the globe, offering an evangelical Christian perspective. Its inaugural issue started with an impressive print run of almost 300,000 copies.

Radio. Television. Movies. Newspaper columns. Books. Magazines. Feature and news stories. Billy was everywhere, in all media, cementing his status as a household name. He was a celebrity, famous not for hitting a ball, slugging a villain, or smooching a starlet, but for spreading the Word of God.

He was the King of all Media and well on his way to becoming an American icon.

CHAPTER TWENTY-TWO

Far East Man

Billy Graham was flying high. The Crusade attendance total had surpassed the 1.5 million mark, with 50,000 recorded decisions for Christ. A year had passed since the Los Angeles campaign had thrust him into the national spotlight, each day bringing a new adventure and opportunities. His calendar filled up quickly, and it was all he could do to keep up with his duties and obligations (including the addition of a new daughter, Ruth "Bunny" Graham, who was born in December 1950).

But not everything went smoothly. Sometimes "busy" inevitably meant making mistakes along the way. The *Atlanta Constitution* gave his "Gate City" Crusade massive coverage, including photographically documenting several scenes that took place in the final meeting. The paper published two pictures side by side: the first depicted ushers collecting "love offerings"—large sums of cash in four big bags. The adjacent picture showed Billy getting into his car, waving farewell to Atlanta, and leaving town. It came across as though Billy was skedaddling with the money and getting out of Dodge.

Billy said the images made him feel like Elmer Gantry, fleecing another flock. He didn't want the photos to characterize or besmirch the ministry, so he immediately addressed the issue.

"I didn't blame the press. I blamed myself," Graham told *Atlanta Magazine* in 1994. "We decided right then and there that we would never take another love offering.... And I was the first [evangelist] who said no."

He also approached Jesse Bader, secretary for evangelism at the National Council of Churches, for counsel. Bader said it would be best to set up a non-profit, elect a board of directors, publish their figures, and pay themselves a salary. He also suggested that Billy take an annual salary of $15,000—the equivalent of what a big-city clergyman received at the time (about $161,000 in 2020 dollars). Additionally, the team pledged not to emphasize offerings in their meetings and to make each Crusade's sponsoring committee handle their income and expenses.

As it turned out, this was the last piece of a puzzle the group had started to assemble back in November 1948 when Billy gathered his evangelistic team to hash out perceived hazards that could sink their ministry if they weren't vigilant. In that important early meeting, Billy, Grady Wilson, George Beverly Shea, and Cliff Barrows met in a motel on Ninth Street in Modesto, California, to discuss tent evangelism, accountability, and how to come up with a set of standards to keep the team above board at all times.

Billy said he felt called to address the pitfalls evangelists had been plagued with in the past and asked the men to go back to their rooms to pray, write down their thoughts, and come back in an hour. When they reconvened, they came up with a list that read like an Encyclopedia Britannica of Sin.

The first on the list was sexual immorality.

This has been the tip of the spear when it comes to ruining a ministry. Unfortunately, when a spiritual leader falls into this sin, it undoubtedly makes headlines. We never hear of the thousands who serve God for decades in pulpits and mission fields, but if leaders fall into this sin, it is the ultimate buzzkill.

And for good reason. People have an expectation that Christians, not to mention preachers, should practice what they preach. And they have every right to hold that view. We should be held to a higher standard.

To remedy this, each member of the team took a vow to never be alone in a room with a woman other than their wives. They were encouraged to avoid such potentially compromising scenarios such as having lunch, counseling sessions, or even something as innocent as a ride to an auditorium or airport without a third party present. When they traveled, they roomed near each other as an added measure of social accountability. They consistently prayed for God's assistance in avoiding temptation.

This has since become known as the "Billy Graham" rule; Vice President Mike Pence lives by the same standard. For some it seems controversial, but for Billy and many others, it was and is an important principle.

The other items covered criticism of pastors and churches and public exaggeration of success. After the *Constitution* photo ran, they added "financial responsibility" to the list. It also led to the formation of the Billy Graham Evangelistic Association in 1950.

The "Modesto Manifesto" established a commonsense template for behavior that served these men well through a half-century of international ministry. I believe the Lord was directing their every step, especially when drawing up this important document.

I know of ministers who have fallen in all those areas. I suppose the devil operates by the old adage "If it ain't broke, don't fix it." He continues to bring down effective leaders with the same old ploys. And when it happens, even if the pastor or preacher is unknown, it makes the news. Then the nonbelievers can wag their collective fingers and say in unison, "Hypocrite!" And trust me, they do.

Billy did not want that to happen to him. And it never did.

Fact is, the Bible promises that with every temptation, there is always a way of escape (1 Corinthians 10:13). Sometimes that is as simple as closing a door, walking out of a room, or using the off button on a remote control. Billy was very careful, and that is why his reputation remained intact throughout his long and very effective ministry.

With a code of conduct established, Billy headed to a place that clearly lacked one. His next milestone took place almost 2,800 miles away from Modesto in the nation's capital. The team held a five-week Crusade in Washington, D.C., from January 13 to February 17, 1952, at the invitation of Democratic and Republican leaders who were hoping for a national awakening.

"This country needs a revival, and I believe Billy Graham is bringing it to us," said Speaker of the House Sam Rayburn, who introduced Billy from the steps of the Capitol Building on February 3. The service was broadcast live on radio and television. Millions across the nation had heard Billy urge Congress to request the president to set aside a National Day of Prayer. Within two years, the legislation was presented to the House of Representatives and passed unanimously. I could hardly imagine such a thing happening in today's politically charged climate.

Still reeling from his earlier encounter with Billy, President Harry Truman chose not to attend the service. However, Billy made a slew of new powerful friends, including senators Richard M. Nixon and Lyndon B. Johnson, two future presidents who would come to count on him for friendship, straight talk, and spiritual counseling. Even more importantly, Billy had taken steps to develop a relationship with the man who would become the next president of the United States: Dwight D. Eisenhower.

A few months before the Crusade in Washington, D.C., Billy had dinner with Texas oil baron Sid W. Richardson and told him how much he admired General Eisenhower, who was serving abroad in France as commander at the Supreme Headquarters of the Allied Powers in Europe (SHAPE). Billy felt the American people needed a candidate who was authentic and embodied integrity and spiritual power. Ike checked all those boxes. Richardson encouraged Graham to write a letter to Eisenhower imploring him to throw his hat into the 1952 election. Richardson personally guaranteed Ike would read it. Some historians have claimed that letter helped inspire Ike to run for president.

It certainly made an impression on him; he wrote Billy back in November 1951. A month later, Billy penned another letter directly to

Eisenhower that reaffirmed his support for his presidential candidacy. He told the general he was praying for him and for God to offer him support, noting that the destiny of the Western World could very well rest on his shoulders. It was a powerful piece of correspondence, and Ike wanted to know from Richardson who exactly was this young man?

He would soon find out.

Billy traveled to Europe after the Crusade in Washington, D.C. Escorted by a military aide, he met Eisenhower in March 1952 at the SHAPE headquarters in Paris. There, Ike, dressed in full uniform and bedecked with medals, greeted him with an outstretched hand and a warm smile. It didn't take long for Eisenhower to speak of his religious upbringing in Kansas as a River Brethren—an offshoot of the Mennonites—where his early life revolved around the church. The River Brethren practiced immersion, foot washing, pacifism, adhering to plain dress, and opposing alcohol, tobacco, and other worldly pleasures. They read the New Testament in the original Greek; Ike had memorized many Scriptures, as Billy had in his youth. Ike was straightforward with Billy, admitting that his military chapel attendance was spotty at best. They also broached the status of the Korean War and the upcoming presidential election during the visit.

Billy was forthright and told Eisenhower that he couldn't publicly support his candidacy. Ike appreciated his honesty and responded that he understood his position. Even though Eisenhower gave no indication that he would run for office, Billy left their two-hour meeting feeling as though he had met the next president of the United States. Several months later, Billy proved to be correct.

When Eisenhower was elected in November 1952, he asked Billy for some Bible verses to use during his inaugural speech. Billy suggested a few, including 2 Chronicles 7:14 ("If my people, which are called by my name, shall humble themselves, and pray, and seek my face, and turn from their wicked ways; then I will hear from heaven, and will forgive their sin, and will heal their land"), which Eisenhower chose to read. In fact, he rested his hand on that passage of Scripture as he took his oath of office.

It was Ike's pastor, Ed Elson, who encouraged him to get baptized on February 1, 1953, just ten days after his inauguration—a move which, I'm sure, was heartily encouraged by Billy. In fact, Ike remains the only U.S. president ever to have been baptized while in office. Eisenhower played a very personal role in popularizing religious faith in America in the 1950s, which included becoming the first commander in chief to attend the Presidential Prayer Breakfast (now the National Prayer Breakfast). Ike credited his relationship with Billy in giving him the courage to put his faith on public display.

A lot of faith was needed where Billy went next: on a Crusade to war-torn Korea.

The trip was inspired by Eisenhower. After petitioning the Pentagon, Billy and his team received military cooperation to visit American soldiers serving in the Korean War. He ended up preaching the Gospel fourteen times to more than seven thousand soldiers during what was the third—and, at that point, bloodiest—year of the Korean Conflict.

When atomic weapons ended World War II, two young State Department aides split the Korean peninsula in half at the Thirty-Ninth Parallel. By the end of the 1940s, two new states had formed: Communist North Korea and anti-Communist South Korea. In June 1950, seventy-five thousand North Korean troops swarmed across the border to take over the South. If South Korea fell, it would lead to a string of other Communist victories across the region. The world was at stake.

So thousands of mostly American troops poured into South Korea. Thousands of Chinese forces fought alongside the North Koreans, raging up and down the peninsula. Seoul changed hands so many times it became almost a deserted ruin. By the time Billy arrived in December 1952 for a Christmas visit, twenty-one thousand Americans had been killed. Peace talks had been underway for a year but progressed slowly. That year had been a series of battles over a series of hills in bloody and sometimes hand-to-hand fighting.

"I thought that if I could see how Christians were suffering in Korea, it would make an impact in my own life, and in turn would enable me to be of greater help to the hundreds of people to whom I have the privilege of ministering," Billy said. "Then, too, the trip would make it possible for me to spend Christmas with the troops, to bring them just a touch of home at Christmastime. That was something I had wanted to do for a long time. During the past two Christmas seasons, I had found it difficult to sit down and enjoy my dinner as I thought of the boys in the cold, muddy trenches of Korea."

Dressed in an army parka and military-issued snow Pac boots, which kept him warm in the sub-freezing temperatures (some days it reached -30 degrees), Billy was literally dressed for battle. But the war he would wage was deeply spiritual. Billy attended war briefings, visited wounded and dying soldiers in a mobile hospital unit, and spent time with patients in a children's hospital, many of whom were orphaned as a result of the conflict. He also delivered sermons to American G.I.s in tents, recreation halls, chapels, makeshift platforms, and open-air venues. He preached to South Korean churches and at street meetings in small villages through an interpreter, offering up the same message he delivered to the soldiers: They were all sinners. But each was forgiven of their sins if they confessed to Jesus Christ and proclaimed Him as their Savior. It was no cakewalk, and it was done off the radar. Billy did it because he cared.

He was also deeply impacted by what he saw; devastation, fear, and despair were everywhere he traveled. Yet he was touched by the Korean people, who smiled widely, though they seemed to have little to smile about, and were deeply grateful to him for caring enough to visit and speak with them. The most moving experience was when he walked through miles of gooey, ankle-deep mud to reach an orphanage for blind children. There, he witnessed a young blind boy stand and sing in English "The Love of God."

Throughout the Korean trip, Billy slept through heavy gunfire, sometimes on a nighttime train passing through territory that was subject to ambushes and enemy fire. But the more dangerous the situation, the more Billy felt the hand of God on him. It was bitterly cold. Snow covered the ground. (Even in black-and-white photos, Billy's nose was clearly red.) He preached on icy mountains in below-freezing temperatures to helmeted men who stood through his sermon. The pictures are propaganda photos that don't show the truth of what was going on, so almost all the troops look healthy, clean-shaven, and energetic—but a few in the background have the thousand-yard stares of men who have been pushed beyond their limits and kept there.

Billy said of that visit: "I wept more in Korea than in all the past several years put together. These experiences changed my life. I could never be quite the same again...I felt sadder, older. I felt as though I had gone in a boy and come out a man."

This was the meanest side of life he had ever seen. These weren't down-and-outers on Skid Row or a rude crowd who talked over his sermon or folks who'd had a few bad turns in life. They were young, cold, and scared. They'd seen their friends machine-gunned and blown to bits, and they had killed men in hand-to-hand combat. The experience gave him a new and bigger perspective, both on life and on his mission. He had a new appreciation for the task God had laid before him and for the awesomeness of his responsibility.

He needed to spread the Word more widely. In his next Crusade, he would do exactly that.

CHAPTER TWENTY-THREE

Yankee Spellbinder

Billy Graham was hot as lava in the early- to mid-1950s.

He was passionate. Fiery. Authentic. And smart enough to realize this was none of his doing. Billy knew the Lord and the Bible well enough to know the Holy Spirit was at work in his life.

Every Crusade had record-breaking crowds. Every stadium was packed. Every sermon was God-inspired. Every audience came in penitent droves. They were moved by the thousands to walk the aisle to accept Christ or rededicate their lives to Him. If Billy had been in another profession, he'd be the home run king, a victorious military general, the heavyweight champion of the world, and a rock star all rolled up into one. He was a modern-day Moses, but with a pinch of genuine Southern panache and sincere humility.

The North Carolina native was bright, funny, self-effacing, curious, quick on his feet, and bold when it came to his convictions. He was a born leader who changed the way the Gospel was spread. People were hungry for God. They saw Christ in Billy and were drawn to him.

He was America's preacher…a Yankee Spellbinder. After the stumbles, the false starts, and the hiccups that always accompany learning, he mesmerized crowds. He had that rare ability to speak to thousands and make them think he spoke only to them.

Billy had also become a beloved figure abroad, which he proved in his goodwill trip to Korea. What wasn't to love? He was a messenger of hope who took peace and joy everywhere he went and united people of all faiths and walks of life.

So when he returned to England in March 1954—a good seven years after the magical Youth for Christ rallies, and was not welcomed with open arms—it mystified him. "Great Britain had a special place in my thinking," he said.

England was strategic for Billy. London, at the time, was the most populated city on Earth, the media center of Europe, and the first official Crusade for the Billy Graham Evangelistic Association outside the United States. England had rolled out the welcome mat for him during the extended Youth for Christ tour in 1946 and 1947. God was truly at work on that visit with thousands coming to Christ, which Billy had not forgotten.

But what a difference a few years can make. Social and spiritual problems had plagued England since the war. Vestiges of it, like destroyed buildings (now simply piles of rubble and bricks), unexcavated bomb craters the size of double-decker buses, and the ugly, cheap prefab buildings were everywhere. Some commodities were still rationed. Butter, meat, tea, and coal were hard to come by. The government offered inedible "egg powder" and decreed that schoolchildren should be made to take a daily dose of castor oil to build up their bodies.

People still grew vegetables in their gardens instead of flowers and lawns. Relatives abroad sent food parcels. Income taxes were twice what they are today, leaving Britons with little disposable income. Housing was at a premium—half the population lived in private rented accommodations, like rooms or studio apartments. Less than a third of all homes were owner-occupied. Britain was the most urbanized and industrialized country in the world—and the most polluted. The Labour government nationalized the coal mines, the railways, the inland waterways, gas and electricity, the airways, the Bank of England, and the iron and steel industry. Most of the countryside was rural and agricultural. People lived in the sorts of places that look very charming on BBC shows now but were in fact a reflection of poverty. Personal telephones were nonexistent. People got around on bicycles. For longer journeys, they took trains. There was one car for every sixteen people.

In short, life wasn't perfect, but it was much better than it had been with Nazi armies raining bombs on their cities. With that crisis over, it remained to be seen whether Britons felt they needed either God or a tall blonde Yank in a double-breasted suit telling them they needed to be delivered from their sins.

The invitation to go to England had been extended two years before during the Crusade in Washington, D.C. That's when two prominent British Christian leaders—a clergyman and a future member of Parliament—spoke to Billy about the possibility of a London Crusade. A few weeks later, Billy was in England addressing approximately 750 British clergymen in Westminster at the administrative headquarters of the Church of England. He spoke for ninety minutes on the new interest in evangelism and the Gospel in America. He also spoke of the principles that guided his organization, including the commitment to work *with* the churches and not apart from them. That got their ears perking.

The following day he met with a group of leaders who wanted to discuss the possible Crusade in more detail. A follow-up meeting took place in the States with John McCordle and F. Roy Cattell, the latter of whom was the secretary of the Evangelical Alliance of Britain. Billy made excellent use of his time as only Billy could—holding a portion of the meeting in Ruth's hospital room as he awaited the arrival of their fourth child and first son, William Franklin Graham III. When Ruth went into labor on July 14, 1952, a nurse wheeled her to the delivery room where a doctor and medical staff attended to her. Meanwhile, Billy and the two men continued their meeting. After two hours, Billy was told that he had a son, known to the world as "Franklin." Six years later, Billy and Ruth added their final addition to the family when Nelson "Ned" Graham was born in January 1958. Today he is a pastor who prints and legally distributes Bibles in China and trains pastors and lay leaders.

Little did Billy realize that this son would, in his own way, impact the world as well. God would not only use Franklin to save souls through evangelistic outreaches like his father, but would also save lives through the Christian humanitarian organization Samaritan's Purse, founded in the 1970s by Billy's friend Bob Pierce.

Billy felt guilty about not being with Ruth when she gave birth to Franklin, but something good did come of it. He locked down a date for the London Crusade: March 1, 1954.

The promotional plans for London were unprecedented and included a staggering fifty-thousand-dollar publicity campaign (almost half a million in 2020 dollars). It was mainly spent on posters, bumper stickers, and handbills to pump up the Crusade. Even more encouraging was the fact that the Alliance locked in Harringay Arena, a twelve-thousand-seat indoor stadium in working-class North London, to serve as the host site for the meetings. Although they secured a three-month option on the venue, most of the committee felt Billy, an untested American evangelist, would only be there three to four weeks, tops.

He prepared for the London Crusade like a boxer would a title fight. He spent hours walking and hiking the mountain trails in Montreat, getting into fighting trim. He walked, prayed, and meditated on those trails, asking God for favor in England.

"In my entire life, I had never approached anything with such a feeling of inadequacy as I did London. If God did not do it, it could not be done," Billy wrote in his autobiography. "But was I, as some critics suggested, too young at age thirty-five for such an awesome responsibility? I felt I was, but I also knew that I was doing what God had called me to do. In my flesh, I too often dwelled on the question, *Who do you think you are?*"

I think I have a little insight into how Billy felt. I too have felt that pressure before speaking at an evangelistic event. Knowing what you're about to do can be overwhelming.

The Bible speaks of spiritual warfare, teaching that the "god of this world" (Satan) has blinded the eyes of the nonbeliever. So when someone like Billy Graham steps into the gap and seeks to call these people out of darkness into the light, opposition from Satan and his minions is to be expected. And something on the scale of this outreach in England? You can be sure the enemy did not take this sitting down.

When we booked the AT&T Stadium in Dallas, Texas, with seating capacity upwards of eighty-five thousand in 2016, I was under extreme spiritual attack. In the months that led up to the event, which we called "Harvest America," I felt as though I was in a vice that kept getting tighter. It certainly improved my prayer life. And it was a great relief when, by God's grace, the event was filled to overflowing, with thousands more watching in churches and homes around the United States and abroad.

I once asked Billy what he personally felt when he extended the invitation for people to come to Christ in his Crusades. He described it as an incredibly emotionally draining experience, saying, "I feel like power is going out of me."

This is a reference to the time when Jesus was walking through a crowd and a woman who was very sick touched the hem of His garment, and He said, "Who touched me?" He said, "I know that power has gone out of me" (Luke 8:46).

Only the evangelist, even more than the pastor, knows the spiritual warfare dynamic in play when an invitation is extended. You can literally feel the spiritual activity, and it is completely exhausting.

The difference I feel between giving a Bible study to our church and speaking in an evangelistic event in a stadium is night and day.

That all happens when the people are there to hear you.

But first, you have to get them in the venue.

Billy based some of his feelings on the fact that the British media were throwing salvos at him in print before he even reached their shores. It's an interesting enigma to foreigners because England is a country that prides itself on impeccable manners. The people are extremely polite, to the point of being over the top, but the British tabloids press can be the opposite of that. England is a small country, but there are lots of tabloids, all in hand-to-hand combat for the juiciest stories. "Gutter press" was one way to describe some of the more venomous ones. In recent years, they have hacked into the cell phones of famous and powerful people and managed to drive the Duke and Duchess of Sussex (Prince Harry and Meghan Markle) clean out of the country. Some of them run daily photos of half-naked women. One critic described them as tapping into "a national delight in base pleasure and ritual cruelty." They are enter-tainment to the working class, a guilty pleasure to the middle class—and an unrivaled parasite to the upper class.

This was the machine that whetted its knives as Billy, Ruth, and the evangelical team were being ferried over from New York on the SS *United States*. The rags gleefully proclaimed gloom and doom, predicting he would fall on his face in "The Great Wen."

A prominent bishop even piled on, promising that Billy would return to the States with his tail between his legs. British journalist Ivor Davis said Billy's arrival aroused great suspicion.

"I remember well there was a skepticism about Billy Graham in London particularly, where many, especially in the media, first thought he was a Bible-toting pitchman," recalled Davis, who wrote for London's *Daily Express*. "I thought he was the Bible equivalent of an American bodybuilder named Charles Atlas who was well known in Britain. There were others who thought he was reminiscent of Sinclair Lewis' satirical Twenties novel, *Elmer Gantry*."

The Brits did not take kindly to big-mouthed American preachers who crossed the pond coming in an attempt to "save them."

They had seen hell up close in the war and were now living out their reward. British church attendance was at an all-time low, but spirits were high—mostly the kinds served in a pub. Another factor to consider was Americans' reputation among Brits. They were, of course, hugely grateful for the American blood and coin shed to keep them free during the war, even though many complained bitterly that the Yanks were a bit late to the fighting. However, it had been a long war, and there was a common expression used about the American army in England: "Overpaid, over-sexed, and over here." Now, in their minds, another boorish American was landing on their shores.

But they did not know Billy Graham. He was not like their stereo-typical view of the Yank.

He had been prepared by God for this mission.

Out on the water, Billy was starting to loosen up. He enjoyed long walks on the deck of the world's largest and fastest ocean liner with Ruth, spending free time with his team in prayer and Bible studies. And to keep warmed up for what lay ahead, he preached a sermon on a Sunday morning in the ship's ballroom. It swayed to and fro in heavy ocean swells, but what perhaps made him seasick was the message the captain relayed to him the next morning: a member of Parliament was contesting Billy's admission into the country in the House of Commons.

The uproar was caused by a *Daily Herald* piece about a brochure the Billy Graham Evangelistic Association had widely distributed in the United States, seeking money and support for the upcoming London Crusade, that carried the following statement: "What Hitler's bombs could not do, Socialism, with its accompanying evils, shortly accomplished."

The captain informed Billy it was a major folly and political insult to Britain's fourteen-million-strong Labour Party. It was the strongest party in the country at the time, responsible for nationalizing scores of industries and implementing the national healthcare system. The term "Socialist" (with a capital S) was almost always synonymous with the Labour Party, and the aggrieved author of the piece, Hannen Swaffer, stated, "Billy Graham has more gravely libeled us more than anyone has dared to do since the war. It is a foul lie…I urge the Bishop of Barking [Hugh Gough, the Crusade's biggest booster] to disown all this ignorant nonsense before the Big Business whom he sponsors opens his Cru-sade…. And I urge him to call Billy Graham to repentance before he has the effrontery to start converting us!"

Another newspaper jumped on the bandwagon and labeled Graham "Silly Billy."

This was nothing more than the devil's doing. I can tell you from experience that Satan works overtime when I host a crusade.

In 2018, our organization paid for billboards that featured a photo of me holding up a Bible with information about the SoCal Harvest evangelistic event we have been holding at Angel Stadium for over thirty years. We also had placed some banners in a local mall, and there were complaints about me holding a copy of Scripture aloft, as though it somehow would be threatening. Ironically, in the same mall, there were advertisements for movies that had violent, threatening imagery, yet the Bible banner is what was flagged.

To make it even more absurd, the book I was holding up did not even have the word "Bible" on it or a cross, or even the tell-tale ribbon marker coming out of the pages. So I guess a nondescript black book is offensive to some people now.

The whole "controversy" around Billy was not actually about Socialism, but about the Gospel, which everyone knew he fearlessly preached. The Brits would realize this soon enough.

When Billy discovered the root of the problem while still in transit, he frantically called Jerry Beavan, already in London, and contacted the Minneapolis office as well about the brochure. The printer's proof showed the spelling of socialism with a lowercase "s," but the newspaper spelled it with an uppercase "S"—giving it a more political connotation. It changed the word from an ideology to the name of a specific group, and that group was not happy.

Beavan issued an explanation, along with an apology for any misunderstanding, to the British press. Billy also wired apologies to members of Parliament, expressing his most sincere—and desperate—regrets. It was doubtful the recipients were gracious in response.

Word traveled fast, even on a cruise ship. A throng of reporters and photographers showed up in Le Havre, France, when the SS *United States* docked briefly. They came on board and swarmed Billy, looking to fan the flames.

"Who invited you over here, anyway?" one of them angrily asked. Another queried, "Do you think you can save Britain?"

But Billy put his best foot forward and was pleasant but careful. He told them that he would straighten everything out once he got to Blighty. He spent several hours with members of Parliament, including time with the offended Labour Party leader, Geoffrey de Freitas. To Billy's great relief, the British politician graciously accepted his apology.

That was classic Billy. Trying to build a bridge, not burn it.

It reminds me of a Crusade he did in a large American city in the later years of his life and ministry. One of the leading churches was not participating, so Billy asked for an appointment with the senior pastor. Billy arrived punctually, as he always did, and was left to sit in the waiting room for over forty minutes. (I supposed the pastor was attempting to establish his importance.) The pastor finally saw Billy and agreed to participate in the Crusade. Billy was world famous at that point and could have easily gone on with or without that particular pastor's support. But his willingness to diffuse conflict and humble himself, if necessary, was part of what we might call his "secret sauce."

When Billy, dressed sharply in an overcoat, tie and white button-down shirt, made his way to the Southampton dock, he was asked questions by at least two dozen reporters and a dozen photographers. One of the first questions he was asked was why he traveled on a big ocean cruise liner and not humbly, like Jesus?

"Well, Jesus traveled on a donkey," Billy said, then paused for effect. "You find me a donkey that can swim the Atlantic and I'll buy him."

After the laughter subsided, a Pathé news reporter asked about his intentions in coming to their home.

"The purpose of coming to Britain is that we were invited by approximately 1,000 churches in the city of London to come and conduct an evangelistic mission. And we're going to conduct this mission very much as we would in the United States," Billy answered. The reporter followed up with a provocative question on how Billy planned to deal with Russia. He laughed heartily.

"That's not in my area at all. I'm not in politics. I'm a minister of the Gospel of Jesus Christ," Billy said. "And I haven't come to Britain with any idea of saving Britain or changing Britain. I've come here simply to present the message of Christ…I've not come to talk about politics."

It was brilliant public relations. Acknowledge the problem, apologize for it, and *voila!* There's no story left for the press to pursue.

Billy's arrival was splashed on the front page of several evening newspapers. He knew one thing to be sure: he was no longer an unknown quantity in England.

After Billy and Ruth made their way through customs, a large crowd of South Londoners greeted him warmly.

"God bless you, sir. I'm praying for you," said one man, echoing the sentiments of hundreds in the crowd.

Those sentiments were a far cry from the British press, who wished him ill. When his train arrived at Waterloo Station the next day, it was like a scene from *A Hard Day's Night* with the Beatles.

Thousands of screaming British fans ran to the station to welcome Billy and his team. A newspaper stated that the group gathered that day was the biggest crowd since 1920, when Hollywood film stars Mary Pickford and Douglas Fairbanks arrived in London to celebrate their honeymoon.

Close to 150 reporters showed up at the next morning's press conference at Central Hall in Westminster. It was one of the largest press conferences in years, a committee member told Billy, who started off with a prepared statement calling for a revival for men and women to live out the teachings of Christ in their daily lives and relationships. Mostly, he was there to deliver a message of hope.

He could have used some of that hope on March 1, 1954—the first day of the Crusade. He spent most of that day in prayer and study, holed up in his room at the Stratford Court hotel off Oxford Street. It was arguably the smallest and cheapest hotel in London, deliberately chosen to bat away any implications of extravagance. But Billy now had bigger troubles than that. He put in a call to Jerry Beavan, who was at the

Harringay Arena. Billy pulled open a curtain to reveal that it was sleeting outside. Was the weather the same at the arena?

Beavan replied it was the same on his end of town. Even more problematic was that the arena was almost empty and not filling up as quickly as he'd hoped. It should have been half-filled by that time. Beavan, not one for sugarcoating his feelings, felt the first night was going to be a flop.

The British press, who were already there in full force (approximately four hundred members), practically outnumbered the people in the stands. They could smell a disaster in the making. In their estimation, this was going to be better than Christmas morning. Photographers were already taking pictures of the thousands of empty seats while reporters were working on clever headlines to mock Billy and make him a laughingstock. The Yank was done for.

A half-hour later, Beavan gave him the update that about two thousand people showed, but the arena seated twelve thousand. Billy was crestfallen.

Before he and Ruth left for the venue, they got on their knees and prayed—hard. When they arose, Billy left it all up to God. His gloom instantly lifted, and he decided that whatever transpired that evening, God would still be glorified because He would ultimately fill the seats. Once again, Billy placed his trust in the Lord.

During the half-hour ride, freezing drizzle and sleet splashed the windshield of the car. Billy placed his hand in Ruth's.

"Let's go face it and believe that God has purpose in it," Ruth said. They rode the rest of the way in silence.

That night they arrived in plenty of time. No lines of cars or people. When Billy and Ruth stepped out of the car at the back entrance, they were rushed by Crusade director Willis Haymaker.

"Billy, the place is packed and there are five thousand people on the other side trying to beat the doors down," Haymaker said.

"Where did they come from?" Billy asked.

"We don't know," Haymaker replied. "God must have sent them."

The scene inside was awe-inspiring.

Hanging in the center of the arena was a large, inspirational sign: "I am the Way, the Truth and the Life." A mixed choir of two thousand people sat above a flower-decked platform while Cliff Barrows led them in a rendition of "All Hail the Power of Jesus' Name."

When Billy walked in, thousands sang in unison. He made last-minute preparations while Dr. Townley Lord, the Baptist leader, came to the front of the stage and read the invocation.

When Billy finally spoke, it was with great clarity and vision—a sermon he titled "Does God Matter?"

He said he was convinced that night could be the beginning of a great movement of the Holy Spirit.

"But I have one tremendous fear," Billy said, "that you may be looking for a man or a team from America to bring revival. There is only one person who can send revival, and that is the Holy Spirit...I believe there is a hunger for God and that by the grace of God, before three months have passed, we are going to see a great revival in the City of London."

If the hundreds of people who went forward that night indicated anything, it was that there would indeed be a great revival in the City of London.

After that, the Crusade caught fire. Despite inclement weather and snarling traffic, the faithful continued to come night after night. By the following Saturday, the arena was packed to capacity a full hour before the service. Close to thirty-five thousand people were outside, with more than one thousand people who'd traveled a good distance from Wales. Even the cynical and jaded journalists—who had not only predicted but, in some cases, lobbied and hoped for Billy's downfall—were now on board and writing glowing stories. The *London Evening News* created a special "Billy Graham Edition" of the paper. Photographers caught heartwarming images of normally reserved Brits with tears streaming down their cheeks falling to their knees and documented life-changing moments.

Even the op-ed writers did an about-face. A scribe with the *Daily Express* penned a public apology: "To be honest, I was prejudiced about him. We have heard so much here about American hot godspellers and their methods of selling religion, which they seemed to have picked up from the salesmen of insurance. And then, just after breakfast yesterday, I met him. I had better say straight away...I may be making a mistake, but I think he is a good man. I am not so sure that he isn't a saintly man. I just don't know. But make no mistake about this...Billy Graham is a remarkable man."

Another highlight of the Crusade was the Children's Rally, which was hosted by Cliff Barrows on March 3, 1954. It featured international movie star Roy Rogers and his equally famous wife, Dale. The "King of the American Cowboys" sat tall on his famous palomino, Trigger, performing rodeo tricks before thousands of children at a dog track next to Harringay. (The horse knew sixty-odd tricks. He wasn't called the "Smartest Horse in the Movies" for nothing.) After Rogers saddled up, he and Dale gave their testimonies to spellbound Brits, who adored American Westerns. Billy really knew what reached the souls of British children, and it wasn't castor oil.

By the end of the first month, the Crusade had become the hot ticket in London. Socialites from the West End and members of the royal family attended services. Bishops proudly sat on the platform. Thousands clamored for admission. They included doctors, dockworkers, housewives, businessmen, "Teddy Boys," pickpockets, Communists, and cops. The Associated Press was wiring two stories a day back to the States, and invitations came pouring in from all over England for Billy to speak, including from many colleges and universities.

But the wear and tear on Billy's health began to show. At the six-week mark, he had lost fifteen pounds, and his eyes were dark and hollow. Sleep was hard to come by, and when he did get it, he'd collapse into bed, essentially comatose.

Each day brought a new adventure and a new venue. Billy spoke at a variety of locations throughout the greater London area, including Trafalgar Square, Hyde Park, and the Odeon theater in Leicester Square in London's fashionable West End. On the Crusade's closing day on May 22, Billy held two separate meetings at the city's two largest venues. Some

65,000 heard the Gospel at White City Stadium. And at the closing event, Wembley Stadium's crowd numbered more than 120,000—despite the rain, sleet, and frigid temperatures.

More than two thousand people, after a two-hour service, waded through the mud to respond to the invitation at Wembley. As Billy and his team exited the platform, the Archbishop of Canterbury, who had just witnessed the largest religious congregation ever seen in the British Isles, told Grady Wilson, "We may never see a sight like that this side of Heaven."

Contrary to the dire predictions that Billy would fail, more than two million people attended the meetings, and close to forty thousand responded—nearly two-thirds of them under the age of eighteen—to the invitation to make a commitment to Jesus Christ.

During the Crusade, London churches demonstrated a level of unity and cooperation previously unheard of. As a result, they were rewarded with a stream of new believers in their congregations. And in the decades since, many Christian leaders and professionals in the United Kingdom have traced the roots of their own ministries to those magical three months in 1954.

"It was like divine adrenaline for a jaded Church," said Reverend Michael Baughen, a former Bishop of Chester, who was a theology student at the time.

As for Billy, the Crusade put him on the international map, setting the pattern for decades of worldwide Crusades that would reach millions with the Gospel.

He had reached the world stage, as recognizable a figure as the queen or the pope. The next day he received a phone call from someone who had been a central figure on that stage for decades.

CHAPTER TWENTY-FOUR

Shaking Hands with Mr. History

The team was exhausted, and a brief holiday in Scotland was in order. Billy had lost thirty pounds and was looking forward to some rest and relaxation. The day before they were scheduled to leave London, Billy received an unexpected early morning phone call from Jock Colville, secretary to Prime Minister Winston Churchill.

At the beginning of the trip, Billy had written to Churchill seeking an audience. Churchill turned him down flat. But after Billy's triumphant appearance at Wembley, he did an about-face. Colville had asked for Billy's availability the following day for a noon lunch.

Billy was flattered but simply drained. Also, he physically couldn't be there, since he and the team would be headed for Scotland.

Half an hour later the phone rang again. It was Colville once more.

"Would you be able to meet with Mr. Churchill at noon *today*?" Colville asked. "He has a lunch scheduled at twelve-thirty with the Duke of Windsor, who is flying over from Paris, but he can see you before that."

Obviously, Churchill really wanted to meet with Billy. He was not a man who was used to being told no.

The meeting was set after some back and forth. Billy had no idea what it was about or what he was in for, but people usually only wanted to see him for one thing: spiritual matters. In this case, that was somewhat odd.

"I could hardly be called a pillar of the church," Churchill once said.

He was not an active Christian. But he'd had a nanny who inculcated the Gospel in him. Her name was Elizabeth Everest, but he called her "Woom" because he was too young to pronounce "woman." He absolutely adored her. His parents spent almost no time with him during his childhood and teens. His mother was a wealthy American beauty who had many affairs. His father was an aloof statesman who, when he paid any attention to his son at all, berated him for spending money like water and having terrible grades. Neither of them visited him once when he was in prep school at Harrow. Woom did, however. Winston met her at the train station, gave her a tour of the campus with his arm around her, and then took her to tea on High Street. This was simply not done at the time. The American equivalent would be a young man taking his teddy bear to boarding school. "It was the bravest thing I ever saw," a schoolmate said decades later.

The little religious instruction Churchill received had come from her. Most historians agree he was something of an agnostic as a young man. He admitted to praying under fire during the Boer War in South Africa and when he was a POW (and subsequent escapee). "The practice [of prayer] was comforting and the reasoning led nowhere," he wrote later. "I therefore acted in accordance with my feelings without troubling to square such conduct with the conclusions of thought."

He described his outlook later.

"If you tried your best to live an honorable life and did your duty and were faithful to friends and not unkind to the weak and poor, it did not matter much what you believed or disbelieved," Churchill once explained.

However, when he was much older, he frequently cited God in his speeches and conversation.

While on a walk in St. James's Park in London during the Blitz, he and his bodyguard, Walter Thompson, narrowly escaped a bomb. Churchill then told Thompson not to worry—that there was Someone else who was looking after him.

"Thompson misunderstood and said, 'Do you mean Sgt. Davis?'" Churchill's great-grandson explained decades later. "And Great Grandpapa gave a small smile and he shook his head and said 'No' and pointed to the sky. He said, 'There's someone up there who has a mission for me to perform and He intends to see that that mission is performed.'"

Churchill openly acknowledged that only God could see Britain through the war. He encouraged the British to put their hope in Him.

Someone once described Churchill as a pillar of the church. He corrected them. "No, no, not a pillar, but a buttress, supporting it from the outside."

Surprisingly, Churchill was nervous about meeting Billy. Colville wrote later that he paced the room, asking, "What do you talk about to an evangelist?"

Can you imagine the man who negotiated with Franklin Roosevelt and Joseph Stalin and faced down Hitler himself being nervous about meeting a man such as Billy? Churchill was clearly out of his comfort zone.

Billy Graham was neither an enemy to be conquered nor an ally to cajole. He was a representative of God Himself, and Churchill knew the Almighty's intervention in his country's salvation.

The tall, blonde Southerner and the tubby, bald aristocrat could hardly have been more different. Billy looked like a movie star. Once, someone presented a newborn to Churchill with the observation, "He looks like you, sir." "All babies look like me," he dryly replied.

Billy was born on a dairy farm. Churchill was born in a palace that had been a gift to his sixth great-grandfather from the queen after a spectacular victory on the Continent.

Billy raised his voice only a few times in his life. Churchill had killed men with revolvers and rifles in India and South Africa and rode in the last charge of the British lancers at the Battle of Omdurman in Sudan in 1898.

Billy and Ruth lived modest lives on modest means. Churchill rarely lifted a finger in his entire life to do anything for himself. When he was an army officer in India, his servants shaved him in the morning while he slept. He got a rash if he slept in anything but silk pajamas. He ran up staggering debts, living far beyond his means.

Billy was a humble man. Churchill once got into an argument with a servant. "But you are wrong, sir," the man protested (and he was right). "That may be, but I am a great man," Churchill huffed.

Billy did not drink or smoke. On the campaign in South Africa during the Boer War, Churchill's baggage took up an entire mule train, including one animal which carried nothing but champagne and brandy. He smoked cigars by the box around the clock.

Billy was a man of peace. Churchill loved firearms and weapons. "There's nothing so thrilling as being shot at and missed," he once said. With his country's back to the wall and his city bombed half into oblivion, Churchill had no compunction about ordering tit-for-tat firebombing of German cities and said he wished he could bomb neutral countries that refused to join the Allies too.

Billy was innately kind. Churchill was relentlessly vicious to his enemies and those who annoyed him. Member of Parliament Bessie Braddock once said to him, "Winston, you are drunk, and what's more you are disgustingly drunk." He replied, "My dear, you are ugly, and what's more, you are disgustingly ugly. But tomorrow I shall be sober and you will still be disgustingly ugly." Socialite and politician Nancy Astor told him at a dinner party she would poison his coffee if she were married to him. "If I were married to you," he replied, "I'd drink it."

There were a few similarities between Churchill and Billy, however. Neither of them was a star student in school, but both did amazing jobs of educating themselves. Both were quick studies of human nature. Both worked extremely hard at speaking and writing. Both were brilliant orators, and both were passionate about their callings.

Billy arrived at 10 Downing Street on Monday, May 24, 1954. He was told the prime minister had exactly twenty minutes to speak with him and was shown into a dimly lit cabinet room. Churchill rose from his chair and shook hands. Billy hadn't realized how short he was (and how old he looked). He towered over the seventy-nine-year-old man, who history says stood five feet six inches tall.

Churchill motioned with an unlit cigar to sit next to him. Three London afternoon dailies were spread out on a table there. The news was troubling.

Earlier that month, the United States, Great Britain, and France had rejected Russian membership in the North Atlantic Treaty Organization (NATO). The U.S. had installed sixty nuclear weapons in Britain. Eisenhower warned of the domino effect in Vietnam, where the French had surrendered to the Viet Minh at Dien Bien Phu. Mao Tse-tung's iron grip on Communist China was clenched.

Communism had been a worry to Churchill well before the Second World War ended. He did not trust the Soviets. American officials knew Britain's power was waning. They had no intention of being used as pawns to help support the crumbling British Empire. He felt the country was as alone as it had been in 1940 at the start of World War II.

When Billy settled into his chair, Churchill congratulated him for his successful London campaign. Billy thanked the prime minister but assured him it was not his doing but God's.

"That may be," Churchill said with a squint, "but I daresay that if I brought Marilyn Monroe over here, and she and I went together to Wembley, we couldn't fill it."

Billy laughed heartily.

Then Churchill got down to business.

"Young man," he said. "I have a question. What do you say to what fills all these big stadiums?"

Without hesitation, Billy gave him his best answer.

"Sir, people are hungry to hear about the Gospel of Jesus Christ."

"That must be it," Churchill replied. A quick moment passed before he posed his next question—perhaps *the* question he wanted to ask all along.

"I am an old man and I don't have any hope for the world," Churchill said. "Do you have hope?"

He may have been talking about geopolitics, but it sounded like a personal plea to Billy. He noticed Churchill mentioned hopelessness no fewer than nine times.

Churchill was plagued by depression much of his life. He famously called it his "Black Dog." When episodes struck, he became so paralyzed by despair that he spent most of his time in bed. He had little energy, few interests, lost his appetite, couldn't concentrate, and was minimally functional. It didn't just happen once or twice. These dark periods would last a few months, and then he'd come out of them and be his normal self. During the war, when that was impossible, his doctor prescribed amphetamines for his depressive episodes and a barbiturate from 1940 on to help him sleep. At the time, Billy was unaware of any of this.

"Mr. Prime Minister," Billy said, "I am filled with hope."

Billy had his New Testament with him. He knew they only had a few minutes left. He immediately explained the way of salvation, watching carefully for signs of irritation or offense. Churchill seemed receptive, if not enthusiastic. He made no comment but listened intently. (Reportedly he displayed a different attitude to most ecclesiastical dignitaries.) Perhaps he heard his beloved Woom speaking to him again.

Billy discussed the meaning of Christ's birth, His death, His resurrection and ascension, and how a man is born again. Billy talked about God's plan for the future, including the return of Christ. Churchill's eyes seemed to light up at the prospect.

At precisely 12:30, ten minutes past Billy's appointed time, Colville knocked to tell Churchill that the Duke of Windsor was in the reception area for his appointed luncheon. Churchill barked that the duke could wait. He motioned for Billy to continue.

Billy spoke for about another fifteen minutes, mostly about the Second Coming of Christ. When he finished, he asked if he could pray. Churchill not only said yes, but that he'd greatly appreciate it.

Billy prayed for the difficult situations the prime minister faced every day. He acknowledged that God was the only hope for the world and for us individually.

When Billy finished, Churchill thanked him and walked him out.

"I do not see much hope for the future unless it is the hope you are talking about, young man," Churchill said. "We must have a return to God."

He leaned toward Billy as they shook hands. "This conversation as long as I live will be confidential and between us. Is that agreed?"

"Yes," Billy affirmed. After the Truman fiasco he never again quoted a leader during his or her lifetime. And he never spoke about his meeting with Churchill until after his death in January 1965.

Churchill never commented on the meeting to his staff, but his private secretaries recalled that he had been terribly impressed and found Billy "most interesting and agreeable."

Outside 10 Downing Street, the cameras flashed, and questions were shouted.

"I felt like I had shaken hands with Mr. History," was all Billy said.

A year later Churchill would step down from office. He had suffered two strokes; his mental and physical capabilities were faltering. Perhaps he clung to Billy's words that God was the only hope for the world and us individually.

Being the only hope for the world had been Winston Churchill's burden for so long that he may have been relieved to know it was in God's hands in the end.

CHAPTER TWENTY-FIVE

Gabriel in a Gabardine Suit

Clearly, God was at work.

After London, Billy became a true globetrotter: Scotland, Finland, Norway, Sweden, Denmark, Belgium, the Netherlands, Germany, France, Switzerland, India, the Philippines, the Caribbean, Hong Kong, Taiwan, Japan, Iran, Australia, New Zealand, Canada, and the United States.

In every city, country, and continent, attendance records were shattered; every Crusade was a milestone, and every visit received unrivaled media attention. The man who *Time* magazine called "Gabriel in a gabardine suit" was now the most discussed and debated religious figure in the world, with the possible exception of the pope.

Since 1949, Billy had preached personally to approximately twelve million people and brought two hundred thousand of them to various stages of Christian commitment. And yet he remained humble.

"I may be a small item on the back page of Heaven's newspaper," he quipped.

His use of a simple authoritative phrase—"the Bible says"—kicked off every Crusade message and perhaps became his greatest legacy from the podium. From there, the mass evangelist preached an authentic, biblical, power-packed Gospel message to the rich and the poor alike during the day and met and befriended professors, theologians, diplomats, tycoons, captains of industry, prime ministers, and royalty at night. In addition to Winston Churchill, Billy either shook hands or broke bread with historical figures such as Generalissimo and Madame Chiang Kai-shek, Prime Minister Jawaharlal Nehru, Prime Minister Yukio Hatoyama, the Duke of Hamilton, the Shah of Iran, John Foster Dulles, C.S. Lewis, Golda Meir, Indira Gandhi, and Martin Niemöller, the Lutheran pastor who was a great hero of resistance against the Nazi regime.

Billy preached in Kottayam, India, where workers—mostly young girls—carved out the entire side of a hill into a three-tiered amphitheater. In Tokyo's Kokusai Stadium, he spoke at a fifteen-thousand-seat venue usually reserved for the ancient sport of sumo. He filled Berlin's Olympic Stadium—the same location where Adolf Hitler had used the 1936 festivities to advance the Nazi cause both inside and outside Germany. He even appeared at Yankee Stadium, where his boyhood hero Babe Ruth slugged homers for fifteen seasons.

Plenty of stars have played stadiums, but few make it to the halls of power: the White House and Buckingham Palace. As head of the Church of England, twenty-nine-year-old Queen Elizabeth II naturally was eager to meet the evangelist who captivated such huge audiences with his inspired sermons.

The relationship between Billy and the British monarch was briefly characterized in the 2018 season of the Netflix series *The Crown*, albeit with a few creative liberties thrown in for good measure. In the episode titled "Vergangenheit," the queen sits rapt as she watches television footage of Billy preaching to the masses on his hugely successful 1954 Crusade. Her interest piqued, she asks for a private meeting with him. Something clearly is on her mind.

In the episode, when they meet at Buckingham Palace, the emotionally bereft queen confesses to Billy that her uncle, the Duke of Windsor, previously associated with the Nazis during the war. She asks Billy what to do when she finds the act of forgiveness a tall order. He instructs her to pray for those she "cannot forgive." The scene is certainly inspirational and made for great television, but was it true?

Well, not exactly.

The pair actually first met in 1955, a year after Billy held his first London Crusade. He had returned to the United Kingdom that year for a tour of Scotland, with a week-long stint in London, ending with another packed crowd at Wembley Stadium. The following day he preached at Windsor Chapel by royal invitation.

Whatever transpired between the two, Billy remained mum on the subject of their friendship except to say that "Good manners do not permit one to discuss the details of a private visit with Her Majesty, but I can say that I judge her to be a woman of rare modesty and character.... No one in Britain has been more cordial toward us than Her Majesty Queen Elizabeth II."

What can't be denied is that they developed an unlikely friendship, sharing some fun and warm moments with each other over the decades. Billy was even made an honorary "Knight Commander of the Most Excellent Order of the British Empire" in 2001. I can hardly believe Billy allowed it, given his humility, but saying no to a queen is not in anyone's DNA.

Billy was more forthcoming about his relationship with President Dwight D. Eisenhower, who invited him to the White House several times after he won the 1952 election in a landslide. They were fond of each other, but Billy had to feign impartiality, or he'd get embroiled in partisan politics. Their interactions were always friendly, but also mostly formal—except when they played golf, which Ike was famous for. Billy recalled an especially warm memory of the president in his autobiography as he watched Eisenhower jumping for joy when his golf partner, Grady Wilson, sank an improbably long putt on the final hole of the El Dorado Country Club in Indian Wells, California. The putt sealed their victory that day over Billy and his teammate, and Ike was deliriously happy.

"Golf games (and other informal encounters) with the President bonded us more closely at the spiritual level," Billy wrote. "I became more and more impressed with his character and the intensity of his growing faith, which he not only formally confessed but also applied to policies and programs."

That included civil rights. Billy had addressed this a few years earlier when he could no longer tolerate segregated seating at his Crusades. It happened at a 1953 rally in Chattanooga, Tennessee, a Southern site of great racial divide.

The city had anticipated his arrival for almost a year and had sped up construction on the new Warner Field House to host the event. The only touch Billy didn't like were the ropes designating the black seating area. Billy, known widely for his conciliatory and gracious ways, could not accept such an injustice. It was racial prejudice on big display and contrary to the very Gospel he preached.

"I was appalled at it and decided that I had to do something about it," he recalled. "I said, 'No more of this.'"

Billy asked the head usher to remove the ropes. He was rebuffed. With holy passion, he took the ropes down himself.

"Either these ropes stay down or you can go on and have the revival without me," he threatened. The head usher resigned, and locally there was some blowback for Billy, including threats against him and his family. However, he weathered the storm. He preached the Gospel, whites and blacks came forward together to receive Christ, and the Kingdom prevailed.

His stance in Chattanooga also opened up a future friendship with Martin Luther King Jr. and other civil rights leaders. (A few years later, Billy refused an offer to travel to South Africa for a Crusade where locals still practiced apartheid.)

"His approach was more of trying to get people into the relationship with Christ, that that they would transform their mindset and the way in which they live, so they would see people differently and thus treat people differently," reflected Bernice King, daughter of the fallen leader.

From that point forward, Billy permanently adopted the policy of holding only integrated meetings.

"Until we come to recognize the Prince of Peace and receive His love in our hearts, the racial tensions will increase, racial demands will become more militant, and a great deal of blood will be shed," Billy said.

Eisenhower also saw how racial discrimination was starting to tear the fabric of the country. That was underscored in September 1957 when Arkansas governor Orval Faubus ordered National Guard troops to prevent nine African-American students from entering the formerly all-white Central High School. It was a ridiculous overreach of power and discrimination, and Eisenhower needed advice before he took action. He called Billy, who was in New York for a Crusade at Madison Square Garden, to discuss the crisis that had erupted into a full-scale riot.

After he was briefed on the situation in Little Rock, Arkansas, Billy was adamant that Ike had no choice: the discrimination must be stopped, and he must intervene.

Many saw this as Billy dispensing political advice to the president, but Billy felt it was more of a "moral and spiritual dilemma," and that Eisenhower needed reassurance. Days later, the former general sent a thousand U.S. Army paratroopers to escort the "Little Rock Nine" into the school. The daring tactic worked, and the students were enrolled without further violent disturbances. It also drew national attention to the Civil Rights Movement and reminded the world not to mess with the man who helped defeat the Nazis.

Billy was also there for Ike when his faith was tested. Eisenhower suffered many physical ailments—including a heart attack and a stroke during his time in office. In August 1955, Billy received a call from his friend Sid Richardson in Fort Worth, Texas. Richardson phoned Billy and told him that Ike wanted to see him on his farm in Gettysburg, Pennsylvania, about ninety miles from the White House. Billy had no idea what Ike wanted, but he prayed that God would give him the words and wisdom to guide the president.

As a student of the Civil War (all the great generals seem to be), Ike gave him a personalized tour of the Gettysburg battlefield, narrating as he drove a golf cart. Ike's ears went up when Billy informed him that both of his grandfathers fought there, and then he took him to the area of the battlefield where Billy's grandfathers' companies might have served during Pickett's Charge.

When they returned to the house, Ike's demeanor changed, and Billy sensed his unease. He then asked Billy if he believed in Heaven. Without any hesitation, he replied that he most certainly did. Ike almost demanded for Billy to list his reasons.

Billy recalled in his autobiography that he opened his New Testament and read several Scriptures that spoke of the afterlife. Ike wanted to know with certainty that he was going to Heaven. Billy explained that the Gospel specifically states that "salvation is by grace through faith in Christ alone, and not by anything we can do for ourselves." The fact that Billy never wavered in that answer or previous answers gave Eisenhower great reassurance.

Eisenhower suffered a "moderate" heart attack following a work-and-play vacation in Colorado, almost a month after Billy's visit. It required several months of recovery. Billy wrote Ike a letter imploring him not to run for a second term, but he did anyway and *won*. Billy suspected that given his earlier questions about Heaven, Ike probably knew he was short on days.

"He knew another truth that too few people understand," Billy said. "Peace between nations depends on goodwill between individuals."

Which explains one of Ike's actions near the end of his life. Billy visited him at Walter Reed National Military Medical Center in Washington, D.C., in late 1968. Ike had suffered heart attacks that April and August and was in bad shape. So was his relationship with his former vice president. Eisenhower had been estranged from Richard Nixon for several years. Nixon, who was about to take office as president of the United States, had a daughter named Julie who was about to marry David Eisenhower, Ike's grandson, on December 22, 1968. Ike wanted to set things right with Nixon now that he was going to be the president and an extended member of the family. He knew Billy was the perfect go-between.

Billy said Eisenhower never discussed their estrangement, but pretty much knew why—Eisenhower was late in endorsing Nixon's 1960 presidential run against John F. Kennedy, and Nixon narrowly lost the election. Nixon, who was publicly loyal to Eisenhower during his presidency, stewed for several years until Ike extended the olive branch through Billy.

It didn't take long for Billy to sort this out. That evening, he was invited to Nixon's apartment in New York for dinner. During their meal, Billy passed along Eisenhower's request. Even though Nixon had the reputation of being an emotionally removed man and cutthroat politician, he was raised as a Western Quaker and had very orthodox beliefs.

"My mother read her Bible and my mother was a saint," Nixon said of Hannah Milhous Nixon, whom he acknowledged as having a tremendous effect on his outlook throughout his life.

Nixon would have made his mother proud, and he promised to call Ike in the morning and follow up with a personal visit that day.

Nixon was as good as his word, and the two men were able to put the past behind them and move forward. It was a time of forgiveness.

C.S. Lewis famously said, "Everyone thinks forgiveness is a lovely idea until they have something to forgive."

Of course, Lewis was right.

But the reality is, when you forgive someone, you set a prisoner free—yourself.

It's always best to bury the hatchet, and preferably not in your opponent's back.

Sadly, Ike was too ill to attend his grandson's wedding. Not long afterward, Billy had another private meeting with him at Walter Reed Hospital, where he was connected to several intravenous tubes. He knew it was probably the last time he'd ever see Ike.

Billy recalled: "He was laying in bed. He wasn't expected to live very much longer. He asked the doctors and nurses to leave the room temporarily. They went out and he reached up and grabbed my hand and he said, 'Billy, you've explained it to me before.' But he said, 'I want to be sure that I know Christ. I want to be sure that I'm going to Heaven.' He said, 'Would you explain it to me one more time?'"

Dutifully, Billy opened his New Testament and once again read to him all the familiar Gospel verses that Ike had heard before, which focused on God's love and eternal life. Then Billy prayed while holding Ike's hand. After Billy said "Amen," Ike thanked him and said, "I'm sure." To Billy, that was a clear signal that Ike was spiritually ready to meet his Maker.

Eisenhower knew Billy was preparing for a special trip abroad. He asked him before he left if he was going to visit the troops in Vietnam. Billy nodded yes.

Ike had one final request.

"Give those old doughboys my greetings, and tell them there's an old soldier here praying for them," he said.

Ike hung on for a few more months, passing away on March 28, 1969, of congestive heart failure. Billy was in Israel when he got the news.

Nixon presided over Eisenhower's funeral in Abilene, Kansas, a few days later. He said in the eulogy, "Some men are considered great because they lead great armies or they lead powerful nations. For eight years now, Dwight Eisenhower has neither commanded an army nor led a nation; and yet he remained through his final days the world's most admired and respected man, truly the first citizen of the world."

Eisenhower saw the same greatness in Billy.

Publicly, when Billy stood up to preach, he was like a lion in the pulpit. He truly had no equal. And, when finished, he was usually soft-spoken and down to earth, not even wanting to discuss what happened that evening.

It's been said, "It takes a steady hand to hold a full cup."

The Lord knew that Billy would be a trusted servant He could use to impact the unknown and marginalized as well as the famous and even the legendary.

Winston Churchill, the Queen of England, Mickey Cohen, Stuart Hamblen, and the president of the United States. Billy shared the Gospel without fear with all of them.

I can tell you from experience that it is an overwhelming thing to stand in the Oval Office and speak to a sitting president. More than one person has been reduced to flattery and capitulation in saying only what they think that powerful person would like to hear. I have personally seen it many times.

Billy Graham spoke truth to power many, many times over.

And God would open even greater doors in the years to come.

CHAPTER TWENTY-SIX

JFK

A new age was dawning as the 1960s approached.

Thanks to the guiding hand of President Eisenhower, the '50s was a relatively stable—and conventional—period for America. The country managed to avoid war (Korea was officially labeled a "conflict"), the economy was booming, technology advanced, and the work force grew. The future offered a source of wonderment and fascination, and Americans were convinced of the superiority of capitalism. We had saved the world and looked good while doing it. Now was our time to shine in the sun.

But in a few short years, America's innocence was shattered, and its harmony unraveled.

The youngest president in American history was elected in November 1960. John F. Kennedy was forty-three when he was sworn in. Handsome and confident, he immediately declared America was going to do great things and not rest on its laurels. JFK was a stark contrast to the grandfatherly Eisenhower. With his beautiful and stylish wife, Jackie, at his side with their children, Carolyn and John, their arrival was both a political and cultural shift.

The youthful Northeasterner had bold plans for the United States of America. Tyranny, poverty, war, and disease were all to be tackled during his presidency. Frank Sinatra even repurposed his hit song "High Hopes" and had new lyrics written to promote that "Everyone was voting for Jack" and that JFK had "high hopes" for the nation.

The world, however, had no such hope for the young idealist. The threat of atomic weapons immediately raised its head via confrontations with the Russian missiles in Cuba. After staring the Soviets down over a thirteen-day period in October 1962—the closest the world has ever come to a nuclear war—Kennedy then sent eleven thousand troops to Vietnam to train the South Vietnamese to fight the northern Communists. All his hopeful plans to tackle the world's great problems were getting lost in a series of events he was forced to respond to.

The decade would see the start of the Civil Rights era, with protest marches and lunch counter sit-ins in the South. The Space Race began when Kennedy declared America would go to the moon. As Bob Dylan famously sang, the times were a-changin'.

Billy was changing too. He had turned forty before the start of the decade and was now officially "middle-aged." That almost immediately made him persona non grata to many youth who adopted the mantra of "Never trust anyone over thirty." These were the same youth who started growing their hair long, practiced free love, smoked those funny little French cigarettes, and badmouthed Uncle Sam whenever they got the chance. Billy was now part of the establishment, whether he liked it or not. That was partly because he held true to the wholesome American values that were suddenly out of vogue with the beat generation.

The other aspect was the company he now kept.

World leaders, captains of industry, connected businessmen, astute politicians, and behind-the-scenes players who made things happen all wanted to meet Billy after the Crusades began. At the top of this list, of course, was the president the United States.

Billy had enjoyed his relationship with President Eisenhower—and through him, his relationship with Vice President Richard Nixon, who seemed likely to win the 1960 election, deepened. The politician was by Billy's side in July 1957 when he preached to more than one hundred thousand in New York's Yankee Stadium, calling it "one of the most courageous spiritual ventures in our generation." They prayed together, read Scripture together, broke bread together, politically strategized together (Billy told Nixon as early as 1957 not to discount John F. Kennedy in the 1960 election, as he would make a "formidable foe"). Pat Nixon and Ruth Graham were friendly and supported each other's causes. Even though Billy couldn't openly endorse Nixon over Kennedy, whom he favored wasn't exactly a military secret in D.C.

On paper it looked like Nixon was a shoo-in for the 1960 presidential election. He not only had the wisdom and experience to run the country, but he also could legitimately lay claim to being a part of the stabilizing force that produced Ike's prosperous America. When Eisenhower had suffered from a stroke and a heart attack, Nixon carefully led the country without attempting to seize power, nor did he allow anyone else in the administration to try. This did not go unnoticed, and Nixon was highly praised. He had been a loyal VP, and now it was his turn.

Despite Kennedy's youth, lack of experience in foreign affairs, and (controversial to some) Catholic faith, the attractive senator from Massachusetts won the Democratic nomination. He pitched himself as a Franklin Roosevelt Democrat, promising a new surge of legislative innovation in the 1960s that would eradicate poverty, promote civil rights, and push forward bold, inventive social programs. Kennedy wisely chose Lyndon B. Johnson as his running mate—an experienced, if not masterful, tactician from Texas who could garner much-needed votes in the Deep South. Over time Johnson also became friendly with Billy, and the two men would develop an intense bond.

Nixon and Kennedy were a contrast in styles and political viewpoints: Nixon was the elder statesman (at forty-seven years old!) with an illustrious career in Congress and the White House who held tightly to traditional American values. Kennedy, a war hero, had a single unremarkable term in the U.S. Senate but seemed to somehow capture the imagination of young Americans who were looking to change the world.

To many of Billy's supporters and other Protestants, Kennedy's affiliation with the Roman Catholic church surfaced almost immediately as an overriding issue. With that in mind, Billy actively sought avenues through which he could help Nixon remain in power, including talking him up on his radio broadcasts and in print. He even implored Eisenhower in a letter to help Nixon in swing-through Southern states where he was still revered. (This proved to be Nixon's undoing. A reporter asked an exhausted Ike, who was not in the best of health, to name some of his vice president's contributions. He replied, "If you give me a week, I might think of one. I don't remember." The Democrats used the clip in a campaign ad, and it practically sank Nixon.)

Billy, however, was solid in his messaging.

"This is a time of world tension," he told a reporter. "It is a time for a man of world stature. I don't think it is a time to experiment with novices."

That statement made front pages around the country. However, Billy had to be careful not to cross the line. He had received many angry letters already. He purposely spent much of 1960 abroad in Crusades in Africa, Europe, and Brazil, avoiding any political talk that could land him in hot water. He also wrote Kennedy a personal letter on August 10, 1960, promising not to publicly stir the pot or harm his campaign. It read:

> *Dear Senator:*
>
> *I trust that you will treat this letter in strictest confidence. There is a rumor circulating in the Democratic Party that I intend to raise the religious issue during the campaign. This is not true. In fact, I would like to commend you for facing it squarely and courageously.*
>
> *There was another matter concerning malicious gossip that I had overheard about you. I took it immediately to two of your closest friends and they clarified it. I promise you it*

has not gone beyond me. It is most unfortunate that political leaders are subject to these types of ugly rumors and gossip.

I shall probably vote for Vice President Nixon for several reasons including a longstanding personal friendship. I am sure you understand my position. However, if you should be elected President, I will do all in my power to help unify the American people behind you. In the event of your election you will have my wholehearted support.

With every good wish, I am,
Billy Graham

During the campaign, Kennedy press secretary Pierre Salinger bumped into Billy on a train and asked if he would consider making a statement calling for religious tolerance in the election. Billy refrained, stating that he did not want to pulled into the political fray and that a statement from him would only heighten religion as an issue. He was also afraid it could be construed by the public as an endorsement.

A few days after Salinger's approach, Billy received a phone call from someone with an inimitable New England accent. Even though he identified himself as John F. Kennedy, Billy, a man not often given to suspicion, had his doubts. The caller wanted Billy to say that religion should not be a campaign issue and that he wouldn't hesitate to vote for a Catholic candidate if qualified. Billy politely said no.

However, he did not deny religion and politics were often intertwined when pressed by the media.

"A man's religion cannot be separated from his person. Therefore, where religion involves a political decision, it becomes a legitimate issue," Billy told a reporter. "But I'm not taking sides." In private, he implored Nixon to concentrate on his base and attempt to solidify the Protestant vote, since Kennedy was sure to capture the Catholic vote. Billy didn't have an issue with a Catholic in the White House, though many in his Southern Baptist denomination most certainly did. When Protestants pressed Billy to come out against Catholics, he refused.

In time, Kennedy's charm and wit began to prevail with the media and then voters, especially after his first televised debate with Nixon on September 26, 1960. To his credit, Kennedy had met with the producer the day before to discuss the design of the set and the placement of the cameras. Nixon, who had just been released from the hospital after a knee infection, did not have the wherewithal to consider this opportunity. He had lost twenty pounds and appeared frail, while Kennedy appeared poised and relaxed, speaking directly to the cameras and the national audience. Nixon was sweaty, could have used a shave, and looked uncomfortable with this relatively new medium called television. His gray suit also seemed to blend into the set while JFK's resplendent blue suit made him appear statesmanlike. Any issues of inexperience and lack of maturity on JFK's part peeled away almost instantly after this appearance. It proved to be a tipping point in the race.

After Kennedy won by the slimmest of margins (the race was decided by 113,000 votes out of more than 68 million cast) on November 8, 1960, Billy offered Kennedy his heartfelt congratulations and promised to do what he could to unite the country behind the new president. Kennedy reciprocated by inviting Graham to lunch and a round of golf in Palm Beach, Florida, a few days before the inauguration—but it wasn't really his idea. His father, Joseph Kennedy, the man who literally pulled the strings (as well as being the one who held the purse strings) in the Kennedy household, told his son to make the overture.

Privately, Billy mourned for Nixon, who wrote to him shortly after conceding the race.

"I have deeply appreciated the spiritual guidance you have given me, but, in addition to that, your political advice has been as wise as any I have ever received from any man I know," Nixon's letter read. "I have often told friends that when you went into the ministry, politics lost one of its potentially great practitioners."

Before Billy met with Kennedy on January 16, 1961, at his Palm Beach estate on Ocean Boulevard, he called Nixon out of loyalty. Despite his gloomy disposition after losing the election, Nixon knew it was a summons that Billy couldn't turn down and told him so. He gave Billy his blessing and instructed him to take the meeting.

The two-story Mediterranean-style home where Billy met Kennedy is reportedly where JFK wrote his Pulitzer Prize–winning book, *Profiles in Courage*, while recovering from back surgery in 1956. Helping to break the ice was Florida senator George Smathers, a JFK loyalist who was friendly with Nixon and Billy and was Billy's golf partner that day. Billy also met briefly with Joe Kennedy at the 1920s-era home before their day got underway. The bespectacled Kennedy patriarch, who was sitting poolside, told his visitor he was there because he wanted Billy to become his son's ally.

Billy knew it was purely a strategic move for the next election, but he assured the elder Kennedy that's exactly what he was. In return, this also allowed Billy to have some sort of Christian influence on the president-elect. And if it gave him the slightest chance to witness to him, then so be it. Billy got his opportunity sooner than even he could have anticipated.

After Kennedy was dressed, he introduced Billy to his beautiful wife, Jackie, and the two men had a quick lunch. Kennedy asked Billy to pray before the meal, which I'm sure was a sincere and earnest prayer. I'd be willing to bet my bottom dollar that JFK was moved. Billy Graham was not a hypocrite, and there is no way that he would have been insincere. Every word he prayed for President-Elect Kennedy would have been from the heart and led by the Holy Spirit.

When they finished their meal, Kennedy loaded Billy and Smathers into a stylish Lincoln convertible and drove them to the Seminole Golf Club in nearby Vero Beach. It was an exclusive members-only club laid out alongside the Atlantic Ocean, where the bluebloods of society played golf and fraternized. The club hosted kings and American presidents, including Dwight D. Eisenhower and Gerald Ford. Other members included industry titans Henry Ford II, Jack Chrysler, John Pillsbury, and Paul Mellon, as well as the Duke of Windsor and Joseph Kennedy. Rose Kennedy wore frilly hats and socialized with the wives of these powerful men on many of these outings, all of whom were there to escape the harsh winters of their respective home states. Countless deals and informal agreements were made on those greens and "the nineteenth hole." And the golf wasn't bad, either. Professional golfing legend Ben Hogan once said of the place: "Seminole is the only course I could be happy playing every single day. If you can play well there, you can play well anywhere."

It is not known if Billy and Kennedy played well that day, but they definitely experienced a nice and casual outing. The conversation was fun and relaxed to the point where Kennedy opened up in the clubhouse. They discussed world events, politics, and how Kennedy thought the '60s would play out. Sadly, he would not live long enough to see how it would all unfold. And neither would his younger brother Robert.

On the way back to the Kennedy compound, which would become known as the "Winter White House," Kennedy turned to Billy at a stoplight and zapped him with a million-dollar question. Billy recalled the exact exchange in his 1997 autobiography:

"Billy, do you believe in the Second Coming of Jesus Christ?" Kennedy asked.

"I most certainly do," Billy replied, almost reflexively.

"Well, does *my* church believe it?"

"They have it in their creeds."

"They don't preach it," Kennedy noted. "They don't tell us much about it. I'd like to know."

To the best of his ability, Billy explained about the first coming of Christ—that He was fully God and yet fully man. And not merely a good man, but the "God-Man."

He essentially told Kennedy what he would later tell journalist David Frost in 1971 about Christ's return: "The only permanent peace the world will ever know is when God intervenes in human history and Jesus Christ is put on the throne. He's going to rule and reign and we're going to have peace. But He will rule with the rod of iron, the Bible says, and that is when death is eliminated, suffering will be eliminated, poverty eliminated."

Kennedy nodded his head, absorbing the information, and told Billy that conversation would be continued for another day. Shortly thereafter, they arrived at the Kennedy compound.

The day didn't end there: Kennedy asked Billy to accompany him to the Hotel George Washington, where approximately three hundred members of the media were waiting for him. It was four days before the presidential inauguration, and Kennedy was expected to make a few remarks. Would Billy mind? Billy was honored...until he got there.

Kennedy, dressed in a stylish tweed jacket, button-down shirt, silk tie, and slacks, joked with the press for a few minutes, then thrust Billy into the spotlight by announcing the evangelist would field some questions. That was news to Billy and, I suspect, some good-natured payback from the thirty-fifth president of the United States.

The soundbite that got the most play that day came from Billy: "I don't think that Mr. Kennedy's being a Catholic should be held against him by any Protestant. They should judge him on his ability and character. We should trust and support our new president."

No doubt Joe Kennedy was pleased by what he heard.

Billy also became friendly with others in the Kennedy clan over the years. He grew especially close to the president's brother-in-law R. Sargent Shriver, head of the Peace Corps, a humanitarian service that Billy saw as parallel to the work of Christian missionaries. (Shriver called Billy "the finest person I know in the Protestant ministry.") Together, Billy and Shriver made a moving documentary film called *Beyond These Hills* about the poverty in the Appalachian Mountains, not far from Montreat. It brought great awareness to their plight.

He also developed a cordial relationship with JFK's younger brother Bobby Kennedy, who served as United States Attorney General from 1961 to 1964. Like Billy, Bobby was a tough crusader in his own right. He took on the mafia, fought for civil rights, and abhorred Communism. And like Billy, he was a great admirer of Winston Churchill. RFK proudly displayed a bust of the English prime minister on his desk and kept a signed copy of his "We Shall Never Surrender" speech to the House of Commons in his office on Capitol Hill.

Billy spoke at the Presidential Prayer Breakfast each of JFK's three years in Washington. There they sat together, prayed together, ate together, spoke of spiritual matters, and agreed that faith was essential in combating the nation's problems. I have no doubt these moments bonded the two men. It was said that Billy was the only Protestant clergyman Kennedy felt comfortable with. In turn, Billy's respect for Kennedy grew exponentially.

I once asked Billy if he had any personal regrets.

He nodded and told me of the last time he saw President Kennedy at the 1963 Presidential Prayer Breakfast on February 7. Billy had contracted the flu, and when the breakfast ended, he walked out of the main ballroom of the Mayflower Hotel with Kennedy. He warned the president of his illness and told him that he would not talk in his face. Kennedy said he didn't mind, suggesting his immune system was strong enough to withstand whatever bug Billy had. At the curb, he asked Billy to ride back to the White House with him.

Apparently, President Kennedy had something pressing he wanted to discuss. Billy kindly protested that he was running a fever and was likely contagious. Fearing he'd make the president sick, Billy suggested another time, perhaps. Kennedy, as usual, was gracious and agreed.

Another time, perhaps.

Billy said he regretted this action and that it haunted him for years. He was left to wonder what was on Kennedy's mind that day, and if there was a spiritual question he could have possibly fielded for him.

The two men remained in touch and exchanged telegrams that June. Kennedy had specifically asked Graham to assist him with civil rights to help build the country's racial harmony. Their correspondence took place the day after Kennedy gave his historic televised address "Report to the American People on Civil Rights," in which he denounced the threats of violence and obstruction on the University of Alabama campus following desegregation attempts by their governor, George Wallace. Kennedy also implored Congress to enact legislation protecting Americans' voting rights, public safety, and equal access to educational opportunities and public facilities.

"The race question will not be solved by demonstrations in the streets, but in the hearts of both black and white," Billy said at the time. "There must be genuine love to replace prejudice and hate. This love can be supplied by Christ and only Christ."

Billy had one last opportunity to communicate with Kennedy; it had to do with Dallas. His friend John Connally, the newly elected governor of Texas, met up with Billy on October 30, 1963, in Houston. That's when Billy made an address in front of five thousand people at Houston Baptist University for its inaugural convocation. After Billy finished, Connally visited him in his hotel room. Connally was particularly worried about Kennedy's visit to Dallas the next month. He said there was simmering animus toward Kennedy in the Lone Star State, and hinted that he was worried not only about how Kennedy would be received but also for the president's safety. The trip wasn't necessary for Kennedy to make, Connally felt, and argued against it. For Kennedy, it was a strategic move to thwart the momentum of Arizona senator Barry Goldwater. The Republican frontrunner in the 1964 election was generating a lot of buzz in Texas with his conservative agenda, and Kennedy wanted to keep the groundswell of support for Goldwater in check while uniting his party at the same time.

Billy, who rarely discussed his past associations with famous people and celebrities, confided in me the following:

About a week before Kennedy's visit to Dallas, Billy's heart became extremely burdened. It was so heavy, in fact, that he called George Smathers to discuss the situation. Smathers's secretary told Billy her boss was on the Senate floor and would return his call when he finished. Smathers skipped the call and sent Billy a telegram, saying President Kennedy would personally respond. Smathers thought Billy wanted to discuss the president's invitation to another golf outing they had scheduled in Florida, which was canceled. However, all Billy wanted to communicate to Smathers was to tell the president not to step foot in Dallas. That type of worry and concern, I can tell you, was not like Billy. He must have felt something very strongly to react and behave this way.

A black cloud hung over Billy and he was struck by what had called an "inner foreboding"—that something tragic might befall JFK. He even mentioned this feeling of dread to a pair of friends while playing golf in the days preceding Air Force One's arrival at Dallas's Love Field. Billy wanted to call Kennedy personally, but he secretly wondered if his weird premonition was actually worth bothering the world's busiest and most powerful man? After much contemplation, he finally dropped the matter.

On November 22, 1963, he wished he hadn't.

CHAPTER TWENTY-SEVEN

The Decade That Took Down a President

John F. Kennedy was dead, his life stolen by an assassin hunkered down inside a book depository in downtown Dallas. The world was in mourning. So was Billy Graham.

Three days after the shooting, Billy was inside the Cathedral of St. Matthew the Apostle in Washington, D.C., sitting next to friends of the Kennedy family for JFK's requiem mass. He was there at the request of Robert F. Kennedy, who invited Billy to mourn with his family. Billy was especially moved by the sight of the Kennedy children, Caroline and John Jr., who would now have to grow up without their father. The day before, Billy had watched Kennedy's flag-draped casket carried on a horse-drawn caisson to the United States Capitol Rotunda, where his body would lie in state. There he also observed JFK's stoic widow, Jackie, from a distance and watched tears roll down the faces of approximately one hundred national and world leaders.

As he sat in the cathedral, Billy's thoughts reverted to his first meeting with Kennedy in Palm Beach a few years before when he asked about Jesus's return. He listened as Cardinal Richard Cushing read the New Testament statement on Christ's Second Coming from 1 Thessalonians

4:16: "For the Lord himself shall descend from heaven with a shout, with the voice of the archangel, and with the trump of God: and the dead in Christ shall rise first" (KVJ). Nothing about Kennedy's assassination made any sense to anyone, but Billy knew the Lord had the answers, and he trusted in that. Or as Nobel laureate and Holocaust survivor Elie Wiesel once said, "Heaven: where questions and answers become one."

Six months after JFK's assassination, a special memorial service and fundraising event for the John F. Kennedy Presidential Library was held at the University of North Carolina campus at Chapel Hill on May 17, 1964. Billy delivered a keynote address at Kenan Stadium in front of ten thousand people, including Governor Terry Sanford, Senator Edward Kennedy, and his mother, Rose Kennedy.

He said of JFK in that address: "He was always interested in the moral and spiritual welfare of the country. He was always asking quick questions. He was one of the most affable men I've ever met. I never agreed with everything he did. Most of us didn't. But I always liked him as a friend and person. I thought there was a certain fairness about him...and he was very anxious to heal the religious breach in the country. And I think to some extent he succeeded."

(Billy also attended Robert F. Kennedy's funeral at St. Patrick's Cathedral in New York City on June 8, 1968. Billy said of his assassination: "I don't weep often, but today I wept for my country.")

Rose was especially gracious to him backstage in Chapel Hill, Billy said. The Kennedy matriarch shared with Billy that even though they practiced different faiths, there was nothing biblically that she disagreed with him on.

Her words not only pleased Billy but gave him much food for thought. It also underscored a notion he had come to understand in the debates a few years before.

"The only hope for finding common ground among Christians of diverse backgrounds and viewpoints was to focus on the Word of God, the ultimate authority for our faith," he wrote in his autobiography.

Billy Graham was one of the most recognized and trusted faces of the twentieth and twenty-first centuries; a confidante and spiritual advisor to presidents, diplomats, and royalty; a civil-rights champion; a president and CEO of a major company; an inventive entrepreneur; and a pioneer of Christian radio, television, and cinema. *(Pexel)*

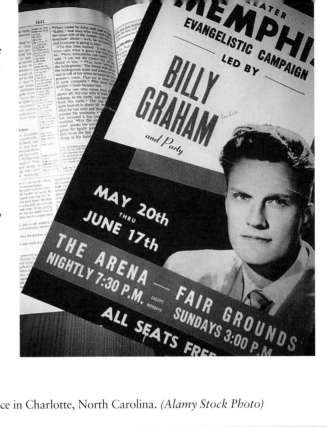

The Billy Graham Homeplace in Charlotte, North Carolina. *(Alamy Stock Photo)*

The kitchen inside the Billy Graham Homeplace. Billy had many home-cooked meals served to him by his mother, Morrow, who also kept the books for the family dairy. *(Alamy Stock Photo)*

The stairway of the Billy Graham Homeplace. Like many homes of that era, it exuded warmth and comfort. *(Alamy Stock Photo)*

An original truck from the Graham family dairy on display inside the Billy Graham Library in Charlotte, North Carolina. *(Alamy Stock Photo)*

The Bostwick Baptist Church north of Palatka, Florida, where Billy Graham preached his first sermon, is now considered a historic site. *(Alamy Stock Photo)*

The sanctuary of Bostwick Baptist Church; this photo was taken the day after Billy Graham died on February 21, 2018. *(Paul Hennessy/Alamy Live News)*

Ruth Bell Graham reading missionary Elisabeth Elliot's book *Through Gates of Splendor*. Ruth and Billy married in August 1943 and together would raise a family, experience adventures across the globe, minister to others, and befriend the world's most powerful and influential people in every field. Their marriage would last until Ruth's death in 2007. *(Alamy Stock Photo)*

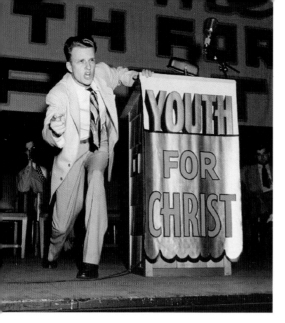

At age twenty-seven, Billy resigned his pulpit to go on the road with Youth for Christ for seventy-five dollars a week. In this September 1947 photo, he's preaching at a rally in Grand Rapids, Michigan. *(Youth for Christ)*

Billy Graham's impact was undeniable, and he managed to accomplish his herculean feats during an era of travel that was not easy or comfortable. Crashes from fog were common. Engines fell off airplanes with such regularity that the incidents weren't even recorded as accidents if the remaining engines landed the plane safely. Turbulence could snap your neck because plane interiors weren't designed for safety. That was the world in which Billy Graham began his travels. *(Youth for Christ)*

Youth for Christ boasted an all-star roster of up-and-coming evangelists, who kneel in prayer before departing for a rally. From left to right: Charles Templeton, Billy Graham, Stratton Shufelt, and Torrey Johnson. *(Youth for Christ)*

At age 29, Billy Graham became the youngest college president in the United States. He was president of Northwestern Schools from 1948–1952. This official presidential portrait looks more like a Hollywood headshot. (*Courtesy of the UNW Archives at the Berntsen Library, University of Northwestern–St. Paul*)

A faculty fun night showing Billy's keen sense of humor. Acting as headmaster in the photo is Richard V. Clearwaters, who intensely disliked Billy because he felt he should have been named Northwestern president. Next to Billy is Marie Acomb Riley, the widow of Dr. William Bell Riley, who named Billy as his successor shortly before his December 1947 death. (*Courtesy of the UNW Archives at the Berntsen Library, University of Northwestern–St. Paul*)

A crowd of several thousand people stand on Capitol Plaza and the steps of the U.S. Capitol in Washington, D.C., to hear Billy Graham preach at a rally on February 3, 1952. Billy is on the platform in the center of the photo. (*Associated Press*)

Billy Graham and President Dwight D. Eisenhower became friends before Eisenhower's election. Shortly before the 1953 inauguration ceremony, Eisenhower asked Billy for some Bible verses to use during his speech, ultimately settling on 2 Chronicles 7:14. The new president rested his hand on that passage of Scripture as he took his oath of office. Billy was also with "Ike" on his deathbed to reassure him of the afterlife. *(National Archives/Dwight D. Eisenhower Presidential Library)*

Billy and Ruth Graham on board the *Queen Mary* preparing for a historic Crusade in England. He once said, "Great Britain had a special place in my thinking." *(Alamy Stock Photo)*

Billy Graham speaks to a rapt crowd gathered at Trafalgar Square in London, England, on April 3, 1954. The Crusade in London was a turning point in his international ministry. *(Keystone Press/Alamy Stock Photo)*

Billy outside 10 Downing Street in London minutes after meeting Prime Minister Winston Churchill. Their half-hour meeting was an uplifting encounter that Churchill carried to his grave. *(Alamy Stock Photo)*

An adventurous Billy riding an elephant in Kottayam, India, during a month-long tour of the country in February 1956. Billy took in the local customs on his international trips and was always up for an adventure. *(Alamy Stock Photo)*

Billy Graham reading from a family Bible with Ruth and their children Franklin and Virginia ("Gigi") in their home in Montreat, North Carolina, in 1957. *(Alamy Stock Photo)*

Billy and Vice President Richard Nixon bow hea[ds] in prayer during the climax of the 1957 Crusade [at] Yankee Stadium in New York City. An estimated 85,000 people filled Yankee Stadium and anothe[r] 2,500 were forced to stand outside the ballpark. [Billy] and Nixon had a long and complicated friendshi[p.] *(Alpha Historical/Alamy Stock Photo)*

President John F. Kennedy and Billy Graham bow their heads at the 1961 National Prayer Breakfast at the Mayflower Hotel in Washington, D.C. Even though the men weren't close, Billy had what he called an "inner foreboding" that something tragic was going to happen to Kennedy. *(John F. Kennedy Presidential Library and Museum)*

Billy Graham playing golf sometime in the 1960s. He was a caddy at the Florida Bible Institute and grew to be decent player (many said he often shot in the 70s). "The only time my prayers are never answered," Billy once said, "is on the golf course." *(Alamy Stock Photo)*

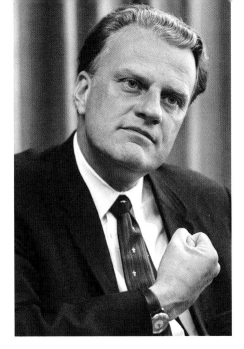

By the mid- to late 1960s, Billy Graham was not only a household name, but also was one of the most revered figures in the world. *(Pixabay)*

President Lyndon Baines Johnson and Billy Graham sharing a laugh in the Oval Office in 1968. LBJ asked Billy to preside over his funeral, which he did in January 1973. *(LBJ Presidential Library and Museum)*

Vietnam erupted in the mid- to late 1960s as tens of thousands of American troops poured into the country. The war was in everyone's living room every night, and Billy made several trips there to give spiritual comfort to American soldiers. In this photo he greets servicemen of I Corps after speaking to more than 1,500 gathered at the Freedom Hill Amphitheater on December 23, 1968. On this trip he came to wish the men and women serving there a "Merry Christmas from the people of the United States." *(USMC archives)*

Billy attending a three-day rock festival in Miami featuring the Grateful Dead in December 1969. He was trying to understand what young people were truly searching for during the counterculture movement. *(Associated Press)*

Billy Graham waving to the crowd as he enters Atlanta stadium with Georgia governor Jimmy Carter and his wife, Rosalynn, on a 1973 Crusade. However, the two men would only develop a friendship after Carter left the White House. *(Alamy Stock Photo)*

Billy and Ruth Graham enjoy a rare time of relaxation at their mountain home in Montreat, North Carolina, in 1972. Billy's hectic schedule meant he was often away from home, and Ruth was equally busy fulfilling her role as wife, confidante, mentor, scheduler, and mother to five energetic children. *(Associated Press)*

Billy's friendship with President Gerald Ford dated back to the 1950s; they often prayed and golfed together. *(Gerald R. Ford Presidential Library and Museum)*

The Grahams and the Reagans after a dinner in the White House in December 1982. Their mutual admiration and love of the Bible cemented their enduring friendship over the years. President Ronald Reagan, Billy noted, had a spiritual side to him that often went unnoticed. *(Ronald Reagan Presidential Library)*

The author relaxing with Billy while on a Crusade in San Juan, Puerto Rico, in March 1995. This photo was taken right before the baptism of one of his grandsons and namesake, William Franklin Graham IV. *(Greg Laurie Collection)*

Spending time with Franklin Graham, Ruth, and Billy at the Billy Graham Training Center at the Cove. The Grahams were fun, kind, and the most gracious people I've ever had the pleasure to know. *(Greg Laurie Collection)*

My wife, Cathe, Billy, and me at the Grahams' home in Montreat, North Carolina. We are standing in front of the fireplace in his front room. The mantle was engraved: "A Mighty Fortress Is Our God" in German. *(Greg Laurie Collection)*

Billy deeply appreciated my friendship with his son, Franklin, whom I've known for more than three decades. My bond with Franklin is a case of opposites attract, but it is sealed by our faith. *(Greg Laurie Collection)*

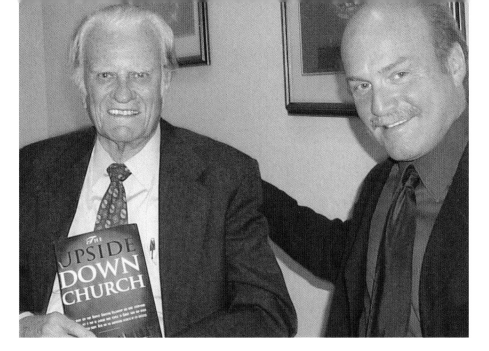

What better endorsement is there than having Billy Graham holding up your book for a photo? He truly enjoyed *The Upside Down Church*, which was written in 2000 to help pastors and lay leaders understand the principles of biblical church growth. *(Greg Laurie Collection)*

Cathe and me spending time with Billy and his brother, Mel, backstage at a Crusade. I got to know Mel very well. He had more classic one-liners and amazing stories than you can imagine. *(Greg Laurie Collection)*

I was present when Billy Graham made his final Crusade appearance in Flushing Meadows-Corona Park in New York City on June 25, 2005. His sermon brought ninety thousand people to their feet at the end. *(Greg Laurie Collection)*

Sharing a special moment with Billy after his final Crusade in Queens. The smile on my face is evidence of how happy I was to be in his presence. He drew that out of almost everyone he knew. *(Greg Laurie Collection)*

The last photo ever taken of me and Billy. It was at the Billy Graham Training Center at the Cove in Asheville, North Carolina. Billy's eagle eyes were softer, his once-strong voice was gentler. He needed a microphone to be heard in the large boardroom, and we had speakers on the table. It was a special day for me because I was able to tell Billy how much he meant to me and the important role he had played in my life. *(Greg Laurie Collection)*

After President Donald Trump, guests, and family departed the official ceremony for Reverend Billy Graham's lying in state, only two honor guards remain prior to the public's being allowed to pay their respects in the U.S. Capitol Rotunda on February 28, 2018, in Washington, D.C. The Baptist evangelist, age ninety-nine, was an informal advisor to twelve presidents and is the first religious leader to lie in state at the Capitol. Photo by Mike Theiler/UPI *(Alamy Stock Photo)*

The Billy Graham Library in Charlotte, North Carolina, was dedicated in May 2007. The ceremony was attended by Billy, former presidents Jimmy Carter, Bill Clinton, and George H.W. Bush, and a crowd of nearly 1,500 people. The building is styled after a dairy barn, and Graham's boyhood home, a short walk away from the library, has been restored. It endeavors to bring inspiration to its guests through the story of a man who shared God's love, strength, hope, and kindness with millions of people around the world. *(Shutterstock)*

On October 15, 1989, Billy Graham became the first clergyman to be honored with a star on the Hollywood Walk of Fame. He was awarded the 1,900th star for his work as a minister of the Gospel using radio, television, and film. He accepted it with great humility and used his special moment to tell others about Christ. "I hope someday somebody will come and say, 'Who is Billy Graham? What did he stand for?' Perhaps a child will ask his parents or grandparents, and they will tell him that he was not a celebrity, not a star, but a simple preacher of the Gospel. And that they might explain the Gospel to him, and that many might find Christ in that." *(Billy Graham Evangelistic Association)*

Billy didn't need to find much common ground with the man who inherited the presidency from Kennedy: Lyndon B. Johnson. They were both charismatic Southerners from humble beginnings, raised in God-centered households. In fact, LBJ had a family legacy of preachers, Bible teachers, and evangelists. Billy noted that LBJ's church attendance was spotless during his presidency, often going two to three times a week. That said, LBJ was no saint, and his misdeeds and complex personality have filled volumes of books and biographies. To his credit, Johnson recognized he was a sinner—which is probably why he went to church so often.

And sin he did. Johnson has often been labeled the most vulgar president in American history by many historians. He burped, farted, and picked his nose. If he had to go to the bathroom during a presidential meeting, he did…and left the door open while everyone gathered around. Billy recognized this complexity in a 1983 interview he gave to the LBJ Presidential Library in Texas.

"He had a conflict within him about religion. One was he wanted to go all the way in his commitment to Christ. He knew what it meant to be saved or lost, using our terminology, and he knew what it was to be born again," Billy said. "And yet he somehow felt he had never quite had that experience. I think he tried to make up for it by having many of the outward forms of religion, in the sense of going to church almost fanatically, while he was president even. Sometimes he'd go to church three times on a Sunday."

Johnson was almost six foot four, and he used his size (along with everything else) to intimidate others into doing what he wanted. His profanity was legendary, and almost every sentence was laced with it. He ignored the idea of personal space. Conversation was a hands-on affair. *Washington Post* editor Ben Bradlee said, "You really felt as if a St. Bernard had licked your face for an hour, had pawed you all over."

He was a civil rights crusader and made huge progress on race relations, but racial slurs dotted his language, nonetheless.

As a politician, he was volcanic. He worked eighteen- to twenty-hour days (but took ten-minute naps all day long). Johnson had thumbnail dossiers of every senator in his mind. One biographer said, "He could get up every day and learn what their fears, their desires, their wishes, their wants were and he could then manipulate, dominate, persuade, and cajole them." During his race against Senator Barry Goldwater, Billy recalled that Johnson had a file on his opponent, which included some very personal medical information.

Getting the full force of his blast was called the "Johnson treatment."

"It was an incredible blend of badgering, cajolery, reminders of past favors, promises of future favors, predictions of gloom if something didn't happen," one contemporary said. "When that man started to work on you, all of a sudden, you just felt that you were standing under a waterfall and the stuff was pouring on you."

Part of the presidency is theater. All great presidents understand that. Johnson had a repertoire of roles he assumed for whatever task lay at hand. Biographer Randall Woods said, depending on the circumstances, he could play:

"Johnson the Son of the Tenant Farmer, Johnson the Great Compromiser, Johnson the All-Knowing, Johnson the Humble, Johnson the Warrior, Johnson the Dove, Johnson the Romantic, Johnson the Hard-Headed Pragmatist, Johnson the Preserver of Traditions, Johnson the Crusader for Social Justice, Johnson the Magnanimous, Johnson the Vindictive or Johnson the Uncouth, LBJ the Hick, Lyndon the Satyr, and Johnson the Usurper."

Johnson also had a charismatic side, but somehow that didn't get through, according to Billy.

"President Johnson, in my judgment, had one difficulty and that was he didn't come over on television like he does in person," Billy said. "In person, he's one of the most charming men I have ever known. But that doesn't somehow come over on television. Now whether some of his managers and handlers kept him from this or not, I don't know. But he's a tremendous person, an overwhelming person. He could walk in this room and you'd be conscious of his presence."

On December 15, 1963, less than three weeks after Kennedy's assassination, Billy's phone rang as he was headed to Annapolis, Maryland, where he would address a group at the United States Naval Academy. It was Johnson. He wanted Billy to drop by the White House the following day. The two men engaged for several hours, even taking a dip in the White House's indoor swimming pool. Billy recalled the nearly unflappable Johnson was shaken up in the aftermath of his predecessor's death. Billy prayed for him, asking God to grant the nation's leader grace and wisdom in the uncertain times. Those intimate moments were followed up by a letter Billy penned to Johnson on December 29, 1963. The letter, which is housed in the LBJ Presidential Library in Austin, Texas, read:

> Dear Mr. President:
>
> Spending those hours with you at the White House was an unforgettable experience. I felt that you gave me an inside look at some of the awesome responsibilities of the presidency. You may rest assured that you, your family and your advisors will be in my prayers constantly.
>
> Just before Moses turned over the helm of Israel's government to Joshua, he said to Joshua: "As thy days, so shall thy strength be . . . Underneath are the everlasting arms." There is no doubt that you are being sustained by the prayers of millions as you lead the free world into this critical period of history.
>
> When Moses died, God said to Joshua: "As I was with Moses, so I will be with thee. I will not fail thee, nor forsake thee." As God was with Washington at Valley Forge and with Lincoln in the darkest hours of the Civil War, so God will be with you. There will be times when decisions come hard and burdens too heavy to bear—that is when God will be nearest to you.

> *Wishing you and Mrs. Johnson and your family a Happy*
> *New Year, I am*
> > *Most cordially yours,*
> > *Billy Graham*

The letter so deeply touched Johnson that he responded a few days later:

> *Dear Billy,*
> > *I hope you will keep writing letters like the one you mailed on December 29. I found in it strength and support.*
> > *Pray for me, too. I cannot fulfill this trust unless God grant me wisdom to see what is right and courage to do it.*
> > *Come back soon and we'll swim again. Only this time I'll try not to be late.*
> > *Sincerely,*
> > *Lyndon*

They saw each other again in February 1964 at the Presidential Prayer Breakfast. Johnson was humble when he spoke that day, asking for grace and the country's prayers: "No man can live where I live, nor work at the desk where I work now, without needing and seeking the strength and support of earnest and frequent prayer." It was a good thing Johnson had his faith, because it would be severely tested like no other president's before or since.

Vietnam was blowing up in his face as no progress was being made, and tens of thousands of American troops poured into the country. The war was in everyone's living room every night. (It became known as the "living room war".) Unlike today, images of dead and wounded soldiers flooded broadcasts. Mothers shoved their children's faces into couch pillows to avoid them.

Civil rights demonstrations blew up all over the country. The counterculture reached its zenith. It seemed like long hair was on everyone under thirty and psychedelic drugs were inside their bodies. About one hundred thousand hippies gathered in San Francisco for the Summer of Love to turn on, tune in, and drop out. They were anti-war, anti-cop, and pro-free love. Acid-tinged guitars and defiant lyrics characterized the music. One of the era's top chants was "Hey, hey, LBJ, how many kids did you kill today?"

CBS News legend Walter Cronkite was at the Battle of Hue during the Tet Offensive of 1968. He returned home and delivered a special report on Vietnam. Almost every person in the country watched Cronkite every night. Johnson watched him too. "If I've lost Cronkite, I've lost Middle America," he said.

It was all taking a toll. The master politician who had spent his whole life fighting his way to the top spot now wanted off the merry-go-round. He would not run for a second term.

Johnson's relationship with Billy wasn't all kumbaya, either. Billy said, if anything, he might have intimidated Johnson and wasn't afraid to correct him when he was wrong or stand up for himself when Johnson might have bullied others into submission. Billy was present at a September 1967 gathering of police chiefs in Kansas City when Johnson said he did not think America's morality was in decline. After the country had spent three months witnessing the Summer of Love, the celebration of psychedelic drugs, and feasting on movies like *Bonnie and Clyde*, *Valley of the Dolls*, and *The Graduate*, Billy begged to differ.

Later that evening when Billy spoke at a Crusade in Municipal Stadium, he hammered on Johnson's earlier comments and expounded on what the Bible taught on the issue. The press jumped on the fact that Billy Graham scolded Lyndon B. Johnson publicly. Billy got an earful the next morning from the president, who was greatly embarrassed. Billy firmly told him that he couldn't be expected to agree with him all the time.

Johnson backed down and never brought up the subject again. The lesson here was that Billy couldn't be bullied, even by the most powerful man in the free world.

Their friendship could also have been compromised during the 1964 election when Johnson ran against Arizona senator Barry Goldwater—a man who was so conservative that he thought *Eisenhower's* policies were too liberal. Billy met Goldwater in the fall of 1963, before Johnson assumed the presidency, and was duly impressed with the former World War II pilot. Goldwater told Billy his message closely aligned with the evangelist's: one preached about national salvation through the Constitution; the other preached salvation through God. Billy tried to stay neutral.

But that became next to impossible when the press claimed Billy was seriously considering running for president or vice president that year as a Republican. A Houston newspaper printed that Texas billionaire H.L. Hunt offered to seed Graham six million dollars to oppose Johnson in a race. Billy's aides say he immediately rejected the offer, but the story was leaked to the Scripps Howard chain, landing Billy on the top fold of many of its papers. His father-in-law, L. Nelson Bell, urged him to call a press conference and kill the story.

Billy did so the next morning, telling reporters in no way, shape, or form was he running for president of the United States—or any office, for that matter. He was called by God to preach the Bible, plain and simple.

Ruth most definitely saw to that. During a White House meal with the Johnsons at the start of the 1964 Democratic Convention, the president gave Billy a sheet listing his potential running mates, an overt act signaling that he was seeking his advice. When Billy started to answer, Ruth solidly kicked him under the table. Surprised, Billy asked Ruth aloud why she kicked him. Johnson also heard the ruckus and wanted to know as well.

Ruth turned to her husband and sternly reminded him that he should stay out of politics and limit himself to "moral and spiritual advice."

When Johnson won the election by a landslide (forty-four out of fifty states, including Washington, D.C.), he and Billy could put politics behind them and focus on what was truly important. Like the time when Billy visited LBJ at his ranch in Stonewall, Texas, about an hour west of Austin.

One evening when they were sitting in Johnson's large convertible and watching the sun go down, Billy was moved to ask him if he had ever personally received Jesus Christ as his Savior. Surprisingly, Johnson, who came from a long line of preachers and evangelists, said he wasn't exactly 100 percent sure. He told Billy he *thought* he was, as he accepted Christ at a revival meeting when he was a boy. Furthermore, Johnson added, he said he accepted Christ several times.

Billy wasn't as sold. For some reason, he just wasn't feeling it.

Johnson shot him a look of bewilderment.

Billy explained that once he accepted Christ, that was it. He didn't need to repeat the act.

Johnson nodded, but Billy felt as if he had said enough. He wanted the former president to ponder his words. Johnson did confess to Billy that he was a sinner, committed shameful acts in his past, but did not get into the weeds on that matter. Johnson also mustered the courage to say he felt he was saved and would spend eternity in Heaven. Billy eventually believed it too. He saw Johnson get down on his knees many times to praise God.

"In fact, a number of times I had prayer with him in his bedroom at the White House, usually early in the morning," Billy recalled. "He would get out of bed and get on his knees while I prayed. I never had very many people do that."

Billy saw Johnson's faith up close. He also saw signs of burnout the year before Johnson's term ended. Despite working hard to pass legislation on civil rights, voting, environment, Medicare, poverty, fair housing, and education in order to build the "Great Society," Johnson's presidency got pulled in another direction during the second half of the 1960s.

Civil rights protests, rioting and looting in the streets, and protests against the Vietnam War—an extremely unpopular conflict LBJ inherited from his predecessor, but which he escalated—ultimately proved to be his undoing. Every time he received a casualty list from Vietnam, he thought about the soldiers' families and how those deaths would impact their lives. Johnson even made it a point to sometimes call soldiers' parents and spouses personally. He was greatly tormented, and the war began to ruin his mental health with bouts of mania and prolonged depression.

Johnson felt great emptiness and was physically worn down from his duties. He confessed to Billy one morning that he was no longer up to being commander in chief. He revealed that many of the men in the Johnson bloodline had heart issues and died in their sixties. He had already experienced a heart attack in 1955 and was now suffering from chest pains. (At the end of Johnson's life, he was popping nitroglycerine capsules.) He told Billy it wouldn't be right for him to run for another term, nor would it be fair to the American people.

"I knew the tremendous tensions he was under and the tremendous work he had to do," Billy said. "Then I'd go into his bedroom at his invitation, and he'd have a great stack of papers that he had to go through before he could go to sleep. The tremendous burdens that a modern president bears is something the average American just doesn't have any idea (about). I think he allowed some of these things to get to him."

Billy was there for the last weekend the Johnsons occupied the White House, before President Nixon's first inauguration in January 1969. He and Ruth were their exclusive guests. After the last official function as president, the Johnsons joined Billy and Ruth for a private screening of *The Shoes of a Fisherman*, a drama starring Anthony Quinn and Laurence Olivier. Billy said Johnson fell asleep, which followed a pattern.

"Every time I ever saw a movie with him, he went to sleep, and he was snoring," Billy laughed. He said Johnson once screened *The Graduate,* starring Dustin Hoffman, for Wunibald Schneider, a Catholic priest and personal friend. Johnson snoozed through that as well.

"So after it was over, the president woke up and he turned to the priest and he said, 'Father, how did you like the movie?' and the priest said, 'Mr. President, it was awful! It was terrible! I'm amazed that you would show that here.' He took delight in telling that story," Billy said.

The couples also attended Sunday church services together, and the following day Billy delivered the inaugural prayer at the Capitol.

He closed that prayer with these words: "O God, we consecrate Richard Milhous Nixon to the Presidency of these United States with the assurance that from this hour on, as he and his family move into the White House, they will have the presence and the power of Thy Son who said, 'I will never leave thee nor forsake thee.'

"What we pray for President Nixon we pray for Vice President Agnew and members of the Cabinet. May they be given a wisdom and a courage that is beyond their own. Bless them as a team to lead America to the dawning of a new day with renewed trust in God that will lead to peace, justice, and prosperity.

"We pray this humbly in the Name of the Prince of Peace who shed His blood on the Cross that men might have eternal life. Amen."

There's no doubt that Billy was at the center of the Oval Office transfer of power that day between Johnson and Nixon. His deep and abiding friendship with both men had a calming influence over such an emotional day in one of the most turbulent times in our nation's history.

When Johnson finally settled into his new life at his ranch, he often invited Billy to visit. This offered Billy a much different glimpse of the man.

"He wanted to do something for the underprivileged and the people that were oppressed in our society, especially black people. I remember after he left office I visited the ranch a number of times," Billy said. "Just to see him with children, little black children, and how he loved them and would take them for rides and take them up in his arms. This had no political motivation whatsoever."

Johnson's extreme loneliness continued after he left public office. It took him a full year to shake off his fatigue. He took up golf, watched movies, spent some time at a seaside villa in Acapulco, Mexico, and raised money for his proposed eighteen-million-dollar presidential library in Austin, Texas. He also resumed a smoking habit he had discarded fifteen years prior; it alarmed family and friends.

Deep down, Johnson felt unappreciated, agonizing over what his presidential legacy would be. His drinking habit kicked in again. He repeatedly listened to Simon & Garfunkel's 1970 classic "Bridge over Troubled Water," wallowing in depression. But his day always brightened whenever Billy would visit him and his wife, Lady Bird, at the LBJ Ranch.

During a 1971 visit, while taking a stroll along the Pedernales River, Billy said Johnson was in a low-key mood. He was remarkably reflective and prescient when he told Billy that one day, perhaps in the very near future, Billy was going to preach at his funeral. LBJ even picked out a shady spot in the family cemetery where Billy would deliver his eulogy. He predicted with great clarity how Billy would read from the Bible and deliver a Gospel message to his family and friends. He also hinted that perhaps Billy might let them know about some of his good works, too. On March 18, 1971, Billy sent Johnson a letter confirming their deal: if Johnson should precede him in death, he agreed to preach at his funeral.

A little less than two years later, Billy fulfilled his end of the bargain when Lyndon Johnson died of a heart attack at age sixty-four, though he looked much older. The sheer weight of the presidency had taken its toll on him in every way.

On January 25, 1973, Billy preached at a graveside service at that very spot Johnson pointed out, which sat next to the graves of his mother and father. Billy told those present as the daylight faded that there was "a massive manhood in Lyndon Johnson. He was a mountain of a man with a whirlwind for a heart…history will never be able to ignore Lyndon Baines Johnson. He was history in motion. He will stand tall in the history that future generations will study."

CHAPTER TWENTY-EIGHT

A Man I Never Knew

The 1970s...
What can I say to properly do the decade justice? I guess you just
had to be there.

If the 1960s was about changing the world, then the '70s was
about changing ourselves. The days of eating lentils in a muddy field
at Woodstock and bemoaning the Vietnam War were over. Jim Mor-
rison, Janis Joplin, and Jimi Hendrix were all dead, and Charles
Manson was in prison.

The new conflict seemed to come from within.

In the "Me Decade," we streaked, roller-skated, and flexed our
muscle cars...until the oil crisis caused our gas tanks to run dry. Men's
hair got longer, and women's skirts got shorter. This decade had it all
and then some: Watergate and water bongs; Indian gurus and Paris Peace
Talks; inflation and recession; domestic terrorism and foreign assassinations; the Pentagon Papers and pungent vapors; serial killers and killer
albums; a presidential resignation and pardon; Kent State and Heaven's
Gate; Pet Rocks and knee-high tube socks.

We listened to eight-track tape players, talked on CB radios, and danced under disco balls. There was also punk, funk, and lots of pop-psychology junk. The Beatles broke up and were replaced by KC and the Sunshine Band.

There were misguided hairstyles, platform shoes, bell-bottom jeans, and leisure suits that made us look supremely wacky and tacky. The '70s birthed Earth Day, the Clean Air Act, and the Clean Water Act, but exposed lots of dirty politicians, including a commander in chief who insisted, "I am not a crook!"

Billy Graham did his best to grapple with what was happening in American youth culture, which rejected almost every value parents had tried to instill—most especially organized religion. Here's a little-known factoid: Billy once attended a music festival in Miami, Florida, on the eve of the '70s that featured the Grateful Dead, Canned Heat, Johnny Winter, and Santana in an attempt to understand these new anti-establishment values.

Concert promoter Norman Johnson invited him, hoping to neutralize some of the opposition he faced from Miami officials. Johnson even offered Billy the opportunity to speak to concertgoers from the stage. But before he did, Billy went "undercover" and strolled the straw-covered grounds, eavesdropping on conversations, listening for what was on kids' minds and hearts, and trying to understand what they were truly searching for.

And he did, to some degree. The tragic assassinations of JFK, Dr. Martin Luther King Jr., and Robert F. Kennedy, combined with America's moral failure in racial equality and the country's involvement in Vietnam, led to widespread disillusionment and cynicism.

Even though it's hard for me to wrap my head around the idea of Billy at a Grateful Dead concert, I love that he had the sincerity, initiative, and fortitude to try to understand what was going on with the counter-culture of the day. Billy genuinely embraced them, dubbing them the "most exciting and challenging generation in history."

That's putting it nicely.

I was part of that generation, and we were very confused. We were rebelling against what is now called "The Greatest Generation." We thought we knew better, and we really didn't. But many in my generation were tired of the emptiness of status symbols and what we perceived as a meaningless life.

The popular Monkees song "Pleasant Valley Sunday" spoke of creature comforts and TVs in every room in "status-symbol land." We were a generation on a search; we just didn't know what we were searching for exactly.

At the festival, Billy got challenged almost immediately when a bearded youth approached him while he was mixing with the crowd. He even confided to Billy that he was high on a couple of substances, including the beloved weed which he'd just smoked.

Billy, keeping the young man's smile, replied that he could also get high on Jesus. He couldn't have looked more out of place in a tan suit and tie, talking with ponytailed stoners wearing bandannas and sunglasses. But photos that ran the next day show Billy with a warm smile on his face, clearly listening intently.

For some reason, Billy expected to hear from the boo-birds when he greeted concertgoers that Sunday morning. He told them he had heard what was on their hearts and minds and also caught on to the messages in their music. Billy reminded them they had more in common with Jesus than not—that He was essentially a rebel and nonconformist who could offer them peace and fulfillment if they chose to follow Him.

His words did not fall on deaf ears. More than 350 people made commitments to Christ and close to two thousand New Testaments were distributed that weekend—all because of Billy's curiosity and temerity.

This reveals perhaps one of the biggest secrets of Billy Graham's success in ministry. Some people, preachers included, reach a certain level of success and stop growing and learning. They rest on their laurels and live in the past.

Not Billy Graham.

He was always a naturally inquisitive person. What he was doing at a Grateful Dead concert was no different from what the Apostle Paul did in ancient Athens. Paul took the time to understand the culture, where he saw myriad statues erected to every imaginable god. He noticed one was dedicated to "An Unknown God" (in case they missed a god, the Greeks included it so all their bases would be covered). He stood in the meeting place and said, "As I was walking along, I saw your many shrines. And one of your altars had this inscription on it: 'To an Unknown God.' This God, whom you worship without knowing, is the one I'm telling you about" (Acts 17:23 NLT).

Billy had the heart of a true soul winner.

He genuinely cared about people who did not know the Lord, and he wanted desperately to reach them. Charles Spurgeon, the great British preacher, once said, "The Holy Spirit will move (nonbelievers) by first moving you. If you can rest without their being saved, they will rest, too. But if you are filled with an agony for them, if you cannot bear that they should be lost, you will soon find that they are uneasy, too. I hope you will get into such a state that you will dream about your child or your hearer perishing for lack of Christ, and start up at once and begin to cry, 'O god, give me converts or I will die!' Then you will have converts."

Billy Graham possessed that rare passion Spurgeon spoke of, and it spurred him on for decades. Long past when most would have retired or just burned out, Billy burned even more brightly.

Perhaps he was partially motivated by the trouble he was having connecting with his own son Franklin.

Franklin and I have been friends for more than three decades. He told me he was in full rebellion mode at that point in his life—drinking and smoking, getting into loads of trouble. Even a couple like Billy and Ruth could not tame their teenaged son. Franklin said his parents were outstanding examples to him; that was never the problem. He just wanted to live his own life, not theirs.

Billy took notice of the fact that Franklin listened to the music of Johnny Cash and saw it as a way to build a bridge to his prodigal child.

I chronicled his friendship with Cash in my 2019 book, *Johnny Cash: The Redemption of an American Icon.*

"America's Evangelist" phoned "The Man in Black," who was riding high with *The Johnny Cash Show*, a popular ABC-TV variety show that consistently drew up to fifteen million viewers a week. He asked if he might be able to visit the country superstar at his home in Hendersonville, Tennessee, just outside of Nashville. Billy wanted to consult with Cash on several matters, including how to connect with Franklin.

Billy met with Johnny and his wife, June Carter Cash, and Johnny's parents, who lived across the street. Their conversation that Sunday night was wide-ranging, lighting on topics as diverse as Vietnam and Cash's most recent triumph—a sell-out concert at New York City's Madison Square Garden.

The two men took an instant liking to each other, and at the end of the evening, Cash said, "If there's ever anything I can do to help you anytime, I wish you'd let me know."

Billy mentioned a Crusade he would be conducting in May 1970 at the University of Tennessee. He wondered if Cash would be interested in performing one of his gospel songs there and maybe even say a few words about his faith in Jesus. Cash readily assented.

It was the start of a firm, enduring friendship between America's favorite entertainer and America's favorite preacher. At every opportunity over the ensuing years, Cash and Billy prayed together, vacationed together, and confided in each other. They discussed their lives, their problems, their hopes, and their fears, and they bucked each other up.

"He's a good man. He is what he appears to be," Cash once said. "Billy's a friend.... We don't talk about the Bible or religion all that much. We talk about life."

Their friendship came with advantages, including Billy's introducing Cash to Richard Nixon.

At one of their parleys, Billy mentioned his friend Johnny Cash and the influence the singer had on young people through his television show, his music, and most especially through his powerful testimony regarding his personal trials and the salvation he credited to God. Not long after-ward, Cash received an invitation to perform for the president and First Lady Pat Nixon at the "Evening at the White House" concert series in the East Room on April 17, 1970.

Cash accepted with great pride and excitement, and his concert was a great success. It also gave Nixon a cool factor that he had not enjoyed before and desperately needed to reach younger voters.

Billy prayed a lot for Nixon as the civil unrest of the '60s spilled over into the '70s, mostly from colleges and universities. Billy saw a need to reach these folks, which is why he helped set up Explo '72 with eighty thousand students in Dallas's Cotton Bowl, Spree '73 in London, Euro-fest '75 in Brussels, and the Brazilian youth congress Generation '79, with five thousand gathering in São Paulo.

Much of Billy's time during the early 1970s was spent overseas, sharing the Gospel in countries torn by chronic strife and division, such as Ireland, which was a hotbed of religious and political conflict filled with bombings and armed attacks by the Irish Republican Army. In South Africa, an integrated audience of forty-five thousand people jammed King's Park Rugby Stadium in the coastal resort city of Durban to hear Billy preach in 1973. At the time, it was the largest multiracial crowd of any kind in South African history.

"Christianity is not a white man's religion, and don't let anyone tell you it's white or black," Billy railed. "Christ belongs to all people."

One of the most meaningful moments in Billy's life, he said, was when he met black baseball star Hank Aaron at the White House with Nixon.

"I was startled when Hank shook the president's hand, then grabbed me around the neck, kissed me on the cheek, and said he would rather meet me than the president," Graham said. "I was so embarrassed, but deeply flattered. Hank and I have been close friends ever since."

That same year—1973—the Billy Graham Evangelistic Association started the World Emergency Fund, which gave extra undesignated income to support other evangelistic enterprises and organizations throughout the world. The money also went to help other countries struck by famine or other natural disasters, including medical supplies and food. It also opened the door for evangelism, praying with survivors, and offering hope in Jesus Christ.

Hope was something Richard Nixon needed in abundant supply as he started his second term. By May 1973, he was deep into the Watergate crisis. The public hearings about the June 1972 break-in at the Democratic Party Headquarters at the Watergate Hotel in Washington, D.C., and the subsequent cover up, were hosted by the Senate Select Committee on Presidential Campaign Activities. It was daily fodder for the media; television delivered live coverage of the dramatic hearings to the living rooms of millions of American households, and only one month after they began, 97 percent of Americans had heard of the scandal. A majority believed Nixon had participated in the cover-up.

Many critics and former associates said Nixon could be devious about political maneuvering. At home and abroad, Billy did whatever he could to help Nixon while he was in office—using his contacts with missionaries in Southeast Asia to come up with a game plan to bring the Vietnam War to a conclusion, and serving as an unofficial diplomat during his evangelistic travels to Europe, Africa, and the Middle East. In the States, Billy's constant presence at Nixon's side helped bolster public support for the president, especially among Christian conservatives in the South. As his 1972 reelection campaign loomed, the president instructed his staff to start an early liaison with Billy's team, a fact affirmed by Charles Colson, Nixon's special advisor and "hatchet man," who later served a short prison term for his role in the Watergate affair. Colson, who famously gave his life to Jesus while incarcerated, then went on to found the influential Prison Fellowship ministry.

"I can think of few other people that Nixon ever spent time with totally alone," Colson recalled. "They had that kind of intimate relationship; he trusted Billy completely."

But Billy was human like anyone else, and sometimes he could be too trusting of people. Some, including Nixon, took advantage of that over the years. I suppose if you are going to have a weakness, generosity of spirit is not the worst one you could choose. The Bible says, "Love believes the best of every person" (1 Corinthians 13), and Billy practiced that to the extreme. I would not necessarily call it naiveté because, in fact, Billy read people well. However, at times he seemed to view them in a light that was not necessarily a true reflection of who they were. I believe that was the case with Nixon.

But Billy's relationship with Nixon also served a purpose, explained Colson, who was charged with mobilizing the religious community, finding disgruntled Democrats and persuading them to vote for Nixon. Colson also befriended many religious leaders and asked for their mailing lists. Pretty much all of them willingly coughed theirs up—except Billy.

"His assistants checked with Billy, came back and said to me, 'Nope, Mr. Graham says he does not want to do that,'" Colson said. "Even for his good friend Richard Nixon, who took him into his confidence and went to his Crusade, flew him on Air Force One, and cruised with him, he would not give up that mailing list. That was good."

As the Watergate scandal slowly unfolded, Billy refused to believe Nixon was involved. He sent him a reassuring note on April 6, 1973.

"I continue to follow all of your activities with tremendous interest, admiration, and prayer. I have marveled at your restraint as the rumors fly about Watergate," Billy wrote. "King David had the same experience. He said: 'They accuse me of things I have never heard about. I do them good but they return me harm'" (Psalm 35:11–12).

Ah, but King David didn't have tapes or transcripts of his dealings. In April 1974, when the secretly recorded conversations in the Oval Office were leaked to the media, Billy slowly started to come around. As he reviewed the transcripts in the *New York Times*, he was disheartened by Nixon's duplicity and especially jarred by his use of profanity. It also made him physically sick.

"Never, in all the times I was with him, did he use language even close to that," Billy later recalled. "Those tapes reveal a man I never knew."

Though Billy ultimately chose to forgive Nixon for Watergate, he did not absolve him; but neither did he judge the man, something he learned from Matthew 7:1–2: "Do not judge, or you too will be judged. For in the same way you judge others, you will be judged, and with the measure you use it, it will be measured to you" (NIV).

Billy did not shrink from commenting publicly on the scandal, stating it wasn't simply a mistake but a sin in God's sight. He called it a "symptom of a deeper moral crisis that affected other nations besides our own."

To Nixon's credit, he didn't want Billy's ministry besmirched by the scandal and kept his distance until he left the White House—a sure sign of his respect.

A few months later on August 9, 1974, Nixon resigned in the face of almost certain impeachment and removal from office. The next day, Billy told the media he felt sorry for the president and his family and only wished him well.

"I shall always consider him a personal friend," Billy said. Nixon surely felt the same way, but he had a hard time expressing it.

But did Billy feel used by Nixon? It was hard for him to believe it, but it was possible.

"Maybe I was naïve at the time," Billy would later say. "Maybe I was used." But he stopped short of saying that Nixon exploited him. Still, Billy felt somewhat burned by the episode. This would certainly manifest itself in his dealings with future presidents. He would become acquainted with each commander in chief until the end of his life but decided that he would be more cautious in the future.

Nixon and Billy discussed Watergate only once afterward, a few months after his resignation. Nixon didn't offer any information that Billy didn't know already. Billy encouraged Nixon to embrace his faith and to be more forthright as a witness for Christ.

He observed that Nixon was private, reserved, and played his cards close to the vest emotionally and spiritually—a fact confirmed by Charles

Colson. He spoke to Nixon after he left the presidency and tried twice to raise the question of Christ. Nixon cut him off both times.

"He would be very likely to talk about it with Graham, especially when he was going through his Watergate experience. Graham told me, 'He prayed to receive Christ,' and I believe him," Colson said. "Whether anything came of it I cannot tell you. Nixon was such a private man. Graham was one of the guys that he let right inside, as close as you can get. I hope when I get to Heaven, I'll see Richard Nixon, and it may be because of Graham. He's the only person who possibly could have done it."

This is probably why Billy maintained his friendship with Nixon after he left the Oval Office, often sending the former president letters and telegrams on a variety of topics. In turn, Nixon offered counsel to Billy when traveling to countries that required some finesse to enter. In fact, Nixon wrote to several world leaders in Eastern Europe and Central America on Billy's behalf when he needed entry, safe passage, or good old-fashioned hospitality.

In July 1990, Billy was reunited once again with the Nixons. That's when the Richard Nixon Presidential Library was dedicated in Yorba Linda, California. By that time, Nixon's public image had been largely rehabilitated and had been recast in the mold of an "elder statesman." Following his reemergence from a long, self-imposed exile, Nixon appeared more relaxed with the public. He was now more candid with reporters than in the past. He offered foreign policy expertise to other presidents and world leaders (but only if asked). He was older, mellower, and less guarded. The public, it seemed, was ready to forgive him for Watergate and move on. The library's construction and dedication were proof of this.

Arrangements were made for Billy to deliver the invocation for the gala event. His services were requested again at a dinner banquet that same evening in Century City to commemorate the Nixons' fiftieth wedding anniversary. Billy was asked to give the blessing. That was a happy occasion. Three years later, he saw the former president under a very different set of circumstances.

Billy conducted Pat Nixon's memorial service in June 1993, which was an intimate gathering of close friends and relatives at the Nixon Library. As Billy entered the grounds, he embraced the former president, who, in an uncharacteristic display of emotion, wept uncontrollably in Billy's arms at the loss of his loyal wife. Billy had a private word with Nixon, no doubt comforting him as only Billy could.

The two men shared a deep bond. Billy said Nixon was an easy man to love, but a hard man to get to know.

"Many people say, 'You couldn't know him completely,' and I suppose that's true of anybody," Billy said. "He might have been more difficult to know because he was reticent. He was reared in a Quaker home and they don't wear their feelings on their sleeves. And there was a shyness to him. I think he found it hard to be a backslapper and glad hander."

One of the last times Billy spent with Nixon was at a New York City restaurant. They sat outside eating their lunch, watching the traffic crawl and people stroll by. They freely discussed whatever was on their minds at that meal, even touching on religion and theology. The spirit of God must have hit Billy at that moment, because he spoke plainly to Nixon that day. Billy told him that their time on this earth was limited and winding down; that they would be wise to use that time as Psalm 2:12 instructs: "Teach us to number our days, that we gain a heart of wisdom" (NIV).

That moment came sooner than either expected. In April 1994, Nixon suffered a major stroke at his home in Park Ridge, New Jersey. Billy, who was in New York City for a United Nations dinner function, went to the emergency entrance of the hospital as soon as he received word. A hospital official escorted him to Nixon's daughter, Tricia. Billy comforted her with some helpful Scripture and then prayed with her. Nixon's other daughter, Julie, arrived a little later and shared another moment of prayer. Three days later, the eighty-one-year-old former president was gone.

Twenty years earlier, Nixon had asked Billy to officiate his funeral. Like Lyndon B. Johnson before him, Billy fulfilled that request. Nixon's funeral was a star-studded affair on the grandest of political stages. It was attended by five living presidents and their wives, high-ranking politicians, foreign dignitaries, and several other noteworthy people. I don't think Billy's words were ever more powerfully arranged and delivered. He gave a eulogy that didn't pay much attention to Watergate but focused on the totality of Richard Nixon as a man, his life in public service, and his achievements in the Oval Office.

"Today, we remember that with the death of Richard Nixon, a great man has fallen," Billy said. "We have heard that the world has lost a great citizen, and America has lost a great statesman. And those of us that knew him have lost a personal friend."

Billy also reminded people of their own mortality before giving them a moment of contemplation regarding their salvation. He started by quoting English scholar and poet John Donne.

"Donne said that there is a democracy about death. 'It comes equally to us all, and makes us all equal when it comes,'" Billy said. "I think today every one of us ought to be thinking about our own time to die, because we too are going to die, and we are going to have to face Almighty God with the life that we lived here.

"There comes a time when we have to realize that life is short, and in the end the only thing that really counts is not how others see us here, but how God sees us, and what the record books of Heaven have to say…"

Billy said that death is not the closing of a door nor the end of our time on Earth; rather, it's access to the Promised Land. This, he explained, means there is hope for all believers.

"Richard Nixon had that hope, and today that can be our hope as well," he said in closing.

Billy always finished with that invitation, another predictable secret to his amazing ministry: tell people about their need for God, then encourage them to respond.

Billy did that until his dying day.

CHAPTER TWENTY-NINE

Revival in a Suitcase

Billy Graham pretty much stayed away from the White House for the second half of the '70s. The whole Nixon and Watergate affair had left a bad taste in his mouth. It was a painful reminder that politics has often been labeled the second-oldest profession and bears a striking resemblance to the first. And besides, as Harry S. Truman once said, "All the president is, is a glorified public relations man who spends his time flattering, kissing, and kicking people to get them to do what they are supposed to do anyway."

So Billy reset his heart and mind on world evangelism. He decided to go big in his next Crusade when he selected Seoul, South Korea. He was hoping for revival, but that came hand-in-hand with nagging doubts about himself. After all his years in ministry, all the triumphs, and all the doors that God opened, Billy never took anything for granted.

"I think the most difficult problem that I have in the ministry is myself, my own limitations, and I have to kneel down before the Lord, day after day and say, 'Lord, help me to make up for my own limitations,'" Billy said when he landed in Seoul in late May 1973. "Many people feel that I come and bring revival in a suitcase. The expectancy is so great that I feel so totally inadequate that I have to say, 'Lord, I have to get out of the way and let You take over.'"

I think it's safe to say the Lord did indeed take over South Korea in those magical five days. It was a country that held a special place in Billy and Ruth Graham's hearts, and it was ripe for the Gospel.

In the twenty years since the Korean War had ended, South Korea had experienced alternating periods of autocratic and democratic rule. It was ostensibly a republic, but citizens only had limited political freedom.

In 1961, a military coup put General Park Chung-hee in power. Under Park the country began to develop industry and march toward economic strength, shifting from one of Asia's poorest nations to one of its wealthiest.

Under Park's reign, South Korea developed a highly skilled labor force and experienced a period of intense industrial development and economic growth in the 1960s and 1970s. Each household enjoyed a per capita income some seventeen times that of their neighbor to the north; theirs was one of the fastest-growing economies in the world. "Development First, Unification Later," became the slogan of the times.

But Park wasn't a savior by any means. Even though he maintained a policy of "guided democracy," it was essentially guided…well, by him! Park restricted personal freedoms, put clamps on the press and opposition parties, and took control of the judicial system and universities. He also organized and expanded the Korean Central Intelligence Agency and put in place a system that looked an awful lot like an autocracy that paid lip service to democracy. He ran the country like a dictator for almost eighteen years. His spy service suppressed any domestic opposition to the regime with wiretapping, arresting, and torturing people without court orders. It was heavily involved in behind-the-scenes political maneuvers. Government crackdowns on demonstrations were usually harsh and left piles of corpses in their wake.

Those crackdowns, a rogue intelligence agency, and a hard-fisted leader were some of the reasons it took three years, hundreds of churches, and several thousand people to coordinate the five-day Crusade with the heads of state, military leaders, and the press. Seven months before Billy arrived, it looked like all bets were off.

That's when Park declared martial law on October 17, 1972, and a month later, he installed an authoritarian regime called the *Yushin* ("Revitalization Reform") order. He also instituted a new constitution that gave him sweeping powers; anyone who dared to cross or publicly criticize him did so at their own peril. So why did he allow a Crusade to take place in his country? Maybe letting Billy come and preach the Gospel bolstered his image to South Koreans and the outside world. It's safe to assume he didn't do it because he was a nice guy.

Meanwhile, Billy simply focused on what was important to God: preaching the Gospel to an audience that was spiritually hungry and ready to listen. (Park met Billy shortly before the Crusade and gave him a Cadillac to drive around the city. Normally, Billy would have considered the car an extravagance and turned it down for a simpler model. However, knowing Park's reputation as a ruthless dictator, he graciously accepted it. As Scripture reminds us, "The heart of the King is the hand of the Lord" [Proverbs 21:1 KJV], and that applies to dictators too. God worked despite Park and accomplished His divine purpose.)

Park gave permission for BGEA organizers to hold the Crusade from May 30 to June 3, 1973, on a mile-long asphalt expanse on Yeouido Island used for official state events and military demonstrations.

Yeouido is an island on the beautiful Han River, which cuts through Seoul. The capital city at that time boasted a population of six million people. In the coming decades, this piece of land would evolve into the city's main finance and banking district, home to Seoul's tallest skyscrapers. But in 1973, it was a spit of sandy earth. Before that, it was a national pasture for sheep and goats—ironic, since Billy would tend to a flock of 3.2 million people by the end of the Crusade.

When Billy and Ruth stepped off the plane on May 30, 1973, they were greeted by a marching band, a choir singing hymns, and thousands of well-wishers waving national flags. It was the kind of welcome usually reserved for national dignitaries and foreign leaders, war heroes, or royalty. To that end, Billy admitted he was in Seoul as an ambassador.

"I'm not here as an American. I represent a higher court than the White House," Billy said into a microphone mere minutes after he stepped off the plane. "I am an ambassador of the King of kings and Lord of lords, and I come in that spirit as His representative."

He said at the same press conference: "Christianity is not a set of ethics. Christianity is a person. And that person is Jesus Christ. And your eternal destiny will depend on your response to His offer of love and mercy. And that essentially is the message I have come to proclaim."

Meanwhile, North Korea did not allow any religious practice of any type (according to one news report, more than two hundred thousand Christians have gone missing since 1953). That country looked upon Billy much differently than its neighbor to the south.

"The North Korean response was 'the witch doctor from America came and performed a witch act,'" recalled Billy Jang Hwan Kim, pastor of the Suwon Central Baptist Church and Billy's translator during the Seoul trip.

Decades before, Kim worked as a houseboy for the U.S. military under Sergeant Carl Powers, who helped him get an education in the United States. Powers enrolled the seventeen-year-old Kim at Bob Jones Academy in Greenville, South Carolina—the sister institution of Bob Jones College.

Kim started as a ninth grader and had to learn quickly, as it was already the second week of the spring quarter. Despite fighting culture shock, severe homesickness, and a limited English vocabulary (he only knew a few swear words, courtesy of American G.I.s), the South Korean transplant rapidly picked up the language, accepted Jesus as his Lord and Savior, became an honor student and role model, and met his future wife, Trudy, who was a student and waitress in the school cafeteria. When he returned to Korea, he had a master's degree in theology and a vision for ministry. Still ministering as I write this, today Billy Kim has been aptly described as the "Billy Graham of Asia."

Even Billy Graham might have agreed with that assessment.

"I would be absolutely nothing were it not for my good voice, Billy Kim," he said at a 1973 press conference in South Korea.

Their friendship started with an official letter from the BGEA a few weeks before the Crusade. It essentially notified him of Billy's plans to hold one in Seoul (which he knew) and asked if he'd be Graham's interpreter. That last bit he had to read over again to make sure his eyes weren't playing tricks on him. Billy Graham had been a role model to Kim; he had attended a Crusade in New York while studying at Bob Jones Academy. Almost a decade later, he followed the BGEA to Berlin, West Germany, and dreamed of becoming a world evangelist. Interestingly enough, two years before receiving Billy's invitation, he had written a letter imploring him to hold a Crusade in Korea.

The letter he now held in his hand not only meant that he was going to meet his evangelistic hero, but also be his interpreter at that Crusade. God indeed worked in mysterious ways.

After Kim accepted the position, he was sent Billy's books, sermon notes, and videotapes of other Crusades, which he intensely studied. The hard work paid off. He had Billy down cold, right down to the accent, gestures, and intonations.

"I felt so incapable. How can I communicate his message to people?" Kim said. "His message was so important for our people to hear...well, once I got in with him, I didn't even know what I was doing. And I think I was completely influenced by the force that, you know, we call the Holy Spirit."

When the two men finally met in Yeouido People's Plaza, backed by a choir of six thousand, the American and Korean evangelists melded together in near-perfect harmony, preaching, interpreting, and leaving a deep impression on the hearts and souls in attendance. The two were in seamless spiritual flow with one another; some were even confused as to who was actually doing the preaching, recalled Cliff Barrows.

"A couple of (G.I.s) at the foot of the platform looked up and said, 'Boy, look at Billy Kim preach. Isn't he preaching a message?'" Barrows said. "And the other one turned to him and said, 'Yeah, and Billy Graham is doing a pretty good job interpreting for him.'"

Billy truly didn't care who got the accolades as long as God received the glory—and He most certainly did.

On the first day of the Crusade, more than three hundred thousand people attended. They sat on newspapers, pads, blankets, and even bedding. The crowd was sprinkled with Christians, Buddhists, Catholics, Daoists, and followers of Confucius.

"All the religions of the world are man reaching towards God," Billy preached. "Christianity is God reaching towards man. God in the person of Jesus Christ."

Each day the Crusade grew in attendance with the finale exceeding 1 million people—the largest crowd ever assembled to hear Billy preach and the largest face-to-face presentation of the Gospel of all time. An estimated 3.2 million people heard the Gospel in that five-day span, smashing the previous record of 2.6 million at a Crusade in Glasgow, Scotland, in 1955. Most important, some 75,000 people submitted cards to indicate they had made a decision for Christ through the Crusade. It was a historic moment for the Korean church, which not only experienced revival, but nurtured the next generation of God's servants. It was a personal milestone for Billy as well.

"I have traveled the world over for a quarter of a century and preached in many of the great stadiums of the world, but I've never seen an outpouring of people as this," he said in a farewell statement. "This is the work of God. There is no other explanation."

Billy Graham did not bring revival to South Korea; revival brought him. But his ministry there resulted in a spiritual reawakening that is still having ripple effects to this very day.

Decades later, when Billy was on his deathbed, Kim visited him at his house in Montreat, North Carolina. Billy smiled at the sight of his old friend, now an international figure himself. Billy, who was bedridden and ailing, had not lost an ounce of his passion or the glint in his eye.

"The last time I met Reverend Billy before he passed away, his condition was so frail it was almost impossible for him to hear or see," Kim recalled. "But the first words he said to me were, 'Let's have another Crusade rally in Korea.'"

CHAPTER THIRTY

The Son Also Rises

A s I review the life of Billy Graham, I am simply amazed by the number of professional milestones he reached. And these milestones, I might add, weren't reached sporadically, by the decade, or on special anniversaries. Every year since he started his ministry, he added new programs to his docket, pushed boundaries, built bridges, broke records, and led the way when it came to spreading the Good News of the Gospel. Billy's hunger and zeal for people to know Christ never waned or let up.

I don't think it is an overstatement to say that Billy Graham was a modern-day prophet. A prophet is not always someone who predicts the future; a prophet is one who speaks for God. Billy did that for decades around the world. No one could have done all Billy was able to accomplish on his own. That only comes through being dependent upon God and empowered by His Holy Spirit.

In late 1966, the BGEA and *Christianity Today* organized the World Congress on Evangelism. Approximately 1,200 preachers, clergymen, church leaders, and theologians representing more than 100 countries attended the ten-day conference at the *Kongresshalle* in West Berlin,

Germany. It was a fitting venue as it was a gift from the United States, designed in 1957 by American architect Hugh A. Stubbins.

The congress, led by Billy and *CT* Editor Carl F.H. Henry, was intended to be a spiritual successor to the 1910 World Missionary Conference in Edinburgh, Scotland. Many evangelical leaders met there for the first time. Despite the fact that it was held in Germany, it was primarily planned, led, and financed by Americans. Its intent was to define and clarify the need for evangelism in the culture among like-minded leaders, establish its relevance to the modern world, and find ways to reach and bring men and women to Christ. It also laid the groundwork for later and larger efforts to assemble evangelicals around the world.

A friend of mine told me he met Billy once and asked him what advice he would give to an older preacher.

"Get yourself a Timothy," Billy said.

That is a reference to the young man the great Apostle Paul mentored. Paul poured into Timothy, writing two letters to him (1 and 2 Timothy) telling him to "do the work of an evangelist" (2 Timothy 4:5), as well as to "teach these truths to other trustworthy people who will be able to pass them on to others" (2 Timothy 2:2 NLT).

That is exactly what Billy and his team were doing at the World Congress on Evangelism.

There would be many other conferences to come in the years to follow, as well as an entire retreat facility dedicated to training people in evangelism, which came to be known as the Billy Graham Training Center at the Cove in Asheville, North Carolina.

One of the most crucial and influential of those conferences took place in the summer of 1974. Billy sensed in his travels that many spiritual leaders felt disconnected from each other, and he felt compelled to bring them together. Wanting to build upon the success of that West Berlin congress nearly a decade before, the BGEA launched a monumental and larger event, this time held in Lausanne, Switzerland, from July 16–25, 1974.

The gathering drew more than 2,300 evangelical leaders from nearly every denomination and 150 countries, along with 1,300 observers and several hundred journalists. The BGEA even had translators in seven languages so everyone understood its mission.

As before, the Lausanne event was intended to train, motivate, and mobilize evangelists around the world. At the start of the conference, Billy said he believed "this could be one of the most significant gatherings, not only in this century but in the history of the Christian Church...we are gathered in Lausanne to let the earth hear His voice."

Leaders participated in plenary sessions, Bible studies, and discussions and debates over theology, strategy, and methods of evangelism. From this gathering, they produced "The Lausanne Covenant"—a declaration that defines the necessity, responsibilities, and goals of spreading the Gospel. Hundreds of organizations subsequently used the covenant as their Statement of Faith.

The congress also created the Lausanne Committee for World Evangelization, which continues to promote the cause to this day.

While Billy's heart and focus were set on preaching the Gospel through mass evangelism, days after Lausanne, he found himself embroiled in Washington politics once more.

On July 27, 1974, the House Judiciary Committee approved its first article of impeachment charging President Nixon with obstruction of justice. Six of the committee's seventeen Republicans joined all twenty-one Democrats in voting for it. The next week, the committee approved two more articles of impeachment for abuse of power and contempt of Congress.

On August 9, Nixon resigned to avoid probable impeachment in the House and a subsequent trial in the Senate. He left the Oval Office with two and a half years of his second term remaining.

"Our long national nightmare is over," declared Gerald A. Ford, the thirty-eighth president of the United States, upon assuming his new duties. But was it? There was still the question of what to do with Nixon once he left the White House. Should he be criminally charged for his role in the coverup or pardoned to end the stench of Watergate?

A month into Ford's presidency, Billy tried to reach him at the White House. He had known Ford since the 1950s when he was an up-and-coming

Republican congressman from Michigan. He knew Ford as a professing Christian, and the two had prayed together many times. Their relationship was warm, and they felt comfortable with each other.

They also shared a mutual friendship with Billy Zeoli, a Christian filmmaker who had met privately with Ford, praying and studying Scripture together. Over the years they grew closer. When Ford became vice president under Nixon in late 1973, Zeoli sent him weekly devotions in the mail, which included Scripture and a prayer. Ford said he believed each one to be "divinely inspired."

Zeoli was in attendance in Lausanne, and he and Graham had an opportunity to discuss his relationship with Ford. Billy told Zeoli he had a responsibility to share the Gospel with the next president but that he did not have a responsibility to be his friend.

"When you get to the White House, don't play golf with him," Billy instructed. "Don't go on (the presidential yacht) with him. Don't make it a social event. Be yourself. You have to try to ground him in Scripture."

What Graham didn't say was that his advice was learned the hard way through his friendship with Nixon. Billy still cared about the former president and went to bat for him when he sensed he was in a bad way, both emotionally and physically.

When Ford finally called Billy back, he told Billy he was giving the pardon serious consideration. Billy did not try to sway him to his way of thinking. Ford knew they were close. However, Billy did say he was constantly praying for the president.

Billy also sought out Nixon at his San Clemente, California, home in late August 1974, a few weeks after his resignation. However, Nixon wasn't taking his calls. His intuition told him that Nixon had dealt with so much internal trauma over the Watergate debacle that he wouldn't be able to survive a trial. Nixon was spiritually, physically, and financially depleted, spending one million dollars on various lawsuits relating to Watergate. He also owed back taxes to the federal government and had to sell off a few of his properties.

Billy also knew that Nixon suffered from thrombophlebitis, a dangerous disease that causes blood clots to form in the legs. Billy suffered from the same ailment. One month after Nixon had left office, his condition worsened when a new clot formed, swelling his left leg to twice its normal size. Billy felt a pardon from Ford would literally save Nixon's life.

Many observers noted the fallen president was a broken man in the throes of severe depression. Nixon usually started his day at 7:00 a.m., but he no longer had much on his plate besides figuring out how to rehabilitate his leg and his public image. Ron Ziegler, his former press secretary, sat alone with him for hours in his home office. Nixon's time away from the White House gave him much time to reflect on his behavior, and remorse finally set in.

"I let down my friends. I let down the country," Nixon finally confessed. "I let down our system of government—the dreams of all those young people that ought to get into government but they think it's all too corrupt...I let the American people down. And I have to carry that burden with me for the rest of my life."

David Eisenhower, Nixon's son-in-law, had also petitioned Ford for a pardon, as did a few others. But he and Billy were in the minority. America wanted to see Nixon punished, and swiftly at that. He was labeled a "crook," and the youth of the day particularly harbored ill will toward him. He represented the "establishment," the man who promised to get us out of the Vietnam War. But he turned out to be perceived as the crook who covered up the Watergate fiasco, making our country the laughingstock of the world. The reality is that other presidents have done far worse and not suffered the consequences that Nixon did. But Nixon knew he had failed.

Billy felt a pardon would quickly close this ugly chapter in American history and allow the nation to move on and heal. Furthermore, it would showcase Ford as a kind and forgiving man. But that act of kindness, however admirable, actually tanked electability in the upcoming 1976 presidential race. Ford knew it, and so did his inner circle, who tried to talk him out of what was tantamount to committing political suicide.

Ford also sought out his old law partner, Phil Buchen, in Grand Rapids, Michigan, to get a different take on the matter. Buchen told Ford that if he was going to put his neck on the line, it would be best to get a statement of contrition from Nixon.

Ford finally called Billy and told him it was a tough decision with many complexities. He also told Billy he was praying hard about the situation. Billy mentioned how hard he was praying for Ford, knowing he was in a rough spot.

Graham's phone call must have carried considerable weight because a few days later, on September 8, 1974, Ford finally granted Nixon a "full, free, and absolute pardon." It ended any and all possibilities of an indictment. Nixon, in turn, offered his statement of contrition: "I was wrong in not acting more decisively and more forthright in dealing with Watergate, particularly when it reached the stage of judicial proceedings and grew from a political scandal into a national tragedy. No words can describe the depth of my regret and pain at the anguish my mistakes over Watergate have caused the nation and the presidency, a nation I so deeply love, and an institution I so greatly respect."

The pardon sent shockwaves through America. Many were thankful the debacle was finally over, but an equal number felt Nixon had received a "get out of jail free" card from a political buddy. Editorials cast as Ford as a villain, and readers mostly agreed.

Predictably, Ford's approval rating tanked by a margin of twenty-five points. This, combined with tensions in the Far East and Middle East and double-digit inflation at home, put the final nails in his political coffin. There was also the fact that the populace wanted new blood in the White House in Watergate's aftermath.

I believe Ford and Billy can be credited for extending Nixon's life, but he was still not out of the woods. In October 1976, Nixon was hospitalized with phlebitis. His veins had become inflamed, impairing his circulation. He was knocking on death's door, going into shock. He eventually pulled through. (During his recovery, Ruth Graham asked a friend to hire a private plane and fly past the hospital with a banner that read: "Nixon—God Loves You and So Do We." You couldn't ask for better friends than the Grahams.) The fact that Billy did all this behind-the-scenes work for a friend and never boasted about it speaks volumes about his character.

On November 2, 1976, Jimmy Carter beat Ford for the presidency. Carter also wanted new blood in the White House, especially where it concerned Billy Graham. Initially, he kept his distance from the evangelist, preferring the company of Jim Bakker, the host of *The PTL Club*, and Pat Robertson, anchor of *The 700 Club*. It was surprising, given that Carter was a conscientious Christian who wasn't complicated like LBJ or private about his faith like Nixon. He, like Billy, was a born-again Southern Baptist firmly reared in the Bible. He even helped organize two Billy Graham Crusades in Georgia and hosted Billy at the governor's mansion. Both men were Democrats who believed in social justice and equality. If any president was destined for spiritual guidance from Billy, it certainly seemed like it should be Jimmy Carter.

Billy personally introduced me to the former president at one of his later Crusades in Atlanta. By then, a lot of water had passed under the bridge, but in the 1970s, their relationship ran hot and cold.

It definitely ran on the colder side when Billy commented to a reporter during the '76 campaign: "I would rather have a man in office who is highly qualified to be president who didn't make much of a religious profession than to have a man who had no qualifications but who made a religious profession." To Carter, it appeared that Billy was giving evangelicals permission not to vote for him. He resented the remark, as did his twenty-four-year-old son, Jeff, who was asked about it by a Tulsa radio personality.

"I hate to talk about religion, to tell you the truth," he started off. "I think the thing that people should watch out for are people like Billy Graham who go around telling them how to live. That's my personal opinion." He further fanned the flames the following day by claiming that Billy had received a doctorate degree for five dollars in the mail. His father immediately apologized to Graham for his son's remarks.

After the election, Billy took the high road and told the press that President-Elect Jimmy Carter was a personal friend and "a leader we can trust and follow." The overture may have helped their relationship because Carter did send an invitation to Billy for his inauguration. However, Billy told Carter he could not attend due to a four-day Crusade he was hosting in Sweden. He also sent a telegram from France saying he would be praying for President Carter. It was a sad milestone of sorts—it was the first time Billy had missed the occasion since attending Eisenhower's inauguration in 1953. He did, however, see Carter in November 1979 for an evening at the White House—the only time he did so during Carter's administration.

To Billy's recollection, he and Ruth, along with Rosalynn Carter, spoke of their Southern upbringings while First Daughter Amy watched television. They also discussed their faith, how much it meant in their lives, and the issues that often divide fellow Christians. They closed the evening in prayer.

After that night, Carter and Billy had improved contact during the rest of his presidency, sending correspondence back and forth, including invitations to attend events at the White House. Many times, Billy was overseas or conducting a Crusade. That's too bad because I'm sure he could have used Billy's spiritual guidance. (They deepened their friendship after Carter left office.)

Jimmy Carter is a good man, and I have spoken with him on three occasions. He was always kind and considerate of others. A true gentleman. Once, I was on a plane, and the former president was going to be flying with us; he took the time to walk the aisles and shake the hand of every passenger. It was a gracious gesture and was much appreciated. He just did not seem to be suited for some of what was required to be the leader of the free world, and he only served one term.

Unlike presidents Roosevelt or Johnson, Carter never projected a big vision to the American people. A highly intelligent man, he became bogged down in policy details without a sense of a larger picture. His speechwriter declared afterward "that Carter believes fifty things, but no one thing."

His presidency was also plagued with crises. Inflation ran wild, there was high unemployment, the Soviets invaded Afghanistan, and a nuclear power plant in Harrisburg, Pennsylvania, almost blew up. Perhaps the worst crisis birthed during the Carter years was when radical Iranian college students took over the American Embassy in Tehran and held the staff hostage. The situation lasted four hundred and forty-four days from November 4, 1979, to January 20, 1981. Every day it led the news, and Ted Koppel made his career reporting on it on his program *Nightline*, keeping a running count of the days that passed. Making it even worse was a failed military rescue mission in the spring of 1980. It just seemed like Carter couldn't win... at anything.

After he left office, he found his calling in peace, diplomacy, and humanitarian work. He declared, like Harry Truman, that he wouldn't use his life after the presidency to become rich. He has worked to promote peace and human rights in Cuba, North Korea, and South Africa, among many other countries. Many people don't fully understand or appreciate the role he played in a helping the United States avert a nuclear crisis with North Korea in 1994. Domestically, he has been a high-profile supporter of Habitat for Humanity, a Georgia-based philanthropic institution that helps low-income working people around the world to build and buy their own homes—and he has done so not by serving on the board, but by swinging a hammer. As of this writing, he remains a deacon and teaches Sunday School at his Baptist church in Plains. (Carter also showed up in Charlotte in 2007, along with former presidents George H.W. Bush and Bill Clinton, for the Billy Graham Library dedication. I had the privilege, along with my wife, to take a photo with him, Bush Sr., and former First Lady Barbara Bush.)

While Carter was still president in September 1978, Billy's son Franklin entered humanitarian work himself at an organization called Samaritan's Purse.

Samaritan's Purse—an evangelical Christian organization that provides aid to people in need as part of its missions work—was founded by Robert Willard Pierce. Pierce was a former Youth for Christ evangelist (he started preaching at age thirteen) and journalist, who later became the organization's vice president. While visiting China on a university lecture circuit, Pierce came upon a group of lionhearted women who gave up their lives back home to live among lepers and orphans, tending to them and sharing the love of Christ. Through their selfless love and devotion, God gave Pierce a vision for ministry.

Pierce was a complicated, stubborn, and temperamental man with a big heart. He was alternatively warm and sensitive, then brazen and abrupt. He was passionate, unorthodox, and given to drama, according to Franklin Graham. He had suffered several tragedies throughout his lifetime: He was ousted by World Vision, the Christian relief agency he founded, by its board of directors in 1967. A year later, his daughter Sharon committed suicide after complaining of his long absences. He also had serious marital issues with his wife, Lorraine, who prayed fervently for him to return home. He never did.

In the wake of being released from World Vision, he founded Samaritan's Purse in 1970 and struck up a friendship with Franklin Graham at a Crusade in Atlanta in July 1973. Their meeting came at a perfect time in Franklin's life. He was at the tail end of his prodigal journey, which including drinking, smoking, fighting, and getting expelled from college. For years he had rebelled against his father's ways, resenting the fact that he was only seen as Billy Graham's son and not an individual.

The bad-boy rebel act was put to rest when he went to the Middle East to help friend Roy Gustafson conduct a summer tour. One night, alone in his room in Jerusalem, he sat on his bed, smoked a cigarette, and picked up his New Testament. He read from John 3, where Jesus told Nicodemus, "You must be born again." If you happen to need a quick refresher: Nicodemus was a respected religious leader in his city. But all of his knowledge and understanding did not guarantee his entrance to Heaven. He had to be born again. That was Franklin's lightning-bolt moment. He put out his cigarette, got down on his knees, poured his heart out to God, and confessed his sins. He repented for his past behavior and promised that if He could put the pieces of his life together, he was His. Franklin asked for forgiveness, to be cleansed of his sins, and recommitted his life to Christ.

As he later said, "the rebel had found the cause."

Shortly after his born-again experience, Franklin returned to North Carolina and married a hometown girl, Jane Austin Cunningham, on his parents' lawn in Little Piney Cove, where he also made a public proclamation of his faith.

"This is a new beginning for Jane Austin and me, and we want you to know we are going to follow Jesus Christ," he said. "Both of us have committed ourselves to serving Him, wherever that path takes us."

In time, Franklin ditched the cigarettes and the alcohol. Soon he began looking for ways to show his faith. That's when Bob Pierce invited him on a six-week mission trip to Asia in October 1975.

Franklin received a hands-on education in hardship and poverty as Pierce exposed him to some of the world's poorest populations: Bhutan in the Himalayas, the jungles of Borneo, and the banks of the Ganges River in India.

They flew small airplanes deep into the jungle and landed on small airstrips. Franklin witnessed people still running around naked, as they had hundreds of years before. He visited villages with no modern conveniences, met witch doctors and Hindu priests who sacrificed live animals, slid across slimy, wet log bridges to cross ravines, and traveled in dugout canoes. Pierce was teaching Franklin about the Gospel on the cutting edge and trying to reach people living in total spiritual darkness.

"Buddy, these people need to hear about Jesus Christ," Pierce told him.

The combination of pure adventure and big faith appealed to Franklin, who took over Samaritan's Purse when Pierce died on September 7, 1978. He proclaimed at the time: "I'm going to travel the gutters and ditches of the world, and I'm going to help people in the name of the Lord

Jesus Christ. My father can go to the big stadiums, but I'll just go to the highways and byways."

Today Samaritan's Purse is a massive operation that deploys thousands of volunteers from around the globe to distribute supplies to those suffering from war, famine, and natural disasters. It stands ready to respond to a crisis anywhere in the world, with medical teams dispatched to the aftermath of disasters in Ecuador, Mozambique, the Bahamas, the Plains of Nineveh in Iraq, the Democratic Republic of Congo, Haiti, and at the site of the Twin Towers after the 9/11 attack. Most recently, it set up a sixty-eight-bed respiratory care hospital in New York's Central Park during the coronavirus outbreak of 2020, which occurred during the writing of this book. In fact, I contracted COVID-19 in October 2020, but my symptoms were fairly mild. It felt like a cold, and I was very fatigued. I also lost my sense of taste and smell. It was much worse for my co-author. His eighty-three-year-old father lost his life to the virus.

Franklin had finally found his mission, and Billy remained steadfast regarding his.

In November 1980, Billy was called to California for a special task. Someone who seemingly had it all was in need.

CHAPTER THIRTY-ONE

California Christians

In late 1980, Billy Graham's star was at its zenith while another pop culture icon's was crashing.

Steve McQueen, cinema's "King of Cool," had been diagnosed with mesothelioma, a rare and deadly form of cancer, the year before. Just months before receiving his diagnosis, McQueen had quietly given his life to the Lord on the balcony of an out-of-the-way church in Ventura, California. Now he was staring down certain death.

I wanted to find out what was behind "The King of Cool's" conversion, and I told that story in a 2017 bestselling book called *Steve McQueen: The Salvation of an American Icon* and a feature documentary called *Steve McQueen: American Icon.*

I have always admired McQueen as an actor and all around "guy's guy"—and because the story includes my friend Billy Graham, some of it bears repeating.

In a Sunday morning service, I briefly told the story of how a troubled boy who became the world's top movie star turned to Jesus after being disillusioned by the sheer emptiness of all he'd accumulated and accomplished.

Afterward, a member of my church, Mike Jugan, asked to speak privately. Mike, a friend and terrific Christian, is a retired pilot for Alaska Airlines. He also was the copilot of the airplane that had taken Steve McQueen to El Paso, Texas, in a last-ditch effort to save the actor's life. He told me then about his encounter with both of my heroes.

On November 3, 1980, Mike was called to the airport in Oxnard, California, to fly a party of three to El Paso. There, he discovered the passengers were actually Steve McQueen and two medical aides.

Mike and his pilot parked far from the terminal in an effort to afford McQueen as much privacy as possible. As they sat in the cockpit waiting for their passengers to arrive, they heard a knock on the side door.

"Are you with the Sam Sheppard party?" asked a tall man wearing an overcoat and hat. It was a code name for McQueen, who'd been hounded by the media ever since the *National Enquirer* broke the story of his cancer. When Mike answered affirmatively, the man stuck out his hand and introduced himself.

"I'm Billy Graham," he said, and climbed aboard.

After a few minutes, a green pickup truck with a custom aluminum camper shell pulled under the canopy that had been set up over the forward part of the aircraft to shield McQueen from paparazzi or other curiosity seekers. McQueen, who had been lying down and receiving oxygen, climbed out of the truck, sporting blue jeans, a T-shirt, and a sombrero, with a bottle of soda in his hand.

"Howdy, fellas," he greeted the pilots as he slipped into a seat on the plane. His two nurses quietly followed.

"I'm standing there," recalled Mike, "looking at my childhood hero, and my heart went out to him. You could see his belly was distended and swollen from the tumors." But Mike also noticed something else: "The look in his crystal blue eyes was predictably fierce. He had this indomitable spirit about him, and he seemed to be at peace."

There were no formal introductions, but Billy did what he had done thousands of times before: he gathered the folks around him and asked God to bless the pilots, the flight itself, and McQueen. Then, before leaving, the famed evangelist leaned in for a final private word with the actor. Except for their hushed voices, there was silence.

When Billy got up to go, he handed his personal Bible to McQueen. On the front inside flap he had written:

> To my friend Steve McQueen.
> May God bless you and keep you always.
> Billy Graham
> Philippians 1:6
> Nov. 3, 1980

Just before Billy exited the plane, Steve called out, "I'll see you in Heaven!"

Many people prayed for Steve McQueen when news of his cancer broke, including former actor Ronald Reagan, with whom he'd been friends since the 1950s. In a more-than-kind gesture, Reagan—the governor of California and a presidential hopeful at the time—even flew a renowned surgeon from Mexico on his private jet to meet McQueen in California days before his final operation.

Sadly, McQueen did not survive his surgery, passing away from complications on November 7, 1980—Billy's sixty-second birthday. When McQueen's son Chad reached his side that morning, he found his father still cradling Billy's Bible in his hands.

"I look back on that experience with thanksgiving and some amazement," Billy later said. "I had planned to minister to Steve, but as a matter of fact, he had ministered to me. His cheerfulness, his bright eyes, his excitement about his relationship with God will never be forgotten. I saw once again the reality of what Jesus Christ can do for a man in his last hours."

I have no doubt that Billy has seen Steve in Glory since then. Imagining their reunion makes me smile.

The day after McQueen departed for Mexico, Ronald Reagan handily defeated Jimmy Carter in the general election to become president of the United States. Although it was a shame that McQueen never got a chance to experience Ronald Reagan's America, which was prosperous, full of hope, and saw a return to national pride, it no doubt pleased Billy, who was an old friend of "The Gipper."

Billy had met Reagan in 1953 at a benefit for retired actors. Their mutual admiration and their love of the Bible cemented their enduring friendship over the years. Reagan, Billy noted, had a spiritual side to him that often went unnoticed. He added that Ronald and Nancy Reagan were both interested in understanding more about the Scriptures, especially Ronald.

Additionally, Billy was drawn to Reagan's quick wit and personality, calling him "one of the most winsome" men he'd ever known.

They socialized, played golf, and even appeared on a *Dean Martin Celebrity Roast* together in 1974. Together they "roasted" the man of the hour, Bob Hope. Before they went on, Reagan warned Billy to be on his toes; some of those powerful people might want to take a shot at him.

Billy appreciated his counsel. He'd had enough experience to know that some people, including some of the most seasoned comedians of that time, might take delight in trying to embarrass a clergyman. They seated him beside the glamorous Hungarian-American actress and socialite Zsa Zsa Gabor, but no one made any attempt to embarrass him. He suspected Reagan may have dropped a hint to them beforehand.

This wasn't Billy's usual crowd. Here was Bob Hope, who had reached legendary status in America and the world for the "road pictures" he did with Bing Crosby, including *Road to Singapore*, *Road to Zanzibar*, and four others. Not intimidated by anyone, including presidents and certainly not a preacher, Hope could take a person down a few notches without even blinking. Hope was also beloved by Americans for entertaining the troops in every war from World War II to the Persian Gulf.

There was also comedian Don Rickles, the bullet-headed imp with a shark's smirk and the eyes of an undertaker. His nicknames "The Merchant of Venom" and "Mr. Warmth" attested to his unique set of skills. Known to a later generation as the voice of Mr. Potato Head in the *Toy Story* movies, in his day he would work a Las Vegas ballroom or *The Tonight Show Starring Johnny Carson* with such acerbic and cutting wit that people would be rendered speechless after he was done, still wanting more.

Billy showed he could project as much star power as any of them, if not more. What's remarkable about the appearance—ostensibly so insignificant when compared to London, Korea, and Hungary—is that Billy held his own so well. Reverse the tables and put Hope, Reagan, and Rickles in front of a million Koreans hungry for the Gospel and imagine how they would have fared.

At his core, Billy was the genuine article, not an actor. He was always the same person who had heard the Word back in North Carolina in 1934. He didn't change. But he did grow. Despite sailing on the presidential yacht, playing golf with world leaders, meeting privately with Winston Churchill, and counseling Hollywood's most dazzling stars and mobsters, he didn't change. None of it turned his head from his calling.

A tuxedoed Billy appeared at the podium and told a funny story about a golfing outing with Hope and even took a few shots from Rickles. Billy, as you would expect, kept his dignity while remaining funny, showcasing to the world that Christians can intermingle with those who don't share a common belief and have a little fun at the same time.

Reagan may have been winsome, but Billy knew how to "win some" with his tact and forthrightness before sharing the unshakable conviction and faith he had placed in Christ.

"There's no pretense when it comes to Bob Hope, except when it comes to counting his golf score," Billy said. "Bob asked me to sign his score card, except I had to refuse on the basis of the ninth Commandment: thou shalt not bear false witness. So Bob signed my name on the grounds that there's no commandment against forgery."

The crowd roared.

His relationship with Reagan took a serious turn a few years later in May 1980, when the presidential hopeful showed up at a Crusade in

Indianapolis. Reagan requested that they meet for breakfast, and when Billy arrived, he hit him up for a favor. Would Billy give him a public endorsement when his campaign reached North Carolina? At the time, Reagan's polling numbers weren't so hot in that state, hovering around 50 percent. He was running against a strong field of candidates that included Kansas senator Bob Dole, former Texas governor John Connally, Senate Minority Leader Howard Baker from Tennessee, Robert John Anderson from Illinois, and George H.W. Bush from Texas, who was his top rival.

Billy explained he couldn't comply because any endorsement of a candidate would taint the credibility of his ministry. Besides, Billy said, Reagan had the Republican nomination in the bag. Furthermore, he truly believed Reagan would defeat Carter to become the next president.

Reagan smiled and graciously dropped the matter. As Billy predicted, Reagan won the election. Voters were troubled by double-digit inflation, Carter's failure to set consistent policy goals, and the Iranian hostage crisis. Despite the fact that Carter was a decent and intelligent man, he was perceived as a weak president. Reagan handily won 489 electoral votes to Carter's forty-nine. It was a landslide and a pivotal moment in American history.

After Reagan's election, he wanted Billy to join him in a variety of inauguration ceremonies, including a prayer service at St. John's Episcopal Church near the White House.

Billy stood next to Reagan on the platform during the administering of the oath of office—a place he had become familiar with over the years. During Reagan's two terms (1981–1989), the Grahams spent many nights at the White House, attending state dinners and ceremonies, often mixing with foreign leaders, royalty, dignitaries, businessmen, sports figures, and celebrities.

One of the few times they didn't see each other at 1600 Pennsylvania Avenue was when Reagan was shot in the left lung outside a hotel in Washington, D.C., on March 30, 1981—a mere sixty-nine days after he took office—by John Hinckley Jr., a drifter. North Carolina senator Jesse

Helms summoned Billy to Reagan's hospital room to offer spiritual encouragement and prayer.

The next day Billy booked a private plane to the District of Columbia, where he was picked up by a White House car. He was rushed to George Washington University Hospital to be by Nancy Reagan's side. He prayed with her and Frank and Barbara Sinatra, longtime friends of the Reagans, who were already there. He also prayed with President Reagan himself, who expressed his desire to forgive his would-be assassin.

Reagan said that while he lay on the operating table, he focused on the hospital's tiled ceiling and prayed—mostly for Hinckley.

"I realized I couldn't ask for God's help while at the same time I felt hatred for the mixed-up young man who shot me," Reagan later said. "Isn't that the meaning of lost sheep? We are all God's children and therefore equally beloved by Him. I began to pray for his soul and that he would find his way."

That cleared the way for Billy to call Hinckley's parents, who, according to an article he had read, were Christians. He phoned them at their Colorado home to let them know they were in his prayers, suspecting their hearts were hurting. (His father, John W. Hinckley, later broke down in court, taking the blame for the shooting because he was estranged from his son and would not allow him to come home.)

That was the special side of Billy, who was so thoughtful of people in almost every circumstance.

Billy was known for his delivery of the Gospel and stands apart in American history as the greatest of the evangelists. But Billy also had a pastor's heart. He cared about individuals and did many kind and caring things for people that were never seen by the general public.

As I have already stated, there were not two Billy Grahams. He was the same man in private that he was in public. In fact, he was even more impressive privately because he had no audience to play to. He was really a genuine, humble country preacher at heart.

Everyone's prayers were clearly answered by the Lord, because that one bullet stopped mere centimeters from Reagan's heart. The wound needed to be stitched immediately, and he needed a lot of blood. His doctors were miracle workers, and Reagan felt his survival was divine intervention.

Reagan famously said before his operation to his surgeons, "I hope you are all Republicans." The doctors and nurses laughed, and one of them, a liberal Democrat, replied, "Today, Mr. President, we are all Republicans."

As he was being wheeled into the operating room, Reagan turned to Nancy and said, "Honey, I forgot to duck!"

Despite his good-natured humor, Ronald Reagan knew he had literally "dodged a bullet" and that God Almighty had spared his life. He shared that sentiment with Billy in a private moment and later again in his diary.

"Whatever happens now I owe my life to God and I will try to serve him in every way I can," he wrote.

Reagan was released from the hospital twelve days later and returned to his Oval Office duties. By the end of his administration in 1989, the United States had enjoyed its longest recorded period of peacetime prosperity, without recession or depression, since Eisenhower's administration three decades prior. He was and still is a beloved president, and his public stature has only grown since his death in 2004. He is rightly regarded as one of the greatest American presidents in history.

While Reagan spent a good deal of his two terms trying to achieve "peace through strength" where it concerned the threat of Communism, including improving relations with the Soviet Union, Billy likewise did the same through his evangelistic ministry.

In fact, Billy got a jump on Reagan regarding the penetration of the Iron Curtain. He had visited Moscow in 1959 and couldn't help but notice the "haunted, tired look on people's faces, along with their fear, insecurity, and what I interpreted in some settings as spiritual hunger and emptiness." He hoped someday to proclaim the Gospel throughout their nation and knelt in prayer in Red Square for God to one day provide that opportunity. It took thirty-three years to fulfill that vision, but Billy waited patiently.

He almost had a chance to preach in Communist Poland in 1966, which would have coincided with the release of a special edition of his classic book *Peace with God*. But twenty-four hours before his team was set to leave, the plug got pulled. Church and government officials could not get it together and iron out the details, so the trip was canceled. Billy felt that even though their planned Crusade had collapsed, he knew God would open that door when the time was right.

That door cracked slightly ajar a year later when Billy finally preached inside a Communist country, Yugoslavia, in July 1967. The country's constitution allowed for a certain degree of religious freedom. This enabled Billy to preach in Zagreb when he was invited by a committee of Protestant churches.

The Catholic Church in Zagreb also pitched in by granting the BGEA permission to utilize a site it owned and maintained through the years. Thousands stood in the rain for hours in a constant downpour for a pair of meetings. They came from as far as Macedonia, Czechoslovakia, Romania, and Hungary. Billy was deeply touched by their dedication and hunger to hear God's word during inclement weather.

That trip increased Billy's yearning to witness to Communist countries, knowing many of them were atheist. However, that largely depended on those nations' political climates. Billy would have to wait another decade to really get his foot through the door.

That finally happened when he visited Hungary in 1977 and Poland in 1978. Each visit was extremely memorable. In a Hungarian church, Billy heard the sound of clicking, thinking that people might be gnashing their teeth at him. When he looked up, he identified the noise: it was the locals handling their personal tape recorders. This was their way of sharing the Gospel with each other. In Poland, Billy had to deflect perceptions that he was anti-Catholic and command the masses to leave the church. Of course, that didn't happen.

At the death camp of Auschwitz, where an estimated 1.1 million people were killed in the gas chambers during World War II, Ruth heard clicks of another kind: cameras from the large press contingent covering their visit. Ruth, however, said those sounds gave her an eerie feeling that guns were being cocked behind them, thinking for a brief moment that she and Billy were the condemned.

What Billy didn't do was badmouth or disparage these countries. On his last day in Poland, Billy said at a Warsaw press conference: "I have come to see that the church can and does exist in every kind of society, including those with Communist governments. I have also discovered that many Christians in these countries have a depth of commitment that puts me to shame...I believe, as time passes, Christians in these countries will be seen more and more as an asset to their societies, and as a consequence the governments will give more recognition to the churches and to individual Christians."

Billy was so well-received that he was invited back to Hungary and Poland in 1981 when he received an honorary doctorate degree from the Christian Theological Academy in Warsaw. That was the same year I met Billy.

I was in Calgary for one of his Canadian Crusades that August. My friend and fellow pastor Mike MacIntosh and I wore the traditional uniform of Southern California—Hawaiian shirts and blue jeans—and over the course of our stay, we were dubbed "The Beach Boys."

Mike was close with Sherwood "Woody" Wirt, the editor of *Decision* magazine, whom we relentlessly hounded for an introduction to Reverend Graham. One day Woody called us to ask if we were ready to meet the man himself.

Do fish swim?

Mike and I, both called to be evangelists, jumped at the chance to meet our hero. Billy was being shuffled from one meeting to another that day and our quick moment took place in a hallway of the hotel where the Crusade was headquartered.

From around the corner, Billy suddenly appeared. He certainly seemed larger than life to both of us, and it showed on our faces. We stood there, stunned to see him in the flesh. We were like kids in a candy store. We were speechless as Billy extended his hand and said, "Hello, I'm Billy Graham." We exchanged a few pleasantries, and then Billy disappeared, off to his next meeting. Mike and I knew we could take that off our bucket lists. But little did I realize then that this would be the first of many other meetings and the beginning of a genuine friendship with the famed evangelist.

The next time Billy and I met, I received something much more meaningful than a handshake and a warm smile: his undivided attention. I'll tell you more about that in a few chapters.

CHAPTER THIRTY-TWO

From Russia with Love

For years, Billy Graham had talked about slowing down to a pace commensurate with his age. In July 1973, when he was pushing fifty-five, he hinted to the media that it was time to stop and smell the roses after decades of hard charging.

"I get weary. I have to rest more now. I stayed in bed from two to five every afternoon during my Atlanta Crusade, conserving my strength for night services," Billy said. "Though I will never retire, I expect to make a shift of gears toward a slightly different direction very soon.

"God has blessed me far beyond anything I could ever dream. If I had my personal choice, I would be a pastor of a small church in the mountains, serving my own little congregation best I know how. But God keeps opening the doors around the world and He keeps telling me to go through those doors with His word. Until He changes His mandate to me and my associates, that little church in the mountains will just have to wait."

What an interesting insight into Billy's heart this is. How many pastors of small churches would gladly swap places with Billy Graham? To have his effectiveness, his reach, and his impact is something others only dream about. But what people don't understand is what that costs.

It's true that Billy was one of the most famous and admired men in all the world. But he bore the burden of a lot of responsibility, a lot of expectations, a lot of pressure, and a grueling schedule.

The most significant thing Billy faced, however, was not what most famous people grapple with. It was the *spiritual pressure*. The devil clearly sets his sights on those who are making the greatest difference in the world for God's Kingdom. He will attack, tempt, harass, and hassle them every way he can. As both a pastor and an evangelist, I can personally attest to this.

The kind of spiritual attack I come under when I am giving a message to our congregation is nothing compared to what I face when I preach the Gospel in a stadium.

Stated simply, Satan hates evangelism and he hates evangelists. Doing these massive events was draining to Billy, and he was wistfully thinking back to simpler times.

As I have also stated, on more than one occasion I heard Billy say, "I'm just a country preacher." And when you get down to it, it was true. He was simply the country preacher that God used to change the world.

Fast forward a decade later. Billy, now nearing his mid-sixties, was still running at full speed and seeking new challenges in the early 1980s. In addition to the Crusades, he was delivering lectures, attending symposiums, conferences, workshops, retreats, and banquets, visiting think tanks, giving guest sermons at churches, making media appearances, and holding press conferences. Keep in mind that fresh sermons and special remarks were required for each occasion. All of this was on top of tending to BGEA business, holding board and committee meetings, and overseeing and tending to all of its subsidiaries. It was a large plate that kept getting fuller each year.

In 1982, the BGEA hosted a mixture of thirty-two Crusades, speaking engagements, conferences, and evangelistic meetings—a number that completely astounds me to this day. It's staggering, actually. When we first began doing our own crusades, I did six in one year, and it just about wiped me out. I was losing my health and especially my voice. I remember during one crusade in Colorado Springs when my friend Dr. James Dobson warned me to start pacing myself better. For Billy to have done so much in one year is simply incomprehensible, especially at his age. A crusade is not the meeting itself; it's planning down to the most minute detail, conferring with and rallying pastors and other spiritual leaders in communities around the event, attending meet-and-greets and banquets, and making endless phone calls.

And that's just the beginning. It's nonstop work. Then there is the preaching itself.

I don't know how Billy did it.

Keep in mind it's one thing to set up a crusade in a city in the United States; it's a whole other thing to do that in a foreign country. In 1982, the BGEA traveled to England, the Bahamas, South Korea, Canada, East Germany, and Czechoslovakia and made a six-day visit to the Soviet Union—a place known for its crushing religious oppression. Officially, only 10–12 percent of the Soviet population at that time were counted as religious believers, but that number was deceptive. Many Christians there refused to be recognized officially because historically they had been subject to harassment and arrests. Despite how hard the government tried to scrub religion from the books, it was believed that many Christians resided in the Soviet Union.

After the 1917 Communist Revolution, the Soviet Union actively attempted to eliminate and erase all religion from society. The government killed or shipped off to prison camps almost fifty thousand priests, monks, and nuns—then seized control of the forty-eight thousand Russian Orthodox churches, allowing about eight thousand to continue operating. New Communist laws restricted the few remaining religious activities. Also, clergy could no longer tend to the sick and poor—or, for that matter, profess their faith publicly. They were stripped of almost everything.

The view commonly held by Soviet leadership was that religion was not only counterintuitive to scientific reason, but also a real threat to state power. Karl Marx called religion "the opiate of the masses" in his *Communist Manifesto*. The government wanted the people to hear one voice, and it certainly didn't want that coming from an entity it could not control.

Penetrating the Iron Curtain at its atheistic apex required years of negotiation and every connection Billy had in the government and foreign churches to make it happen. The trip was originally scheduled for late 1979, but it was postponed when Russia invaded Afghanistan. In the ensuing years, Billy's negotiating team had to work through myriad religious and political issues with the Kremlin and the Politburo to get him cleared.

At the time, the Soviet Union still had plenty of its own issues. Its economy was a disaster. The Russians imported grain from the U.S. throughout the 1970s. When President Leonid Brezhnev died in 1982, Afghanistan was well on its way to turning into the Russian version of the Vietnam conflict. Defense spending ate most of the country's budget. Gross domestic product was almost at zero. Brezhnev's successor, Yuri Andropov, was a KGB ascetic who believed in restoring discipline and order to society. The government still adhered rigidly to Marxist-Leninist doctrine, which kept the people ignorant and away from Christianity. Human souls and a hunger for God had been suppressed for decades. Christianity was barred from newspapers and television, except as a target for ridicule or atheistic propaganda.

Reagan called the Soviet Union "the Evil Empire" in a famous speech. And he was right.

His administration's policy was called a Second Cold War. Reagan carried it out by massive military spending the Soviets couldn't possibly match, especially on technology. In American popular culture, the Soviets were Hollywood's go-to villains. Everyone from Rocky to James Bond to Clint Eastwood to Chuck Norris fought them...and won. Billy would fight them too...and win!

In May 1982, the Russian Orthodox Church planned the clumsily titled "World Conference of Religious Workers for Saving the Sacred

Gift of Life from Nuclear Catastrophe," an international peace conference held in Moscow. The event was expected to draw hundreds of world church leaders and representatives from all major religions, and Billy was invited to address the gathering.

As enticing as the offer sounded, instincts told Billy this event could be a trap. He knew that peace conferences there often served as fronts for Soviet propaganda and were tightly controlled by the government. Not only were they political in nature, but they were often critical of the United States. Billy did not want to be party to negative talk about his native country, nor did he want to glorify Communism or dishonor God.

Through a contingency of ambassadors and contacts in Washington, D.C., and Moscow, Billy was able to negotiate three crucial points in advance:

- He would go as an observer, not a full delegate
- If he spoke at the conference, he would have complete freedom to speak from the Bible on any topic of his choosing
- He would be allowed to preach at two Moscow churches, one Orthodox and one Baptist

Still, Billy had some major reservations. For weeks, he and Ruth alternately debated and prayed about the trip. They also honed the draft of his proposed conference speech in case he decided to go.

Billy also called Richard Nixon for advice. The former president told him that yes, the Communists would try to use him for their own purposes—that was to be expected—but suggested Billy go anyway. So did a few other high-level businessmen and politicians whom Billy trusted, including President Ronald Reagan, Vice President George H.W. Bush, and geopolitical consultant Henry Kissinger. They reached the same consensus: go, but step lightly.

However, not everyone was in agreement about the opportunity, including a few members of the BGEA executive board. Billy was always good about taking their counsel to heart, and in a rare move, he vetoed them because he felt the Lord's urging him to go. Alexander Haraszti—Billy's emissary and translator in Eastern Europe (he spoke eight languages)—said if Billy nixed the Soviets' invite, he'd never receive another offer to any Communist Bloc nation. That bothered Billy, who instinctively knew there was a hunger in these countries for the Gospel. And he wanted to deliver it to them.

I remember this event well. I also remember Billy was roundly criticized by many, including some Christian leaders in America, for agreeing to the trip. But to me, it would be like critiquing the Apostle Paul for going to Mars Hill in Athens, which at the time was the intellectual capital of the world. It was also a very secular place. And that is exactly why Paul went.

The evangelist takes literally the command of Jesus to go into "all the world" to preach the Gospel (Mark 16:15), and that includes Communist countries. This was an open door for Billy, and he simply knew he must walk through it. He would resonate with Paul's words, "Preaching the Good News is not something I can boast about. I am compelled by God to do it. How terrible for me if I didn't preach the Good News!" (1 Corinthians 9:16 NLT).

After the Moscow trip was announced, thousands of letters a day began pouring into the BGEA office in Minneapolis. Billy noticed that only a small percentage was critical. The rest praised him for his bravery and passion. It was confirmation that he was on the right track.

Billy arrived in Moscow on May 7, 1982. He said at a press conference that day he hoped his visit would foster a better understanding between the United States and the Soviet Union and was looking forward to meeting with government leaders. After his remarks, an American reporter approached Billy and discreetly placed a piece of paper into his hands. It contained the names of several "Soviet prisoners of conscience." The journalist implored Billy to publicly condemn the Soviet government. This type of display had become familiar to Billy on foreign visits. However, he wasn't going to act hastily. That would not only be unwise, but also would jeopardize his entire trip.

Billy turned the paper over to a Soviet authority and gently expressed his concern for the well-being of the people on the list. However, he knew any further action would be futile and that the real change agents were government leaders. Still, he cared about their plight. It was a tight spot, but his church hosts lauded Billy for his discretion and assured him he'd done the right thing.

Many Christians traveled from various parts of the Soviet Union—including Uzbekistan, Ukraine, Estonia, and Siberia—to attend Billy's two services. Despite the fact that this was in essence a humanitarian effort, Billy's every step was closely monitored by uniformed policemen, plainclothesmen, and members of Komsomol, the Young Communist League.

I find it interesting that Billy was only allowed to speak in a church and a cathedral, but not in large auditoriums, halls, or stadiums, which he certainly could have filled. His Sunday morning sermon was delivered at the Moscow Baptist Church, a place he'd visited in 1959 as a tourist. Then it was virtually empty. On this day, the 2,500-seat church was filled to capacity. Outside, a couple hundred people sang Christian hymns behind police barriers.

When Billy's sermon concluded, he was taken to Moscow's Cathedral of the Epiphany, a Russian Orthodox church, where the service was already underway. It was Billy's first time in an Orthodox setting, and he marveled at the cathedral's majestic beauty.

The seventeenth-century church didn't have a sound system or podium, and early into his sermon, the congregants began to shout. Billy thought perhaps it was a demonstration or revolt, but he learned they were simply calling for his interpreter to speak louder.

That wasn't the case at the May 11 peace conference, the last meeting of his Soviet trip. Everyone there could clearly hear his speech, "The Christian Faith and Peace in a Nuclear Age." Billy's message found its target with audience members.

The hundreds of Jews, Baptists, Buddhists, Hindus, Muslims, Russian Orthodox clergy, and atheists assembled there heard Billy make a biblical case for the answers to world problems and the nuclear threat. He explained he was there as a Christian and that "everything I have ever been, or am, or ever hope to be in this life or the future life, I owe to Jesus Christ."

Billy proclaimed he was not a pacifist, nor was he in favor of unilateral disarmament because every nation had a right to defend itself against an attack. He said peace will come from another source.

"Lasting peace will only come when the Kingdom of God prevails. The basic issue that faces us today is not merely political, social, economic, or even moral or humanitarian," Billy said. "The deepest problems of the human race are spiritual. They are rooted in man's refusal to seek God's way for his life. The problem is the human heart, which God alone can change."

When Billy finished, trickling applause turned into a thunderous standing ovation.

On that same historic trip, Billy also took the time to meet with Boris Ponomarev, a polite but powerful member of the Communist Party. Ponomarev was the chairman of the Foreign Affairs Committee of the Supreme Soviet of the USSR and a member of the Politburo.

Ponomarev took Billy on a personal guided tour of the Kremlin, even showing him President Leonid Brezhnev's office, down the hall from his (today it is occupied by Vladimir Putin). He saw the historic palace's gold-leafed chamber, stained glassed windows, hand-painted ceramic tiles, and ornate chandeliers. Billy found everything exquisitely decorated, with doors mysteriously opening for them and staffers gently bowing as they made their way through the building. Billy concluded that if push came to shove, the Soviet leaders would never dare push the red button and start a nuclear war because they would not want to lose their lavish perks and lifestyles. It was an astute observation.

The meeting with Ponomarev went far better than the subsequent one with the "Siberian Seven," a family of Siberian Pentecostals who had taken up residence in the basement of the American Embassy in June 1978.

They had seen photos of the American evacuation from Saigon and thought the same could be done for them. Wayne Merry was a consular/internal political officer at the embassy from 1980 to 1983. It was his unenviable task to look after them.

"It was quite a job to persuade them that we could not fly a helicopter into the middle of the Soviet Union, land on the roof of the U.S. Embassy, and take (them) off to live happily ever after in the USA—that took a lot of persuading," Merry said years later. "I had an Air Force colleague speak to them about it.... That was only one aspect of a continuing effort to convince them that we were their friends and champions and not their enemies. That's what I spent my time doing, dealing with things like the helicopter fantasy. In addition, they did not actually want to go to the United States, which they regarded as hopelessly decadent, but to the biblical kingdom of Israel. Not the contemporary State of Israel, mind you, but its Old Testament predecessor. Kind of hard to issue visas for that."

At home, American Pentecostals screamed bloody murder over the affair, asking why the seven couldn't simply be stuffed into diplomatic pouches and flown out.

Meanwhile, the Soviets simply said the same thing for the entire five years: "They have to go back to (their hometown) and apply for exit permission just like anybody else." Back then, no one emigrated from Russia. No one. For any reason at all. *Nyet.* You were the property of the state. Closed case.

The Soviets allowed Billy to visit them. His visit was strictly supervised, and no photographers or television cameras were allowed. That turned out to be a blessing in disguise.

Consular officer Wayne Leininger, who worked in Moscow from 1980 to 1984, briefed Billy in advance.

"We tried to warn him that if he went in to have a prayer session with these folks regarding them as meek-and-mild, fold-your-hands, bow-your-heads Christians, they were going to eat his lunch," Leininger said years later. "They were going to put him and his whole organization on the spot. 'What are you going to do for us? Whom are you going to talk to while you are here? What are you going to do when you leave? Who are you going to talk to in the outside world? How are you going to help us?'

"He shrugged that off and said, 'Don't worry about that. I have talked to people under stress before.'

"He got in there, and within five minutes his face was pale. He was sweating. He couldn't speak in a complete sentence. I have never seen anybody so otherwise self-possessed become so thoroughly discombobulated before. But then, he had never met anybody like these people before."

Because of Billy's reputation, the Seven thought of him as a miracle worker who could free them instantly. That certainly wasn't a reasonable expectation. Billy did, however, work behind the scenes with Alexander Haraszti, a former Baptist minister and physician, to help negotiate their release almost a year later. The Soviets allowed them to finally leave on June 27, 1983. They eventually ended up in the United States. Billy, of course, gave all the credit to Haraszti, who he said knew more about Eastern Europe than Henry Kissinger. Their release was a day to savor. Billy felt the same about his 1982 trip to Russia.

He had preached to tyrannized people under great pressures and restrictions and was well received in a mostly atheist country. He came away with a lasting impression.

"I found the Soviet people, in their hunger for the Word of God, the same as I have found people in every part of the world," Billy said.

He took some flak from journalists for not speaking out against religious abuses in the Soviet Union. But he had gone as an invited guest and had no plans to denounce his hosts. He felt it wasn't the time or place to discuss the matter.

The way I see it, Billy was wise. There were rules to his visit, and he stuck to them. By doing so, he was allowed to return to the Soviet Union again in 1984 (a twelve-day visit that included twenty-three speaking engagements), in 1988 (when he celebrated the 1,000th anniversary of the Russian Orthodox Church), and in 1992 during a Crusade in Moscow's Olympic Stadium, which drew more than 155,000 people and almost 43,000 inquirers. And those trips were bigger and grander affairs, allowing Billy greater access to the furthest reaches of the Soviet Union, to preach to more people, and to visit other Communist countries in the 1980s and 1990s, including East Germany, Czechoslovakia, Romania, China, and North Korea.

Years later Billy marveled at the spiritual transformation that eventually took hold in these countries as Communism crumbled.

"Who would have ever dreamed that Eastern Europe would be opened up? Or that Russia would be pleading for Bibles and evangelists and preachers?" Billy said. "And that you could go to any school in Russia and open the Bible and talk about Christ? And that they are wanting teachers to come and teach the Bible in the schools in the Soviet Union, when they're banned by the schools in this country, if you can imagine such a thing?"

His friend Ronald Reagan was a missile-wielding hardliner who stared the Soviets down and told Premier Mikhail Gorbachev to tear down the Berlin Wall. But Billy's soft power penetrated the Iron Curtain more deeply than any warhead ever could. He was not only an evangelist. He was a world-class statesman—and even more importantly, an ambassador for the Kingdom of God.

Transitions

By the mid-1980s, Billy Graham had gone from strength to strength, glory to glory. He still maintained his moniker as "America's Preacher" and continued to offer counsel to the world's most powerful and influential people, including the U.S. president.

Billy's ministry was still going strong as mine began to flourish. His started in the 1940s in the aftermath of World War II. By the grace of God, mine was born during the Jesus Revolution of the 1970s. In fact, Billy legitimized that movement when he appeared at Explo '72 (short for "Spiritual Explosion") in Dallas, Texas.

It was hosted by Bill Bright's Campus Crusade for Christ (now called Cru), which congregated eighty thousand young people from more than seventy-five countries to praise Jesus in June 1972.

The massive four-day event attempted to make Christianity relevant to a new generation that yearned for more than the status quo, did not trust anyone over thirty, and talked of fulfilling a spiritual yearning in their souls. It was a paradigm-shifting moment in the history of evangelicalism and one of the signature events of the Jesus Movement.

More than one hundred thousand people attended. Billy Graham, who co-sponsored it and gave the keynote address, referred to it as the "religious Woodstock."

Billy's participation was crucial. Without question, he was the most visible representative of evangelicalism around the world. And since then, no one has taken his place. He embraced the passion and deep commitment to Christ evidenced by the "Jesus People." He even grew his hair longer, which I remember noticing on the photo on the back cover of his book *The Jesus Generation*. Consciously or not, Billy's hair was never longer than it was in the early 1970s.

This is one of the reasons I wrote this book. Three of my heroes— Steve McQueen, Johnny Cash, and Billy Graham—had many things in common. They were all famous, charismatic, and very talented people. Of course, they were all Christians. And they were all, in a word, cool.

Absolutely.

McQueen was the personification of that word, even known as "The King of Cool." Cash was the same, becoming known as the "Godfather of Cool." I submit to you that Billy may have been the coolest of them all.

So what does it mean when we say that?

To me, being cool means to be real, authentic, and original. It's not the person who morphs with the latest trends. It's the person who stays true to who he is.

And Billy was certainly all those things.

He was also kind because he invited those same young people to his Crusades (which didn't always go over so well with the older attendees). But Billy knew in order to grow the Church, you constantly have to reach out to the younger generations. He was quick to embrace the future when other evangelists stuck with what was safe.

The church was starting to change, and Billy knew it.

My ministry started in 1974 in Riverside, California, thanks to Chuck Smith, my pastor, who franchised his Calvary Chapel church to me after his Costa Mesa site exploded with success. Kids with long hair, shorts, and sandals flooded his mid-week services because Calvary

Chapel veered away from traditional hymns and broke the mold by singing Christian praise music that was heavy on guitars. These worshippers were essentially hippies with a heart for Jesus. However, on Sunday mornings, Calvary Costa Mesa was still a traditional suit-and-tie environment. I respected that, but I wanted to try something different from what I had seen in most Sunday morning services of that time in our Riverside sanctuary.

I wanted contemporary worship and casual dress, not just on Sunday nights, but on Sunday mornings as well. But even though our *style* would be contemporary, they still were going to get an old-time Gospel message. I'd seen many preachers adjust their message and lose the truth in the process. I would preach the Bible as the authoritative Word of God and Jesus Christ, the same yesterday, today, and forever—just as Billy did.

I also wanted to surround myself with quality people, as Billy had. The very first thing I did was seek out people whom God was calling to ministry in the same way. Specifically, I wanted people who were smarter and more gifted than I was. I was young, but I knew enough to understand that ministry is a team effort, not a one-man show. The ones who went the route of no accountability often flamed out or blew off course. I wanted to build from the ground up a ministry with strong foundations and honest communications. I was very intentional in the design of the church, and it worked out well.

Our original three-hundred-member congregation grew to eight thousand strong by 1984. I received a call from a person at an organization that specialized in megachurches. I was not even familiar with the term at that point, but this man told me that our little church—the one no one wanted in the beginning—was now one of the largest churches in the United States.

With a new sanctuary and campus location came a new name: Harvest Christian Fellowship.

I also had changed quite a bit in those ten years. The long hair, the beard, and the hippie threads were long gone. I was clean-shaven, my hair was cropped short, and I showed up for church in Ralph Lauren sweaters and brightly colored button-down shirts (but I did not ditch the jeans). Cathe and I had our first child, Christopher, purchased our first home, and were no longer driving beater cars. Our congregation grew up right alongside us, and we considered them part of our family.

I was much more presentable the second time I saw Billy. That occurred in July 1985 when the Billy Graham Crusade came to Anaheim Stadium, and I was asked to help plan some of the special youth events and offer the opening prayer at the stadium one evening.

By then I had become a friend to Billy's son Franklin. I met him through our mutual friend Dennis Agajanian, who was a frequent guest at Billy's Crusades and had played at our church many times.

My friendship with Franklin is a case of opposites attract. Even though we are almost the same age (only five months apart) and have the same cultural touchstones, he is at heart a North Carolina country boy. I am California-born and bred. He is a rugged, outdoorsy type who likes to hunt, fish, and fly planes. At that point in my life, I rode dirt bikes, hung out at the beach, and loved art and design. The real glue to our relationship has been our mutual love for Christ, and, of course, his dad. Franklin knew I had the greatest respect for his father.

Over time, we grew closer. He invited me to sit on the board of directors for Samaritan's Purse. Franklin impressed me with his commitment to Christ and absolute fearlessness in whatever he tackled. If he believed something was God's will, neither Hell nor high water would hold him back. It did not seem that the word "can't" or the phrase "not possible" were even in his vocabulary.

Billy appreciated my friendship with his son and urged me to continue to encourage Franklin. Maybe including me in the Anaheim Crusade was Billy's way of showing his gratitude. Nonetheless, before the evening was finished, I wished I had made a better first impression on him.

The big night came, and there I sat on the stage with Billy and his faithful team of so many years—music and program director Cliff Barrows, soloist George Beverly Shea, longtime friend and confidante

T.W. Wilson—as well as pastors and civic leaders from around Southern California.

I had been given an agenda and was told to study and follow it closely so that I'd know the exact moment to get up and offer the opening prayer. But I was so caught up in the excitement that I completely missed my cue. Cliff Barrows, normally an easygoing, affable fellow, finally barked at me, "Get up there, man, and pray!"

I jolted out of my seat and practically sprinted to the podium. I manically gripped the sides of Billy Graham's own pulpit and wondered if these folks knew what they were doing, allowing me to stand up there and represent them.

I took out the paper on which my prayer had been written, and my brains turned to mush. I decided to wing it—bad move. I have absolutely no recollection of what came out of my mouth. I recall sitting back down and thinking that I really blew it, big time. I also expected a posse of guards to rush me as far away from Billy Graham as they could and get the stink of me off the stage. Thankfully, that didn't happen.

The rest of that evening I sat there spellbound, observing Billy closely as he moved about with certainty, speaking with deep conviction about God's love with that captivating, down-to-earth quality and charm he possessed.

I paid tribute to Billy later that year with a crusade in the Philippines called Decision '85. It was an exhaustive effort and a nice success, but nowhere near the scale of a Billy Graham Crusade.

But Billy noticed.

About two years later he invited me and my wife, Cathe, to his mountain home in Montreat, North Carolina. This was the Grahams' private retreat, visited by their closest friends, church leaders, CEOs, and presidents Nixon and Obama. Frankly, an invitation to the White House would not have captivated me as much. Cathe and I were both in awe as we stood on the porch of the Grahams' rambling cabin.

Visiting their home was like a trip back in time. The immense beams of the house had been reclaimed from the western region of the state; the house was smartly decorated with antiques from that era as well. From their porch, you could see for miles in every direction.

When we came in for dinner, the smell of comfort food overwhelmed our senses, and we could not wait to dig in. Ruth made a tasty pot roast, mashed potatoes, and hot, buttery rolls. It was delicious, and we washed it down with Southern iced tea. Cathe stayed behind with Ruth while I had some alone time with Billy, sitting in his front room before a roaring fire and admiring the mantel, which had German words carved on it. I asked Billy what they meant. He responded, "A Mighty Fortress Is Our God."

Of course. They were the words of the great hymn written by the leader of the Protestant Reformation, Martin Luther.

Because Billy was such a hero of mine, I was floored when he fixed me with his eagle gaze and said words I'd never even dreamed he'd say: "Greg, I've been thinking about you."

That got my attention real quick. *Billy Graham was thinking about me?*

"I think you should leave your church and go into full-time evangelism," he said. "I think you should do Crusades with us here at BGEA."

It was as if my life flashed before my eyes and then spun forward. Consciously or subconsciously, I saw my broken beginnings, the esteem in which my grandparents held "Dr. Graham," my reverence for Billy as a champion of the Jesus Movement, then my increasing love and respect for him over the years as the man who shot straight with the Gospel, no matter the setting or the audience. I could not get over the fact that my dysfunctional life had somehow arrived at this Hallmark moment: Billy Graham—America's Preacher—telling me that I should come work with him?

If God had spoken to me from a cloud, I doubt I could have been more stunned.

It was indeed a wonderful and unexpected surprise. But what was even more unbelievable (and somewhat unexplainable as I look back) was my response. I had actually come to the point in my journey where I could tell the difference between God and Billy Graham.

"Billy, you know that when you tell me that, it's like Moses proclaiming God's will from on high," I began. Billy smiled.

"I can't tell you how much that means to me," I continued. "But I know what God's calling me for right now. It's to pastor our church and also to do evangelism. It's not the same for everyone. But for me...right now...I need to do both for each one to be fruitful on its own."

In retrospect, I could have added (because I knew it was true), "Your son, Franklin, has been uniquely called and gifted to help fill your shoes."

Billy's crystal-blue eyes pierced right through me, and for a moment I didn't know what to think. However, he seemed satisfied with my halting answer. He nodded affirmatively, smiled again, and then we talked of other things.

That conversation took place many years ago, but I think of it often. What I told Billy that night was the plan I've stuck to in the years since. In August 1990, Chuck Smith and I hosted our first crusade (called "Summer Harvest" at the time) at the Pacific Amphitheatre in Costa Mesa, where close to eighteen thousand people attended each of the five nights. It was modeled loosely after the Billy Graham Crusade, but with a more contemporary twist as we pioneered a new template, which was effectively a worship band in the place of the choir. It was envisioned by my friend Chuck Fromm of Maranatha Music and led by Love Song band member Tommy Coomes. It was truly groundbreaking.

We don't even blink when we see bands leading worship in churches today with guitars, electric keyboards, and drums, but back then, it was a new paradigm. One person called it a "sanitized Woodstock." Fair enough, if that's what got people to come, but the Gospel message they received was totally raw and unfiltered.

Each evening featured some of the greatest Christian contemporary music, and I preached for forty-five minutes. After dark, I gave an invitation for people to come forward and accept Christ. People got up by the hundreds and streamed to the stage. Several times the music paused, and I made another appeal. To my wonder, more people got up and came forward. Each time the crowd stood up and applauded those making life-altering decisions. It got to the point where no one could squeeze into the aisle or get to the front of the stage. We had more than six thousand professions of faith over five days.

It was magical.

It was glorious.

It greatly exceeded expectations.

And it was all God.

As wonderful as it turned out, it was just a small taste of what Billy experienced more than four hundred times in his decades-long career. Yet he was still gracious enough to recognize this personal milestone in a September 26, 1990, letter to me. It read:

> *My dear Greg,*
>
> *Praise God for the tremendous crusade you had at the Pacific Amphitheatre. I appreciate your thoughtfulness in writing to tell me about it, and also for your humble and gracious comments about the input that my Team and I have had in your ministry.*
>
> *You and Chuck Smith are certainly doing great things for the Lord in California and we thank God for your vision and for His evident blessing on both of your lives.*
>
> *With warmest Christian greetings and appreciation for all that you mean to the Kingdom of God, I am*
>
> *Cordially yours,*
>
> *Billy*

Ruth also wrote to me a very kind letter of congratulations:

> *Dear Greg:*
>
> *Thank you for the report on your meeting in the Pacific Amphitheatre in Orange County. It was absolutely thrilling and I'd love to see Anaheim Stadium packed out next year. It would be a tremendous encouragement to Bill to see how, as his ministry is coming to a close, the Lord is raising up*

others to carry on faithfully the proclamation of the Gospel of Jesus Christ.

We thank God for you and all the others who are a result of Chuck Smith's faithful witness to Jesus Christ and His power to redeem and enable.

Our love to you and Cathe.

Warmly,

Ruth

As Ruth hoped, the event expanded to Angel Stadium in 1991, where it has been held every year since. Crusades like this have also been held in other cities across the country and in Australia and New Zealand. Total attendance has now topped the five-million mark.

Maybe that's why in 1994 Billy asked me to become a BGEA board member and assist him with illustrations in his messages. This time, I immediately took him up on the offer. And I'm proud to say that I'm still a BGEA board member more than a quarter-century later.

Why did Billy seek me out? That's a question I've pondered for decades. The best answer I can give is that he most likely saw a fellow evangelist, and he knew how important it is to have as many of us out there as we can. We are a lot rarer for some reason than those who are gifted to teach.

Pastors are many, but evangelists are few.

An evangelist is someone who has been gifted by God to both articulate the Gospel and call people to repent of their sins and follow Christ. This calling is not lesser or greater than that of a pastor; it is simply different. And it is needed, just like the other gifts that God gives His Church.

I also believe Billy wanted some younger blood on the BGEA board. Almost all the board members were Billy's contemporaries—in their mid-seventies and older. In July 1992, Billy was diagnosed with Parkinson's disease, a progressive and incurable nervous disorder that marked the beginning of his physical decline. He was looking to the future, which is why he wisely installed Franklin as the board's vice chairman and eventual president.

He also expanded the organization's training of young evangelists by conducting Schools of Evangelism on every continent designed to raise up future Gospel messengers all over the globe.

It was apparent that Billy wanted new blood throughout every part of his organization. New blood brings fresh ideas and perspectives, and I know he wanted some of those fresh ideas to come from me.

All well and good, but who was I to give Billy Graham advice on something he'd done well since the 1940s? At one meeting I preached from Luke 5, which tells of how Jesus recruited the disciples and describes His teaching and healing ministry. Billy, Franklin, Cliff Barrows, and T.W. Wilson all had their eyes trained on me. But the only pair I saw were Billy's steely blues. They literally stopped me in my tracks when I looked up from my sermon notes. My heart was pounding in my chest because I was so intimidated by speaking in front of him. I much preferred it the other way around, which was the case when we were out on the road on one of his Crusades.

One of the first things I did for Billy was to find him a cap. He was constantly being recognized and often tried to hide his appearance in his down time. But when you have a profile that could fit comfortably on Mount Rushmore, that's tough.

I can't recall what city it was, but Billy had misplaced his hat and asked if I would go and find him another. As far as I was concerned, it was a full-on mission for God. I went to a local mall looking for the perfect hat for Billy to wear. I discovered a store I think may have been called Lids; it had an unbelievable selection that completely overwhelmed me. After much deliberation, I finally made a selection, returned to the hotel, and presented it to Billy. He looked at it, smiled, put it on his head, and thanked me.

The next day I did not see him, but I spotted a photo of him on the front page of the paper—getting into a car and wearing the cap I bought him. I proudly announced to anyone within earshot, "That's the hat I bought Billy yesterday!" (He misplaced the hat not long afterward, but it was always my honor to assist him in any way I could.)

After that, Billy started asking for my help with his messages. I was very honored. But I also wasn't timid or shy about what he was asking of me. I felt I could be of service to him with this.

I have always had an interest in pop culture, history, and politics. I like collecting interesting stories, statements, and things that arrest my attention as potential illustrations for sermons down the road. I keep them in a box or in files and type them into documents I keep on my computer.

Frankly, I was more pumped up about working on Billy's sermons than on my own, so I expended a great deal of effort researching and carefully studying his earlier works. Billy had a highly personalized delivery—a cadence—in his preaching style. He'd make a point. Build on it. Build higher. Then boom! The punch!

My illustrations ran the gamut of pop culture, timely articles, and biblical examples. They touched on topics like the shooting death of rapper Notorious B.I.G. (Christopher Wallace), the pessimistic outlook of Generation X, the movie *Leaving Las Vegas* starring Nicolas Cage, and an alternate introduction to the Prodigal Son message.

If Billy was intrigued with an idea, I'd meet with him in his hotel room and explain the context of the message, how it should be used or illustrated, who the players or artists were, and why I felt it would resonate. Of course, there was always Scripture to back whatever message I tried to convey. If Billy didn't like something, he'd stare and say nothing. But if he did, he'd reach for the phone, punch in the number to his secretary, and say, "Stephanie, I want you to add this to my sermon tonight—the thing that Greg wrote."

Perhaps my crowning achievement was the night Billy used some illustrations I wrote regarding the Smashing Pumpkins' 1995 song "Bullet with Butterfly Wings."

The leadoff single from the alt-rockers' double album *Mellon Collie and the Infinite Sadness* perfectly captured the spirit of the times. It was dark, lyrical, and angry. Writer and lead singer Billy Corgan was comparing his newfound fame as a rock star with biblical suffering and misunderstandings. The song resonated with me; not only was it current, but it also had some interesting lyrics.

Billy delivered the message at the Crusade's Youth Night in Minneapolis, Minnesota, in June 1996. He said it almost verbatim as I had written it, and I got chills up my spine. When the assembled applauded, Billy's team members looked at me and gave me the thumbs up.

It truly was one of the greatest moments of my life.

The interesting thing is, whenever there was a national or global crisis, nobody cared about what was hip or relevant anymore. They simply wanted answers from someone who could be trusted to make sense or draw meaning from a tragedy—and that mantle naturally fell on Billy's shoulders. Like in the April 1995 Oklahoma City bombing and the 9/11 attacks on the World Trade Center in September 2001. Only Billy could come up with the words to comfort millions, to explain the evil that men do, what we could learn from such a tragedy, and how we could heal as a nation.

Three days after the 9/11 attack, he reminded people that God is not the author of evil and is full of love, mercy, and compassion in a time of suffering. That day he spoke powerfully of hope, faith, and the love of Jesus Christ when he addressed the nation from the National Cathedral in Washington, D.C.:

> *We say to those who masterminded this cruel plot, and to those who carried it out, that the spirit of this nation will not be defeated by their twisted and diabolical schemes. Someday those responsible will be brought to justice.*
>
> *But we especially come together to confess our need of God. We have always needed God from the very beginning of this nation, but now we need Him especially. We're involved in a new kind of warfare, and we need the help of the Spirit of God.*

The Bible's words are our hope, "God is our refuge and strength, an ever-present help in trouble. Therefore we will not fear, though the earth give way and the mountains fall into the heart of the sea."

Billy concluded with this:

My prayer today is that we will feel the loving arms of God wrapped around us and will know in our hearts that He will never forsake us as we trust in him.
We also know that God is going to give wisdom and courage and strength to the president and those around him. And this is going to be a day that we will remember as a day of victory.
May God bless you all.

The truth was, the nation especially needed Billy that day to deliver that message. A rock of faith for decades, a trusted advisor to presidents, someone whose message never deviated despite the changes in the times.

It had been one of the most awful and disturbing days in American history, a day when civilians were attacked out of the blue in the heart of the country. Pearl Harbor veterans thought it worse than that day of infamy in the 1940s. "At least we had guns to shoot back with," one said. These weren't trained soldiers staggering through the dust and smoke of lower Manhattan; these were executives and secretaries, office workers, waiters, delivery people.

Wherever you were on that day, and whatever you thought, Billy knew exactly the words to slake your soul, give you comfort, and reassure you that God was with you.

In many ways, it was the most important address of his life.

CHAPTER THIRTY-FOUR

Lion in Winter

After the new millennium dawned, the world suddenly seemed a darker and more dangerous place. The formerly carefree pleasure of getting on an airplane changed dramatically. Large metal or concrete barriers appeared in front of government buildings to prevent car bombs. Office buildings now had large security details and check-in processes. A whole list of exotic countries suddenly became too dangerous to visit. Shocks to global order were coming faster than anyone ever would have imagined.

More and more people were unsettled and looking for reassurance, stability, and a sense of safety and hope. However, they weren't willing to turn to the Bible as they had been in previous decades. People had become skeptical and unbelieving about Christianity and turned to spiritual practices that had nothing to do with God.

Technology advanced inexorably, either leaving people behind or pulling them in faster than they ever expected, making it harder for them to get off the merry-go-round. Today we no longer have to go to the library because we can download a book instantly. We don't have to go to a shopping mall and linger because the shopping mall now comes to our door via the internet. We can have a four-course meal delivered to our house in less than a half hour, thanks to our smartphones. It truly boggles the mind.

What's even more mindboggling is that Billy spoke of this decades ago.

"Before He comes again the world is going to go through many convulsions, the Bible teaches," Billy said in 1971. "There will be worldwide lawlessness, there will be an overemphasis on sex, there will be an acceleration of technology."

The Digital Age did force Billy to adapt his ministry. He had tested the internet waters and wisely developed a BGEA website and online counseling service. He also used the airwaves to conduct a Crusade in San Juan, Puerto Rico, that was beamed over a satellite network to more than 165 countries to an estimated audience of a billion people. As he had done decades before with radio, television, and motion pictures, his organization adopted the latest communications tools to spread the Gospel of Jesus Christ. Undoubtedly, this new way of communicating pleased Billy because it is what God had created him to do.

But as the world was speeding up, Billy Graham physically was starting to slow down. Even though he never expressed it or complained, I doubt it pleased him at all.

As he entered his eighties, his great head of hair turned snowy white, and he managed to acquire a list of physical ailments and maladies common to octogenarians. Billy had several falls, ending up with fractures and a case of hydrocephalus—a buildup of excessive fluid deep within the brain. He addressed his emotional and physical afflictions in an interview with journalist David Frost, and he made it a teaching moment for everyone.

"(God) allows it. And He allows it for a purpose that I may not know. I think everything that comes to our lives, if we are true believers, God has a purpose and plan," Billy said. "And many of these things are things that cause suffering or inconvenience or whatever. But it helps to mature me because God is molding and making me in the image of His Son, Jesus Christ. Jesus Christ suffered more than any other man that ever lived, because when He was on that cross, He was bearing the sins that you and I have committed."

Ruth, too, began to have medical issues, suffering from spinal meningitis. Her frail condition was compounded by arthritic pain in the back and neck that started in 1974 when she fell out of a tree while testing a pipe slide for her grandchildren. She woke up in the hospital with a shattered left heel, a broken rib, a crushed vertebra in her neck, and a concussion. This accident later resulted in chronic back pain. She also had dual hip replacements.

Ruth rarely accompanied Billy during the last few years of his ministry, but she did visit North Korea with him in 1997. She remained a bedrock source of inspiration and support. As always, she offered prayer and wise biblical counsel to him.

Despite his physical ailments, Billy's mind remained sharp, and he continued to move forward. He wrote bestselling books (*Nearing Home: Life, Faith, and Finishing Well* is arguably the seminal book on death), conducted Crusades, and continued to offer spiritual counsel to presidents when called upon. He was at the White House with George H.W. Bush and his wife, Barbara, the night the U.S. launched the Persian Gulf War against Iraq. He also discussed spiritual matters with George W. Bush, who credits Billy with helping him turn his life around and ultimately leading him to accept Christ. Billy gave the invocation at both Clinton inaugurations and forged a strong bond with the Arkansas native.

He insisted—much to the public's relief—that he had no immediate plans to retire and would continue preaching "as long as God gives me breath." He had not read in the Bible where man retired from sharing the Gospel. Billy, it appeared, was going to live as long as Methuselah.

Even though Billy was becoming less visible in the new millennium, there was still a great need for him. In 2003, he was listed (again) by Gallup as among the top ten men Americans most admired—the forty-fifth time since the list's inception in 1948. Second place wasn't even close: Pope John Paul II appeared twenty-five times.

I continued to see Billy a few times a year. It was mostly at BGEA meetings, national conferences, Crusades, and at the Billy Graham Training Center at the Cove. This facility is surrounded by 1,200 acres of some of the most gorgeous countryside I've ever seen, and it was the site where Billy and I had some of our best and most intimate visits.

The Cove is a very homey and inviting place. I remember when we dedicated it to the Lord out in the pouring rain. We were all given green-and-white umbrellas with "Billy Graham Training Center at the Cove" printed on them. Cathe and I still have ours.

When you walk into the lobby, you are greeted by large portraits of the Grahams on the walls; Billy on one wall, Ruth on the other. This was not Billy's choice, but that of his family and team. Billy honestly did not like all the attention he garnered throughout his life, but along with the great platform and influence the Lord had given him came notoriety. People who were employed by Billy genuinely loved the man.

The Cove's décor is country style—rocking chairs everywhere, with a beautiful view of the forest that surrounds the main building. The smell of popcorn is in the air, and there is even soft-serve ice cream 24/7.

It was a place that both Billy and Ruth frequented, and it was not unusual for people to see them sitting in on sessions, as they were life-long Bible students.

The people who are asked to speak stay in cabins tucked away up a road with their own porches and more rocking chairs. Each cabin was decorated by Ruth herself.

There are books to read, but no televisions. That is by design. Ruth wanted it to be a place to retreat from all the noise of the outside world. I have many fond memories of staying there that I will treasure always, but most of all, a personal letter from Billy after I spoke there one year.

> *Dear Greg:*
> *Greetings from Montreat.*
> *The last couple of days I have heard you late each after-*
> *noon over our radio station. What a powerful message God*

gives you. I wish I had your youth, energy, strength, and knowledge of the Bible. You have certainly been one of God's faithful servants. I am more than grateful for your standing by Franklin.

I just wanted to let you know how much I personally appreciate your coming to teach at The Cove. Since I am scheduled to be away at the time you are scheduled to speak, I wanted to write and apologize in advance that I wouldn't be able to come and hear you. We are thankful for your interest and prayers for The Cove.

Again, I want to thank you and send love from Ruth and me with the warmest Christian greetings and the prayer that God may continue to bless you and yours.

Cordially yours,

Billy

I also treasured being present for Billy's 417th and final evangelistic campaign in June 2005 at the World's Fair site in Flushing Meadows–Corona Park in Queens, New York. Almost fifty years before, he held a heralded Crusade at Madison Square Garden. But even that venue was too small to accommodate the crowds that wanted to say farewell to him.

The three-day event that June drew more than 230,000 New Yorkers of all faiths and denominations. Billy, who was eighty-six at the time and dependent on a walker due to a pelvic fracture, gave one of the most heartfelt sermons I'd ever seen him deliver. He used his aging body and frailty to urge those in the audience to repent of their sins and accept Christ as their Savior.

His entire family was present—children, grandchildren, and great-grandchildren. Billy beamed with joy to see them all. Everyone knew this was the last time this warrior for Christ would speak publicly. As he was assisted to the platform, he looked out at the crowd, and said "God loves you!" pointing in one direction. "And you," pointing the other direction. I doubt I was the only one there who had goose bumps.

His words were so simple and pure, and they really represented who Billy was. Not the fiery preacher of the tent in Los Angeles in 1949, but a seasoned saint, a lion in winter, a kindly grandfather speaking undiluted truth.

I choked up, tears welling in my eyes. This was the end of the line for Billy—as a preacher, that is—and I knew it. It was his hope to do one last Crusade in England, but sadly, that never came to pass. It truly was the end of an amazing era of proclamation evangelism that I was privileged to see up close and personal. I was not there for the whole race, like his faithful team members Cliff Barrows and George Beverly Shea. But I was there for the last laps, and it was a glorious thing to behold. I shall never forget it.

After Shea, then ninety-six, sang a beautiful song, Billy personally thanked him and said the first thing on his mind: "I know that it won't be long before both of us are going to Heaven. You know, Jesus said, 'Be ready, for in such an hour that you know not, the son of man comes.' In Amos, the fourth chapter, it says, 'Prepare to meet your God.' Are you prepared? Have you opened your heart to Jesus? Have you repented of your sins?"

I watched from the side stage, but I roamed the crowd intermittently. Billy's sermon was translated into thirteen languages, including Arabic. The message was alternatively apocalyptic and hopeful, touching upon the days of Noah and discussing current events—including the mysterious disappearance of Natalee Holloway, an eighteen-year-old Alabama high schooler who had vanished from the Caribbean island of Aruba a few months before.

Billy implored the assembled to remember that tomorrow is never promised and to give themselves to Christ to be born again.

"You come to this Crusade to live many more years, but you don't know," Billy said. "This may be the last day of your life. You never know. The Bible says today is the accepted time. Today is the day of salvation."

He received a very long and robust standing ovation from the ninety thousand people in attendance that day.

I saw Billy gaze out over the crowd one last time, with thousands of people coming to the front to either get one last look at the modern-day Moses or to accept Christ as their Savior. The response was huge; it was such an amazing experience to witness up close.

When Billy was finished, he donned his sunglasses, and with the aid of his walker and Franklin, slowly walked away from the pulpit for the final time.

As I watched Billy leave the stage, it reminded me of a very special time I had with him in Portland, Oregon: After the final invitation, I accompanied Billy and several of his associates through the narrow hallways underneath the stadium. We were surrounded by security men, who were necessary because of the many threats always received on the road. (Billy's FBI file documents threats that date back several decades and are filled with so much vitriol and hate.) The team escorted us into a four-door sedan, and police cars led us out of the stadium and into the street, their lights flashing and swirling.

I couldn't help but feel as if I were in the company of the president of the United States. Given this type of access, I watched Billy closely. Specifically, I wanted to see how he responded to the attention of others. I must say, it was interesting.

While the others excitedly talked about the highlights of that evening, Billy grew quiet, peering out the window. When we arrived at his hotel suite, he ducked into his room for a few minutes. The rest of us continued talking. Before the start of the Crusade, a local pastor had delivered several bags of barbeque sandwiches, but hours later they were cold. I wondered if Billy would stand for this. Or perhaps we'd go out to eat or stay in and order room service.

When Billy finally emerged from his room, he had changed into a pair of cotton pajamas. I was quite surprised.

He had forgotten to pack his slippers because he was still wearing his dress shoes. He looked endearingly unstylish, and he was completely unselfconscious about his look.

We sat down, and someone brought over some paper napkins, then Billy doled out the cold barbeque sandwiches. It did not dampen the mood in the room as we ate, laughed, and visited. We talked about a lot of things—fun things, ordinary things. Not once did Billy bring up the Crusade.

Sitting there with him in his old-fashioned cotton PJs and shiny dress shoes, I saw one of the greatest antidotes to the pride that can come with the intense celebrity spotlight that shines on stadium evangelists. The lesson he taught all of us, without uttering a single word, was how to cultivate a keen sense of the ordinary.

Billy didn't sit there and relive the evening's moments of glory. He knew there were hidden dangers in doing something like that—fishhooks that could snare his pride and tempt him to think it was all about him.

Billy knew it was all about God.

I have followed his example to this day. After a crusade, I go back to my hotel room, clean off my desk, play with the grandkids, catch up on my emails, or eat a sandwich.

Even though my visit with Billy the evening of his last Crusade was uplifting, I had just witnessed the end of an era. Millions and millions of people had come to his Crusades, held on almost every continent, some in hostile countries. With gentleness and strength, he had taken the Gospel from the Mordecai Ham days of aggression, guilt, and judgment to a place of kindness and true love personified. He was the most non-judgmental person I have ever met. He won over everyone he came in contact with, and many remotely. Atheists, Communists, gangsters, movie stars, presidents, and every kind of sinner and unbeliever recognized his name, trusted him, and listened to him. He became part of the foundation of America, a bedrock institution in his own right. Now it was time for him to fade into the sunset, like all American heroes do.

Billy was going home, this time for good.

He used the time wisely, relaxing at his mountain home in Montreat, North Carolina, with Ruth, filling their time with deep talks, reading, watching movies, and keeping up with the news. He also spent time with his three dogs—Pala, Chyna, and Theo—and played fetch or slowly walked them on their spacious property.

Ruth, who now required round-the-clock care, had a favorite armchair by the front window of the house. From there, draped in an afghan, she read, wrote letters, received visitors, and loved on her children (several of whom had ministries of their own), grandchildren, and great-grandchildren.

Slowly, her health began to deteriorate. The degenerative back disease left her bedridden most of the time and in a great deal of pain. Now married for more than sixty years, Billy declared that he loved her more than ever.

"It's hard to sit and watch when I love her so much…" he told a *Time* magazine reporter.

Eighty-seven-year-old Ruth Graham finally passed on to Heaven on June 14, 2007, at their home at Little Piney Cove in Montreat. And that's exactly where she wanted to be. Naturally, this came as a massive blow to Billy.

"Ruth was my life partner, and we were called to God as a team," he said. "We've rekindled the romance of our youth, and my love for her continued to grow deeper every day. I will miss her terribly and look forward even more to the day I can join her in Heaven."

I attended Ruth's memorial service at the Anderson Auditorium at the Montreat Conference Center in North Carolina two days after her passing. Sitting in the front pew, Billy hung his head in deep sorrow. It was devastating to lose the love of his life. Yet Billy somehow managed to address the room, which was full of two thousand close friends and associates.

"She's so beautiful," said Billy, who stood with the assistance of a walker in the front pew. "I sat there a long time last night, looking at her. And I prayed because I know she had a great reception in Heaven."

Ruth's children followed, all paying tribute to their mother. She was the glue that held everything together and protected Billy.

Ruth's final resting place is at the foot of a cross-shaped walkway in the Prayer Garden on the grounds of the Billy Graham Library in

Charlotte, North Carolina, which had opened to the public a month before her death.

She insisted on being buried in a common coffin constructed of birch plywood that was made by a convicted murderer in Louisiana named Richard Liggett. He also made one for Billy. They were purchased for $215 each. She also insisted that an unusual statement be placed on her tombstone.

End of construction,
Thank you for your patience.

It was classic Ruth wit on display. She got her wish—and more than a few laughs from visitors who came to pay their respects at her gravesite.

Naturally, when one spouse dies the other deteriorates quickly. Billy spoke glowingly of Ruth a few months after her death in June 2007. Franklin wheeled him into the dining room as our BGEA board of directors' meeting at the Cove broke for lunch. Billy's eagle eyes were softer, his once-strong voice was gentler. He needed a microphone to be heard in the large board room; we had speakers on the table. He conveyed to us how much he missed Ruth since she'd gone to glory. But this was not a maudlin affair. He lifted our spirits and actually made us laugh as he described how he recently spent a couple of hours holding the hand of another woman.

Emily Cavanaugh Massey had been his fiancée when they were attending Florida Bible Institute in the 1940s, but she had suddenly broken up with him without warning. At the time, she strangely thought that Billy was not spiritual enough or that he would not amount to much in life! Her rejection of him had spurred Billy to a deeper commitment to Christ. Now, decades later, her husband, Charles, was ill. She'd asked Billy to come and pray for him. Billy had rolled in, held her hand, and prayed at the bedside of her ailing husband and his former Wheaton classmate—the man who stole her away from him so many decades ago.

Years after the two were married, Ruth met Emily at a Billy Graham Crusade, and they enjoyed each other's company. Ruth was not the jealous type. In fact, she thanked Emily for breaking up with Billy, and thus, an old friendship was renewed. (The Masseys both passed away in 2008.)

A few weeks before that incident, Billy informed me that he had flown to the White House. President George W. Bush met him in the driveway, and to the amazement of his aides, he pushed Billy's wheelchair around all afternoon.

Billy Graham's life was definitely not typical, even in old age.

Billy's mood was so jovial in recounting these stories that I was moved to ask him a question that had been nagging me for some time.

"Billy," I said to him, "that reminds me of an urban legend I've often heard about you." I told him of the story that circulated periodically of a time when a limousine was sent to pick him up at the airport. As they drove, Billy politely asked the driver if they could change places, just for a while. Always the curious sort, Billy wanted to see what it felt like to drive a long, black limo.

I'm sure the guy got that request a few times over the years, but this was Billy Graham, after all. How could he say no?

And so they switched seats. Billy took the wheel and drove the limo out on the open highway, and that's where he lit it up. He gunned the motor and was zipping along at about eighty-five miles an hour when a police car spotted them and pulled them over. Billy sheepishly handed him his license.

The officer went back to his squad car and got on his radio to talk to his boss at headquarters. "I've pulled over a limo."

"So?" barked his patrol sergeant. "Who's in it?"

"I don't know," the officer whispered. "But it must be someone really big. All I can tell you is that *Billy Graham* is the driver!"

Billy grinned wide but didn't say anything. Lunch was over. I had so many things I wanted to say, and so little time. I knew his end was near.

These unfamiliar emotions had suddenly welled up inside me, and I leaned down to say words that don't come easily to me—words I almost never say to anyone other than my wife and family. I never heard them growing up, so it was hard for me to say them to anyone else. They are words I never dreamed I would one day say to my personal hero. I never knew my father, so Billy, in many ways, was a paternal figure to me.

He meant so much to me in ways he could never know. But perhaps he sensed it.

I leaned down to look him in the eye. Billy's spectacular mane of snowy white hair shone so bright that day. His eyes were clear, and so was his mind. And yet, I felt like he had one foot in this world and the other in Heaven with Jesus and Ruth.

"I love you, Billy," I said, nearly choking.

He smiled back. "I love you too, Greg."

That was the last time I ever saw Billy on this earth, but I know it won't be the last time I see him.

Billy often said he looked forward to Heaven, to reuniting with friends and loved ones who had gone on before, to freedom from sorrow and pain.

"I also look forward to serving God in ways we can't begin to imagine, for the Bible makes it clear that Heaven is not a place of idleness," he said.

Once, at the Cove, my friend John asked me if I would introduce him to Billy. I took John over and said, "Billy, this is my friend. He wanted to meet you personally." Billy smiled and greeted John warmly.

"Mr. Graham," John said, "I want to thank you for your faithfulness to God over these many years."

Billy looked John in the eyes and said, "I wish I could have done more."

It's hard to imagine Billy doing more than he did in his lifetime, but that was the way he saw things, and perhaps it was a real insight into his great effectiveness for God's Kingdom.

Billy is sorely missed, and no one will ever take his place in American or world history.

I am sure the Lord will raise up another great evangelist in the days to come because they seem to come in waves—Whitefield, Moody, Sunday, and of course, Graham.

I have studied the lives of all of these great men of God, but I must say without hesitation that the greatest of them all was the dairy farmer's son from Charlotte, North Carolina—William Franklin Graham.

Or as he always preferred to be called, just "Billy."

Afterword

Reunion

Billy Graham died on February 21, 2018. He was ninety-nine years old.
He had told anyone within earshot that when the news of his death was finally announced to the world, they shouldn't believe a word of it.

"I shall be more alive than I am now," he said. "I will just have changed my address. I will have gone into the presence of God."

And there's no doubt he was.

Billy's departure was a significant moment for all of us who knew him, as well as the millions of people he touched around the world. Though we all knew his death could come any day at his advanced age, just knowing Billy was still with us brought a certain reassurance.

But now he was gone.

The Church was losing a champion, the world was losing a hero, and while history was still being made, history lost with his death. But with Billy's passing, Heaven opened up and God received a most humble and faithful servant.

Because there was no shadow of a doubt where Billy went, it only stands to reason his funeral was a celebration of a life so wholly dedicated

to God. Everybody of importance to Billy was there, but none as important as the man himself.

There were approximately two thousand guests, including two hundred members of Billy's family. It was a global event, with close to four
hundred members of the press recording every word and posting and
beaming them out to the planet.

Political figures ranging from former New York mayor Rudy
Giuliani, former Alaska governor Sarah Palin, Housing and Urban
Development secretary Ben Carson, Vice President Mike Pence—and
most notably, President Donald Trump and First Lady Melania Trump—
were there. (Former presidents Bill Clinton and George W. Bush had gone
to Charlotte a week earlier to pay their respects.)

Christian leaders—ranging from Catholic and Eastern Orthodox to
evangelical—from fifty countries clamored for seats.

As I walked around the tent and saw Jack Graham, Brian Houston,
Max Lucado, Joel Osteen, and Robert Jeffress, I thought, *Who else
would have such a broad connection to people like these?* It made me
think of Heaven. It was like a great family reunion.

And it was.

The Christian press even decided to quote me on that.

Cathe and I took our seats toward the front behind the Graham
family. The sun was shining, but there was a strong, cold wind whip-
ping through the flaps of the massive twenty-eight-thousand-square-
foot tent that had been erected for Billy's funeral. It was both functional
and symbolic, reminding everyone that Billy's ministry effectively
started in a tent in Los Angeles in 1949. Now, in a fitting send-off, it
would end in one.

Beyond the platform was Billy's boyhood home, where he had milked
cows and never in his wildest dreams imagined touching the world as an
international evangelist. Next to that sits the Billy Graham Library, a
place for visitors to come and learn about North Carolina's favorite son.
There is a parkway leading to the library named after him as well.

Members of the Graham family took the stage and spoke of Billy as
a brother, a father, and a grandfather.

None of the political figures spoke that day—not even President Trump. Trump greatly respected Billy, having gone to one of his Crusades as a young man at Yankee Stadium with his father. The young man who became the forty-fifth president of the United States never forgot what he saw and witnessed there—a true man of God.

With the presidential limo known as "The Beast" idling nearby, Trump listened, laughed when funny anecdotes were shared, and prayed with all of us.

To me, one of the most moving moments was when Billy's daughter Ruth Graham mounted the stage and told a story of when she—just like a prodigal—had returned home to her parents after a tempestuous second marriage went awry.

To back it up a bit: feeling unhappy and unloved, Ruth divorced her first husband after twenty-one years of marriage and shortly thereafter moved to a different town. She met a widower, and they quickly fell in love. Though her kids, her parents, and friends all warned her to take it slow, their whirlwind romance was capped by a quickie marriage on New Year's Eve. Ruth later said that within twenty-four hours, "I knew I'd made a terrible mistake."

Her new husband had a volatile temper and threatened her with violence. She feared for her safety, and after five weeks of marriage, fled to her parents' home in Montreat. It was a two-day trip, and she did a lot of thinking behind the steering wheel on the way. Mostly, she feared the damage her quickie marriage and divorce would do to her father's reputation as "America's Preacher."

Poor Ruth beat herself up on that long drive, and many questions (and doubts) swirled around in her head.

"What was I going to say to Daddy? What was I going to say to Mother?" Ruth shared. "What was I going to say to my children? I'd been such a failure." She added, "Women don't want to embarrass their fathers, but you *really* don't want to embarrass Billy Graham!"

As Ruth made the long and winding trek to Little Piney Cove, she saw her tall, commanding father standing outside, waiting for her. She took in a deep breath and opened the car door, expecting to be chastised.

"As I got out of the car, he wrapped his arms around me and said, 'Welcome home,'" Ruth recalled. "There was no shame. There was no blame. There was no condemnation. Just unconditional love.

"And you know, my father was not God, but he showed me what God was like that day."

That was Billy...and Ruth in a nutshell.

Now they are together in Heaven.

Franklin Graham, Billy's oldest son and successor in the ministry that bears his name, quoted his father that day. He said:

"For the Christian, death can be faced realistically and with victory because he knows that 'neither death nor life...will be able to separate us from the love of God' (Romans 8:38–39 NLT). But thanks be to God, who gives us the victory through our Lord Jesus Christ" (1 Corinthians 15:57 ESV). He added, "My father preached on Heaven, told millions how to find Heaven, wrote a book on Heaven, and now he's in Heaven. His journey is complete."

It certainly was.

I could hardly write a book on Billy Graham without talking about the Gospel he preached.

Having worked from transcripts and recordings of hundreds of his messages over the years, I strongly believe one of the secrets to his success was the simplicity of his message. He never deviated from his objective.

This outline is from a message Billy preached. I adapted it, adding some of my own thoughts, and use it to close almost every crusade message I preach now.

If you want to go to Heaven—if you want to know that your life is right with God—read this now:

No. 1—Realize that you are a sinner.

The Bible tells us that "All have sinned and fallen short of God's glory" (Romans 3:23 NIV).

To sin means both to fall short of a mark and to cross a line. God has set a mark for humanity that none can reach. Jesus said, "Be perfect as my Father in Heaven is perfect" (Matthew 5:48 NKJV).

Who can aspire to that? Answer: no one. But that is where Jesus comes in.

To sin means to cross a line. The Bible speaks of how we are "dead in our trespass and sin" (Ephesians 2:1 NASB).

We all have seen signs that say, "No trespassing." We have all crossed that line and broken God's commandments.

No. 2—Recognize that Christ died on the cross for you.

Jesus came to this earth on a rescue mission two thousand years ago for us. He died on that Roman cross because there was no other way to satisfy the righteous demands of God that we all have violated.

With one hand, Jesus took hold of sinful humanity. With the other hand, He took hold of the Father. The Romans drove spikes through those hands as He bled and died for your sins and mine.

I love how the Apostle Paul summarized it when he said, "He loved me, and He gave himself for me!" (Galatians 2:20 NIV).

Jesus died for you.

Christ Himself said, "For God so loved the world that He gave His only begotten son, and whoever believes in Him should not perish but have everlasting life" (John 3:16 NIV).

No. 3—Repent of your sin.

The Bible reminds us that "God has called everyone, everywhere to repent" (Acts 17:30 NLT). The word "repent" is a military term that means "do an about face."

Turn from your sin and put your faith in Jesus Christ.

No. 4—Receive Jesus Christ into your life.

Being a Christian is a relationship with God. It's Christ Himself taking residence in your heart and life as your Savior and Lord.

Jesus says, "Behold, I stand at the door and knock, if any man will hear my voice and open the door I will come in" (Revelation 3:20 NLT).

Only you can open the door of your heart and ask Jesus to come in. He just a prayer away.

No. 5—You must do it now.

Don't put this off.

You may never have another moment like you have right now to ask Christ to come into your life. The Bible reminds us that "today is the day of salvation" (2 Corinthians 6:2 NLT).

This is your moment to have your eternal address changed from Hell to Heaven.

Billy would conclude his evangelistic messages by saying, "You must do it publicly!" Jesus said, "If you will confess Me before people I will confess you before the Father and the angels in Heaven."

Then Billy would say, "I'm going to ask you to get up out of your seat and come down here and stand in front of the platform and make your public stand for Christ!"

And millions came over the decades, most often to the streams of the song "Just as I Am."

But you can pray and ask Christ to come into your heart right now. You don't need to walk forward in a stadium. You can do it right where you are, right now.

Simply pray this prayer out loud from your heart:

> *Lord Jesus,*
> *I know that I am a sinner.*
> *But I know that you are the Savior who died on the cross for my sin.*
> *I am sorry for that sin, and I turn from it now.*

I put my faith in you as my Lord and God and friend.
Thank you for hearing and answering this prayer.
In Jesus's name I pray,
Amen.

Acknowledgments

Because of the length of Billy Graham's life and the breadth of his work, this book you hold in your hands was given a deadline three times longer than the other two *American Icon* books I wrote on Steve McQueen and Johnny Cash. To get Billy Graham's story right required an awful lot of research.

My collaborator, Marshall Terrill, and I have consulted a veritable library of Graham books, articles, periodicals, YouTube videos, and thousands of documents on the internet, including the 1,004-page file the FBI kept on Billy. Research reached as far back as the Civil War. This book contains dimensions of Billy's life and background which have never been explored anywhere before.

However, this book simply would not have been possible without the blessing of Billy's son, Franklin Graham, who has been my friend for many years. I'm so thankful for Franklin's grace. As I embarked on this undertaking, I had some inkling as to what Billy had accomplished, but I now have a much better understanding. I wasn't close. Now I think of it in these terms: Billy's life and work were as substantial as any U.S. president's. Add to that the fact that Billy kept up this blistering pace for almost six decades, while each commander in chief had either four or eight years. Lucky for me, Billy also did an exceptional job of document-ing his life—material I was able to access. I was also fortunate to have the wise counsel of a few others who knew Billy: Paul Saber, who has served with me on the Billy Graham Evangelistic Association board for many years; Dennis Agajanian, a musician who has toured with the Billy Graham Crusade since the 1970s; and Tom Phillips, who is the vice president of the Billy Graham Evangelistic Association.

A most sincere thanks to Stephanie Wills, Billy's personal secretary, for her eagle eye and fact-checking talents. My gratitude is also extended to Donna Lee Toney, assistant to Franklin Graham and David Bruce and personal assistant to Billy Graham. These three remarkable people devoted hours of time to this manuscript and their contributions were invaluable to this project.

A special thank you must go to HarperCollins Publishers for the use of material in *Just as I Am,* Billy's 1997 autobiography, to help tell his epic story again.

I must also thank Robert and Erik Wolgemuth of Wolgemuth & Associates for their wonderful literary representation; developmental editor Scott Seckel, who devoted months of his life to this manuscript; and Cara Highsmith, who served as the line editor on the first draft. Special thanks go to Lee Strobel for allowing us access to his 1998 book, *The Case for Christ: A Journalist's Personal Investigation of the Evidence for Jesus,* and his exclusive interview with Charles Templeton near the end of his life.

Others who helped in this endeavor I'd like to thank in alphabetical order: Karla Dial, Ivor Davis, Pete Ehrmann, John Hellin, Tim Peterson, Gregory Rosauer, Carolyn Terrill, Mike Terrill (who passed from COVID-19 during the course of the writing of this book but read the finished manuscript), Will Vaus, and Austin Wilson.

The challenge I posed to my collaborator, Marshall Terrill, was to show a side of Billy Graham that very few have ever seen. Knowing him personally, I can say that he was even more impressive one-on-one than he was in front of the millions who heard him speak.

It is not an overstatement to say that Billy Graham was one of the great-est preachers in the history of the Church and that he was the single greatest evangelist of all time. Don't take my word for it; history bears that out.

About the Authors

Greg Laurie is the senior pastor of Harvest Christian Fellowship in Riverside, California, and the founder of Harvest Crusades, a nationwide evangelistic event that has drawn more than 10.4 million in stadiums and arenas around the world with over 550,000 professions of faith since 1990. Greg was invited by Billy Graham to serve on the board of directors of the Billy Graham Evangelistic Association in 1994 and still serves today.

Greg is also the featured speaker of the nationally syndicated radio program *A New Beginning* and hosts a weekly television program on the Trinity Broadcasting Network. He has authored over seventy books, including *Steve McQueen: The Salvation of an American Icon*, which was accompanied by a film in 2017, and *Johnny Cash: The Redemption of an American Icon* in 2019. Greg has been married to Cathe Laurie for more than forty-five years, and they have two sons: Christopher, who was killed in a car accident in 2008, and Jonathan, who is the campus pastor at Harvest Orange County. Greg and Cathe have five grandchildren.

Marshall Terrill is a veteran film, sports, and music writer and the author of twenty-five books. They include bestselling biographies of Steve McQueen, Johnny Cash, Elvis Presley, and Pete Maravich. He also served as the executive producer of the 2017 documentary film *Steve McQueen: American Icon.*

Selected Bibliography

Adams, Carl L. *Wanted: Lost Souls*. Bloomington, Indiana: Xlibris Corporation, 2001.

Aikman, David. *Billy Graham: His Life and Influence*. Nashville, Tennessee: Thomas Nelson, 2007.

Allison, Lon. *Billy Graham: An Ordinary Man and His Extraordinary God*. Orleans, Massachusetts: Paraclete Press, 2018.

Brown, Mary Beth. *The Faith of Ronald Reagan*. Nashville, Tennessee: Thomas Nelson, 2011.

Cable, Mildred, and Francesca French. *The Gobi Desert*. London: Hoddon & Stoughton, 1942.

Churchill, Winston. *The Story of the Malakand Field Force*. London: Longmans, Green and Co., 1898.

Cornwell, Patricia. *Ruth, a Portrait: The Story of Ruth Bell Graham*. New York, New York: Doubleday, 1997.

Dalhouse, Mark Taylor. *An Island in the Lake of Fire: Bob Jones University, Fundamentalism and the Separatist Movement*. Athens, Georgia: University of Georgia Press, 1996.

Edwards, Mark T. *Christian Nationalism in the United States*. Basel, Switzerland: MDPI, 2017.

Ellis, William T. *Billy Sunday, the Man and His Message*. Philadelphia, Pennsylvania: John C. Winston, 1914.

Frost, David. *Billy Graham: Candid Conversations with a Public Man.* Colorado Springs, Colorado: David C. Cook, 2014.

———. *Billy Graham Talks with David Frost.* Philadelphia, Pennsylvania: A.J. Holman Company, 1971.

Hosansky, David. *Eyewitness to Watergate.* Washington, D.C.: CQ Press, 2007.

Gibbs, Nancy, and Michael Duffy. *The Preacher and the Presidents.* Nashville, Tennessee: Center Street, 2007.

Graham, Billy. *Billy Graham, God's Ambassador: A Celebration of His Life and Ministry.* New York, New York: HarperOne, 2007.

———. *Death and the Life After.* Nashville, Tennessee: Word Publishing, 1987.

———. *I Saw Your Sons at War: The Korean Diary of Billy Graham.* Charlotte, North Carolina: Billy Graham Evangelistic Association, 1953.

———. *Just as I Am.* New York, New York: HarperCollins Worldwide, 1997.

———. *Nearing Home: Life, Faith and Finishing Well.* Nashville, Tennessee: Thomas Nelson, 2011.

———. *Where I Am: Heaven, Eternity, and Our Life Beyond.* Nashville, Tennessee: W Publishing Group, 2015.

Graham, Franklin. *Rebel with a Cause.* Nashville, Tennessee: Thomas Nelson, 1995.

Graham, Franklin, and Jeanette Lockerbie. *Bob Pierce: This One Thing I Do.* Nashville, Tennessee: W Publishing Group, 1983.

Graham, Franklin, and Donna Lee Toney. *Through My Father's Eyes.* Nashville, Tennessee: W Publishing Group, 2018.

Graham, Ruth Bell. *Footprints of a Pilgrim: The Life and Loves of Ruth Bell Graham.* Nashville, Tennessee: W Publishing Group, 2001.

———. *It's My Turn.* Grand Rapids, Michigan: Fleming H. Revell Company, 1982.

———. *Legacy of a Pack Rat.* Nashville, Tennessee: Oliver Nelson Books, 1989.

Groom, Winston. *Ronald Reagan Our Fortieth President.* Washington, D.C.: Regnery Publishing, 2012.

Ham, Edward E. *50 Years on the Battlefront with Christ: A Biography of M.F. Ham.* Old Kentucky Home Revivalist, 1950.

Hansen, Jake. *Igniting the Fire: The Movements and Mentors Who Shaped Billy Graham.* Uhrichsville, Ohio: Shiloh Run Press, 2015.

Harpur, Thomas. *There Is Life after Death*. Markham, Ontario: Thomas Allen Publishers, 2011.

Jenkins, Jerry B. *In His Own Words: Inspirational Reflections on the Life & Wisdom of Billy Graham*. Carol Stream, Illinois: Tyndale Momentum, 2018.

Khan, Ashley, Holly George-Warren, and Shawn Dahl. *Rolling Stone 1970s*. Boston, Massachusetts: Little, Brown and Company, 1998.

Kim, Billy. *The Life of Billy Kim: From Houseboy to World Evangelist*. Chicago, Illinois: Moody Publishers, 2015.

Laurie, Greg. *Lost Boy*. Allen David Books/Kerygma Publishing, 2008.

Laurie, Greg, and Marshall Terrill. *Johnny Cash: The Redemption of an American Icon*. Washington, D.C.: Salem Books, 2019.

———. *Steve McQueen: The Salvation of an American Icon*. Grand Rapids, Michigan: Zondervan, 2017.

Long, Michael G. *The Legacy of Billy Graham: Critical Reflections of America's Greatest Evangelist*. Louisville, Kentucky: Westminster John Knox Press, 2008.

Martin, William. *A Prophet with Honor: The Billy Graham Story*. Grand Rapids, Michigan: Zondervan, 2018.

Manchester, William. *The Last Lion: Winston Spencer Churchill*, Vols. 1–3. Boston, Massachusetts: Little, Brown and Company, 1983, 1988, 2012.

Millard, Candice. *Hero of the Empire: The Boer War, a Daring Escape, and the Making of Winston Churchill*. New York, New York: Penguin Random House, 2016.

Myra, Harold, and Marshall Shelley. *The Leadership Secrets of Billy Graham*. Grand Rapids, Michigan: Zondervan, 2005.

Pollock, John. *A Foreign Devil in China*. Houston, Texas: World Wide Publications, 1988.

———. *Billy Graham: The Authorized Biography*. New York, New York: McGraw-Hill Book Company, 1966.

———. *Crusades: 20 Years with Billy Graham*. Houston, Texas: World Wide Publications, 1969.

———. *The Billy Graham Story*. Grand Rapids, Michigan: Zondervan, 2003.

Ragsdale, Grady. *Steve McQueen: The Final Chapter*. Baltimore, Maryland: Vision House, 1983.

Roe, Earl E. *Dream Big: The Henrietta Mears Story*. Carol Stream, Illinois: Tyndale House, 1990.

Strobel, Lee. *The Case for Faith: A Journalist Investigates the Toughest Objections to Christianity*. Grand Rapids, Michigan: Zondervan, 2000.

Strober, Gerald S. *Graham: A Day in Billy's Life*. New York, New York: Doubleday, 1976.

Templeton, Charles. *An Anecdotal Memoir*. Toronto, Ontario: McClelland and Stewart Limited, 1983.

Vaus, Will. *My Father Was a Gangster: The Jim Vaus Story*. Washington, D.C.: Believe Books, 2007.

Wacker, Grant. *America's Pastor: Billy Graham and the Shaping of a Nation*. Cambridge, Massachusetts: Belknap Press of Harvard University Press, 2014.

Ward, Mark. *Music in the Air: The Golden Age of Gospel Radio*. Greenville, South Carolina: Emerald House Group, 2004.

Wellman, Sam. *Billy Graham: The Greatest Evangelist*. Uhrichsville, Ohio: Barbour Publishing, 1996.

Whalin, W. Terry. *Billy Graham: America's Greatest Evangelist*. Bloomington, Minnesota: Bethany House Publishers, 2002.

———. *Billy Graham: A Biography of America's Greatest Evangelist*. New York, New York: Morgan James Faith, 2014.

Wilson, Grady. *Count It All Joy*. Nashville, Tennessee: Broadman Press, 1984.

Wirt, Sherwood Elliot. *Crusade at the Golden Gate*. New York, New York: Harper & Brothers, 1959.

Woods, Randall. *LBJ: Architect of American Ambition*. Cambridge, Massachusetts: Harvard University Press, 2006.

Sources

Chapter One: The Dairyman's Son

1. "He'd get drunk...." John Pollock, *Crusades: 20 Years with Billy Graham* (Houston, Texas: World Wide Publications, 1969), 1.
2. "A hard-drinking, hard-cursing veteran...." Billy Graham, *Just as I Am* (New York, New York: HarperCollins, 2018), 3.
3. "I used to have to get up by at least three o'clock," Guy Laurence, "Interview with Dr. Billy Graham" from 1984, YouTube, April 9, 2014, https://www.youtube.com/watch?v=RjhbR8yW4jo.
4. "Billy never liked (milking cows)," Melvin Graham, interview with University of North Carolina-Charlotte, J. Murrey Atkins Library, May 21, 1996.
5. "About three o'clock in the morning...." David Frost, *Billy Graham Talks with David Frost* (Philadelphia, Pennsylvania: A.J. Holman Company, 1971), 17.
6. "Maybe that is where the seeds of some of my ecumenical convictions...." Graham, *Just as I Am*, 7.
7. "I remember one night Mother and Daddy...." Catherine Graham, interview with University of North Carolina-Charlotte, J. Murrey Atkins Library, June 6, 1996.
8. "I think all that yelling helped develop his voice...." W. Terry Whalin, *Billy Graham: America's Greatest Evangelist* (Bloomington, Minnesota: Bethany House Publishers, 2002), 14.
9. "Every day was a different Scripture...." Billy Graham, interview with Charlotte Mecklenburg Library, "Billy Graham: Growing Up in Mecklenburg," https://www.cmstory.org/exhibits/billy-graham-growing-mecklenburg/billy-graham-growing-mecklenburg.

10. "That the Lord has come in and lives...." John Pollock, *Billy Graham: The Authorized Biography* (New York, New York: McGraw-Hill Book Company, 1996), 4.
11. "Just laid hold of the Lord...." ibid.
12. "I guess they're some fanatics...." Graham, *Just as I Am*, 24.

Chapter Two: No Angel

1. "During the service, he'd sit kind of in the back...." Melvin Graham, interview with University of North Carolina-Charlotte, J. Murrey Atkins Library, May 21, 1996.
2. "I'd get out and shake my fist at him...." W. Terry Whalin, *Billy Graham: America's Greatest Evangelist* (Bloomington, Minnesota: Bethany House Publishers, 2002), 14.
3. "My father and mother were both disciplinarians...." Billy Graham, interview with Charlotte Mecklenburg Library, "Billy Graham: Growing Up in Mecklenburg," https://www.cmstory.org/exhibits/billy-graham-growing-mecklenburg/billy-graham-growing-mecklenburg.
4. "He was a gangly knot of undirected energy...." David Aikman, *Billy Graham: His Life and Influence* (Nashville, Tennessee: Thomas Nelson, 2007), 24.
5. "I do feel that I could...." David Frost, *Billy Graham: Candid Conversations with a Public Man* (Colorado Springs, Colorado: David C. Cook, 2014), 161.

Chapter Three: A Bespectacled Messenger

1. "We newcomers glared at the students...." Billy Graham, *Just as I Am* (New York, New York: HarperCollins, 2018), 14.
2. "The Bible says if I do anything...." David Frost, *Billy Graham Talks with David Frost* (Philadelphia, Pennsylvania: A.J. Holman Company, 1971), 28.
3. "My hormones were as active...." Graham, *Just as I Am*, 17.
4. "They would have whaled the tar out of me...." Billy Graham, *Billy Graham, God's Ambassador: A Celebration of His Life and Ministry* (New York, New York: HarperOne, 2007), 24.
5. "Ham compared Charlotte to Sodom...." "Prophet Ham Lambasts Sin in Charlotte," *Elizabeth City Independent*, October 12, 1934.
6. "There are a lot of Christians who are halfway fellows...." E.E. Ham, *50 Years on the Battlefront with Christ: A Biography of M.F. Ham* (Old Kentucky Home Revivalist, 1950), 86–87.
7. "Why don't you come out and hear...." Billy Graham, interview with Charlotte Mecklenburg Library, "Billy Graham: Growing Up in Mecklenburg," https://www.cmstory.org/exhibits/billy-graham-growing-mecklenburg/billy-graham-growing-mecklenburg.
8. "Is he a fighter?..." ibid.
9. "I figured he was the same way...." John Pollock, *Billy Graham: The Authorized Biography* (New York, New York: McGraw-Hill Book Company, 1966), 6.

10. "I have no recollection of what he preached...." Graham, *Just as I Am*, 26.
11. "He didn't know really what...." Pollock, *Billy Graham*, 6.

Chapter Four: The Old Has Gone, the New Has Come

1. "Get your heart right with the Lord...." Melvin Graham, interview with University of North Carolina-Charlotte, J. Murrey Atkins Library, May 21, 1996.
2. "He made it very vivid...." ibid.
3. "In a word, I was spiritually dead...." Jeri Menges, "Young Billy Graham: 'In a Word, I Was Spiritually Dead,'" *Decision*, December 1, 2017.
4. "Grady Wilson was one of my closest friends...." "Grady Wilson Dies at 68," *Christianity Today*, December 11, 1987.
5. "There's a great sinner in this place tonight!..." Michael G. Long, *The Legacy of Billy Graham: Critical Reflections of America's Greatest Evangelist* (Louisville, Kentucky: Westminster John Knox Press, 2008), 5.
6. "My tailor friend helped me to understand...." Billy Graham, *Just as I Am* (New York, New York: HarperCollins, 2018), 30.
7. "I'm a changed boy...." Sam Wellman, *Billy Graham: The Greatest Evangelist* (Uhrichsville, Ohio: Barbour Publishing, 1996), 28.

Chapter Five: Rose-Colored Glasses

1. "Billy realized that he had to break up...." Grady Wilson, *Count It All Joy* (Nashville, Tennessee: Broadman Press, 1984), 7.
2. "Sir don't do that...." John Pollock, *Billy Graham: The Authorized Biography* (New York, New York: McGraw-Hill Book Company, 1966), 10.
3. "If you come to one of my movies...." Alex Falsetto, "The Woody Allen Special [1969] (Guests: Candice Bergen, Billy Graham and the 5th Dimension)" from 1969, YouTube, September 8, 2016, https://www.youtube.com/watch?v=rfY_xwSTztA.
4. "Now we come to God's second question...." Wilson, *Count It All Joy*, 22.
5. "I'm glad to see so many of you...." ibid., 23.
6. "My technique was to offer...." David Frost, *Billy Graham Talks with David Frost* (Philadelphia, Pennsylvania: A.J. Holman Company, 1971), 19.
7. "We combined our selling...." Wilson, *Count It All Joy*, 21.
8. "Grady, did you bring your gun along?..." ibid.
9. "Buddy, we're okay...." ibid.
10. "I was naturally sort of a shy fellow...." Frost, *Billy Graham Talks with David Frost*, 20.

Chapter Six: God's Not Deaf

1. "I didn't have the slightest idea what kind of school [Bob Jones] was...." Mark Taylor Dalhouse, *An Island in the Lake of Fire: Bob Jones University and the Separatist Movement* (Athens, Georgia: University of Georgia Press, 1996).

2. He was "doing more harm to the cause...." Paul Hyde, "Billy Graham Had a Rocky Relationship with Bob Jones University and Its Past Presidents," *Greenville News*, February 21, 2018.
3. "If a hound dog barks for Jesus...." William Martin, *A Prophet with Honor: The Billy Graham Story* (Grand Rapids, Michigan: Zondervan, 2018), 246.
4. "He didn't have any purpose...." John Pollock, *Billy Graham: The Authorized Biography* (New York, New York: McGraw-Hill Book Company, 1966), 11.
5. "Although converted, Billy and I...." Grady Wilson, *Count It All Joy* (Nashville, Tennessee: Broadman Press, 1984), 23.
6. "Hey, God's not deaf!..." ibid., 24.
7. "If you leave and throw your life away...." John Pollock, *Crusades: 20 Years with Billy Graham* (Houston, Texas: World Wide Productions, 1969), 13.

Chapter Seven: New Horizons

1. "I had just stepped outside...." Lois Ferm, "Billy Graham in Florida," *The Florida Historical Quarterly* 60, no. 2 (October 1981).
2. "Like an animal that had...." John Pollock, *Billy Graham: The Authorized Biography* (New York, New York: McGraw-Hill Book Company, 1966), 13.
3. "The fellows would wash the dishes...." ibid.
4. "I had no purpose...." ibid., 15.
5. "No, Billy's going to preach...." Ferm, "Billy Graham in Florida."
6. "He had a bit of difficulty...." Pollock, *Billy Graham*, 15.
7. Billy's appearance was "big doings in those days...." John B. Hannigan, "Historical Marker Dedicates Site of Billy Graham's First Sermon," *Florida Baptist Witness*, April 21, 2011.
8. "I never thought at that time...." ibid.

Chapter Eight: God Speaks, on the Eighteenth Hole

1. "If I play ten hours a day...." Scott Ostler, "He Turned a Dream into a Reality," *Los Angeles Times*, October 28, 1987.
2. This incident "caused me to look to God...." John Pollock, *Billy Graham: The Authorized Biography* (New York, New York: McGraw-Hill Book Company, 1966), 16.
3. "I have something to tell you...." ibid.
4. "She wanted to marry a man...." David Aikman, *Billy Graham: His Life and Influence* (Nashville, Tennessee: Thomas Nelson, 2007), 40.
5. "Oh God, if you want me...." Billy Graham, *Just as I Am* (New York, New York: HarperCollins Worldwide, 1997), 53.
6. "One of two things can happen...." John Pollock, *Crusades: 20 Years with Billy Graham* (Houston, Texas: World Wide Productions, 1969), 21.

Chapter Nine: Ready to Roar

1. "Old timers say that last night's meeting…." Lois Ferm, "Billy Graham in Florida," *Florida Historical Quarterly* 60, no. 2 (October 1981).
2. "I stood right in the door…." John Pollock. *The Billy Graham Story* (Grand Rapids, Michigan: Zondervan, 2003), 26.

Chapter Ten: Knees Down! Chin Up!

1. "There is more power…." William T. Ellis, *Billy Sunday, the Man and His Message* (Philadelphia, Pennsylvania: John C. Winston, 1914), 240.
2. "The more I prayed…." John Pollock, *Billy Graham: The Authorized Biography* (New York, New York: McGraw-Hill Book Company, 1966), 23.
3. "God has chosen a human…." ibid., 24.

Chapter Eleven: The Twenty-One-Year-Old Freshman

1. He found Wheaton "a new and strange place…." John Pollock, *Billy Graham: The Authorized Biography* (New York, New York: McGraw-Hill Book Company, 1966), 24.
2. "He was so much taller…." David Dresser, interview with Wheaton College, June 30, 2010.
3. "He was tall and lanky…." Pollock, *Billy Graham*, 24.
4. "We would take turns praying…." ibid.
5. "Other fellow students there…." W. Glyn Evans, interview with Wheaton College, April 21, 2010.
6. "He (Billy) was not a person to entertain…." ibid.
7. "This student who went forth…." ibid.
8. "We weren't too interested…." ibid.
9. "He not only did the driving…." ibid.
10. "Life and death were not abstractions…." Billy Graham, *Just as I Am* (New York, New York: HarperCollins Worldwide, 1997), 68.

Chapter Twelve: Saved by a Bell

1. "I noticed what they were wearing…." Jane Levring, interview with Wheaton College, August 3, 2010.
2. "She's so spiritual that she gets…." Patricia Cornwell, *Ruth, A Portrait: The Story of Ruth Bell Graham* (New York, New York: Doubleday, 1997), 74.
3. "At that moment…." Billy Graham Evangelistic Association, "Footprints of a Pilgrim—Remembering Ruth Bell Graham (Full Program)," YouTube, November 8, 2016, https://www.youtube.com/watch?v=is9MrevpN88&lc=Ugh5Y6DBpKcIAXgCoAEC.
4. "They ran a tight ship…." AnneGrahamLotz(Official), "A Conversation with Ruth Bell Graham," YouTube, April 29, 2014, https://www.youtube.com/watch?v=pBS23WonTSc.

5.   "We children were not the only ones...." ibid.

6.   "And to my innocent child's mind...." ibid.

7.   "Almost nothing remains...." Will Ripley, "Billy Graham's North Korea Legacy: From 'Witch Doctor' to Honored Guest," CNN, March 2, 2018, https://www.cnn.com/2018/03/02/asia/billy-graham-asia-north-korea-intl/index.html.

8.   "She was very outgoing...." Jeanne Smith Burton Wheaton, interview with Wheaton College, April 20, 2010.

9.   "Finances were tight...." Autumn Ellis Ross, "Remembering Ruth," *Wheaton* (Autumn 2007): https://alumni.wheaton.edu/s/1156/images/editor_documents/wheaton_magazine/autumn2007.pdf?sessionid=c75624a4-a92d-48a0-b156-f27f7e4677b8&cc=1.

10. "There was a seriousness about him...." John Pollock, *Billy Graham: The Authorized Biography* (New York, New York: McGraw-Hill Book Company, 1966), 26.

11. "She had her eyes on him...." Burton, interview with Wheaton College.

12. "On the way back...." Billy Graham Evangelistic Association, "Footprints of a Pilgrim."

Chapter Thirteen: A Marriage Made in Heaven

1.   "He was so very serious...." John Pollock, *Billy Graham: The Authorized Biography* (New York, New York: McGraw-Hill Book Company, 1966), 26.

2.   "Missionary life...." James Donaldson, "Unsung Heroes No. 3—Amy Carmichael," Church Mission Society, July 12, 2009, https://churchmissionsociety.org/our-stories/unsung-heroes-no3-amy-carmichael/.

3.   "Mildred Cable's most famous quote...." Mildred Cable and Francesca French, *The Gobi Desert* (London: Hoddon & Stoughton, 1942).

4.   "A good marriage...." Billy Graham, "Billy Graham Trivia: What Was Crucial to Billy and Ruth's Happy Marriage?" Billy Graham Evangelistic Association, February 8, 2017, https://billygraham.org/story/billy-graham-trivia-what-was-crucial-to-billy-and-ruths-happy-marriage/.

5.   "I don't recall reading in Scripture...." "Ruth Graham, 87; Had Active Role as Wife of Famed Evangelist," *Los Angeles Times*, June 15, 2007, https://www.latimes.com/la-me-graham15jun15-story.html.

6.   "Well, I don't recall...." ibid.

7.   "God had brought them...." Pollock, *Billy Graham*, 26.

8.   "The Lord leads me...." ibid.

9.   "A Christian wife's responsibility...." Ruth Bell Graham, *It's My Turn* (Grand Rapids, Michigan: Fleming H. Revell Company, 1982), 54.

10. "Raced right out and spent...." Billy Graham, *Just as I Am* (New York, New York: HarperCollins Worldwide, 1997), 76.

11. "She had long, straight hair...." ibid.

12. "Do not disturb our dear Billy...." Pollock, *Billy Graham*, 28.

Chapter Fourteen: It Takes a Village

1. "The building had a low ceiling...." Grosvenor C. Rust, interview with Wheaton College, September 23, 2010.
2. "I think it is very important...." John Pollock, *Billy Graham: The Authorized Biography* (New York, New York: McGraw-Hill Book Company, 1966), 29.
3. "It is not wise to disagree...." Ruth Bell Graham, *It's My Turn*, (Grand Rapids, Michigan: Fleming H. Revell Company, 1982), 54.
4. "After I wrote the article...." David Frost, *Billy Graham Talks with David Frost* (Philadelphia, Pennsylvania: A.J. Holman Company, 1971), 40.
5. "The worst fit of stage fright...." John Pollock, *Billy Graham*, 32.
6. "Some of you need to confess...." Patricia Cornwell, *Ruth a Portrait: The Story of Ruth Bell Graham* (New York, New York: Doubleday, 1997), 101.

Chapter Fifteen: London Fog

1. "We used every modern means...." Mark T. Edwards "Christian Nationalism in the United States," *Religions*, published by MPDI (June 2017): 118, https://www.mdpi.com/books/pdfview/book/326.
2. "When we met, Billy looked...." Billy Graham, *Billy Graham, God's Ambassador: A Celebration of his Life and Ministry* (New York: HarperOne, 2007), 32.
3. "This is what I hoped would happen...." Mark Ward Sr., *Music in the Air: The Golden Age of Gospel Radio* (Greenville, South Carolina: Emerald House Group, Inc., 2004).
4. "Lord, come down...." Charles Templeton, *An Anecdotal Memoir* (Toronto, Ontario: McClelland and Stewart Limited, 1983),33.
5. "When they came off the train...." Eric Hutchings, "The Apprenticeship of Billy Graham, 1937–1949," interview with Billy Graham Archives Center.
6. "Billy was amazed at the numbers...." Eric Hutchings, interview with Billy Graham Archives Center, "The Apprenticeship of Billy Graham, 1937–1949," May 9, 2009, https://www2.wheaton.edu/bgc/archives/Papers/BG3749/BG3749.htm.
7. "Billy Graham at that time...." Canon Thomas Livemore, interview with Billy Graham Archives Center, "The Apprenticeship of Billy Graham, 1937–1949," May 9, 2009, https://www2.wheaton.edu/bgc/archives/Papers/BG3749/BG3749.htm.
8. "They enjoyed the way he said things...." ibid.
9. "Torrey Johnson...." Torrey Johnson, interview with Billy Graham Archives Center, "The Apprenticeship of Billy Graham, 1937–1949," May 9, 2009, https://www2.wheaton.edu/bgc/archives/Papers/BG3749/BG3749.htm.
10. "Cliff Barrows...." Cliff Barrows, interview with Billy Graham Archives Center, "The Apprenticeship of Billy Graham, 1937–1949," May 9, 2009, https://www2.wheaton.edu/bgc/archives/Papers/BG3749/BG3749.htm.
11. "He challenged those who were ready...." Eric Hutchings, "The Apprenticeship of Billy Graham, 1937–1949."

12. "I gave him my testimony...." William Martin, *A Prophet with Honor: The Billy Graham Story* (Grand Rapids, Michigan: Zondervan, 2018).

Chapter Sixteen: Evangelism Races, Education Plods

1. "That young man rarely misses...." John Pollock, *Billy Graham: The Authorized Biography* (New York, New York: McGraw-Hill Book Company, 1966), 42.
2. "I sent him a letter from Winona Lake...." Billy Graham, interview with Billy Graham Archives Center, "The Apprenticeship of Billy Graham, 1937–1949," May 9, 2009, https://www2.wheaton.edu/bgc/archives/Papers/BG3749/BG3749. htm.
3. "He looked at me with fire...." Curtis Gilbert, "Rev. Billy Graham's Rise Began in Minnesota," *Winona Daily News*, February 21, 2018, https://www. winonadailynews.com/rev-billy-grahams-rise-began-in-minnesota/ article_5aeedbf2-05d7-51ea-9f0b-26b9689154f0.html.
4. "Evangelism races, education plods...." Pollock, *Billy Graham*, 45.

Chapter Seventeen: Inexperienced, but Enthusiastic

1. "I didn't know that would grow...." Jenny Collins, "A Reluctant Leader Leaves a Legacy," *Pilot*, February 28, 2009.
2. "T, you better do the rest...." John Pollock, *Billy Graham: The Authorized Biography* (New York, New York: McGraw-Hill Book Company, 1966), 46.
3. "When she gave advice...." Grady Wilson, *Count It All Joy* (Nashville, Tennessee: Broadman Press, 1984), 34.
4. "Nobody came into Billy's office...." Collins, "A Reluctant Leader Leaves a Legacy."
5. "I greatly admired Billy...." ibid.
6. "He came in through the door...." ibid.
7. "He really threw himself...." ibid.
8. "He was handed an institution...." ibid.
9. "He had invited me...." Mark W. Lee, interview with Wheaton College, October 4, 2010.
10. "The challenge really worked...." Collins, "A Reluctant Leader Leaves a Legacy."
11. "I could hardly keep up...." Luvern Gustavson, interview with the University of Northwestern-St. Paul, "A Reluctant Leader Leaves a Legacy," February 28, 2009.
12. "Billy was able to put forth...." Collins, "A Reluctant Leader Leaves a Legacy."
13. "When Billy Graham left Northwestern...." Greg Roseauer, personal interview, February 26, 2020.
14. "When I neglect my correspondence...." Pollock, *Billy Graham*, 46.

Chapter Eighteen: Two Evangelists, Two Crises of Faith

1. "There seemed to be little concern...." Charles Templeton, *An Anecdotal Memoir* (Toronto, Ontario: McClelland and Stewart Limited, 1983), 67.
2. "How could a loving God...." Lee Strobel, *The Case for Faith: A Journalist Investigates the Toughest Objections to Christianity* (Grand Rapids, Michigan: Zondervan, 2000), 13.
3. "I doubt if any other woman...." Earl E. Roe, *Dream Big: The Henrietta Mears Story* (Carol Stream, Illinois: Tyndale House, 1990).
4. "Lord, what shall I do?..." John Pollock, *Crusades: 20 Years with Billy Graham* (Houston, Texas: World Wide Productions, 1969), 57.
5. "Oh God; there are many things...." Billy Graham, *Just as I Am* (New York, New York: HarperCollins Publishers, 1997),139.
6. "That was the beginning...." Billy Graham, "Celebrating 80 Years," video on ForestHome.org/about/.
7. "I have often pondered...." Templeton, *An Anecdotal Memoir*, 71.
8. "I oppose the Christian Church...." James D. Davis, "Ex-Evangelist Dumps God," *South Florida Sun Sentinel*, July 11, 1999.
9. "Actually, I'm dying," Strobel, *The Case for Faith*, 13.
10. "No. No. There cannot be...." ibid., 15.
11. "No question...." ibid., 16.
12. "You sound like you really...." ibid., 17.
13. "Well, yes, He's the most...." ibid.
14. "And if I may put it this way...." ibid., 18.
15. "Enough of that...." ibid.
16. "Look at them, look at them!..." Thomas Harpur, *There Is Life After Death* (Markham, Ontario: Thomas Allen Publishers, 2011).

Chapter Nineteen: Kissed by William Randolph Hearst

1. "There was one thing...." Lawrence Young, interview with Wheaton College, July 14, 1971.
2. It was "the greatest flop they ever experienced...." Jon Brown, "Scratching Coals from the Furnace: A Millennial's Perspective of Billy Graham," The Daily Caller, March 2, 2018, https://dailycaller.com/2018/03/02/snatching-coals-from-the-furnace-a-millennials-perspective-on-billy-graham/.
3. "We were praying about it...." Young, interview with Wheaton College.
4. "We knew that we might...." ibid.
5. "You ready to go?..." "Stuart Hamblen: October 8, 1908 to March 8, 1969," Hamblen Music Company, https://www.hamblenmusic.com/home/stuart-hamblen/pages.
6. "There is someone in this tent...." John Pollock, *Crusades: 20 Years with Billy Graham* (Houston, Texas: World Wide Productions, 1969), 61.
7. "It was very slow going...." Young, interview with Wheaton College.

8. "You've been kissed by...." John Pollock, *Billy Graham: The Authorized Biography* (New York, New York: McGraw-Hill Book Company, 1966), 59.

Chapter Twenty: Cowboys, Heroes, and Mobsters

1. "Hearst newspapers...." Lawrence Young, interview with Wheaton College, July 14, 1971.
2. "And he went—reluctantly...." Louis Zamperini, interview with Wheaton College, May 16, 1976.
3. "I got under conviction...." ibid.
4. "Of all my near-death experiences...." ibid.
5. "I knew I was through...." ibid.
6. "Well, honey, let's go...." Jim Vaus, personal interview with Wheaton College, May 26, 1976.
7. "Brother, are you saved?..." ibid.
8. "All I could think about...." ibid.
9. "There is a man in this audience...." Will Vaus, *My Father Was a Gangster: The Jim Vaus Story* (Washington, D.C.: Believe Books, 2007), 55.
10. "OK, I'll go," Vaus, personal interview with Wheaton College.
11. "God, if You'll mean business...." Vaus, *My Father Was a Gangster*, 56.
12. "I don't think Cohen...." David Frost, *Billy Graham Talks with David Frost* (Philadelphia, Pennsylvania: A.J. Holman Company, 1971), 59.
13. "No! And if that guy...." Vaus, *My Father Was a Gangster*, 66.
14. "The revival that started here...." Cecilia Rasmussen, "Billy Graham's Star Was Born at His 1949 Revival in Los Angeles," *Los Angeles Times*, September 2, 2007.
15. "Something was happening...." Billy Graham, *Just as I Am* (New York, New York: HarperCollins Worldwide, 1997), 152.

Chapter Twenty-One: King of All Media

1. "Boys, if you ever pray...." Michael T. Benson, *Harry S. Truman and the Founding of Israel* (Westport, Connecticut: Praeger, 1997), 45.
2. "Is there anything *we* can do...." Geoffrey C. Ward, "Straighten Up and Fly Left," *New York Times*, August 25, 2002.
3. "And of course that was taking advantage...." Chuck Raasch, "When Harry Met Billy: The Beginning of Rev. Graham's Presidential Relationships," *St. Louis Post-Dispatch*, February 28, 2018.
4. "It was a terrible mistake...." Raasch, "When Harry Met Billy."
5. "I did not know that you...." David Frost, *Billy Graham: Candid Conversations with a Public Man* (Colorado Springs, Colorado: David Cook, 2014), 10

Chapter Twenty-Two: Far East Man

1. "I didn't blame the press...." Steve Walburn, "The Third Coming of Billy Graham," *Atlanta*, October 1994.
2. "This country needs a revival...." Terry W. Whalin, *Billy Graham: A Biography of America's Greatest Evangelist* (New York, New York: Morgan James Faith, 2014), 84.
3. "I thought that if I could see...." Billy Graham, *I Saw Your Sons at War: The Korean Diary of Billy Graham* (Charlotte, North Carolina: Billy Graham Evangelistic Association, 1953).
4. "I wept more in Korea...." Billy Graham, "Billy Graham's Korean Issued Boots," Billy Graham Library, July 1, 2014.

Chapter Twenty-Three: Yankee Spellbinder

1. "In my entire life...." Billy Graham, *Just as I Am* (New York, New York: HarperCollins Worldwide, 1997), 213.
2. "I remember well there was a skepticism...." Ivor Davis, interview, April 1, 2020.
3. "Billy Graham has more gravely...." Graham, *Just as I Am*, 214.
4. "Who invited you over here...." John Pollock, *Crusades: 20 Years with Billy Graham* (Houston, Texas: World Wide Productions, 1969), 127.
5. "Well, Jesus traveled on a donkey...." David Frost, *Billy Graham Talks with David Frost* (Philadelphia, Pennsylvania: A.J. Holman Company, 1971), 31–32.
6. "The purpose of coming to Britain...." British Pathé, "Thousands Mob U.S. Evangelist," video, 1954, https://www.britishpathe.com/video/thousands-mob-u-s-evangelist.
7. "That's not in my area at all...." British Pathé, "Thousands Mob U.S. Evangelist."
8. "God bless you, sir...." Pollock, *Crusades*, 127.
9. "Let's go face it...." ibid., 130.
10. "Billy, the place is packed...." Frost, *Billy Graham Talks with David Frost*, 58.
11. "But I have one tremendous fear...." "From the Archive of Billy Graham, London 1954," *Church Times*, February 22, 2018, https://www.churchtimes.co.uk/articles/2018/23-february/news/world/from-the-archive-billy-graham-in-london-1954.
12. "To be honest, I was prejudiced...." Harold Myra and Marshall Shelley, *The Leadership Secrets of Billy Graham* (Grand Rapids, Michigan: Zondervan, 2005).
13. "We may never see a sight...." Graham, *Just as I Am*, 233.
14. "It was like divine adrenaline...." Gayle White, *Atlanta Journal Constitution*, "Evangelist Billy Graham is Dead at 99," February 21, 2018.

Chapter Twenty-Four: Shaking Hands with Mr. History

1. "Would you be able...." Billy Graham, *Just as I Am* (New York, New York: HarperCollins Worldwide, 1997), 235.
2. "I could hardly be called a pillar...." Andrew Roberts, "Churchill Proceedings—Winston Churchill and Religion—A Comfortable Relationship with the Almighty," International Churchill Society, November 2013.
3. "It was the bravest thing...." William Manchester, *The Last Lion: Visions of Glory 1874–1932* (Boston, Massachusetts: Little, Brown and Company, 1983, 1988, 2012), 157.
4. "The practice [of prayer] was comforting...." John Broom, "Winston Churchill and Christianity," FaithInWarTime.wordpress.com, January 22, 2015, https://faithinwartime.wordpress.com/2015/01/22/winston-churchill-and-christianity/.
5. "If you tried your best to live...." Broom, "Winston Churchill and Christianity..
6. "Thompson misunderstood and said...." Heather Sells, "Divine Destiny: Churchill's Faith and the Defeat of Evil," CBN News, December 29, 201.
7. "He looks like you, sir...." Manchester, *The Last Lion*, 36.
8. "There's nothing so thrilling...." Winston Churchill, *The Story of the Malakand Field Force* (London: Longmans, Green and Co., 1898), 107.
9. "Winston, you are drunk...." Richard Langworth, "Drunk and Ugly: The Rumor Mill," International Churchill Society, January 2011, https://winstonchurchill.org/publications/churchill-bulletin/bulletin-031-jan-2011/drunk-and-ugly-the-rumor-mill/.
10. "Young man, I have a question...." *Billy Graham: God's Ambassador*, Gaither Film Productions, 2006.
11. "Sir, people are hungry...." ibid.
12. "That must be it...." ibid.
13. "I am an old man...." ibid.
14. "Mr. Prime Minister...." John Pollock, *Crusades: 20 Years with Billy Graham* (Houston, Texas: World Wide Publications, 1969), 139.
15. "I do not see much hope...." John Pollock, *Billy Graham: The Authorized Biography* (New York, New York: McGraw-Hill Book Company, 1966), 132.
16. "This conversation as long as I live...." *Billy Graham: God's Ambassador*.
17. "I felt like I had shaken hands...." Pollock, *Billy Graham*, 132.

Chapter Twenty-Five: Gabriel in a Gabardine Suit

1. "I may be a small item...." "A New Kind of Evangelist," *Time*, October 25, 1954.
2. "Good manners do not permit...." Billy Graham, *Billy Graham, God's Ambassador: A Celebration of his Life and Ministry* (New York, New York: HarperOne, 2007), 4.
3. "Golf games with the President...." Billy Graham, *Just as I Am* (New York, New York: HarperCollins Worldwide, 1997), 200.
4. "I was appalled at it and decided...." Billy Graham Evangelistic Association, "Taking Down the Ropes of Segregation—Part 2," YouTube, January 8, 2018, https://www.youtube.com/watch?v=EQuFvvwnKRE.

5.   "Either these ropes stay down...." ibid.
6.   "His approach was more...." ibid.
7.   "Until we come to recognize...." ibid.
8.   "Salvation is by grace...." Graham, *Just as I Am*, 204.
9.   "He knew another truth...." ibid.
10. "My mother read her Bible...." Kelsey Dallas, "Q & A: Finding Richard Nixon's Faith in a Legacy of Scandal," *Deseret News*, May 31, 2017, https://www.telegram.com/news/20170531/qa-finding-richard-nixons-faith-in-legacy-of-scandal.
11. "He was laying in bed...." EvangelioGospel, "Billy Graham Meeting with Dwight Eisenhower Just before He Died," YouTube, October 8, 2011, https://www.youtube.com/watch?v=u9Dry6K1a88.
12. "Give those old doughboys...." ibid.
13. "Some men are considered...." Andrew Glass, "Eisenhower Dies at Age 78, March 28, 1969," *Politico*, March 28, 2018, https://www.politico.com/story/2018/03/28/eisenhower-dies-at-age-78-march-28-1969-484631.

Chapter Twenty-Six: JFK
1.   "One of the most courageous spiritual...." Nancy Gibbs and Michael Duffy, *The Preacher and the Presidents* (Nashville, Tennessee: Center Street, 2007), 75.
2.   "If you give me a week...." David A. Graham, "If You Give Me a Week, I Might Think of One," *The Atlantic*, May 27, 2016.
3.   "This is a time of world tension...." *TIME, Billy Graham: America's Preacher, 1918–2018* (February 23, 2018), 66.
4.   "A man's religion cannot...." "Billy Graham Gives Implied Nod to Nixon," *Charlotte Observer*, May 21, 1960.
5.   "I have deeply appreciated...." Gibbs and Duffy, *The Preacher and the Presidents*, 106.
6.   "Billy, do you believe...." Billy Graham, *Just as I Am* (New York, New York: HarperCollins Worldwide, 1997), 395.
7.   "The only permanent peace...." David Frost, *Billy Graham Talks with David Frost* (Philadelphia, Pennsylvania: A.J. Holman, 1971), 46.
8.   "I don't think that Mr. Kennedy's...." Graham, *Just as I Am*, 396.
9.   "The race question will not...." Pollock, *Crusades: 20 Years with Billy Graham* (Houston, Texas: World Wide Productions, 1969), 280.

Chapter Twenty-Seven: The Decade That Took Down a President
1.   "He was always interested...." HelmerReenberg, "Reverend Billy Graham Reaction Following the Assassination of President John F. Kennedy," YouTube, October 21, 2012, https://www.youtube.com/watch?v=PsjlnHHZYjk&lc=UggUK6k3AAWigXgCoAEC.

2. "I don't weep often...." Rick Hampson, "The Lost Day: How We Remember, and Don't, the 26 Hours after Robert F. Kennedy Fell," *USA Today*, June 18, 2018.
3. "The only hope for finding...." Billy Graham, *Just as I Am* (New York, New York: HarperCollins Worldwide, 1997), 401.
4. "He had a conflict...." Billy Graham, "Billy Graham Oral History, Special Project," LBJ Library, October 12, 1983.
5. "It was an incredible blend...." Lisa Suhay, "Is Trump 'Un-Presidential?' Not Compared to Some Past Presidents," *Christian Science Monitor*, August 10, 2015, https://www.csmonitor.com/USA/USA-Update/2015/0810/ Is-Trump-un-presidential-Not-compared-to-some-past-presidents.
6. "Johnson the Son of the Tenant...." Randall Woods, *LBJ: Architect of American Ambition* (Cambridge, Massachusetts: Harvard University Press, 2006), 639.
7. "President Johnson, in my judgment...." David Frost, *Billy Graham Talks with David Frost* (Philadelphia, Pennsylvania: A.J. Holman Company, 1971), 69.
8. "No man can live...." Lyndon B. Johnson, "Remarks at the 12th Annual Prayer Breakfast," American Presidency Project, February 5, 1964, https://www. presidency.ucsb.edu/documents/ remarks-the-12th-annual-presidential-prayer-breakfast.
9. "If I've lost Cronkite...." Joel Achenbach, "How Walter Cronkite's Broadcast changed the Vietnam War," *Washington Post*, May 25, 2018.
10. "In fact, a number of times...." Graham, "Billy Graham Oral History, Special Project."
11. "I knew the tremendous tensions...." ibid.
12. "Every time I ever saw...." ibid.
13. "O God, we consecrate...." Billy Graham, "1969 Inaugural Prayer," Billy Graham Center Archives, https://www2.wheaton.edu/bgc/archives/inaugural05. htm.
14. "He wanted to do something...." Graham, "Billy Graham Oral History, Special Project."
15. "A massive manhood...." Jon Thompson, "Billy Graham Preaches at LBJ's Funeral Service in Stonewall, Texas," YouTube, January 30, 2012, https://www. youtube.com/watch?v=Ejfui4W2GVk.

Chapter Twenty-Eight: A Man I Never Knew

1. "The Holy Spirit will move...." Charles Spurgeon, *The Metropolitan Tabernacle Pulpit, Volume XXII* (Passmore and Alabaster, January 1, 1877), 148.
2. "If there's ever anything I can do...." Greg Laurie with Marshall Terrill, *Johnny Cash: The Redemption of an American Icon* (Washington, D.C.: Salem Books, 2019), 177.
3. "He's a good man...." ibid.

4. "Christianity is not a white...." "Billy Graham: Six Things He Believed," BBC News, February 21, 2018, https://www.bbc.com/news/world-us-canada-43144752.

5. "I was startled when Hank shook...." Jack U. Harwell, "A Look at the Man in His Prime," *Baptist Press Features*, July 5, 1973.

6. "I can think of few other people...." Mark Galli, "Inside the Nixon Years," *Christianity Today*, 2012, https://www.christianitytoday.com/ct/2018/billy-graham/inside-nixon-years.html.

7. "His assistants checked with Billy...." ibid.

8. "Never, in all the times...." *TIME, Billy Graham: America's Preacher, 1918–2018* (February 23, 2018), 68.

9. "I shall always consider him...." ibid.

10. "Maybe I was naïve...." ibid.

11. "He (Nixon) would be very likely...." Galli, "Inside the Nixon Years."

12. "Many people say...." Billy Graham, *Good Morning America*, 1994.

13. "Today, we remember...." Billy Graham, "Eulogy for Richard Nixon," AmericanRhetoric.com, April 27, 1994, https://www.americanrhetoric.com/speeches/billygrahameulogyrichardnixon.htm.

14. "Donne said that...." ibid.

15. "Richard Nixon had that hope...." ibid.

Chapter Twenty-Nine: Revival in a Suitcase

1. "All the president is...." David McCullough, "The Language of Leadership: The Words of Harry Truman," *Los Angeles Times*, January 17, 1993.

2. "I think the most difficult problem...." Jooyoung Lee, "For One More Revival, Rise Up Korean Churches, Remember Billy Graham in Korea 1970s," YouTube, November 22, 2014, https://www.youtube.com/watch?v=qFJVdAQi8Ko.

3. "I'm not here as an American...." ibid.

4. "The North Korean response...." ibid.

5. "I would be absolutely nothing...." ibid.

6. "I felt so incapable...." ibid.

7. "Isn't he preaching...." Billy Graham Evangelistic Association, "Seoul, South Korea: Billy Graham's Largest Ever Crusade," YouTube, February 8, 2018, https://www.youtube.com/watch?v=PQDLjd57vdE.

8. "All the religions of the world...." "For One More Revival, Rise Up Korean Churches, Remember Billy Graham in Korea 1970s."

9. "I have traveled the world...." ibid.

10. "The last time I met Reverend Billy...." Will Ripley, "Billy Graham's North Korea Legacy: From 'Witch Doctor' to Honored guest," CNN, March 2, 2018, https://www.cnn.com/2018/03/02/asia/billy-graham-asia-north-korea-intl/index.html.

Chapter Thirty: The Son Also Rises

1. "This could be one of the most significant...." "Let the Earth Hear His Voice," Lausanne Movement, July 16, 1974, https://www.lausanne.org/content/let-earth-hear-voice.
2. "Our long national nightmare is over...." "Our Long National Nightmare Is Over," *Los Angeles Times*, December 28, 2006, https://www.latimes.com/archives/la-xpm-2006-dec-28-na-oath28-story.html.
3. "When you get to the White House...." Nancy Gibbs and Michael Duffy, *The Preacher and the Presidents* (Nashville, Tennessee: Center Street, 2007), 234.
4. "I let down my friends...." James Wieghart and Frank Jackman, "President Nixon to David Frost: I Let Down My Country," *New York Daily News*, May 25, 1977.
5. "I was wrong in not acting...." David Hosansky, *Eyewitness to Watergate* (Washington, D.C.: CQ Press, 2016), 291.
6. "I would rather have a man...." Stephen P. Miller, *Billy Graham and the Rise of the Republican South* (Philadelphia, Pennsylvania: University of Pennsylvania Press, 2011), 198.
7. "I hate to talk about religion...." Gibbs and Duffy, *The Preacher and the Presidents*, 251.
8. "That Carter believes fifty things...." James Fallows, "The Passionless Presidency," *The Atlantic*, May 1979.
9. "The rebel had found the cause...." Franklin Graham, *Rebel with a Cause* (Nashville, Tennessee: Thomas Nelson, 1995), 123.
10. "This is a new beginning...." ibid., 138.
11. "Buddy, these people need...." ibid.
12. "I'm going to travel...." Paula Zahn, "The Prodigal Son Comes Home," CNN, 2001, https://www.cnn.com/CNN/Programs/people/shows/graham/profile.html.

Chapter Thirty-One: California Christians

1. "Are you with the Sam Sheppard party?..." Greg Laurie with Marshall Terrill, *Steve McQueen: The Salvation of an American Icon* (American Icon Press, 2017), 17.
2. "I'm Billy Graham...." ibid.
3. "Howdy, fellas...." ibid., 1.
4. "I'll see you in heaven!..." Laurie with Terrill, *Steve McQueen*, 288.
5. "I look back on that experience...." Grady Ragsdale Jr., *Steve McQueen: The Final Chapter* (Baltimore, Maryland: Vision House, 1983), 177.
6. "There's no pretense...." Billy Graham, *The Dean Martin Celebrity Roast: Bob Hope*, October 31, 1974.
7. "I realized I couldn't ask...." Winston Groom, *Ronald Reagan Our Fortieth President* (Washington, D.C.: Regnery, 2012), 99.
8. "I hope you are all Republicans...." ibid., 98.

9. "Whatever happens now...." Mary Beth Brown, *The Faith of Ronald Reagan* (Nashville, Tennessee: Thomas Nelson, 2011), 196.
10. "Haunted, tired look on people's faces...." Billy Graham, *Just as I Am* (New York, New York: HarperCollins Worldwide, 1997), 382.
11. "I have come to see that the church...." ibid., 486.

Chapter Thirty-Two: From Russia with Love

1. "I get weary...." Jack U. Harwell, "A Look at the Man in His Prime," *Baptist Press Features*, July 5, 1973.
2. "Everything I have ever been...." Billy Graham, *Just as I Am* (New York, New York: HarperCollins Worldwide, 1997), 505.
3. "Lasting peace will only come...." John Pollock, *The Billy Graham Story* (Grand Rapids, Michigan: Zondervan, 2003), 180.
4. "It was quite a job...." Association for Diplomatic Studies & Trading, "The Siberian Seven: Escaping Religious Persecution in the U.S.S.R.," November 9, 2016, https://adst.org/2016/11/siberian-seven-escaping-religious-persecution-u-s-s-r/.
5. "They have to go back...." ibid.
6. "We tried to warn him...." ibid.
7. "I found the Soviet people...." Pollock, *The Billy Graham Story*, 181.
8. "Who would have ever dreamed...." David Frost, *Billy Graham: Candid Conversations with a Public Man* (Colorado Springs, Colorado: David Cook, 2014), 87.

Chapter Thirty-Three: Transitions

1. "Greg, I've been thinking about you...." Greg Laurie, *Lost Boy* (Allen David Books/Kerygma Publishing, 2008), 145.
2. "Billy, you know that when...." ibid., 146.
3. "We say to those...." Billy Graham, *Just as I Am* (New York, New York: HarperCollins Worldwide, 1997), 751–54.

Chapter Thirty-Four: Lion in Winter

1. "Before He comes again...." David Frost, *Billy Graham Talks with David Frost* (Philadelphia, Pennsylvania: A.J. Holman Company, 1971), 83.
2. "He allows it...." David Frost, *Billy Graham: Candid Conversations with a Public Man* (Colorado Springs, Colorado: David Cook, 2014), 90–91.
3. "I know that it won't be long...." Andy Newman, "Graham Ends Crusade in City Urging Repentance," *New York Times*, June 27, 2005.
4. "You come to this Crusade...." ibid.
5. "It's hard to sit and watch...." *TIME, Billy Graham: America's Preacher, 1918–2018* (February 23, 2018), 91.

6.   "She's so beautiful...." Tim Funk, "Nearly Festive 2007 Service Honored Ruth Graham's Devotion to Family, Christ," *Charlotte Observer*, June 16, 2017.

7.   "I also look forward to serving God...." *TIME, Billy Graham: America's Preacher, 1918–2018*, 81.